Forever Familias

Forever Familias

Race, Gender, and Indigeneity in Peruvian Mormonism

JASON PALMER

UNIVERSITY OF ILLINOIS PRESS
Urbana, Chicago, and Springfield

Library of Congress Cataloging-in-Publication Data
Names: Palmer, Jason (Jason Charles), 1979– author.
Title: Forever familias : race, gender, and indigeneity in Peruvian
    Mormonism / Jason Palmer.
Description: Urbana : University of Illinois Press, [2024] |
    Includes bibliographical references and index.
Identifiers: LCCN 2023048398 (print) | LCCN 2023048399
    (ebook) | ISBN 9780252045851 (cloth) | ISBN
    9780252087950 (paperback) | ISBN 9780252056734 (ebook)
Subjects: LCSH: Church of Jesus Christ of Latter-day Saints—
    Peru. | Latter Day Saints—Peru. | Identity (Psychology)—
    Peru—Religious aspects—Church of Jesus Christ of Latter-day
    Saints. | BISAC: RELIGION / Christianity / Church of Jesus
    Christ of Latter-day Saints (Mormon) | SOCIAL SCIENCE /
    Race & Ethnic Relations
Classification: LCC BX8617.P4 P34 2024 (print) | LCC BX8617.
    P4 (ebook) | DDC 289.3/85—dc23/eng/20240104
LC record available at https://lccn.loc.gov/2023048398
LC ebook record available at https://lccn.loc.gov/2023048399

To
Elvira, Sajama, Zelanda, Harika, and Milagro
and to
el barrio

¡Wallatas por siempre!

In memory of Mathias

Contents

Acknowledgments

I am grateful to my forever familia for joining my journey to the center of Zion. That familia includes Elvira, my daughters, my mom and dad, my grandparents, my brothers, my cousins, my aunts, my uncles, mis concuñas, "and even more and more" . . . hasta la suegra.

Barrio Periféricos and Pioneer Trail Ward, you are at Zion's center. This project would have been impossible without your patience and openness.

I am indebted to the following professors of anthropology at the University of California, Irvine. Leo Chavez, you struck the perfect balance between expertise and curiosity. Susan Bibler Coutin, thank you for living what you publish. Eleana Kim, your kind guidance gave this project its theoretical ground. Valery Olson, you were the first one to believe.

I am also indebted to the following Weber State University professors. I thank Linda Eaton who introduced me to a form of cultural relativism from which I am still reeling, Richard Pontius for listening to my anthropological imaginings as we hiked the Wasatch, Alicia Giralt for teaching me street Spanish, and Brooke Arkush for showing me the spiritual qualities of material research.

Much thanks goes to the following scholars who workshopped my project: Nandita Badami, Ante Nikola Bagic, Joseph Barnett, Evan Conway, Katie Cox, Ryan Cragun, Collin Ford, Manuel Galaviz, Kelly Hacker, Forest Haven, Amy Hoyt, Angela Jenks, Caroline Kline, David Knowlton, Gregory Kohler, Horacio Legras, Neaks Loucks, Lilith Mahmud, Kyrstin Mallon Andrews, George Marcus, Patrick Mason, Armand Mauss, Michael McBride, Chandra Middleton, Michael Montoya, Alejandro Morales, Thomas Murphey, Sarah Newcomb, Kristin Peterson, Taylor Petrey, Rebecca Richart, Jana Riess, Elizabeth Hanna Rubio, Jacobo Sefamí, Gary Shepherd, Gordon Shepherd, Anya

Tinajero, Roxanne Varzi, Sujey Vega, Erica Vogel, Melissa Wrapp, and Nima Yolmo.

Financial support from Claremont Graduate University's Global Mormon Studies Research Grant allowed me to pay my illustrious bilingual transcribers, Karla Milicich and Alberto Vargas.

Alison Syring, thank you for your unceasing advocacy throughout the peer review process.

Map of Peru

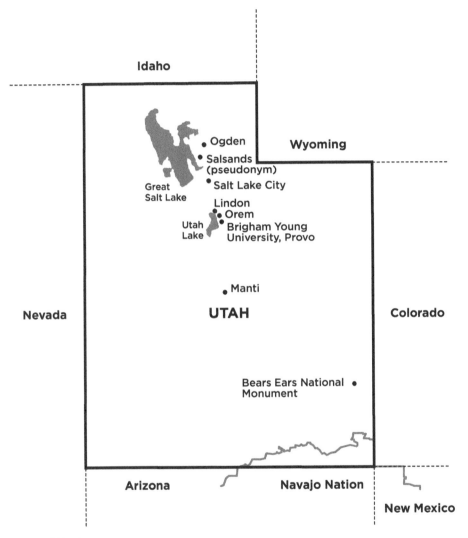

Map of Utah

Forever Familias

Categories

We will adopt US law as our own and take it upon
ourselves. The US has order and cleanliness that
is very different from here in Peru. So, to live, to
raise my children, going to the US would be better because practically La Familia entera [the
entire family] is over there. That made me really
emotional because they just happen to be in Utah
where a large number are Mormons, and we are
members of that church in Utah, right?

So, back to your question, my image of Utah is
that it is a peaceful place, that it is a place where
you can educate your kids, and that the main
temple is there, in Salt Lake City, right? I am excited to be able to finally see it. Even though I
can't maybe go to the temple during the first
month because everyone in La Familia works and
I'll be alone, simply being able to palpably feel
that I am close, that I am closer to the holiness—
because I don't know the laws and the highways
and I don't drive—but just the mere fact of being
close makes my little lightbulb light up.[1]

—Sofi[2]

Essentialism and Constructivism

Sofi spoke these words in the Lima, Peru, airport shortly before immigrating
to Utah. Her words are complex. Understanding the complexity of her words
and those of Saints like her requires an introduction to both Mormonism and
Peruvianness. Unpacking the spiritual portent and migratorily dynamic context of her words will foreground this book's central argument. I argue that the
Peruvian Mormons in my study rearticulated Anglo Mormon (SL) domains in
ways that exposed cracks in the dominance of a colonial system. That system,
which subsumed both the United States and Mormonism, wielded gender,

race, and family in an attempt to cement leaders, government, legacy, holiness, future, marriage, and independence—this book's chapter titles—into essentialist categories designed to replace Peruvianness and other permutations of indigeneity with whiteness.

An essentialist categorization considers people, places, things, and times as having an immutable essence or a preexisting set of properties that automatically or, as people with essentialist categorizations like to say, "naturally" cause them to belong to a specific classification. Alternatively, a constructivist categorization understands people, places, things, and times as having changeable properties that only exist through human and nonhuman construction. Societies that are more essentialist see their categories as acorns. Oak seedlings can grow differently in different environments, but their essence as individual oaks is predetermined and natural. Societies that are more constructivist see their categories as clay. Clay can be molded into many things and stretched to encompass many more.

Different societies have different ways of categorizing the phenomena that make up the shared aspects of their lives. The categories of the Church of Jesus Christ of Latter-day Saints (alternately, the church) were originally forged in the 1820s among highly essentialist European settlers and their descendants who actively dispossessed Indigenous people of the territory that would become the western United States. As a result, contemporary Peruvians like Sofi with ties to an indigeneity that tended toward constructivism found themselves struggling to rejigger those categories in order for their Peruvianness to fit their Mormonism and vice-versa. The research questions that I explored in Utah and Peru from 2014 to 2021 that catalyzed my anthropological encounters with Sofi before and after her immigration to Utah were these: What new Mormonisms emerged from the categorical struggle between Anglo (PL) and Peruvian members of the church? How did Peruvians spatially, relationally, and emotionally establish and live those Mormonisms without losing their Peruvianness?

"Peruvianness" was a common term in my Peruvian study participants' lexicon. More than simply being from the nation-state of Peru, Peruvianness connoted a fragile oneness achieved between influences both foreign to Peru and originating in Peru. While my Peruvian study participants, regardless of religion, felt comfortable using the term "Peruvianness" to express their understanding of Peruvian peoplehood, the feelings of both Anglo and Peruvian members of the church regarding the term "Mormonism" were fraught. A "Mormon" in my usage is an individual who claims ties to the mid-nineteenth century, US religious movement known as Mormonism, founded by the Prophet Joseph Smith. During my study, there were dozens of religious institutions that claimed such ties, but I mostly followed members of the Church of Jesus Christ of Latter-day Saints, headquartered since 1847 in Salt

Lake City, Utah. That institution considered the Prophet Joseph Smith's successor to be the Prophet Brigham Young rather than one of a handful of other possible successors, many of whom began their own institutional churches. The sixteenth prophet of Brigham Young's church, Russell Nelson, announced in 2018, midway through my study, that the approximately sixteen million baptized and, therefore, registered members of his international institution should no longer refer to themselves as "Mormons," hence the contestation of the term "Mormonism" among my study participants.

Still, despite the Prophet's wishes and the wishes of the majority of my study participants loyal to him, I cling to the identity category "Mormon" in this book. This is because "Mormon" encompassed individuals in my study who did not adhere to all aspects of the dogma of Nelson's international church—a church that he legally owned as a US corporate president—but who still considered themselves to be Mormons, Latter-day Saints (LDS), or simply Saints. Part of that dogma included the belief that Nelson and his predecessors—all Anglo males—had not earned or constructed their prophetic leadership positions through study, charisma, spiritual prowess, electoral politics, application processes, or personal drive. Instead, they had been unassuming people carrying a hidden essence that had required Jesus Christ Himself, the true leader of the church, to personally detect and, in my Mormon study participants' lingo, "call" forth.

Part of navigating different societies' categories involves translating between different languages. This does not merely involve national languages, such as English, Spanish, and Quechua (or Runasimi, as my Quechua-speaking study participants preferred to call it). It also involves the meanings that, for example, Mormons in my study expressed with the term "call" versus the meanings that my non-Mormon study participants expressed with that same term. Therefore, to succinctly designate which society's lingo I am using when I introduce a new term, I will employ the following codes: ML-Mormon lingo, PL-Peruvian lingo, PML-Peruvian Mormon lingo, AL-Anglo lingo, AML-Anglo Mormon lingo, and SL-scholarly lingo. The glossaries contain the definitions of all coded terms.

As you peruse the glossaries, please note a deliberate change in publishing style regarding the demarcation of non-English words. Publishers in the United States have traditionally italicized non-English words. Many writers, such as journalist Patricia Escárcega (2020) exposed that practice as part of a colonial logic meant to naturalize English as the default human language and to mark all non-English languages as "other." To divest from that logic in this book, I indicate new non-English terms using the same parenthetical coding system that I use to indicate new English terms.

Though I apply only one code to each new term throughout this book, there were overlaps among different linguistic groups' usages of each term.

This book's argument rests on Mormonism's need to simultaneously require and resist those overlaps. By denying categorical overlaps, Anglo Mormons in my study were able to incorporate unanalyzed US norms into their doctrines (ML) and consider them divine. As a result of the cultural work that it took to conceal categorical overlaps, Peruvian Mormons in my study often felt that they had to acculturate themselves to whiteness (SL) before determining their own destinies as Saints.

Indigeneity and Coloniality

Through interacting with Mormons who upheld a diverse array of dogma—much of which involved the peopling of the Americas—I came to understand Mormonism and Peruvianness (PL) as having the following relationships to indigeneity (SL): The mission of Mormonism was to explain, pedestalize, absorb, and ultimately eliminate indigeneity. The mission of Peruvianness was to grant the power to all Peruvians to define indigeneity for themselves and to be as apologetically or unapologetically Indigenous as they wanted to be.

In those two statements, Mormonism appears anti-Indigenous while Peruvianness appears pro-Indigenous. The two missions, therefore, seem mutually exclusive. However, the experiences of Peruvian Mormons like Sofi with claims to indigeneity have proven to me not only that both missions can simultaneously help and harm Indigenous people, but that Mormonism and Peruvianness can coexist.

Sofi grew up in the northern maritime city of Chimbote, Peru, during a time, the 1980s, when many Runasimi-speaking highlanders were migrating to work in her city's fish canneries. Within contemporary Peruvian thought (part of Peruvianness), Runasimi is an Indigenous language, meaning that it was spoken on the land before those believed to be antithetical to Runasimi speakers—the Spanish-speaking colonizers—arrived. That construction pits indigeneity against coloniality (SL) in a never-ending battle that helps define Peruvianness. But what are indigeneity and coloniality?

The interplay between indigeneity and coloniality—and the slightly overlapping interplay between constructivism (SL) and essentialism (SL)—generates the core of both Mormonism and Peruvianness. Indigenous Mormon and anthropologist of Mormonism Arcia Tecun defined indigeneity as pointing to "living ancestral connections that serve as portals beyond the paradigm of coloniality through original people's ancestral memories of being 'human' whether they are still in a site of creation or have been displaced or have become mobile from that site while still maintaining an Indigenous consciousness and way of being and doing" (Hernández 2021, 3).

Coloniality, on the other hand, is a mindset and process that violently severs established relationships of mutual indebtedness between human and nonhuman entities and replaces them with unsustainable relationships that siphon off those entities and accumulate them in distant places, far from their original ecosystems (Coulthard 2014). Settler coloniality is the particular form of coloniality that early Anglo Mormons unwittingly built into categories that they deemed universal and unchanging rather than culturally specific and ever evolving. Settler coloniality is insidious because it involves humans invading an ecosystem that had already fully incorporated humans. The invaders, feeling that they know a better way to relate to the ecosystem than its original human members, seek to replace those humans with themselves. Since this replacement is accomplished in face-to-face human interactions, it produces guilt in the invaders, who would like to *belong* in the ecosystem. Once the invaders realize the value of what was lost as they replaced sustainability with extraction—thus knocking the ecosystem out of balance—nostalgia is also produced (Rosaldo 1989). To overcome their guilt, the invaders, through their stories, myths, and histories, depict themselves as the one true group of humans destined to rule the ecosystem (Hurwitz 2017). To overcome their nostalgia, they narrativize human relatedness itself as separate from Earth's ecosystems (Anderson 2010). "The violence of settler-colonialism is therefore also intensely spiritual and symbolic, because the obliteration of Native society and culture becomes the prerequisite for the colonial settler's ability to make meaning and value within the society he invents upon the stolen land of another people" (Zahzah 2022, 47).

Understanding the church through that settler colonial theoretical frame allowed me to see the top leaders of the official church in Salt Lake City as relentlessly channeling Peruvian Mormons' religious energy to fuel Utah's extractive project. It also allowed me to witness Peruvian Mormonism subverting that project with equal relentlessness. That feedback loop produced constant categorical reconfigurations that I detected in everyday lives.

Likewise, analyzing the United States through that same framework of settler coloniality allowed me to understand its continued existence as dependent upon the ultimate annihilation of the land's original inhabitants and their forms of kinship or relatedness (Yazzie 2015). It allowed me to understand that when US policies ended up harming indigeneity, those policies were not failing. Rather, they were doing precisely what the United States was founded to do (Cook-Lynn 2001). Therefore, understanding the United States as a state built to perpetuate settler coloniality (a settler state) means understanding the United States to be irredeemable (Horne 2020). Since there is no legitimate basis for its existence upon land that it stole, it cannot make full restitution for its crimes against indigeneity without ceasing to exist (Todorov 1984).

As long as there are Indigenous people on the land, Indigenous relations will be uncomfortable reminders to settler forms of governance that they are precisely that: settler forms, as opposed to original and, therefore, legitimate forms that have been interwoven with local ecosystems since time immemorial. The sheer existence of people in the United States with ties to the original people who existed on the land before borders lacerated it remind settler governments that, no matter how hard they try, they will never be Indigenous and that their settler ways of relating to the land are fragile and doomed (Dunbar-Ortiz 2021). During my study, Sofi and other Peruvian Mormon migrants living in Utah included themselves among the people who represented such an unsettling (pun intended) reminder to contemporary Mormon settler colonists.

Mormon Racism

The original seed of the multiple global Mormonisms that exist today in the discipline of Mormon Studies' various scholarly formulations, such as my designation of Anglo Mormonism (SL) and Peruvian Mormonism (SL), sprouted as a single organization in the early 1800s that struggled with schismatics from the outset. Mormonism was one of many utopian movements on the US frontier meant to compensate for the dystopia that settlers created as they actively fought for their frontier's westward creep into Indian Territory (Jennings 2016). Mormonism was a religious revival, but it was also a revival of settler hope. Mormon settlers not only hoped that they could become Indigenous, but they also hoped to restore to Indigenous people the right kind of indigeneity. The kind of indigeneity for which settlers hoped was one that quietly acquiesced to settler ways of being the Leaders (PL), forming governments (SL), living legacy (ML), establishing holiness (ML), seeking future, defining marriage, and navigating independence.

Such hope was canonized in *The Book of Mormon*, which is where Mormonism got its name. *The Book of Mormon*, published in 1830 by Mormonism's first leader, the Prophet Joseph Smith, made explicit that the differences in skin pigmentation between settler colonists and Indigenous people were divinely embedded within differences of morality and decency. While the United States' and *The Book of Mormon*'s constructions of race contrasted with and influenced each other in complex ways (Mueller 2017), they both contained the same core tenants of what anthropologist Alejandro Lipschütz (1967) called pigmentocracy. They agreed that dark skin denoted immorality, and they agreed on the doctrine of genocide (Green 1988). Within the doctrine of genocide, Indigenous people were the antithesis of the settler project and either had to be eliminated bodily, or their *indigeneity* had to be eliminated from their otherwise salvageable bodies. That doctrine's mantra was, "the fewer Indigenous people, the more land." It contrasted with the US doctrine of slavery's mantra, which was, "the more Black people, the more labor." In that imagined calculus, being identifiable as Black benefited settler colonialism economically. Being identifiable as Indigenous did not. Therefore, while a single Black grandparent made a grandchild immutably Black, if the daughter of two Indigenous people acted morally—meaning beneficial to settler colonization—she could theoretically lose her indigeneity and morph into the elite group that labeled itself "White" provided that she sufficiently assimilates into the culture—whiteness—of those who saw themselves as naturally—biologically—inhabiting that elite group.

The Book of Mormon constructed a category of race for individual Indigenous people that would allow them to both join whiteness and become biologically light-pigmented during their own lifetimes. In my interpretation, Mormonism invited Indigenous people to willingly abandon their indigeneity and, in so doing, symbolically grant that indigeneity's inherent land claims—its authenticity—to settlers. Joseph Smith's magical production of *The Book of Mormon*—which may have involved the use of ransacked Seneca grave goods as seer stones (Murphy 2020)—encapsulated the US settler colonists' thirst for authenticity. Channeling grave robbing into book publishing, it was as if Smith were taking the morbid words of poet William Carlos Williams to heart: "The land! don't you feel it? Doesn't it make you want to go out and lift dead Indians tenderly from their graves, to steal from them—as if it must be clinging even to their corpses—some authenticity?" (McGuire 1992, 816).

The book—a compendium of ancient records from the Americas that the Prophet Mormon etched onto sheets of gold in 400 CE and that Joseph Smith discovered and, through seer stones, translated into English 1,400 years later—was only able to orchestrate such a semiotic and somatic exchange between indigeneity and coloniality by harnessing the power of story (Said 1993). Its story depicted a light-pigmented, Israelite family led by Lehi, who was of the Hebrew subtribe of Manasseh (mentioned in Genesis). He, his wife Sariah, their four sons—Laman, Lemuel, Nephi, and Sam—and their unnamed and uncounted daughters fled Jerusalem during the reign of Zedekiah (mentioned in 2 Kings) to arrive in 600 BCE at what many Peruvian Mormons in my study argued was an uninhabited American continent. Lehi's god promised the Americas to Lehi's descendants, but that promise was contingent upon their righteousness. If they ever became unrighteous, they would lose the land, and that loss would be their own fault.

Before Lehi's family members populated the Americas and built it into what they called Zion (ML), Laman and Lemuel became cursed. God cursed them because they did not organize their lives according to His one true definition of family (AML), which I will discuss below. In a coterminous event that many of my study participants liked to interpret as being somehow unrelated to the curse so as to make it sound less racist, Laman's and Lemuel's skin tone darkened.

Lehi's righteous son Nephi prophesied that, though his siblings' dark-pigmented descendants—the Lamanites (ML)—would end up killing off all his "white" (J. Smith 1830, 73) pigmented descendants—the Nephites—the Lamanites would one day be restored to the true forms of relatedness as outlined in *The Book of Mormon*, and their skin would be restored to whiteness (Boxer 2009). Early adherents to *The Book of Mormon* spread Nephi's whitening prophecy abroad. As an Anglo Mormon in Buenos Aires stated in his 1925 prayer dedicating the "land of South America" for Mormon missionary work, "the Indians of this land, who are the descendants of Lehi . . . [will] again become a white and delightsome people" (Christensen 1995, 23).

Nephi also prophesied that the mechanism of the restoration of truth and whiteness to his brothers' brown descendants—the Lamanites—would include European settler colonists, whom he saw in a dream and described as "white and exceedingly fair and beautiful" (J. Smith 1830, 29). According to Nephi, the latter-day colonists' propitious removal of the more wicked among the Lamanites (Native peoples) would prepare the way for a Euroamerican nation-state that would one day allow for the religious freedom necessary to bring *The Book of Mormon* out of its hidden New York repository—where Joseph Smith found it in 1820, led by an apparition of the Prophet Mormon's son Moroni (ML)—and into the heathen hands of the Native descendants of the book's Lamanite protagonists.

In the 1830s, that book provided New York settler colonists a justification for their participation in genocide (Boxer 2019). Conveniently, "white Mormons found that their scripture could support both the veneration and eradication of indigenous people" (Hendrix-Komoto and Stuart 2020, 28). Furthermore, the book's view that Indigenous people were swept away "due to their ancestors' unrighteousness [placed] the fault of genocide at their own feet" (Newcomb 2021, 112) rather than at the feet of settlers.

In a popular, settler interpretation of *The Book of Mormon*, Lamanites (Native peoples) rightfully lost Zion (the Americas) through their lack of leadership capabilities. Therefore, the city of Zion had to be rebuilt on the continent by those with divine know-how: settler colonists (Singer 2021). That interpretation made Anglo Mormons into both the true pioneers (ML), an identity that was vital to many Mormons in my study, and the rightful Indigenous: the predestined governors of Zion. Many Anglo Mormons in my study identified so strongly as pioneers—by which they meant descendants of the historic Great Plains–crossing Mormon Pioneers (AL)—that they felt slighted when Lamanite-identifying Mormons identified as pioneers too. To strengthen the symbolic power of settlers over indigeneity, *The Book of Mormon* sacralized the periodic colonial encounters between light-pigmented Nephite people and dark-pigmented Lamanite people as providential encounters between adults and children, between people who knew how to use the land and people who did not. The book fed off the same supposition that Thomas Jefferson and other settler colonists in the eighteenth century used to spin archaeological myths, justifying the colonists' conquest of the Americas. The supposition was that any land use in pre-Columbian America that White people found praiseworthy, such as Serpent Mound and other striking earthworks in the Moundbuilders' territory around the Mississippi, must have in fact been orchestrated by an early race of light-pigmented Indigenous people whom "merciless Indian savages" (per the Declaration of Independence) later killed off (Colavito 2020).

That Anglo Mormons during the late 2010s continued to find solidarity in whiteness with that extinct race of light-pigmented Indigenous people—the Nephites—was evident in an ethnographic film documenting a "Lands of *The Book of Mormon*" cruise ship tour of ancient Mesoamerican archaeological sites. One of the sixty Anglo Mormons on the tour, a female, argued with a male non-Mormon Mexican tour guide who claimed that his ancestors built Chichén Itzá. She countered that White Mormons were actually the ones with rights to "affiliate kin—family—to the people who built these [temples] in a religious sense" (Chamberlain 2019, min. 14:23). Her kinship with Mexico's ancient inhabitants stemmed from the whiteness that she shared with the Nephites. Refracted through *The Book of Mormon*, her visit to the spectacular Mayan temples restored her kinship to both whiteness and indigeneity.

Joseph Smith's new religion, therefore, was restorationist in many ways. First, it restored the true justification behind what he felt was light-pigmented people's rightful theocratic authority over the American continent. Second, it restored the power necessary for the remnant of the original inhabitants of that continent—the Lamanites—to leave behind their savagery and return to the whiteness of their forefather, Lehi. However, those two principal restorations required many other more material and logistical restorations. In addition to receiving visitations from ancient American prophets, some of whom, according to *The Book of Mormon*, became apostles (ML) when Jesus Christ visited the New World days after his resurrection in the Old World, Smith also received the keys of the priesthood (ML) directly from the resurrected, angelic hands of Christ's biblical apostles Peter, James, and John. They placed their hands upon Smith's head and conferred upon him the priesthood keys necessary to restore Christ's biblical church. Smith then gave those keys to other men through the laying on of hands (ML), who gave them to other men and so on down the same textual lineage of authority through which all contemporary priesthood-holding Mormon males in my study could trace their power directly back to Christ. The keys required restoration because they had been lost during the European Dark Ages. From the time of the apostle Peter's death until 1830 when those powers were restored to Smith, nobody on Earth had the authority to conduct Christ's church, to legitimately initiate members into His church through the waters of baptism, or, as will become important below, to marry and produce a proper family.

The priesthood keys allowed Smith to reestablish what he felt to be the same leadership hierarchy that existed during Christ's life, with one exception: in Christ's temporary absence, Smith would be the interim leader. He would be the Prophet (ML) in council with his twelve apostles who, in the structure of the official church during my study, supervised General Authority Seventies (ML) covering the planet, who supervised Area Authority Seventies covering a few nation-states, who supervised stake presidents (ML) covering large portions of cities, who supervised bishops (ML) covering neighborhoods, who supervised elders (ML: adult males in those neighborhoods), priests (ML: sixteen- to seventeen-year-old males), teachers (ML: fourteen- to fifteen-year-old males), and deacons (ML: eleven- to thirteen-year-old males). The people who occupied those various offices in the male-only priesthood hierarchy—and other people, including females, who occupied leadership positions in the church's auxiliary organizations (ML)—were understood to be assigned by Christ Himself through the voice of His servants. Many such divine assignments were made during my study, and both Anglos and Peruvians often found it difficult to have faith that such callings (ML) were backed by Christ's will rather than His servants' whims.

Once Christ had a New Jerusalem from whence to rule the world—a Zion—He would return, and a prophet would no longer be necessary. Early followers of Smith, whom he baptized by immersion through the authority of Christ's restored priesthood, expected that the Second Coming of Christ would happen during their lifetimes. Accordingly, they prepared one spiritual Zion after another in the form of material cities—Kirtland, Ohio; Jackson County, Missouri; and Nauvoo, Illinois—from whence they were expelled for various reasons in 1838, 1839, and 1846 respectively.

One of the main impetuses for these peregrinations across different US conquests, aside from persecution from other settler colonists, was the desire to restore the proper essence of indigeneity to Native nations. One of the first things that Joseph Smith did, not six months after establishing his new church in 1830, was to share *The Book of Mormon* with Seneca people on the Cattaraugus Reservation near Buffalo, New York. He did not personally have success in converting any of them to his new religion, but he still felt that God the Father and His Son Jesus Christ, through the Holy Ghost, were communicating to him that he should continue to call males in his tiny, all-Anglo congregation to missionize "the Lamanites," by which he meant Native peoples. Thus, the famous Mormon missionary movement was born through a desire to save Native people from their improper indigeneity. That movement wielded military metaphors from the start because it was seen as a spiritual rescue mission to people who were literally at war with the US army.

The Mormon missionary movement had immense success in getting converts from England and Scandinavia to join the Mormons' sojourn in Nauvoo because, Smith explained, "We believe in the literal gathering of Israel and in the restoration of the Ten Tribes; that Zion (the New Jerusalem) will be built upon this continent" (J. Smith 1842, 710). That article of faith, which Mormon youth all over the world still memorized during my study, was taken to mean that global Mormons had to migrate to wherever the largest body of American Saints happened to be.

Global Mormons in 1846 included thousands of British people, but almost no Native people. This disparity spawned speculation that quickly became an official doctrine regarding the different faith capacities among different "races" of people. One way in which Scandinavian and British converts to Mormonism became "native" when they became "American" to distinguish themselves "from those they considered the true colonizers" (Canessa 2012, 88) was by claiming that they were actually of the lost subtribe of Israel—Ephraim—scattered among the "gentiles," by which they meant European non-Mormons. The reason that they were able to believe in Mormonism in the first place was because they carried Israel's "believing blood" (Mauss 2003, 32), which was thought to react to the sound of the Mormon message, causing automatic, synaptic acceptance. Technically, according to *The Book of Mormon*, all Native people on the American continent were also of the house of Israel through Ephraim's younger brother Manasseh (Laman's ancestor) meaning that they also had believing blood, albeit not as receptive as Ephraim's first-born, birthright blood.

According to believing-blood theory, the Seneca and other Native nations should have been more receptive to the Mormon message. They were supposed to have been carrying an elect essence. Therefore, they should have been converted and baptized in quantities, if not surpassing, at least comparable to those of the British. Yet, for some reason, Native people were not accepting the message meant for them. Early Anglo Mormons with missionary fervor felt that perhaps the true descendants of the Lamanites, the very people to whom *The Book of Mormon* was written according to that book's title page, lived elsewhere in the Americas.

As Anglo Mormons moved west among all kinds of Indigenous nations undergoing their own forced removals, their vision of where the believing-blood-toting Lamanites dwelled kept getting pushed farther before them. As early as 1831, a year after both the church's founding and Andrew Jackson's signing of the Indian Removal Act, apostle Oliver Cowdry already had his missionizing sights set far to the west, on those he considered "more civilized tribes," such as "the navahoes" (Mueller 2017, 100). The predominant sentiment among Anglo Mormons was that the uprooted, decimated, and "degraded Indians" (Taylor 2000, 180) surrounding them in places like Ohio could not possibly be the same Lamanites whom *The Book of Mormon* prophesied would join with them in the Earth's latter days to "build a city, which shall be called the New Jerusalem" (J. Smith 1830, 501).

Finally, in 1847, impelled by missionary zeal and expelled by US antebellum politics, the still largely Anglo body of Saints, numbering about 12,000, left the United States entirely and became the famous Mormon Pioneers. Salt Lake City, Utah, became their Zion.

Arriving in Utah and still failing to see the mass conversions that believing blood was supposed to produce in the biological descendants of Lehi (Laman's father), the apostle Parley Pratt sought them in South America. During a reconnaissance mission in 1852, he concluded that "perhaps nine-tenths of the vast population of Peru, as well as of most other countries of Spanish America, are of the *blood of Lehi*" (1888, 447). The church did not establish an official mission in Peru until 1959, but its eventual success there and across Latin America certainly confirmed Pratt's notion that the right kind of indigeneity had finally been found. The Lamanites—the foreordained recipients of *The Book of Mormon*—were in Latin America.

Peruvianness

The sort of indigeneity that Anglo Mormons found in Peru involved a multiplex mix of millenarian locality and cosmopolitan exoticism that many Peruvians in my study called Peruvianness. My Peruvian study participants often described Peruvian cuisine and its iconic beverage—Inca Kola—as a microcosm of the way Peruvianness combined tradition with newness. That combination produced what Anglo Mormon missionaries in Peru during my study somehow felt to be the right kind of indigeneity.

According to Peruvian chef Mitsuharu Tsumara, Peruvianness contained three elements: millenarian Indigenous tradition, biodiverse ingredients, and—most importantly—foreignness (Ara 2017). Peruvianness celebrated outside influences on the shifting civilizations aboriginal to Peru. That some of those influences were colonial and thus recognized as nefarious did not diminish the acknowledgment of them as an integral part of Peruvianness. Sofi, along with most Peruvian Mormons in my study, had a complex relationship to both indigeneity and Mormonism that deepened the contradictory nature of her Peruvianness. Not only did Sofi not speak the language in Peru that was emblematic of indigeneity, Runasimi, but she also actively participated in the stigmatization of her Runasimi-speaking classmates in grade school. Since her own paternal grandparents were monolingual Runasimi speakers, Sofi later came to believe that her self-hate sparked her bullying.

She portrayed her stigmatization of indigeneity in a nation-state founded upon indigeneity as a paradoxical part of Peruvianness that created many ironic situations for her. Even as she was making fun of people who spoke a quotidian dialect of Runasimi, she, along with Peru's nationalized social studies curriculum, was celebrating in her public school's patriotic pageants the regal dialect of Runasimi that the mythological founding fathers of Peru—the Incas—spoke. In other words, Sofi grew up within a social milieu that treated indigeneity in much the same pedestalizing yet patronizing way that the successors of Joseph Smith, the prophets and presidents of the Church of Jesus Christ of Latter-day Saints, would come to treat indigeneity.

Around the time of the church's founding, Peru's anti-indigeneity was worsening among Peru's settler colonist, White class: criollos (PL). With the criollo-controlled Peruvian republic's independence from Spain in the 1820s, Indigenous ayllus (PL) no longer had the Crown to protect their documented land from hacienda (PL) slavery, an entrepreneurial form of feudalism wherein the new individual usurper of a land deed—the hacendado—became the de facto owner, guardian, and educator of that land's previous stewards (Arguedas [1964] 1973). Male hacendados colonized Indigenous lands and seized the sexual rights to Indigenous men's wives and daughters, encouraged as part of "whitening" the new nation-state (M. E. García 2021).

In a deliberate attempt to make Peru a settler state, its government used hacendados to employ eugenics, reeducation (Lajimodiere 2019), and other forms of genocidal statecraft perfected in the United States (Speed 2019). Seeking escape from this forced assimilation, Indigenous highlanders migrated from rural areas. They came to make up about 10 percent of the populations of coastal Lima and inland Arequipa by 1956 (Durand 2010). By 2021, they and their descendants made up approximately 80 percent (M. E. García 2021) of those two metropolises.

In 1969—in a move that I observed many upper-class Peruvians and their Anglo Mormon mine-owning corporate partners continue to verbally resent during the late 2010s—Peru emancipated hacienda-enslaved people. Though the violence of hacienda slavery was not comparable to that of chattel slavery, its removal was "akin to the abolition of [chattel] slavery in the Americas" (Mayer 2009, 3) in many ways. For one, the beneficiaries of slavery found ways to reinscribe it: US-owned company towns (Morales 2010) in existence since the late 1800s were at the ready to displace and underpay formerly enslaved people in the continual removal of precious metals from Peru. One US company's mining town near the southern Andean city of Arequipa at its height from 1958 to 1963 included as many as forty Anglo Mormon male overseers and their nuclear families. They congregated, without Peruvians, in Peru's first Mormon-built chapel (ML).

In reaction to this "benevolent colonialism" (Robinson 1983, 239) that enriched foreign profiteers in Peru at the expense of most Peruvians, the highland Shining Path guerrilla movement began in the 1980s. The Shining Path War, as my study participants discuss in chapter 2, was a watershed moment for Peru, for Peruvianness, and for Peruvian Mormonism. It was a complex civil war over indigeneity itself and over whether Indigenous people should function communally within a nation-state ruled by non-Indigenous Peruvians (criollos) and foreign interests or whether they should overthrow that rule. Those who wanted to overthrow the settler state were called terrorists by those who did not. Throughout the two-decades-long war, its multiple factions blurred in Peruvian discourse until indigeneity itself became associated with terrorism within the construct of Peruvianness. The result was that, during my study, Peruvians who dared identify as Indigenous, even presidential candidates, were often suspected of terrorism. Naturally, these negative associations with indigeneity affected Peruvian Mormons' Lamanite identity, which I discuss in chapter 3.

President Alberto Fujimori's counterinsurgency to the Shining Path in the 1990s sparked more migration from the highlands to Arequipa and Lima (Gandolfo 2009). All this displacement put highland Indigenous people—insulted as "cholos" (PL)—into places where they were gazed upon as pollutants, not only of hygiene, but also of pure racial categories (Spalding 1970). In 1986, Hernando de Soto (who went on to run for president in 2020) proposed that Indigenous people be required to carry an internal passport in order to restrict their movements and cure their condition of being undocumented in their own country. During my study, that people who made up 45 percent of Peru's population were still not considered citizens of Peru was evidenced in official state texts—from museum maps to history books—that labeled highland Peruvian migrants "immigrants" (Museo Cultural de Arequipa, n.d.) as if they were foreigners.

Newly arriving Runasimi speakers, whose Spanish ancestry made them technically mestizos (PL), were phenotypically indistinguishable from the elite coastal mestizos accustomed to "breeding out the brown" (Larson 2005). This produced a threat to the social order. Highland mestizos able to pass as coastal mestizos created a new kind of mestizaje (mixing) that was doubly hybrid (De la Cadena 2005). In Peru, fear of this pernicious in-betweenness so threatened elite identities that it was defining the mestizo, not the differences between indios (PL), criollos, and negros (PL), that fueled twentieth-century Peruvian social distinction (Romero 2004). Perceived skin tone became a vital marker of such distinction within Peruvianness, especially among Peruvians who believed in *The Book of Mormon*, which is why I often mention skin pigmentation throughout this book. My designation of "perceived skin tone" rather than "verifiable skin tone" is deliberate. Part of Peruvianness during my study was the ability to quickly distinguish one's place on Peru's social hierarchy relative to others through differences in a complex amalgamation of hair color, surname, hometown, accent, educational attainment, and dress (Sabogal 2005), all of which seemed to me to determine skin tone designations to a far higher degree than the determiners' rods and cones.

In the late 1900s, the epithet "cholo" took on new valences to accomplish the task of distinguishing the kind of mestizo who acted indigenously from the kind who acted decently (PL). The hierarchy became so finely gradated that virtually every Peruvian simultaneously had somebody to call cholo and was somebody's cholo (De la Puente 2012). The only people who were nobody's cholo were those who were socially White enough to call anybody cholo.

As a result of its distance and altitude, midway between the coast and the Andean altiplano, its long history of interracial relations, and—as concerned Peruvian Mormons in a nation-state wherein one was "Peruvian and therefore Catholic" (Vogel 2020, 88)—its reputation as the Vatican of Peru, the city of Arequipa complicated the falsely dichotomous racialization of geography between the "white coast" and the "brown Andes" (De la Cadena 2000, 21). This is one of the reasons why I chose Arequipa as my principal Peruvian field site for this study of Peruvianness and its navigation of Mormonism's categories.

During my study, a large minority in Arequipa hailed from the altiplano city of Puno. Puneños (PL) occupied Arequipa's lowest social category, that of recién bajados (recently come down from the mountains). They were thought to require the most de-Indianization (SL) (De la Cadena 2000, 6) in order to change their indigeneity into a more socially acceptable form of indigeneity captured in the identity category "arequipeño neto" (PL). Those who already considered themselves arequipeños netos welcomed neither puneños nor their squatter communities on the outskirts of the city, which were called "invasions" (PL). Puneños were said to have a darker skin tone than arequipeños netos, many of whom admitted to me that their city was called the White City for reasons more racially complex than the white volcanic stone out of which many of its sixteenth-century buildings were hewn.

Arequipa's complex indigeneities and their various blends of essentialism and constructivism were scarcely contained within Peruvianness (Palmer 2021). In fact, Peruvian media spoke of Arequipa as if it were its own nation-state, and customs officers at the Arequipa airport often jokingly demanded my arequipeño visa. To make a long story short, Arequipa generated an ever-multiplying form of secessionist indigeneity perfectly primed for the ultimate arrival of an equally dizzying form of secessionist coloniality: Mormonism.

It makes sense, therefore, that some of the very first people to combine Mormonism with Peruvianness were arequipeños (people from Arequipa). In fact, after being baptized at the hands of young Anglo Mormon missionaries from Utah, the first Peruvian Mormon to be assigned to embark upon her own official proselytizing mission was arequipeña Ruth Ojeda. In 1961, Sister Ojeda (ML) was called to serve (ML) in the Andes Mission, headquartered in Lima (Christensen 1995). She, along with her Anglo Mormon companion (ML), taught her fellow Peruvians that the church to which she belonged was the only church on the face of the Earth that had the legitimate power to baptize and to speak on behalf of Jesus Christ Himself. She also taught that the sole mouthpiece of Christ on Earth was an elderly White male in Salt Lake City whom most of the approximately two million Mormons worldwide and most of the approximately two thousand Peruvian Mormons in Peru at the time considered to be a living prophet.

Prophetic Paternalism

Just as most of my Peruvian Mormon study participants knew the succession of Inca kings by name, most also knew the church's succession of seventeen prophets by name, each of which began his role as Christ's one true living mouthpiece on the Earth soon after the death of the previous prophet. The Prophet during the last few years of my study was Russell Nelson. He was flanked by his two councilors in the First Presidency (ML). The First Presidency oversaw the Quorum of the Twelve Apostles (ML: hereafter, the Twelve). Most of my Mormon study participants, whether Peruvian or Anglo, knew the names of all fifteen of those men, and could recognize their faces. Those fifteen men (or Jesus Christ through them, depending on one's belief) called the shots in what I refer to as "the church" or, when I need to emphasize their specific Salt Lake City influence as trumping Peruvian influence, "the official church." The homage paid to central leadership among Mormons was similar to that paid to the pope among Catholics. However, it was unusual among followers of other US-based Christian movements such as Jehovah's Witnesses or Seventh Day Adventists, most of whom would not be able to recite the names of their contemporary leaders. The reason such recognition occurred among Mormons probably stemmed from the fact that the words of those fifteen men—often spoken at a live, biannual television event called "General Conference" (ML) and then published in the church's official magazine, *Liahona*—became scripture, tantamount to the holy writ found in Mormonism's four canonical books. Those books were, in order of the importance that my study participants granted them in their daily lives: *The Book of Mormon*, the *Doctrine and Covenants* (a collection of Jesus Christ's dictations to Joseph Smith), the Holy Bible, and the *Pearl of Great Price* (more of Joseph Smith's translations of ancient records including Egyptian papyri).

The member of the Twelve most intimately involved in opening the church's first official evangelizing mission in Peru in 1959 was Spencer Kimball. He was also the man most involved in calling off the gathering of Israel (ML) to Zion. He wrote profusely that Utah was no longer the one and only Zion on Earth and that "the 'gathering of Israel' is effected when the people of the faraway countries accept the gospel and remain in their native lands. The gathering of

Israel for Mexicans is in Mexico" (Kimball 1975, para. 18). Kimball, who later became the Prophet, wanted his new Latin American flock—and their various indigeneities that were disturbing his settler sensibilities—to stop immigrating to Utah. Therefore, he made it possible for Zion to become bureaucratically reproducible anywhere in the world. He made Zion into a correlated franchise, similar to McDonald's. Ever after, the church's Zion became just as much a set of administrative regulations with growth metrics, scalability, and mission statements as a metaphorical mindset or a palpably holy place.

During my study, there were two overlapping governing structures that managed the church's Zion franchises and prevented their splitting into independent local Mormonisms: the mission district (ML) and the stake of Zion (ML). From what I could gather, after the Kimball era, it was through those governing structures that Mormons materially built Zion and filled it with meticulously quantified, newly baptized Saints.

The first governing phase was the mission district. This was a probationary structure under the jurisdiction of a governing body called the Area Presidency (ML), which worked directly under the Twelve. The mission district included cartographically delimited congregations called branches (ML). Local members of branches usually met for worship services in rented venues or even in each other's homes. In Peru, young male missionaries, largely Anglo, ordained with keys of the priesthood oversaw those branches and were themselves overseen by a mission president (ML) who was also, in my experience, usually Anglo. Each mission president's many missionaries, usually around 250 per mission region, were happy to teach anyone, regardless of gender, about Mormonism. They were happy to baptize anyone into the church. However, since the official church's leadership structure only functioned through the power of the priesthood and since that power could only be held by males, missionaries could not establish locally run congregations unless they baptized males. Therefore, throughout this book, when I describe congregations as not having enough male membership, I do not mean that there was a paucity of males compared to females, I simply mean that there were not enough people who held what many Mormons believed to be the essence of leadership: masculinity. Though the male-to-female ratio was fairly equal in the demographics of the congregations that I visited and joined, female membership numbers did not count for much in the algorithms that the official church used to decide where in Zion to allocate its buildings and funds.

If the missionaries' efforts resulted in the baptism of enough Peruvian males who went on to receive the priesthood themselves, one of those males would be called to be a bishop, and his entire congregation would graduate up from the probationary status of branch to the permanent status of ward (ML). When this happened, the central church, headquartered in Salt Lake City, would use its inhouse architectural, social science research, and legal firms, staffed almost exclusively with Anglo males, to purchase land and design and build a chapel on it for that new ward in Peru.

Wards in Peru and Utah were not merely congregations of people who participated in a liturgy once a week and went their separate ways. Rather, they were ward families (ML) bound together through near-daily communal experiences, both spiritual and recreational (Black 2016). The ward family unit highlights one of the main differences between Utah's Mormonism and Peru's. In Utah, elite Mormons controlled civic, educational, and other ostensibly secular aspects of society. As a result, many Anglo Mormons in my study claimed that Utah's culture and government reflected their values. However, since many Peruvian Mormons in Peru were the only Mormons in their families, workplaces, and schools, their ward family became their only refuge from the World (ML) of profane dancing, drinking, swearing, and immodestly dressing non-Mormons around them. Peru's society was at odds with Peruvian Mormons' values. A Peruvian ward's chapel, therefore, often became its members' only venue for what they deemed wholesome togetherness: scripture study, prayer, ceremony, sports, pageants, dances, potlucks, and talent shows.

Ironically, many Peruvian Mormons in Utah felt that Utah's culture—what they called "la gringada" (PL)—was equally at odds with their values, but for different reasons, which I describe in chapter 7. As a result, Spanish-speaking Mormon wards in Utah (Embry 1997) became refuges, not only from irreligious society, but also from Anglo Mormonism (Romanello 2020).

Many Peruvian ward family members in Peru, like their Peruvian counterparts in Utah, also sought such refuge from Anglos. In their case, it was because Anglos surveilled the mission district inside which Peruvians found themselves geographically bound. Refuge from Anglo surveillance was only possible after enough wards coalesced inside a confined geographical area. Once the concentration of wards was high enough, the Anglo-controlled Area Presidency would shift governance over those wards from the mission district, led by Anglos, to the second phase of franchise-control called the stake of Zion or simply the stake. Stakes in Peru were led by stake presidents who, in my experience, were almost always Peruvians. For a stake to be up and running in Peru, it usually had to include a Peruvian stake president (who was sufficiently acculturated to Anglo Mormonism's categories), his two Peruvian councilors, and his twelve Peruvian high councilors. As a group, those fifteen Peruvian men with stake-level callings oversaw seven or eight wards, each led by its own Peruvian bishop. When the transition from mission district to stake of Zion was thus completed, local Peruvian members became largely free of direct foreign oversight from Salt Lake City's Anglo emissaries.

However, paternalism still seeped into the grassroots. In a compilation of Anglo Mormon missionary records in Peru that former mission president

Dale Christensen self-published in 1995—the year when non-US Mormons outnumbered US Mormons for the first time (Bartholomew 2020)—Peruvians from 1925 to 1995 were described variously as "the blood of Israel" (Christensen 1995, 60), "dirty little boys and girls, in tatters" (98), "of the lineage of the prophets" (99), "ignorant and backward local resident Indians" (105), "a highly superstitious people" (132), "our own people" (136), "innocent" (141), "the Indian people" (141), "very friendly Lamanite people of the jungle" (147), "[God's] covenant people in the highlands of the Andes" (203), and "pre-programmed, like computers, toward the gospel" (204). In addition to paternalism, almost all of those phrases betrayed a certain essentialism, which was necessary for the colonializing category of race. According to those Anglo mission presidents, Peruvians had an essence that was "pre-programmed" rather than constructed. Anglos felt that it was their job to help Peruvians discover and live up to that essence.

Peruvian Mormons internalized, resisted, and amalgamated Anglo Mormon essentialist categories to various degrees, creating unique indigeneities that they passed on to their descendants, a few of whom were fourth-generation Mormons during my study. Many Peruvians in my study did not appreciate such Anglo paternalism, however, and did not agree with many of the Anglo values that created Mormonism. Why then did Peruvians want to be baptized into the Anglo Mormons' church in the first place? I avoided that question because all of my study participants resented it. First of all, they did not believe that it was the Anglo Mormons' church; they believed it was Christ's church. Second, it was not that they wanted to join the church because it offered them the most advantages in the growing "religious market" (Gooren 2003, title) of a rapidly de-Catholicizing Peru. It was that Jesus Christ Himself, sometimes quite audibly, sometimes through otherworldly messengers, told them to join.

Though the previous sentence sounds inappropriate coming from a social scientist who should be concerned with objectivity, this book will contain many such sentences because of my practice of what anthropologists Rane Willerslev and Christian Suhr (2015) called "methodological faith" (SL). Methodological faith provides a "radical reorienting shift in perspective" (20) gleaned not through the alterity of the ethnographic other, but through "a form of otherness that does not belong to oneself or the ethnographic other, but entirely subsumes them both" (18). I was not one to say whether that otherness was Jesus Christ or some alternate force, so I had faith in my study participants' faith. I also had faith in their ability to speak for themselves, which was why I fought to keep large stretches of uninterrupted and relatively unanalyzed interview transcript in this book. My methodological faith demanded of me that I use the tools of social science sparingly when analyzing faithful discourse. I felt that faithful discourse needed to be analyzed with its own tools, and I am confident that my readers of faith will possess more of those tools than

I did. Therefore, I occasionally leave readers to draw their own conclusions from the raw—albeit carefully selected, curated, and translated—transcripts.

However, the most important ramification of my methodological faith was that it allowed me to quickly put to rest the sociological question of why Peruvians became Mormons. I answered that question early on with a simple, yet unobservable answer: God wanted them to be. This freed up time for the following, more observable question. Given that some Peruvians in the late 2010s were Mormons, how did they navigate the fact that their church's centralized structure had been, since its founding, largely staffed with non-Peruvians?

Migratory Dreams

Even when Peruvian Mormons busy building their local Zions in Peru were not operating under the gaze of older Anglo leaders, they interacted with young Anglo missionaries on an almost daily basis because the largely Anglo-run mission district always grew in tandem with, and cartographically overlapped with, the largely Peruvian-run stake of Zion. Since the president of the Peru, Arequipa Mission District who participated in my study assigned his young missionaries to live in different neighborhoods in Arequipa, they became members of the ward families covering those neighborhoods. However, they were not beholden to the Peruvian bishops of those wards. Instead, they were only beholden to their Anglo mission president who would assign them to live in a different part of the Peru, Arequipa Mission every eight to twelve weeks. As a result, local church members perceived them to be highly migratory and aloof from the vicissitudes of nonmigratory arequipeño Mormon life and its ecclesiastical and topographical limitations. The missionaries' apparent financial independence accentuated that perception. During my study, funding for the eighteen-month (for females) to twenty-four-month (for males) unpaid missions of Mormon youth usually came either from their parents in the cases of most US missionaries or from their hometown wards' mission funds and ward families' donations in the cases of most Peruvian missionaries. The money would be prepaid to a mission account and distributed directly toward each missionary pairs' room and board, such that missionaries wanted for nothing and rarely handled money at all. This aura of mastery over material and spiritual concerns often lent the words of male eighteen- to twenty-year-old elders or female nineteen- to twenty-one-year-old sisters (ML) more sway than those of Peruvian church leaders who were decades their elders and who had been Mormons longer than the missionaries had been alive.

During my study, though there were Mormon missionaries in Arequipa from many places, including other parts of Peru, there was a disproportionate number from Utah. As a result of those demographics, many Peruvian Mormons in my study had a word for Utah. They called it "la fábrica" (the factory), meaning the production plant from whence Mormon bodies were reproduced and distributed to the world. The cosmopolitan, super-migratory "demonstrations of wholesome white masculinity" (Campbell 2020, 252) that were the bodies of Anglo Mormon male missionaries from la fábrica, combined with their aforementioned immunity from terrestrial problems, could not help but sanctify the image of Utah (Appadurai 1991) in the nascent Mormon dreams of already xenophilic Peruvians seeking escape from their own terrestrial problems through immigration (Altamirano 1999).

Sofi was one such Peruvian. She exemplified many others who were drawn to Utah despite their church's rhetoric—which had become increasingly doctrinal since the Kimball era—that "members of the Church [should] remain in their homelands rather than immigrate to the United States" (Church 1999, para. 1–4). When she moved to Peru's capital city of Lima in the early 1990s to matriculate at a technological institute, she met a pair of young men with white shirts and ties. One was from Utah, one of the least populous states in the United States. The other was from Peru's second most populous city, Arequipa. Elder Johnson and Elder Abedul were Mormon missionaries with a two-year, fulltime mandate to take the message of the newly restored church of Jesus Christ to the world, but particularly to a group of people whose ancestors, they believed, wrote *The Book of Mormon*.

The Book of Mormon made the process of adjusting and forceably fitting various Peruvian cultural categories into Anglo ones all the more complex for Sofi because it was through reading that book that she felt the desire to see herself as Indigenous for the first time. At the same time, it was only through reading that book that she first felt the desire—the call—to see herself as Mormon. Those desires could not be extricated from her underlying desire of thirty years, and that desire did not make her ultimate baptism into Mormonism any less genuine. That underlying desire was to reunite with her already-Mormon, Lamanite-identifying family by immigrating to Utah. Yet, as previously stated, her church leaders did not want her to leave Peru. They certainly did not want her Indigenous body entering the central church's historic Zion that the Mormon Pioneers founded.

Pioneer Indigeneity

This book engages the contradictions that Lamanites like Sofi navigated as a people included in a holy book but excluded from a holy place. Part I of this book engages the specific contradictions that indigeneity generated inside both Mormonism and Peruvianness. As a result of phenomena like *The Book of Mormon* and the Shining Path War, my Mormon study participants—even those who identified as Lamanites—often saw indigeneity in opposition to being a good Latter-day Saint. Furthermore, even though the sight of Indigenous people accepting Mormonism was a sign that the one true Zion, the New Jerusalem, was about to be completed, early Anglo Mormons had had to remove Indigenous people from the Salt Lake valley in order for that valley to become Zion. Salt Lake City required settler coloniality for its existence as a Zion (Parry 2019). Since the settler colonists who built Salt Lake City called themselves pioneers, the term "pioneer" got caught up in so many of Mormonism's origin myths associated with Anglo settler coloniality and Zion-building in Utah that "pioneer" became virtually synonymous with "Anglo Mormon" in the utterances of my Peruvian Mormon study participants.

Analyzing those utterances, it seemed to me that in the minds of Peruvian Mormons, being a true Saint required also being a pioneer. Did that mean that one also had to be White to be a Saint? Could people with ties to indigeneity, through Lamanite identity, also be pioneers? Chapters 1 through 4 explore questions having to do with the tension between pioneers and indigeneity. "Chapter 1: Leaders" wonders whether Lamanite-identifying Peruvians, who were not automatic pioneers by virtue of ancestral essence, would ever be able to take the reins of Zion-building in their own country. "Chapter 2: Government" asks how Peruvians used Mormonism's craft of origin mythmaking to wrest the pioneer title from the exclusive grasp of Anglo Mormonism and emblazon it onto a newly sovereign Peruvian Mormon self-government. "Chapter 3: Legacy" explores the question of whether Peruvian Mormon Lamanites could ever truly harness pioneer legacy. "Chapter 4: Holiness" analyzes the terrestrial valences of sacredness and wholeness that Peruvians gauged in order to plant *The Book of Mormon*, a settler colonial text, into an Indigenous Peruvian setting.

Since the first four chapters of the book all revolve around indigeneity and pioneers, terms that could easily become mutually exclusive or ring dichotomous, I came up with a shorthand term meant to encapsulate my argument, which is that they are neither mutually exclusive nor dichotomous. That term is "pioneer indigeneity" (SL).

Pioneer indigeneity is partially a reaction to colonization in that it helps me reveal how coloniality worked in the lived realities of my study participants. Pioneer indigeneity is an important aspect of Mormonism for all Saints regardless of nationality. It is present when Saints are unashamed at benefiting from both indigeneity and its antithesis. Pioneer indigeneity offers a view unencumbered by the anthropological temptation to sift subjects into the categories of resisting other and complicit other that delayed the development of an anthropology of Christianity until the 2000s (Bialecki, Haynes, and Robbins 2008). In other words, pioneer indigeneity is one of many new anthropological "frames that reject victimization and recognize a more complex engagement with power, one that doesn't necessarily 'look like' resistance but in fact speaks back to power" (M. E. García 2021, 152).

Pioneer indigeneity is a dialectic term, meaning that its dynamic opposition generates a third connotation that has more power than that which pioneering or indigeneity would be semantically allowed to exert separately. Since pioneer indigeneity applies differently to different positionalities, its dialectic strength for Anglo Mormons might go toward codifying their justification of land ownership in the Americas. For Peruvian Mormons, pioneer indigeneity might point to the ways in which they are even more "Mormon" than Anglos. In the end, I coined "pioneer indigeneity" because it allows me to concisely explain how Peruvian Mormons could be both Indigenous and members of what many Native scholars (Crowfoot 2021) consider a fundamentally US— and therefore, anti-indigenous—religion.

Temples

Part II of this book explores the contradictions inherent in family as a cross-culturally misinterpreted category. Across all the Mormonisms of my study, whether Anglo or Peruvian, family implied temple work (ML): the culmination of Zion. Temple work was the pinnacle of Zion's contradictorily inclusive exclusivity. On the one hand, the church's official mission was to use temple work to ceremonially bind all humans into one universal kinship (McKay-Lamb and Jensen 2015). On the other, that kinship's ultimate symbol, its architectural culmination, and the only spot of Earth wherein such an inclusive binding together of humanity could be done was a Mormon temple (ML), the same sort of temple that excluded all but the most worthy (ML) of Saints who happened to have what their official church counted as family.

The priesthood keys that Joseph Smith received from Peter, James, and John included many powers, but not the ones that allowed family relationships to remain bound together, or sealed (ML) in the afterlife. Those keys were particularly important for Mormons in my study because their official church taught that humans and others, including Jesus Christ and Satan, existed as siblings in one grand nuclear family under Heavenly Father and Heavenly Mother in the preexistence (ML) of this planet. To remind themselves of that primordial siblingship (SL), Mormons quotidianly referred to each other with the titles brother (ML) and sister (ML) during my study. Their belief held that in order that we mortals, as future gods, might become heavenly mothers and fathers to our own planets full of our own future offspring, our families needed to be sealed together as nuclear, heterosexual, couple-centric units ritually connected back to the first human couple on this planet, Adam and Eve.

However, before receiving the keys to seal relationships eternally, Joseph Smith's followers had to build an edifice, the crown jewel of Mormon Zion. They called it the temple. On April 3, 1836, the biblical prophet Elijah visited Smith in resurrected form inside the walls of the Mormons' newly finished temple in Ohio and gave him the power to seal couples in matrimony for time and all eternity (ML) so that Mormon families could be reunited in the afterlife.

Recall Sofi's mention of the Salt Lake City temple in the epigraph to this introduction. I will now explain how Sofi's words, and their templar context, demonstrated how her category of familia (PML) was fundamentally different from her Anglo-dominated church's category of family. On July 18, 2016, I digitally recorded her epigraphic words during an interview together with her husband, Rafa, in the Lima, Peru, airport. Sofi was a Peruvian Mormon soon-to-be immigrant to Utah. I was an Anglo Mormon anthropologist of Mormonism. Sofi's "husband," Rafa, was a Peruvian Catholic. My use of scare quotes for "husband" and my use of Spanish for familia signal the untranslatability of kin categories between Anglo Mormonism and Peruvian Mormonism. Such untranslatability is one of this book's themes.

For the first few years of my study, I took the words of Peruvian Mormon immigrants to Utah like Sofi at face value. I interpreted them to mean that Utah remained a mecca for Mormons, that Mormons felt an inexplicable draw to its pioneer-sculpted landscape and architecture, and that Mormons felt that Utah was indeed the one true Zion, the city of God. It took me a few more years of deeply hanging out with Peruvian Mormons to realize that Zion, for them, was inchoate. Rather than revolving around Utah for Sofi, the places and sentiments of her Peruvian Mormon Zion revolved around the temple, and the temple revolved around familia. Therefore, while the Lima temple had existed since 1986, Sofi still wanted to immigrate to Utah because La Familia mostly lived within driving distance of its Salt Lake City temple.

Sofi and I were both members of La Familia, a large group of mostly Peruvians and mostly Mormons who spread across Peru and Utah through the 1970s immigration of my spouse, Elvira's, tía (PL) Jacoba Arriátegui and tío (PL) Arcadio Costa. However, Sofi and I had never met before our airport interview because she was one of La Familia's last daughters to immigrate from Peru to Utah, and I was a relatively recent addition to La Familia through marriage. My positionality as both an Anglo Mormon and a member of a Peruvian Mormon family gave me valuable access to the inner workings and outer limits of what constituted the category of relatedness for both groups.

In my estimation, the category of relatedness contained the principal difference between Anglo Mormonism and Peruvian Mormonism. During my study, not to mention the preceding five centuries, Anglos and Peruvians regardless of Mormonism existed on a geopolitical power dynamic that favored Anglos. Therefore, what might have been considered a benign difference between two equally powerful societies regarding what could be categorized as family was instead placed under the colonial power dynamic and converted into an excuse for both Anglo and Peruvian Mormons to see Peruvian Mormon familias as less worthy than Anglo Mormon families.

Unsealability

Since the temple was almost synonymous with marriage and nuclear family in official church manuals, biannual church General Conference speeches, and church magazines (all published in and distributed from Salt Lake City), the temple became the site wherein the power that Anglo Mormons brandished over Peruvian Mormons reached its apogee. During my study, Mormon temples were where Anglo-defined, patriarchal, nuclear families, as opposed to Peruvian-defined, often matriarchal (Palmer 2022), expansive familias, were sealed or bound together for eternity. Unsealed families could not be together in the afterlife, and many Peruvian Mormon familias in my study tended to be nearly unsealable. Their unsealability was due to the official church's policies (ML)—decided upon by the First Presidency and the Twelve in Salt Lake City from an outsider perspective but decided upon by Christ Himself from an insider one—that constrained temple rites.

First, unlike chapels wherein visitors were welcome, temples were only for baptized members of the church whom two male interviewers—a bishop and a stake president—had deemed worthy and had granted temple entry cards called "temple-recommends" (ML) that expired every two years. Temple-worthiness often had as much to do with what the particular interviewer thought of the member's familial situation and civil status as it did with the member's ability to answer affirmatively the pat temple-recommend interview questions from the official church's handbook of instructions. Those questions dealt with belief in Jesus Christ, in His living prophet, in following His ten biblical commandments, and in the importance of paying one-tenth of one's income to His church's Salt Lake City coffers. Whether or not a temple-recommend was granted, however, ultimately depended upon the interviewer's phenomenological ability to discern temple-worthiness in the interviewee. This meant that any number of factors internal to the male interviewer—for example, racism, sexism, stance on immigration, jealousy, or morning mood—could, especially when exacerbated by the aforementioned power dynamic between Anglos and Peruvians, temporarily preclude a Peruvian member's ability to enter the temple at all, let alone enter for the purpose of being sealed to a loved one.

Sofi, knowing that she would soon be close enough to enter the holy Salt Lake City temple, got an appointment with her stake president in Lima for a temple-recommend interview. The stake president, unlike most stake presidents in Peru, happened to be an Anglo Mormon (he was a US diplomat stationed in Lima). He refused to sign off on her temple-recommend card even though her Peruvian bishop had already signed it. Her stake president's refusal to sign was not because she failed to answer all questions satisfactorily but because, in planning to immigrate to Utah, Sofi was planning on breaking the Lord's longstanding counsel found in a letter from the First Presidency that her stake president had recently read from the pulpit. That letter was similar to the aforementioned letter from 1999, which reiterated that the church's peripheralized parishioners needed to "remain in their homelands rather than immigrate to the United States" (Church 1999, para. 4). Therefore, though her immigrant visa would soon allow her body entry into the bounded center of the US settler state, her lack of a temple-recommend would bar her soul entry into the most holy of Mormon Zion spaces therein. Understandably, Sofi resented her church's anti-immigration letter and her stake president's interpretation of it as affecting temple-worthiness. Though she was already plotting ways to circumvent her stake president, such as scheduling an interview with a new stake president once in Utah, the sentiments she harbored were almost identical to those of an Indigenous farmer who participated in anthropologist Maria Elena García's (2021) study of Peruvian gastropolitics. The farmer said, "The problem is that we are seen as clinging to our lands, being almost part of our lands, and we can't move from there. They don't want us to move from there" (131).

Even when my Peruvian Mormon study participants like Sofi procured a temple-recommend and were physically, logistically, financially, and legally able to travel to the nearest temple (Rodríguez 2018)—the only terrestrial place wherein relationships could be immortalized—many found themselves inside temples surrounded by loved ones with whom they still could not be sealed. This was because of a second set of constrictions on temple rites. There were only two sorts of relationships that could be temple-sealed according to the official church's policy of familial nuclearization during my study: husband-wife and couple-child.

One husband-wife sealing ceremony that I witnessed during my study took place in a small, ornately decorated but virtually colorless room in the upper floor of the Ogden, Utah, temple. A priesthood-holding, Spanish-speaking, Anglo male whom God had vested with the keys of sealing and whom the state of Utah had vested with the authority to marry, read the liturgy. He pronounced the couple—a Peruvian American groom and a Mexican American bride—legally married for their time on this Earth, and granted them a destiny wherein they would become a joint god/goddess dyad that would reproduce infinitely.

The first child born of that couple after their sealing ceremony in the temple was considered already sealed to them. Her name was Jessica. The official church designated Jessica as born in the covenant (ML), meaning that she was automatically, eternally connected to both of her parents. No temple-sealing ceremony would be necessary for her except one, the one that would connect her to her future husband and, therefore, to her resulting future offspring. If both of her parents had also been born of Mormon temple-married parents, then she, upon birth, would have also been automatically connected through their covenant lineages to all four of her grandparents who, if they had been born of Mormon temple-married parents, would have connected her to all eight of her great-grandparents and so on through unbroken lines of blood descent tracing back to Adam and Eve.

However, if Jessica's deceased maternal grandfather, for example, had never been Mormon and thus never able to seal himself to his deceased Mormon wife in the temple, Jessica could, provided that she knew his name, birthdate, and birthplace, print his name on a card from her church's genealogical website, Familysearch.org, and ask a male friend to be baptized in the basement of the temple on her dead grandfather's behalf. Jessica could then become a proxy bride representing her grandmother who would be temple-sealed to her newly Mormonized grandfather vicariously in a marriage for the dead. Once Jessica's dead maternal grandparents were temple-sealed, she could then fix the rupture that had separated those grandparents from being sealed to her living, Mormon, temple-worthy mother. This would require that Jessica's mother undergo the couple-child sealing ceremony wherein proxies would represent Jessica's dead grandparents and Jessica's mother would represent herself.

All of that complexity was temple work. Its goal was to seal the ruptures between couples and their children up the generations in straight lines until each family that ever existed on Earth was properly nuclearized and connected back to Adam and Eve, forming one universal group that got to count as a family in Anglo Mormonism.

Of course, Peruvian relatedness was not as easily worked into straight lines back to Adam and Eve as Anglo relatedness was. Therefore, temple work excluded many of my Peruvian Mormon study participants from sealability. For one thing, most Peruvian Mormons were either single mothers themselves or came from situations of generational single motherhood and unmarried serial polyandry, which produced anything but tidy, nuclear, arboreal lines of genealogy. Being unmarried posed a problem for patching (sealing) generational rifts because children could only be sealed to married couples, not to individual parents. For another thing, most of the Peruvian Mormons in my study represented the first generation of Mormons in their extensive, non-Mormon familias. Therefore, they lacked the automatic sealing that came with being born in the covenant. Furthermore, they often lacked the textual and photographic records of their ancestors that many born-in-the-covenant Anglo Mormons took for granted by virtue of having parents, grandparents, and even great-grandparents who, being Mormon, knew the importance of curating their own ancestors' data for temple work.

Still, Peruvian Mormons in my study were resourceful. Often, when they did not qualify for a familial rite according to the Anglo Mormon category of relatedness, they would rewire it into a Peruvian Mormon category that allowed them to qualify (Palmer forthcoming). As Sofi's story will depict below,

Peruvian Mormons' creativity was not limited to circumventing their official church's familial strictures. It also involved circumventing US legal ones.

Family

The ways in which my study participants went about circumventing what others might have categorized separately as "US law" and "LDS religion," demonstrated that such separations were arbitrary. Sofi's actions below, therefore, lend credence to the historical theory that the US government and the Mormon religion were co-constructs (Gordon 2002) and to the Native studies theory that the two remained codependent facets of the same settler colonial project (Estes 2020).

I arranged Sofi and Rafa's interview to happen right before their inaugural flight to the United States. It was to be their "before-immigration" interview. Soon after arriving in Utah, they would attend Jacoba and Arcadio's son Hector's chicken-frying fundraiser (pollada) on July 28, Peru's Independence Day, where they agreed that I could conduct their "after-immigration" interview. I thought that by comparing the two interviews, I would be able to contrast Sofi's imaginings of Utah-as-Zion against her immediate perception of its reality. I ended up witnessing more of a contrast than I had expected.

When it came time for our "after-immigration" interview, I could not find Rafa or Sofi anywhere among the seventy Peruvian and Latinx partiers of all ages inside Hector Costa's middle-class, suburban, single-family, Utah home. However, when I escaped the huayno dance, "Pío Pío," to check the chicken friers outside on the deck—while Runasimi/Spanish lyrics and stomping feet reverberated through the drywall—I saw Sofi sitting alone on a patio chair. In comparison to her formal, stilted comportment during our "before" interview wherein she focused on the sanctity of both US law and the Salt Lake City temple, she now seemed relaxed, maybe even a little conspiratorial. Gesturing to the large quantity of chicken that was meant to be sold to Hector's Anglo neighbors and fellow English-speaking ward family members to raise funds for the victims of flash flooding in Piura, Peru, she criticized "those gringos" (PL) for not supporting the pollada: "They can very well afford to fork over 10 percent of their incomes in tithing, but they can't even give so much as $10 to help a flood victim?"

Struck by her comfort in critiquing Anglo Mormon hypocrisy and by her subtle disparaging of the sacred Mormon practice of tithe paying, I felt that she trusted me—one of "those gringos"—too much for me to retain from her my secret: thanks to my spouse Elvira, Sofi's prima (PL), I knew the truth behind everything that she had said in the "before-immigration" interview about her marriage to Rafa.

When I told her this, she was visibly relieved that I had not been offended about her real motivation for participating in the interview: to use both it and my White, US-male status as a simulation for what she later confronted in the person of the White, US-male embassy official whose job it was to phenomenologically discern her US-worthiness and the legitimacy of her marriage to Rafa. She then clarified the extent of her sincerity regarding other aspects of our interview. Ultimately, she had deliberately left out the nuance in most of what she had said regarding the holiness of Utah. This mean that her epigraphic excerpt mostly reflected what she thought that I—a Utah Mormon—wanted to hear. She further clarified that it was not only her lack of a Utah driver's license that would preclude her immediate trip to the Salt Lake City temple, but her lack of a temple-recommend. Though she desired to be sealed to La Familia for eternity inside a temple, she had never been temple-worthy, had never experienced a Mormon male stake president discern worthiness in her body or spirit, and had never even been inside the Lima temple. She most certainly had never been inside the iconic Salt Lake City temple, the cinematographically intense images of which had graced the projection screen of her Lima chapel every six months during the previous twenty years of her church's broadcast of its General Conference.

She then told me about how her childhood in Chimbote ended up sparking her matrimonial creativity with Rafa. Although she grew up as a hermana (PL) by Peruvian constructivist kinship standards to the children of her Tía Kimberly, who was Jacoba's niece, she was biologically their cousin by US essentialist standards. This meant that when Kimberly's daughter Eva married an Anglo Mormon from Utah, became a US citizen, and began to petition her "siblings and half-siblings" (a non-Peruvian distinction) for immigrant visas to the United States, Sofi did not qualify.

In Peruvianness, Sofi was just as much a sibling to Kimberly's children as they were to each other because they all grew up constructing that siblingship by eating the same food under the same roof. In Peru, relatedness was more a construction that required togetherness in place and over time than something already attached to the essence of biological reproduction. Peruvians constructed their relatives. They were not merely born with them. Therefore, relatedness—together with most of the other categories that this book explores—was more constructivist than essentialist for Peruvians. However, for the United States, which based its category of relatedness increasingly upon genetics ever since the 1953 popularization of DNA as the mechanism of biological inheritance, Sofi was merely a cousin. In the United States, shared genes and matrimonial/adoption law contained the essence of true relatedness. Therefore, its category of relatedness was more essentialist than constructivist. Consequently, Sofi did not fall under the United States Citizenship and Immigration Services' (USCIS) sanctioned category of direct family that allowed US citizens to apply for visas only for children, spouses, parents, siblings, and the direct nuclear dependents of the same. Though most of Eva's dozen siblings immigrated to Utah within a decade, Sofi stayed behind in Peru for three decades, stuck in the US-defined and vilified category of "extended family" (AL), a category that did not exist in Peruvian vernacular and that had no translation in Spanish or Runasimi.

However, Sofi eventually found a loophole in US immigration law: Eva could petition her own father Rafa for an immigrant visa, and Sofi could become his wife. Eva and Rafa accepted this plan. Sofi married Rafa. Thereafter, Sofi figured as the dependent spouse on a valid, US immigrant visa petition. Sofi had successfully rewired her familia to make it legible enough in the United States as family to unite it. Sofi legally became her sister Eva's stepmother, a relationship that counted as family for USCIS purposes when cousin did not. Sofi's new husband—her sister's father—was only in Utah for two days before returning to Peru, hence his absence from the pollada. But Sofi was in Utah to stay.

Her relief in discovering that despite already knowing most of that story, I still respected her, stemmed from her original fear that I, being an Anglo Mormon, would accuse her of making a mockery of US immigration law. Since many Mormons, both Anglo and Peruvian—in line with scriptural evidence from Mormonism's canonical books—believed that US legal documents were divine, she thought that I would berate her about not coming the "right" way into the United States. In fact, she suspected that the Anglo stake president had somehow discerned her creative marriage as the true source of her immigrant visa. She feared that he had denied her temple-recommend because of that and not because, as he had claimed, of the First Presidency's anti-immigration letter.

I assured her that I was not her Anglo stake president. I told her of my border abolitionist stance, of the historical recency and xenophobia of the claim that only romantic love could make a marriage legitimate, and of my anthropological awe at her kinship ingenuity. We laughed together at the Peruvian adage, "papelito manda" (at the tiny paper's command), which indexed the simultaneous silliness and holiness of colonial statecraft's obsession with documents, such as marriage certificates and visas. She even commented on the remarkable similarity between the process of procuring an LDS temple-recommend and the process of procuring a US visa. Both processes were meant to block the profane from crossing borders into the sacred.

Sofi's contrived before-immigration interview and her confessionary after-immigration interview provided me a window into Peruvian Mormon Zion's interwoven layers of complexity regarding relatedness. One layer involved the overlap between USCIS and LDS notions of family. Both notions were narrow in only recognizing as USCIS-petitionable or LDS temple-sealable a handful of relationships. Just as Eva could not petition a cousin's visa as a matter of US policy, she also could not seal a cousin relationship in the temple as a matter of LDS policy, even if said cousin were worthy to enter. However, while LDS and USCIS kinship categories overlapped significantly, LDS kinship notions remained far narrower than USCIS notions. If one was an unwed parent, for example, one could be reunited with one's child through a USCIS petition, but one could not be eternally united to one's child through an LDS sealing.

Another layer of Peruvian Mormon Zion that Sofi's interviews peeled back involved how her material desire to cross borders in order to be reunited with La Familia in this life related complexly to her spiritual desire to cross temple doors in order to be ritually sealed, and thus reunited with La Familia in the afterlife. Sofi's Mormonism sanctified a unidirectional, arboreal model of ancestor-to-descendent relatedness based on the essence of shared DNA. Her Peruvianness, on the other hand, constructed relatedness among humans, nonhumans, and generations—as chapter 6 analyzes—through the multi-directional, rhizomatic sharing of other substances, such as food and drink (Weismantel 1995). In an act that transgressed her Mormonism, she married her sister's father, thus genealogically rewiring the individuating, patrifocal nuclear family that her official church's leaders considered the immutable forever family (AML). Simultaneously, in an act that strained her Peruvianness, she utilized that rewiring in order to physically join, far from Peru, the communally constructed, matrifocal familia that both her religion and its incubator—the US settler state—demonized in ways that I discuss in chapter 5.

Familia

In being both Peruvian and Mormon, Sofi embodied the melding of many categories, such as coloniality and indigeneity, that often seemed polar opposites to my Anglo Mormon study participants. However, such a melding was nothing new in the Andes, the greater geographic cultural area that included much of Peru. In the Andes, things that Anglo Mormons classified into opposing, impermeable categories often existed as one whole category. For example, many Indigenous Andeans placed both good and evil into one category called "saxras," poorly translated as "sacred" (O. Harris 2006). As this book demonstrates, the Andes' holistic, permeable categories affected Peruvian Mormonism's reconfiguration of Anglo Mormonism's narrow, binary categories.

At the root of family—one of this book's key objects of study—there existed a foundational set of categorical opposites for Anglo Mormons that did not exist as starkly among Peruvian Mormons. That set involved nature versus culture (Douglas 1966). According to Andean philosopher of the late 2010s Conibo Mallku Bwillcawaman (2015), since many Andean societies were not divided along a nature-versus-culture axis, the European categories that inhered to nature, such as sex, and to culture, such as gender, did not exist there. Within Andean ideals, so-called gender roles had to be played, but their playing involved neither an essential, genitalia-assigned category of sex nor an essential, God-given category of gender (Rivera Cusicanqui 2010). Furthermore, unlike Anglo Mormon gender roles, man and woman complementarity did not imply a zero-sum game wherein "when one side expands, the other side necessarily contracts" (Patterson 2020, 70). Instead, complementarity involved a constructed, community-assisted balance wherein man selves and woman selves caused each other to exist and become one "full related selfhood" (E. A. Johnson 1996, 68) called the ayllu in Runasimi.

This all meant that gender, like relatedness, was more constructivist among Andeans and more essentialist among Mormons. Among Andeans in my study, familia was generally seen as constructed through human volition. Among Mormons in my study, family was generally understood as already containing an unchosen essence. In the end, I found that the question over where to draw the line between essentialism and constructivism regarding relatedness generated productive controversies in the lives of Andeans who became Mormons.

One effect of these controversies' productivity was linguistic: the melding of constructed relatedness with essential relatedness produced new ways of using words and mixing languages. Again, I highlight that production by distinguishing familia from family throughout this book. The Runasimi word "pacha" (SL) adds another tone to the depth of meaning within familia that makes it resonate too differently from family to be synonymous. Understanding pacha requires understanding the Andean allyu and its lack of individuality. Upon death, human ayllu members ideally reentered the inner world as a fully polarized but genderless collective soul, part of which could properly inhere to the raw materials of an as-yet-unsexed, potentially human infant but only with work involving a cyclical exchange between human ayllu members, such as farmers, and nonhuman ayllu members, such as corn (Canessa 2012). In that cycle, both ancestors and the past were up, down, ahead, and behind. There were no descendants just as there were no individuals. The collective was its own ancestor. Linear blood descent—upon which LDS genealogical strictures were patterned for the temple-sealing of individual dead ancestors and upon which the USCIS's definition of direct family was likewise patterned—made little sense in the Andean nonlinear, ungendered category of relatedness. That holistic category was called pacha in Andean academic philosophy (Mallku Bwillcawaman 2015). Pacha, which meant both earth and familia, was similar to the Hawaiian word 'āina (Silva 2017) in that it encompassed everything that European colonization separated into the stark domains of science, religion, kinship, sex, and gender. Pacha was also similar to the Dakota word tiyośpaye, a federation of families. As with pacha, in the closeness of tiyośpaye "lay such strength and social importance as no single family, however able, could or wished to achieve entirely by its own efforts" (E. C. Deloria 1988, 20).

Settler scholars have conducted countless studies of various Indigenous kinship systems. They seek the source of those systems' linguistic incompatibility with colonizing tongues. During such studies, members of Indigenous groups who usually favored the scholars' colonial language would often momentarily switch to their ancestral languages in order to replace the colonial word for family with a holistic word akin to pacha. For example, many monolingual English-speaking Diné participants in such studies used the word k'e because they sensed in it something both broader and deeper than the English word kinship (Bluehouse and Zion 1993). The English-speaking Māori used whānau because it denoted relationality to both human and nonhuman people and geographies in ways that "family" could not (Walker 2017).

Likewise, my monolingual English-speaking Peruvian American study participants born in Utah seemed to subconsciously perceive an incommensurability between Anglo and Peruvian categories. They almost invariably said "familia" in the midst of an English sentence instead of "family." Throughout the second half of this book, I honor that practice by applying it to the following recurring question: if terms like pacha, 'āina, tiyośpaye, k'e, whānau, and familia worked to reunite Indigenous wholes that European coloniality divided into discrete categories, what categorical understandings might the theories and experiences of Peruvian Mormons reconfigure, and what seepages between colonializing categories might their language expose?

Forever Familia

During my study, the church used "a forever family" as an advertising slogan to distinguish itself as the only organization on the planet with the power to have "sealed in heaven" (J. Smith 1830, 435) certain kin relationships that were forged either genetically or legally (the only two options) on Earth. As captured in a 2018 article in the church's globally distributed magazine, *Liahona*, achieving forever family status not only improved a family's celestial living arrangements in the afterlife, but it also conferred upon a family's earthly home a "happy and warm" (McBride 2018, 69) feeling unavailable to families whose relationships were not sealed.

The spiritual, historical, topographical, and architectural culmination of Mormon Zion was the temple precisely because the temple was the place wherein temporary groupings became forever families. This transformation depended on a heteronormative, monogamous, husband-centric category of kinship established through the historic interplay of US settler colonialism and US Mormonism (Ulrich 2020). The US-centric nature of Mormonism's archetypal category of relatedness meant that family signified something different to the official church than its translation, familia, signified to my Mormon study participants who were not from the United States. To magnify that categorical misalignment—and the others that it produced within future (chapter 5), marriage (chapter 6), and independence (chapter 7)—I coined the Spanglish term, "forever familia" (SL).

Forever familia recalls two intersectional difficulties. One was the difficulty that Peruvians encountered while trying to make their pacha familias legible as Mormon families. The other was the difficulty they encountered while trying to force a "forever" sort of future-centrism onto Peruvian temporal categories that contained no stark divisions between past, present, and future. I chose Spanglish for forever familia because it was the language of my in-laws, La Familia. In 2018, most of its members lived in the same up-and-coming Utah suburb—Salsands—and called their group "La Familia" even when speaking English. This book explores the quotidian reasons why La Familia and other nonnuclear Peruvian Mormon familias did not easily fall into the category of forever family—or even family—in many formulations of Zion.

However, this book also explores La Familia's uncategorizability in general and how its categorical in-betweenness threatened Anglo Mormonism's strict categorical separations. For one thing, whether members of La Familia could be categorized as immigrants to or indigenous to "America" depended upon the legitimacy of artificial borders that cut across both the northern and southern portions of that single landmass (Walia 2021). Peruvian grade school texts considered that landmass to be one continent. US texts considered it to be two. Furthermore, members of La Familia were nationally uncategorizable. They lived both their Peruvianness and their Mormonism in the destination place of their religion's origin story (Utah), in the unplaceable space of Zion, in the US settler state, in the land promised to their Jewish migrant ancestors, and in Peru where they constructed/found more members of La Familia to help migrate. This palimpsestic existence—ostensibly living in one place but inhabiting multiple realms—created an ambiguity common to many migrants that feminist anthropologists Nina Glick-Schiller, Linda Basch, and Cristina Blanc-Szanton called "transnationalism" (1992, 1). The transnationalism of La Familia was further complicated by its fluid class status (Pereyra 2015) stretched across various systems amalgamated through migration, unmarried serial polyandry with members of other nation-states, and generational matrilocality (SL: when a husband moves into his mother-in-law's household). In sum, for La Familia and other transnational migrants, "the division between home and not-home and insider and outsider [was] simplistic" (Alcalde 2018, 11).

Therefore, La Familia menaced colonial taxonomies. It was uncategorizable. Its transnationalism, indigeneity, class complexity, and religion combined to threaten the tidiness of the economic category of nation-state and its germ—family—upon which both Zion and the United States depended.

La Familia's threat exposed the fragility of the façade that portrayed the LDS and the USCIS category of family as universal. In order to demonstrate how Peruvian Mormon forever familias revamped their official church's category of family, the final three chapters of this book investigate a few of the constitutive categories of forever familia. "Chapter 5: Future" examines how Peruvian spacetime placed future outside of Peru, causing migrations of people and changes to their ways of being relatives and Saints. "Chapter 6: Marriage" scales Mormon punctuality out to the existential level through the situations of two unmarried Peruvian women who struggled to stick to Mormon life-schedules. "Chapter 7: Independence" follows Anglo and Peruvian Mormons as they navigate the dialectic of Peruvian collectivism versus US individuality and its interplay with Peruvian Mormons who were both collectivists and individualists.

Methodology

To explore the complexity of Peruvian Mormon Zion's reconfiguration of categories that Sofi's marriage of convenience to Rafa exemplified, I gathered ethnographic data through three summers of preliminary research from 2014 to 2016 in Peru and Utah. I followed that with two, six-month phases of fulltime "observant participation" (Bernard 2011) with Spanish-speaking, Mormon wards, one in Salsands, Utah, in 2017 and the other in Arequipa, Peru, in 2018. From 2019 to 2021, I collaborated with a few key study participants (particularly the real people behind the composite characters of Sofi, Jacoba, Collin, Pasi, Ofelia, Simón, and Basilio) to vet drafts of this book. Their revisions helped temper my critical analysis with methodological faith.

Sites

Both of my principal field sites were home to about 20,000 active Mormons (ML: Mormons who continue to participate in their ward family's activities after baptism), but Arequipa's total population was 900,000 and Salsands's was 29,000. The Latinx population of Salsands was probably less than 1,000 and included about 300 Peruvians, 100 of whom were members of one of La Familia's many overlapping cadres. I chose Salsands because it was the nexus of La Familia's many complex networks of family-based migration, and I was already a member of La Familia. Though I chose Salsands largely for convenience in accessing study participants with whom I already had a relationship of trust (except for the Costa faction of La Familia, whose trust I still had to earn), its Spanish-speaking ward, Pioneer Trail, gave me access to many other Peruvian and Anglo Mormon study participants who were not members of La Familia. Even if I had limited myself to participating with La

Familia for the duration of this study, the sheer diversity of that family along the spectrums of race, class, immigration status, mode of US arrival, religious devotion, Indigenous identity, and even national origin gave me confidence that I was approaching the full picture of what the categorical chapter titles of this book meant for various Mormons and non-Mormons.

In order to access the geographical core of forever familia creation in Zion, I also chose Arequipa, Peru, as a field site. That city first caught my eye because in 2012, the Prophet Thomas Monson slated Arequipa as the site of Peru's third and the globe's 163rd Mormon temple. For the Prophet to have selected Arequipa as a temple site, local Mormons in the city had to have multiplied their wards enough to be geographically bound into many, relatively Peruvian-governed stakes of Zion rather than remaining under one large, Anglo-controlled mission district. The conglomeration of those stakes (Arequipa had seven), each with their seven or eight wards, had to have encompassed enough temple-worthy, tithe-paying families to warrant the multimillion-dollar construction of a temple that was to be funded, designed, and contracted entirely by church headquarters.

Since only members of worthy families could achieve forever family status, my preliminary research among arequipeños while they were making themselves and their city worthy of a Utah-directed temple construction project caused me to notice a categorical mismatch between family and familia. During temple construction, arequipeño Mormons seemed more aware than ever of their perceived status among Anglos as unworthy nonnuclear familias rather than as worthy nuclear families. In other words, the temple—because it was both a metaphor for Zion and "the fully material construction zone" (Maffly-Kipp 2020b, 147) of Zion—was one of the places wherein forever familia distinguished itself from forever family most strikingly. I felt that if I could inhabit a place that was transitioning to full Zion status through temple construction, then I could witness a people's transition, or failure to transition, to a status that was fully worthy of that temple. Therefore, I chose to live in Arequipa.

Arequipeño Mormons' negative opinions of their own familial progress toward "forever" status provided an interesting contrast to their official church's opinions because, seen through the numerical, corporate lens that considered Zion and its categories to be internationally transplantable, Peruvian families appeared quite worthy. With 600,000 baptized members, 200,000 active members (my own estimate), 112 stakes of Zion, and three temples, Peru ranked fifth in the world behind the United States, Mexico, Brazil, and the Philippines in physical Zion-building during my study according to the algorithm that central church statisticians used to calculate a nation-state's status as a Zion. By the time this book is published, there will likely be nine completed or nearly completed temples in Peru. This will mean that Peruvian

Mormonism's rate of organizational growth, starting with an active membership of only 300 in 1959, will continue to be one of the church's highest.

Data

Data for this project took three principal forms: fieldnotes of interactions at congregational and familial activities, photographs of those activities, and audio recordings of 468 interviews with people contacted through those activities. After transcribing the interviews and coding them using qualitative data analysis software, which I then paired with over 4,000 pages of single-spaced field notes and over 16,000 photographs, patterns began to emerge that depicted my Peruvian study participants as a community engaged in building, merging, puncturing, and renaming their cultural categories so as to find space for themselves in the ultimate Mormon category: Zion. Of course, with that much data, I ran into the same limitation that Third Nephi, a descendant of Lehi's son Nephi, faced two millennia prior, meaning that "this book cannot contain even a hundredth part of what was done among so many people" (J. Smith 1830, 463). Therefore, there are many pressing questions that I will have to explore in future publications.

Positionality

Another limitation was that the principal instruments of data collection for this project were my eyes and ears, both of which captured stimuli filtered through my biases and preconceived notions of what was important. I must, therefore, dwell somewhat on the creation of those biases and notions.

I am a generational, born-in-the-covenant Mormon with what Anglo Mormons call "pioneer ancestry," meaning that I, and most of my great-grandparents, grew up in the Utah church. I could not extricate the experiences that I had during my official, Institutional Review Board–approved fieldwork for this project (2014–2021) from the experiences that I have had my entire life (I was born in 1979) as an integral part of Mormon wards across the world—Utah, Bolivia, Taiwan, Turkey, Japan, California, and Peru—during my various careers as a religious missionary, K–12 educator, and anthropologist.

My partner, Elvira, is Peruvian and was baptized into the church in Chiclayo in 1983 along with her mother and brothers. On July 28, 2001, we were sealed for time and all eternity inside the Salt Lake City temple in a ceremony that was too sacred (ML) for our non-Mormon kin to attend. Our Peruvian Mormon prima Sofi also could not attend. Not only was she not temple-worthy, but she was not legally worthy to enter the US settler state. We now have three daughters and a growing, conglomerated familia—La Familia—that is mostly comprised of Peruvian Mormons.

In 2013, I offered a project for acceptance into an anthropology PhD program at the University of California, Irvine. I proposed to study my own familial situation, specifically focusing on why so many Peruvian Mormons immigrated to Utah, giving that state the highest concentration of Peruvians in the United States outside of the Eastern Seaboard (US Census Bureau 2010). I assumed that it had something to do with Utah continuing to be felt as sort of Zion for Peruvian Mormons. However, also in 2013 and unbeknownst to most of my in-laws—who would go on to make up about 150 of my approximately 1,000 study participants—Elvira and I underwent a change in our way of living our Mormonism that was more drastic than the constant changes that had previously gone unnoticed during our international lives.

The change was sparked on April 8, 2013, when Anglo Mormon Jean A. Stevens became the first female to pray at General Conference, the most significant Mormon religious gathering of the year (Berkes 2013). Rather than celebrate her prayer as progress, we had a feminist awakening.[3] We already knew that, since the 1950s (Bowman 2020), only men could hold the priesthood—which was not the state of being a priest (Stapley 2020) but rather the power (ability/charisma) and authority (permission/office) of a phenotypically male God to act in His name (Toscano 2020)—and we had consciously reconciled that divine sexism as one of His many mysteries that could be mentally stored away for future elucidation (Rivera Wright 2021).

However, in official church doctrine, public prayer did not require priesthood. As critically conscious Saints, how had we not noticed that from 1830 (the church's inaugural year) to 2013, women were excluded—without theological justification—from praying at the very conferences that guided our saintly formations? We wondered what other manifestations of sexism our faith had caused to escape our consciousnesses and what would stop our daughters from internalizing that sexism.

The obvious solution would have been to stop associating with the church. However, faith, for us, was not a glib thing that could simply be discarded. Furthermore, we felt that a faith crisis did not establish a simple polarity between believers and unbelievers, especially since "Mormonism never was simply a faith; it always was a 'way of life'" (Van Beek 2005, 25).

During this time of rapid evolution in my faith, UCI accepted my ethnographic proposal. Going to church was now to be both my academic job and my spiritual journey. This created a seven-yearlong dilemma that I faced every time I participated with Mormons in performing Mormonism. I agonized over the ethics of my ultimate decision to "stay Mormon" during my study of Mormons. Was I staying in order to secure greater ethnographic access, or was I staying in order to secure greater spiritual salvation? I could not deny that it was logistically advantageous for me to utilize my continued membership in the church in order to officially join Mormon ward families as an active member, which often involved accepting a calling and participating in near-daily communal activities rich with ethnographic experiences. To make my dilemma more complex, if I wanted any clout in those wards, Mormonism's focus on the nuclear family—a form of kinship that became, in the late 1800s, the US standard by which all other forms were judged (Coontz 2016)—would make it advantageous to have my spouse and daughters attend church with me, a church, mind you, with an official leadership that we now suspected of deliberately inculcating sexism. For the entire seven years of this project, we joined Spanish-speaking ward families in Utah (Iber 2000), California, and Peru in this uncomfortable state of what we constantly feared would be exposed as a sort of staged orthopraxy meant to disguise our unorthodoxy.

We did not lie about our supposed unorthodoxy, which at times verged on atheism, but we also did not go out of our way to disabuse our fellow ward family members in Salsands's Pioneer Trail Ward4 (many of whom were also La Familia) or in Arequipa's Barrio Periféricos (Peripheral Ward) of what we assumed was their assumption that ours was a properly "Mormon" forever family in Zion. Much assuming was afoot. We assumed that if our coreligionists only knew what we truly believed, then they would consider us impostors. However, interviewing Mormons about their true beliefs taught me something: most Latter-day Saints felt like impostors. Therefore, I fit right in. Peruvian Mormonism taught me that there was no such thing as a Mormon orthodoxy. There was no such thing as a true believer. In fact, belief or unbelief was not at issue at all. What was at issue was a willingness to be one with the Saints. And that was something that I could genuinely be.

Participation

During the seven years that I spent in and around my chosen field sites, I proselytized with Mormon missionaries, visited Mormon homes, socialized with temple construction workers, became a temple ritual worker, baptized two of my daughters, and worked alongside Peruvian Mormons in their professions. Through one 2015 activity in Utah—an irreverent Mormon Comic-Con of sorts called the Sunstone Symposium—I met a Mormon woman from Cusco named Pasi who ended up occasionally directing my research toward Mormons in that city as a supplement to my research in Arequipa. In Arequipa and Cusco, I participated in dozens of events at which I was probably the only Mormon, such as Catholic pilgrimages, carnavales, and patron-saint "cargo" festivals that involved ritual negotiations of Catholic indigeneity through dance and drink. With La Familia and other Mormons in Arequipa, Cusco, and Salsands, I joined and/or organized multitudes of worship services, baptisms, talent nights, committee meetings, weddings, Family Nights (ML), open-houses, leadership trainings, FIFA World Cup parties, Self-Reliance Initiative courses, Pioneer Day parades, and mountain excursions.

I captured the thoughts of the participants in those activities by digitally recording semi-formal interviews, public meetings, and semi-spontaneous focus groups. Rather than asking about the categorical chapter titles of this book, my initial questions in each interview revolved around Zion: where it was, what it was, and what it had to do with Utah and Peru. However, once interviewees began talking about topics of importance to them, I would simply ask follow-up questions related to those topics rather than returning to my prepared list. Those topics, tabulated, became this book's seven chapter titles.

Table 1 demonstrates interlocutor characteristics relevant to those chapter titles. Numbers in the table only represent the number of participants whose words happened to be digitally recorded and not the approximately 500 unrecorded people with whom I interacted for purposes of this project. Data is neither generalizable to greater populations nor to the post-2019 situations of my study participants.

TABLE 1. Study Participant Characteristics

Digitally recorded participants	542
Interviewees (including focus-group members)	468
Interviewees in La Familia	38
Interviewees with less than one hour of audio	368
Interviewees with between one and two hours of audio	67
Interviewees with between two and ten hours of audio	29
Interviewees with over ten hours of audio	4
Interviewees in La Familia with over ten hours of audio	1
Non-interviewees (usually public speakers)	74
Females	213
Males	329
Over age thirty	345
Under age thirty	197
Spanish recordings	273
English recordings	60
Bilingual Spanish/English recordings	24
Recorded in Peru	183
Recorded in Utah	140
Recorded over internet	34
People who identified as Peruvian (hereafter "Peruvians")	358
Peruvians still living in Peru	269
Peruvians with family in Utah	144
Peruvians who had never been to Utah	233
Peruvians still living in Peru, but who had spent over six months in Utah	16
Peruvians born in Peru, but who now lived in Utah	72
Peruvians born in Utah	17
Peruvians with informal US entry (clandestine border-crossing)	5
Peruvians with US immigration informality (usually a tourist visa overstay)	64

TABLE 1. continued

Peruvians naturalized as US citizens	21
Peruvians who were Mormon before immigrating to Utah	47
Peruvians who became Mormon after immigrating to Utah	15
Peruvian Mormons	298
Peruvian Mormons who attended church regularly	272
Peruvian Mormons known to have a "White passing" phenotype	3
Peruvian Mormons who considered themselves biological descendants of Laman	268
Peruvian Mormons with at least one Runasimi- or Aymara-speaking grandparent	183
Peruvian Mormons whose first language was Runasimi or Aymara	3
Peruvians who learned Runasimi or Aymara after becoming Mormon	1
Peruvian non-Mormons	60
Temple-recommend-holding Mormons	312
Temple-recommend-holding Peruvian Mormons	211
Peruvian Mormon women	106
Peruvian Mormon unmarried women	50
Peruvian Mormon unmarried mothers	24
Peruvian Mormon unmarried fathers	2
Peruvian Mormons who had not been ritually sealed to their coresident family	148
Peruvian Mormons who had served missions	145
Peruvians born into an already Mormon family	57
Peruvians with at least one Peruvian parent who was also born into a Mormon family	2
Peruvians who married an Anglo	9
Peruvians who married a Peruvian	207
Peruvians who married a non-Peruvian Latin American or US Latinx	14
Anglo Mormons	76
Anglo non-Mormons	9
Native Mormons	1
Native non-Mormons	5
Black Mormons	1
Non-Peruvian Latin American/US Latinx Mormons	71
Non-Peruvian Latin American/US Latinx Non-Mormons	21

One demographic that this book's frames of pioneer indigeneity and forever familia will unpack in particular is that of the 148 "Peruvian Mormons who had not been ritually sealed to their coresident family" either because they were too Indigenous to qualify for temple entry based on worthiness standards meant for "pioneers" or because their familias were too excessively coresident to fit their church's official category of family at all. Understandably, the stressful imaginings of how unsealed genealogical nodes might dissolve pacha in the afterlife generated a destructive anxiety within those 148 Saints. However, their imaginings were also productive. They motivated the kin-building that drove Peruvian Mormon Zion's rewiring of all seven of the kin-limiting, Anglo Mormon categories that I will now proceed to dissect.

PART I

Pioneer Indigeneity

CHAPTER 1

Leaders

We'll find the place which God for us prepared,
Far away in the West,
Where none shall come to hurt or make afraid;
There the Saints will be blessed.
—"Come, Come, Ye Saints" (Clayton 1985, 30)

Essentialist Constructs

At every reenactment of the Mormon settler colonists' exodus to Utah that I attended or heard about, participants sang the above hymn in English or Spanish. Its lyrics demonstrate the essentialism as opposed to the constructivism of Mormonism's categories. In the above verse, the category of place is revealed as essentialist. God endowed an essence upon the West that made it already the Saints' place, their Zion. According to the hymn, the Saints did not construct the West as their place. Instead, its essence—its destiny—was already manifest as belonging to them.

As it was with place, so it was also with leaders. Many Peruvians in my study believed that leaders were constructed socially through lifetimes of honor, humility, perseverance, charisma, and respect. Conversely, many Mormons in my study believed that leaders were literally foreordained in the preexistence by the laying on of hands to become such. The primordial essence of leadership was already upon leaders. Essential leaders were out there just waiting to be found and called forth. As Peruvians who happened to also be Mormons looked around themselves during my study, they found that their most important leaders were disproportionally Anglo males. This might have revealed to them something about their religion's category of leaders, namely that it emerged along with the Anglo cultural categories of race and gender, which were also essentialist as opposed to constructivist. In Anglo Mormonism, there was an ancestral essence of subordination upon all Lamanites and a primordial essence of subservience upon all females that tended to disqualify both from the category of leaders.

In this chapter, I explore how that tendency materialized within Anglo and Peruvian interactions. Specifically, I explore how Anglo Mormonism disguised its essentialist category of leaders so that Peruvian Mormons would not detect it as a racist and sexist cultural construct. Ultimately, I argue that Anglo Mormonism concealed the true criteria of its "leaders" category so that everyone, including both Anglo and Peruvian Mormons, would accept Peruvian subservience to Anglo males as part of a divinely appointed—rather than a culturally constructed—holy order.

The Shining Path of Zion's Camp

The most expensive and time-intensive Mormon Pioneer reenactment in which I participated happened years before I began this study. It was called the Trek (ML). It involved my camping out along the actual Mormon trail in Wyoming among Peruvian American and other Latinx teenage members of a Spanish-speaking ward in Utah who lived in the same stake of Zion as Anglo members of English-speaking wards. Other reenactments that I heard about during my study involved arequipeño Mormon leaders wearing what they imagined to be Mormon pioneer outfits while orchestrating police escorts in order to facilitate pushing makeshift covered wagons through Arequipa's busy streets. In Barrio Periféricos, the ward that I joined in Arequipa as part of this study, pioneer reenactments sometimes simply involved dressing up as the Mormon Pioneers while having a potluck in our chapel's cultural hall (ML). The cultural hall was a multipurpose gymnasium that functioned as a dance hall, a Sunday School (ML) classroom, and even an extra seating section when attendees to our Sunday worship services overflowed the accordioned rear wall of our ward's sacrament hall wherein the eucharist was prepared by fourteen-year-old male teachers, blessed by sixteen-year-old male priests, and distributed by eleven-year-old male deacons every Sunday.

In all cases, the principal purpose of the US Great Plains–crossing, Pioneer reenactments was not simply to playact the historical event whereby Anglo Mormon leaders tamed the West and secured a permanent Zion—Utah—for their followers. It was not simply to meld past and present temporalities between Peruvian and Utahan spatialities to produce a Peruvian Mormon spacetime wherein centuries-old leaders, contemporary leaders, and millennia-old leaders all participated simultaneously in the same territorial project of Zion-building. Instead, the principal purpose of reenacting the Anglo Mormon origin myth was to publicly enact Mormonism's long-held tradition of making its own entertainment separate from that of the World. Since such a feat required organizational skills, the Mormon Pioneer reenactments were an invitation to that outside world's potential Mormon converts to come and experience Mormon pioneer leadership for themselves and to wonder what the requirements might be to become pioneers, a word that my Mormon study participants used to mean not only leaders, but the first Leaders.

Whether the reenactments took place in Arequipa among Peruvian descendants of the Incas or in Utah among Anglo descendants of the actual Mormon colonizers, many reenactors told me that they felt unity as they stamped pioneer identity into the earth with each footfall along the simulated trail of sacrifice toward Zion. Indeed, despite the otherwise essentialist aspects of their "leaders" category, Mormons felt they that were actively constructing identities as pioneers, the principal determinant of leaders.

Mormon pioneer pageantry, therefore, made leaders into both a constructivist and essentialist category. According to Mormon pageantry's narrative norms—part of what the official church deemed gospel culture (ML) during my study in the late 2010s—leaders were constructed, not simply preordained. Sacrifice constructed leaders. In pioneer narratives, sacrifice and suffering were the only things capable of winnowing down a ragtag group of lazy followers into a refined generation of self-governing leaders. In Anglo Mormon stories, such leaders became the Mormon Pioneers. Could Peruvian Mormons also be the Mormon Pioneers? Could they be Zion's leaders? Chapter 2 entertains Peruvian Mormon answers to those questions. However, to scrutinize the protective crust that Peruvian Mormons had to remove from the Anglo Mormon category of leaders in order to reconstruct it into Peruvian Mormon self-government, the present chapter focuses on Anglo Mormon answers—including my own and those of the Arequipa temple construction site's official photographer.

The juxtaposition of the following two scenes offers a gateway into our answers because both scenes depict the same sort of suffering through which leaders were paradigmatically constructed and through which their essence was selected in Mormon mythology. However, one scene is about an Anglo Mormon male while the other is about a Peruvian Mormon female. Placing both on the same mythological plane will highlight the equivalency of their power, thus accentuating the fact that there was nothing inevitable about Mormonism's exclusion of Peruvians and females from its "leaders" category. The juxtaposition demonstrates that, where there exists a will to expand them, Mormonism's narrative norms can become capacious enough to allow non-White non-men room within "leaders."

This first scene depicts a rained-out skirmish between a group of Anglo Mormons and a Missouri militia in 1834—a time when Missouri was fast becoming Zion for all Mormons.

Joseph [Smith] had high hopes for his small band, which he called the Camp of Israel. Although they were armed and willing to fight, as the ancient Israelites had been when they battled for the land of Canaan, Joseph wanted to resolve the conflict peacefully. . . .

Twenty minutes later, hard rains tore through camp [thus making it impossible for the Mormons' enemies to attack]. . . .

Wilford Woodruff and others in the camp found a small church nearby and huddled inside while hail pelted the roof. After a moment, Joseph burst into the church, shaking the water from his hat and clothes.

"Boys, there is some meaning to this," he exclaimed.

"God is in this storm!" (Church 2018, 199, 203–4)

The second scene is an excerpt from my 2018 interview with a Peruvian Mormon woman in Arequipa named Delia who lived through Peru's Shining Path guerrilla war in Lima in 1991. Her greater narrative is the focus of chapter 2. Delia and I were both members of Barrio Periféricos. Delia's theories regarding low church attendance among the contemporary youth in our ward prompted my clarification question.

> JASON: So, you are saying that its laziness? And nowadays, kids in Peru are too lazy to even go to church?
>
> DELIA: It's laziness, pure laziness, unlike during our time. Back in the nineties, I remember one young woman, Abish [named after one of only three female *Book of Mormon* characters], from our church youth group in Lima who made the mistake of running from the Path's bombs.
>
> We would always say, "When the bombs sound, don't run." You had to walk because if not, it was a sign that you had been the one to plant the bomb.
>
> But she ran, and the police took her away. They tortured her, and she was in jail for over a month. It was horrible for her, but even so, she went on her mission. She is still strong in the church to this day.
>
> Those are the types of young people that we had in that generation, at least in Ayacucho and Lima where the terrorism was at its strongest. That is why I say that the terrorism was a good thing.

Church historians' official account of what they called "Zion's Camp" and Delia's recollection of the lives risked to attend church during the Shining Path had something in common. God was in the terrorism just as He was in the storm.

The church's historians and Delia used gospel culture's narrative norms to forge "a good thing" from the ashes of trauma. The young man Wilford would emerge from his trials to become the Prophet fifty-five years later. The young woman Abish, whom Peruvian military police said disappeared on her way to a youth activity at her ward's chapel, would emerge from her trials to become a missionary. Though separated by time and space, those two young people, one Anglo Mormon and one Peruvian Mormon, became united under a single generation, "that generation": the generation of leaders.

However, Zion's implicit criteria for the category of leaders disturbed their union. When Spanish-speaking Mormons in my study referred to "the Leaders" with a capital L they often implied masculinity, pioneers, and whiteness (SL). In my mind, those concepts recalled sexism, anti-indigeneity, and White supremacy respectively. In some of their minds, masculinity, pioneers, and whiteness formed gospel culture: the unremarkable, tacit expression of Zion-worthy lifeways thought to automatically accompany church membership. Under the Anglo Mormon gaze, Peruvian Mormons were only leaders to the extent that they could first distinguish and then live gospel culture. Therefore, this chapter's interrogation of gospel culture is an interrogation of "leaders" as a Zion category. Unlike much scholarship on "global Mormonism" (Shepherd, Shepherd, and Cragun 2021, title) that left "sub-standard leadership" (Gooren 1999, 85) unquestioned as if it were a natural characteristic of humans from the Global South, this chapter troubles the category of "leaders" itself. In other words, this chapter assumes Mormon leadership deficiencies to be attributes of the category, not of the Peruvian humans who hoped to occupy it. Though this chapter focuses on Anglo Mormonism's anchoring of leaders to the colonial categories of gender and race, it lays ground for the next chapter—presaged by Delia's narrative above—wherein Peruvian Mormonism untethers gender and race from a new configuration of leaders under Peruvian pioneer indigeneity's own version of gospel culture.

Gendering Leaders

To begin troubling leaders, I provide my own highly gendered story of pioneering arequipeño Mormon anthropology. The miniskirt anecdote below demonstrates that Anglo Mormonism's category of leaders was too gendered for Peruvian Mormon frameworks. In other words, gender was one aspect of "leaders" that Peruvian Mormons needed to rework in order to keep their Peruvianness while simultaneously convincing an Anglo-controlled church that Peruvians could be competent leaders.

Not six days after arriving in Arequipa—a city nestled at 7,500 feet above sea level on a 19,000-foot-high volcano—my wife, Elvira, and I found ourselves in the bishop's office of the large, contextually mismatched chapel of Barrio Periféricos, the name of the Mormon ward to which we were assigned by virtue of happening to choose an Airbnb rental that was within its socioeconomically diverse cartographic boundaries. Bishop Paucar interviewed us, ostensibly so that he could get to know us and transfer our electronic membership records to his ward, but really so that he could size us up for one of the lay leadership roles that all active members played in the ward, including himself.

Bishop Paucar was a cusqueño (person from Cusco) migrant who made his living delivering cellphone-minute vouchers to kiosks throughout Arequipa on his motorcycle. Given Peru's inverted topographic hierarchy of difference wherein the higher the elevation of one's hometown, the lower one's status, cusqueños were not as stigmatized as puneños, but they were still thought of as requiring significant de-Indianization in order to assimilate into arequipeño society. Bishop Paucar had joined the church only ten years prior and was already in his fifth year as bishop, the highest leadership position in a ward and a virtual beacon of de-Indianization. Interestingly, Bishop Paucar's superior, the stake president, was a puneño whom many in Barrio Periféricos considered a model of the properly de-Indianized Lamanite.

Bishop Paucar, his spouse, and two school-aged kids lived alone as a nuclear family in an overcrowded tenement five minutes by taxi from our flat. Though his coresident family-shape matched the norm for those whom God usually called to be Mormon bishops, his income level did not (Knowlton 1996). Usually, bishops in Peru were selected from neighborhoods like our gated and guarded one (Zhang 2010), a subdivision that caused ward members, whenever I would tell them our address, to stick up their noses in mock haughtiness and snort "pituco" (PL)—Peru's epithet for criollo snobbishness (see figure 1).

In the bishop's eyes, my whiteness, maleness, and middle-class place of residence meant that I was the racial, gendered, and geographical embodiment of leadership. Indeed, there was a global "tendency among Latter-day Saints of color . . . to defer in decision-making to those . . . who [were] white heritage Mormons with generations of LDS ancestry" (Straubhaar 2018, 107). I was terrified that this "tendency" would land me a problematically high leadership position in Barrio Periféricos, one that would not only confirm the central role that sexism and anti-indigeneity played in the Mormon category of leaders, but one that would place me in that role.

Instead, the bishop relayed to me the Lord's calling that I was to become the first councilor in the Elders Quorum presidency, a male-only organization integral to every ward. That position did not make me feel too complicit in the church's history of only applying "leaders" to three out of four possible binary gender dynamics—male over male, male over female, female over female, but never female over male (O'Brien 2020)—because, as I told myself, at least there existed a female counterpart to my leadership position: the first councilor in the female-only Relief Society (ML) presidency. My illusion of gender parity dissipated when I discovered that the only first councilors included in Executive Committee Meetings, which made decisions for all ward members regardless of gender, were male. Such remained the case even when said meetings convened immediately after all-gender meetings held in the home of the Relief Society president, requiring her to temporarily vacate her own living room.

Another reason for my initially easy conscience was that "first councilor" was not a big job in any of the many age-, civil status-, and gender-specific

FIGURE 1. Our neighborhood. Few arequipeños owned cars, much less garages. Therefore, this photo depicts the epitome of the middle-class, pituco lifestyle. June 2018. Photo credit: Jason Palmer.

presidencies that made up Mormon wards. First councilors merely supported their organization's president. Furthermore, compared to other ward organizations in my experience, Mormons never expected much of Elders Quorum. Unlike most Mormon organizations for males (Deacons Quorum, Teachers Quorum, and Priests Quorum), there was no specific age in Elders Quorum at which one automatically graduated into the next highest group up the hierarchy, which was the High Priests Group. Elders Quorum was, therefore, a group of males over the age of eighteen whose distinguishing characteristic was that they were not phenomenologically associated with the category of leaders tightly enough to be high priests.

However, Elders Quorum was about to receive a worldwide boost. Three months after I became a first councilor, our ward witnessed the Prophet decree during the global broadcast of the church's 186th semiannual General Conference—always convened near Salt Lake City's Temple Square—that the Elders Quorum and High Priests Group would be combined into one greater body uncreatively dubbed "Elders Quorum."

Current presidencies from both groups were thereby dissolved. Stake presidents were instructed to ask God to call, post haste, a new presidency for each ward's "Super Quorum," as our puneño stake president more aptly named the new Elders Quorum. One week after the Prophet's announcement, the stake president spoke in our ward's Sacrament Meeting (ML) and hyped up said Super Quorum. He proclaimed that gone were the days of Elders Quorum members sitting idly by while the bishopric and the Relief Society did all the leadership work in the ward. He did not focus on how heavy that work was because we all knew. It involved visiting less active (ML) members and trying to reactivate them by sharing spiritual messages and inviting them to activities. It demanded organizing bus trips to the Lima temple. It necessitated scheduling dinner invitations at ward members' homes for the ward's current set of fulltime missionaries. It required motivating ward members to compete in crowd sourcing, ancestor-name digitizing contests so that those ancestors' temple work could be completed. It entailed teaching members how to use Familysearch.org to do genealogy. It obligated rehearsing for the next folkloric dance competition against other wards in the stake. In short, being a leader in the ward encompassed a multitude of arduous activities that erased the lines between materiality and spirituality. Many hands made light work, according to the stake president. Therefore, the new Super Quorum president was not only to take charge of his all-male quorum, but was also to become a "second bishop" for all ward members, both male and female.

A week later, I—the most transitory, the most pituco, and perhaps the least temple-worthy member of the ward—stood in front of my coreligionists to be recognized as the new Super Quorum president. The combination of racism and sexism infused into my calling to that brand-new Mormon position with no female equivalent was undeniable. I had already begun to draw theoretical parallels between Mormon Zion-building in Peru and British colonialism in India through the writings of critical theorist Homi Bhabha, and it was becoming clearer why dozens of highly qualified, Peruvian male ward members were overlooked for the leadership calling that I had received. Perhaps God—or the stake president—considered them to be more *Mormonized* than Mormon, similar to the way British colonial officials saw Indians as "the effect of a flawed colonial mimesis, in which to be Anglicized, [was] emphatically not to be English" (Bhabha 1984, 128). To extend the British analogy, I was now a colonial official. I was one of the Leaders.

On May 13, 2018—Mother's Day in Peru—and about one month into my tenure as the Super Quorum president, I arrived home from our ward's Sunday services to see a WhatsApp message from Bishop Paucar containing a link to the church's modesty-in-dress standards from their web-based pamphlet, *For the Strength of Youth*, and an excerpt from that link stating, "Young women should avoid short shorts and short skirts" (Church 2011, 7). This was one of many church teachings that overvalued "female purity, often to the detriment of young women whose spiritual formation [was] closely tied to their sexual experience and sense of self" (Moslener 2020, 279) and was one of the justifications for placing Mormon women into segregated, age-specific organizations "under constant male surveillance" (Crawford 2020, 381). The bishop followed his post with the short comment, "Brother, please interview Sister Safira Gonzalez regarding dress standards, thanks."

Apparently, under the bishop's weekly surveillance of the female bodies in his congregation, Safira's was detected as being immodest. I was confused. For one thing, his detection seemed to have happened, given the timestamp, during Sacrament Meeting—the most sacred time of the Mormon week—when, according to my Anglo Mormon upbringing, Mormons were supposed to be meditating upon their own indebtedness to Jesus and not upon the unwieldy "nature" of the female body (Bordo 2004). For another thing, within my worldview, Sister Gonzalez was an adult, not a youth.

I felt sick. How could a religion that believed in a God who "denieth none that come unto him, black and white, bond and free, male and female" (J. Smith 1830, 109) also believe that I, an Anglo man, should deny a Peruvian woman the right to an unsurveilled embodied experience in what was supposed to be the most sacred moment of her week? I had a great relationship with the bishop by that point, and I knew that he hated being in the tower of the panopticon (Foucault [1977] 1995) just as much as he hated dragging me up there with him, but—himself surveilled by the stake president—he apparently felt dutybound to detect and exclude impurities and miniskirts in his little piece of Zion.

According to the way in which my Anglo society's category of gender interacted with its category of leaders, the bishop's request felt inappropriate. However, instead of confronting the bishop about that inappropriateness as I would have done had I truly cared about Safira's spiritual safety, I convinced the bishop to ask the Relief Society president—a female—to talk to Safira. In other words, I cared more about saving myself from direct involvement in what I felt to be Zion leadership's inherent sexism than I did about helping my spirit sister escape what I felt to be one of its symptoms.

In this example, the colonializing categories of race and gender reassembled to produce "leaders" in the Peruvian Mormonism that I studied that did not equate to "leaders" in the Anglo Mormonism that raised me. When I wrote about the miniskirt event in my field notes, I focused on Bishop Paucar's sexism because my settler upbringing had naturalized misogyny in my mind as an essential part of Latin American masculinity and leadership. Like the Anglo feminists whom anthropologist Saba Mahmood (2005) critiqued in her book about hijab use among Muslim women in Egypt, I desired to rescue an oppressed woman whom I deemed helpless from an oppressed man whom I deemed backward.

Reflecting on my bias as I reviewed my notes years later, I realized that Bishop Paucar's surveillance and subsequent request had nothing to do with a purportedly innate machismo and everything to do with how gender itself lay at a point of misalignment between Peruvian and Anglo versions of "leaders." For the bishop, the mismatch between my gender and Safira's was inconsequential, and so he asked me, a male, to interview her, a female, about her revealing attire. In reaction to what I misrecognized as his categorical oversight, I, like many Mormon Studies scholars before me, accused a Latin American male and, by extension, "the local cultures of Latin America" (Gooren 2008, 373) of "leadership atrocities" (Tullis 1980, 72) when I critically noted his uncouthness in being incapable of seeing the gender inappropriateness of his request.

I assumed that my sense of morality regarding gender was somehow more enlightened than that of Bishop Paucar. In reality, however, my cultural category of gender was limiting my understanding. I was only capable of categorizing Safira's miniskirt under "gender," so my solution was to pawn off responsibly onto another leader with a matching gender. In my essentialist mindset, miniskirts were part of the essence of femininity. The bishop, on the other hand, categorized Safira's miniskirt as "stewardship." Stewardship was an aspect of leadership that, for Bishop Paucar, was quite separate from gender because in many non-Mormon aspects of his life, communities had constructed women as stewards over men just as often as they had constructed men as stewards over women. Bishop Paucar's mother, for example, was the center of her matrilocal (SL) household in Cusco where she held immense power over her coresident sons-in-law. Bishop Paucar was the head of his own household, but his five brothers' households were headed by their mothers-in-law. Furthermore, even Bishop Paucar's arequipeña neta boss at the cell phone company was an unmarried matriarch with her own large, matrilocal household.

This is all to say that in Peruvianness, stewardship and gender did not overlap automatically. Leadership was, therefore, not as gendered in Peru as it was in the United States. In Peru, there existed no essence of domination attached to masculinity. Male dominance over females could and did exist, but that dominance had to be constructed. It was not seen as automatic, natural, or God-given. In the settler society in which I was raised, however, stewardship was always already gendered in the same unidirectional, binary way as it was in the settler religion in which I was raised: male over female.

Female over male leadership was remarkable in US society in the late 2010s, and societies usually only remark upon phenomena that threaten previously unquestioned categorical conflations, such as the conflation of stewardship and gender. When I was nine years old, the possibility of "leaders" as a category independent of "gender" so threatened US settler society that the Council on Biblical Manhood and Womanhood (1988) published "The Danvers Statement," which attempted to ecumenically cement across evangelical Christianity the euphemistic complementarity of husband-and-wife gender roles. In the statement, a prominent group of theologians, homemakers, and seminary presidents contradictorily denounced both machismo and female leadership:

"husbands should forsake harsh or selfish leadership and grow in love and care for their wives; wives should forsake resistance to their husbands' authority and grow in willing, joyful submission to their husbands' leadership" (2). Seven years later, the LDS church's all-male First Presidency, without consulting the all-female General Relief Society presidency (Maffly-Kipp 2020a), distributed an adaptation of "The Danvers Statement." They called it "The Family: A Proclamation to the World" (hereafter "The Family"), and it established a similarly sexist "equality" between the gender roles of leadership and submission (First Presidency 1995).

From 2015 to 2018 during a home décor analysis based on convenience sampling, I found that "The Family," as a single-page, often framed document (Campbell 2020) that looked from afar similar to a facsimile of the US Declaration of Independence, was prominently displayed in eighteen out of twenty Peruvian Mormon homes (ten in Peru and ten in Utah) and in only three out of twenty Anglo Mormon homes (all in Utah). Those results seemed contradictory because the document implicitly disparaged the matrifocal, conglomerated familias of coresident siblingship common in Peru and explicitly established the husband-led, suburban Utah, 1950s nuclear family as the sole archetype for the forever family.

Yet, given the aforementioned rules of societal remarkability, the near ubiquitous display of "The Family" in my Peruvian Mormon study participants' homes made sense. Since, relatively speaking, it clashed with Peruvian society but matched the taken-for-granted essence of Utah settler society, Anglos did not think to display it as often as Peruvians. Other items that Peruvian Mormon homes displayed more often than Anglo Mormon homes included "photographs and artwork of predominantly male religious leaders" (Stanton 2020, 343). These of course, functioned "to influence Saints' conflation of leadership with the male gender" (343), a conflation that was not yet complete in Peru, thus requiring more architectural reinforcement.

In my reaction to Bishop Paucar's request, my religion's essentialist categories showed me no alternatives to my society's essentialist categories. The lack of visible alternatives solidified the illusion in my mind that the more gendered, more essentialist Anglo Mormon category of leaders made universal sense while the less gendered, more constructivist Peruvian Mormon category of leaders had not "matured" (Moffat and Woods 2020, 434). Using the analogy of maturation, many Mormon Studies scholars infantilized the practitioners of non-Anglo Mormonisms during my study. At the time, I could not blame them. Even though I was critical of both settler society and Anglo Mormonism, I still shared their inability to see leaders as a category of something other than a colonial construct, in this case, gender.

This is not to say that I should have simply followed my leader's request to interview Safira about her miniskirt. Such a course of action would have been wrong in my culturally constructed sense of morality. It is simply to say that Bishop Paucar had a differently constructed sense of morality in which asking me to do so was not necessarily wrong, or at least not for the same gendered reasons. In the end, Safira surely had her own verdict regarding the appropriateness of her two bishops' outsized interest in her choice of Sacrament Meeting attire.

Pioneering Leaders

Gender was not the only colonial construct under which Anglo Mormonism placed the category of leaders during my study. "Leaders" also fell under the colonial constructs of race and kinship and sat squarely atop the pioneer extreme of coloniality's pioneer-versus-indigenous binary. The beloved Mormon term "pioneer" involved a temporal question regarding rightful leadership in Mormonism: Who was first in the God-prepared space of Zion? Though the notions of time and space upon which that question rested varied within and across both Anglo Mormonism and Peruvian Mormonism, in both Mormonisms, "leaders" hinged on the label "pioneer" and on what it shared with and stole from indigeneity, namely, being first.

The Book of Mormon prophesied that Latin American Mormons would be last in Zion. They came from a cursed lineage, the Lamanites. Joseph Smith canonized into perpetual futurity the day when the curse would be lifted and they "shall blossom as the rose" (Smith et al. 1835, 192) and build the New Jerusalem. However, a stark division of time labeled "future" was incongruous to the continent that descendants of the Inca—whom many Mormons believed to be Lamanites—called "Abya Yala" (Mallku Bwillcawaman 2015). As if a prescient contestation to the future tense of Joseph Smith's demeaning "shall blossom" prophecy, Abya Yala (PL), a placename that Runasimi-speakers used during my study, was in the present progressive tense. It meant "earth in the blossoming" (Mallku Bwillcawaman 2015, 232). Using Abya Yala to refer to the Americas both north and south—as I will do for the remainder of this book—is an intervention meant to imply that Lamanites are blossoming now. Peruvian Mormons are not merely destined to one day blossom in some settler futurity or science-fiction "Great American Indian novel" wherein "all of the white people will be Indians and all of the Indians will be ghosts" (Alexie 1996, 95). Abya Yala signifies that Indigenous Peruvian Mormons are pioneering the New Jerusalem upon Abya Yala as you are reading these words.

In theory, the conceptual unity of time and space expressed in Indigenous rights activists' placename for both North and South America—Abya Yala—is similar to that which Mormon Zion conjures—one indivisible place that does not segregate based on time of arrival. In practice, however, the essentialist structure of pioneer discourse caused Zion spacetime to splinter into ante-cedent-descendant hierarchies and land disputes that summoned a colonial formulation of power that anthropologist Elizabeth Povinelli called "the gov-ernance of the prior" (2011, 25). Mormon coloniality constructed itself as the free "governing prior" by ridding the present of the "governed prior"—the Indigenous—either through genocide, through perpetual futurization, or through discursive banishment into a past of the merely "customary" (24).

In the Anglo Mormon origin myth that my study participants loved to reenact, Anglo Mormon colonists were the governing prior, the Mormon Pioneers, and the first true inhabitants of Utah's Zion. As a missionary in Bolivia in 1998, I found it important to share that my ancestors were leaders of Zion's genesis in Utah because "to a Mormon, heritage is not something to be taken lightly" (Oman 2015, 78). The Anglo Mormon Heather Oman, who made that understatement in the edited volume *A Book of Mormons: Latter-day Saints on a Modern-Day Zion*, went on to claim, "this heritage, this church, it's in my blood" (79). Lucky for Oman, the religion "where God wants everyone to be" (82) just happened to be the religion that was a part of her inherited essence, her blood.

During my study, such a figuration of the Mormon Pioneer as the para-digmatic leader capable of siring descendants who were Mormon by blood created a division between two sorts of Mormons. Those with "believing blood" who felt "the sanctity of the sacrifices" (Oman 2015, 79) that their ancestors made upon arrival to a mythically uninhabited Utah were unmarked "Mormons." Those with a Native ancestry canonized in *The Book of Mormon* as being full of incorrect "traditions" and "abominations" (J. Smith 1830, 28) were "Peruvian Mormons."

Culturing Leaders

Therefore, I found "Peruvian Mormon" to be a marked category (Brekhus 1998) for both my Anglo and Peruvian Mormon study participants. In this section, I will argue that through categorical manipulations, such as leaving key identities unmarked, Anglo Mormons in my study constructed Peruvian Mormons as personifying insufficient leadership.

For my Anglo Mormon study participants living in Peru, "Peruvian Mor-mon" designated both a divisiveness that was tribal and biased—Peruvian—and a solidarity that was universal and objective—Mormon. As sociologist Wayne Brekhus (1998) posited, unmarked nouns, such as "man," were under-stood as the default state of their category—in this case, "person"—because they were thought to automatically fulfill all of its requirements. They captured its essence. Alternately, nouns that did not quite fit the categorical essence were marked with a modifier, such as "wo-," as in "wo-man."

From Mormonism's initial decades, belonging to the unmarked category "Mormon" hinged upon what made proper familial leaders, or heads of households. As mentioned, one essential aspect of that headship was masculinity. The Anglo Mormon pioneers deliberately intertwined their ideas of masculine headship together with ideas of more efficient settler colonization to form a new colonizer-indigenous kin entity, or "settler adoption fantasy" (Tuck and Yang 2012, 14). As historian Matthew Bowman (2020) put it, "they drew both on ideas embedded within Mormonism itself and on the norms and mores of American culture and worked out a new gendered cultural synthesis which incorporated elements of each" (129).

Yet, even as they were ultra-cognizant of the doctrines (ML) that they included in their synthesis, they were completely unaware of what else they included, namely, their version of "leaders," which involved an essentialist, as opposed to a constructed, kin notion. Their kin notion posited that true kinship flowed mainly through a linear blood descent extending from textually verifiable antecedents in the past to biologically verifiable descendants in the future regardless of whether one had personally spent time with—or had elected—any of those individual relatives. This kin structure matched an ancient Athenian leadership structure, part of the basis for Western democratic thought, wherein leadership was selected by lottery—called—rather than cultivated or earned.

Mixing both notions, Anglo Mormons during my study chose neither their ancestors nor their leaders. In this way, Anglo Mormon leadership, like Anglo Mormon kinship, was more essentialist than constructivist. For many Peruvian Mormons on the other hand, such impersonal notions of leadership stood in contrast to the relatedness that they had cultivated through a lifetime of "negotiated obligations and possibilities within the general field of local social belonging" (Povinelli 2011, 25). The official church's seemingly arbitrary practice of calling non-applicants into leadership and then suddenly releasing (ML) them from leadership—both without explanation—was difficult for many in Barrio Periféricos to accept. It was difficult because it contradicted the "immanent practices of affiliation" (Povinelli 2011, 25) and charismatic "personalism" (Cooper and Hernández de Olarte 2020, 385) that determined the winning and losing of leadership positions and kinship roles in so many other aspects of their lives wherein "true authority [had] to be earned, not assumed by virtue of occupying an institutional position" (Van Beek, Decoo, and Decoo 2020, 522), a biological sex, or a biological lineage that supposedly held the essence of leadership.

During my study, the group of twelve Utah-dwelling males—the Twelve—whom many of my study participants considered to be the twelve modern apostles of Jesus Christ, unwittingly intensified the difficulty that Peruvian Mormons had in infusing the church's category of leaders with different valances of gender, constructivism, and essentialism that were more steeped in Peruvianness. The Twelve did this by constantly insisting through their publications and broadcasts that the official church's bureaucratic leadership notions, like its kin notions, were divine essentialisms, not cultural constructs. In the Twelve's phraseology, its leadership notions were divinely dependent, unchangeable doctrines as opposed to culturally dependent, revisable policies. Yet, the Twelve could only sort items between doctrine and policy when they were cognizant of them. As their church became increasingly global, I imagine that they must have sensed that there were tacit aspects of correct leadership—such as those involving personhood, space, and time—that were divine but indeterminate. My theory is that they decided to form a miscellaneous category for all such items and that, as a label for that category, they coined the term "gospel culture."

According to a speech that member of the Twelve Dallin Oaks "broadcast to Africa" (2012, 40) in 2010, gospel culture was "a distinctive way of life, a set of values and expectations and practices common to all members [of the church]" (42). He then pointed to the aforementioned document "The Family" and designated its depiction of a fully nuclearized, postwar US family as "a beautiful expression of this gospel culture" (42). Next, searching for a nonexample, he turned to the Global South. "Some cultural traditions in parts of Africa are negative when measured against gospel culture and values. Several of these concern family relationships—what is done at birth, at marriage, and upon death" (43). Finally, while *The Book of Mormon* claimed that traditions could be incorrect, Oaks went a step further in claiming that entire cultures could be false: "When it comes to giving up false traditions and cultures, we praise our younger people for their flexibility and progress, and we appeal to our older members to put away traditions and cultural or tribal practices that lead them away from the path of growth and progress. We ask all to climb to the higher ground of the gospel culture" (43).

I believe that Oaks asked his followers to "put away" entire lifeways because he wanted the church to be a "totalistic organization . . . [wherein] values, practices, rituals, and relationships . . . [would] not only extend to the member's everyday life but play a primary role" (Hinderaker 2015, 93). Oaks's words seemed to show that the institutional church was attempting to become "complex and powerful enough to create its own hegemonic values, structures of power, and senses of centrality and marginality" (Chen and Yorgason 2020, 42). Within those structures, "whiteness, maleness, Americanness, and married heterosexuality [would] hold particularly privileged positions" (42). That privilege would mean that settler Mormons like Oaks would have the luxury of considering that, when Saints were good, gospel-loving people, gospel culture was just the way things were done. However, since gospel culture, like any colonializing mechanism, was "that which authenticated, and set the terms for, difference" (M. E. García 2021, 98), Indigenous Mormons deemed too different did not have the same luxury. In fact, Indigenous studies theorist Boatema Boateng (2019) defined indigeneity itself as "the condition in which you do not have the luxury of considering that your way is simply the way things are done" (1).

In Arequipa, many Anglo Mormons on various temporary church assignments involving missionization and temple construction expected Peruvian Mormon leaders to simply know how things were done regarding those projects. When Peruvian Mormon leaders did not know, some Anglo Mormons brandished one of their most insidious binaries—"gospel culture" versus "Utah Mormon culture"—and theorized that Peruvian ignorance stemmed from the innate Peruvian inability to distinguish the one from the other. By placing tacit Anglo Mormon common sense together with church doctrine into the category of gospel culture while tossing humorous Utahan idiosyncrasies into the category of Utah Mormon culture, Anglo Mormons in my study were able to mask their racism with self-deprecation and draw attention from the fact that gospel culture *was* Utah Mormon culture. Through this and other artifices, they were able to include unquestioned settler colonist norms, such as leadership characteristics, into their gospel and pretend that those were divine, unchanging doctrines rather than fluid cultural preferences specific to settler society and forged in colonial violence (Colvin 2017). In this way, "gospel culture [was] not innocent, it [was] paternalistic, demeaning, and willfully evasive to historical and contemporary power dynamics" (Hernández 2021, 5). Nevertheless, through their conceptual manipulations, Anglo Mormons during my study—including myself—unwittingly defended gospel culture as innocent. In so doing, they painted settler society as divine and Indigenous society as deficient, not fully "Mormon," and not capable of producing leaders.

Whitening Leaders

True leaders, in the Anglo Mormon conception, were those capable of distinguishing between the church's doctrine and the World's culture. Collin Daly was a case in point. He was a member of our informal association of Anglo Mormon expatriates in Arequipa that we called "Taco Tuesday" wherein we would eat weekly at one of Arequipa's few Mexican restaurants, call ourselves gringos in "mock Spanish" (Hill 1998), and imagine ourselves connoisseurs of Peruvianness. Though I am critical of Collin's thought processes in this book, he became my friend for a reason: we shared many of those thought processes. Whether we were collecting local knowledge or collecting local souls, we were both pursuing what we thought to be noble and even liberatory goals in Arequipa. However, our goals could not be extricated from the goals of the colonial regimes—the US church and the US academy—that our very presence in Peru upheld. However lofty, our goals did not exonerate us from the unintended violence that our actions caused in Peru.

A generational Mormon in his late thirties from Colorado and a graduate of Brigham Young University (BYU, a church-owned university in Utah), Collin had been hired as the official Arequipa temple construction photographer. His boss, an Anglo Mormon from Utah also in his late thirties, was the site manager of the entire Arequipa temple construction project. His job was to adhere to the "'standard plan' for architecture that [made] Latter-day space consistent across countries" (McDannell 2020a, 21) lest it become too saturated with local meaning to remain faithful to the supposedly placeless Zion archetype modeled after the place of Utah.

Collin's high position as a temple construction photographer in the corporate side of the church seemed to give him greater authority over the temple site than even the highest levels of the local ecclesiastical side occupied by Peruvian church leaders. Those leaders were often rebuffed from even visiting the construction site unless they were lucky enough to get a construction job with the Peruvian subcontracting companies that won the bids to build the temple. Conversely, Collin gave me permission to enter the completely walled-in site as often I pleased. All I had to do was make a prior appointment, promise not to tell my ward family members in Barrio Periféricos who would have gone green with envy, and delay publishing anything about my visits until the temple was completed. I spent a total of eighty hours on the temple construction site from February to June 2018. During that time, I interviewed the all-Anglo, all-Mormon five-person team that represented the central church as the owner of the temple project. That team included Collin, his boss, an architect, and an elderly married couple called to serve a "temple construction mission" with the objective of proselytizing among the construction workers. I also interviewed individuals from all levels of the different Peruvian and Colombian construction companies working on the project. Mostly, I hung out at the segregated lunch tent. There, I would chat with the high-end caterers who served the engineers their artisanal arequipeño cuisine. Then, I would cross over to the street vendors who served the construction workers their meals. Occasionally I watched FIFA World Cup games with all the workers on an improvised projection screen when their need to support Peru's national team outweighed the urgency of temple completion. I also attended a few of the prayer and scripture study meetings that the construction missionaries would facilitate to start each workday on a spiritual note for their captive audience of approximately 150 workers, two of whom were active Peruvian Mormons and three of whom were inactive.

One day, in March 2018, I recorded the below conversation with Collin inside the airconditioned portable office shared by the all-Anglo temple team. We talked, mostly in English, about what it was like for him to grow up only seeing the ecclesiastical side of the church wherein people were called by God to unremunerated positions and then suddenly to be thrust into the corporate side wherein people were hired by fellow mortals. He claimed that his semi-liberal, non-Utah Mormon, Colorado upbringing prepared him to "see how the sausage is made." In his estimation, unlike some of the Peruvian Mormons and Utah Mormons with whom he worked on the site, he was able to dissociate the questionable decisions that humans influenced by Utahan or Peruvian cultures made within the church from the church's divine doctrine—its gospel.

> One of the construction foremen was a member of the church, a Peruvian. I think he was a high councilor [one of a stake president's twelve emissaries] here in Arequipa. He mentioned how there was swearing on the temple construction site and that I needed to get my boss to do something about it.
> "We can't have that on the temple site," he said.
> I said, "Yeah, well, you know, we do everything we can to help teach them that this is something different, but in the end, they are construction workers. It's a construction site, and to me, the Lord is going to accept this building and their work regardless of their language."
> And he seemed to understand, but I know that sometimes Peruvians think that since this is a temple, everyone should be temple-recommend-holding members of the church to build it, and, you know, that's not how the Lord runs His corporation.

Collin used the word "corporation" not to mean the "body of Christ" but to mean its opposite. The corporation of the church, as opposed to its gospel, included all the messy carnality required to make a celestial organization, led by God, function on a fallen planet. According to Collin, the high counselor should not have expected people in the corporation to behave like Saints. In criticizing the Peruvian leader's expectations of saintliness and decency on a construction site, Collin was attacking his leadership style even as he unintentionally echoed a latent racial discourse called indigenismo—specific to 1920s Cusco, but palpable in 2010s Arequipa—that glorified the Inca ancestry of the underclasses while considering their uncouthness innate (De la Cadena 2000). "Construction workers will be construction workers," might not have sounded racist in certain US contexts, but, on Collin's jobsite, perceived skin color gradations mapped almost precisely onto pay grades. Of course, "skin color" in Arequipa was not about phenotypic, verifiable hue, but about comportment, dress, education, and—often—hair color/texture, all of which could change (Scorza [1970] 2002). This meant that as one moved up the jobsite hierarchy from cement mixer to structural engineer one "whitened," and one's vocabulary became decent (PL), meaning less Indigenous. Temple construction workers were mostly migrants from Puno who, had they lived in Arequipa in the late 1800s, would have been called "towns-children," an expression that simultaneously dignified and infantilized indigeneity (Nieves y Bustamante [1892] 2010). The few temple engineers who were locals were mostly arequipeños netos whom their subordinates sometimes identified racially as "upstanding people."

Collin subtly belittled the Peruvian high councilor for not being advanced enough a leader to see beyond the merely cultural prohibition of foul language at the temple construction site. For Collin, the temple was not made holy by the language through which it was constructed. Instead, it was made holy by what went on inside it once it became dedicated (ML). After the dedication ceremony, unclean things, mouths, and peoples were no longer allowed to enter. The symbol of its cleanliness from profanity was the color that saturated everything about a completed temple's interior design, from the neckties of the males who guarded its gates to the mallets that knocked the ritual doors of its replica of heaven. The color was white. However, in Collin's mind, white the pigment, vital to a temple's holiness, had nothing to do with the whiteness that the Peruvian high councilor thought temple construction workers should express in their speech patterns.

In the high councilor's opinion, indecent language during construction would diminish the temple's holiness at completion. Collin noted that opinion and submitted it as evidence to support his greater commentary that Peruvians were not capable of seeing what was truly important—the core of what made a temple holy. In other words, the Peruvian leader was incapable of reading the true meaning behind the words emblazoned on the exterior walls of all Mormon temples in Abya Yala in the language of each nation-state's dominant colonizing force: "Holiness to the Lord." As such, he did not fit into Collin's category of "leader."

On another occasion that was not audio recorded, Collin more candidly criticized what he felt was a uniquely Peruvian incapacity for sifting doctrine from culture, this time regarding the baptismal ceremonies that converts to Mormonism underwent at font-equipped chapels across Arequipa. Each enclosed baptismal font had an aperture exposing to the public the baptizer and the baptizee standing waist-deep in a pool of water. That aperture could be closed with shutters. The Peruvians in Collin's ward family thought that it was important to close the shutters immediately after each baptismal rite. He, however, instructed them that shutter-closing was not a vital aspect of the rite. He said, "It is kind of nice to leave the shutters open so that family members can take photos of the participants" while they are still wet and dressed in white—meaning often sheer—clothing. In his mind, the symbolic power of white pigment—equivalent to holiness—needed to be allowed to shine forth, trumping both the demands of modesty and the physics of the white t-shirt effect. He mentioned that President Miller—an Anglo, Utahan millionaire called to preside over the Peru, Arequipa Mission for three years—agreed with him that the Peruvian shutter-closing behavior needed to stop. In fact, President Miller personally stopped the practice during a baptism that I attended in Barrio Periféricos.

Collin found comical the Peruvian inability to see the silly shutter-closing practice for what he thought it was, just another incorrect Peruvian Mormon tradition and not a vital aspect of the ceremony. To me, the comedy was Collin's inability to see as equally silly or traditional the aspects of the ceremony that he considered doctrinal. At a baptism that I organized as the Super Quorum president, I invited Collin to be one of the two witnesses because the person whom I had previously selected for that responsibility had unexpectedly dropped out. According to official protocol, if witnesses caught errors in the rite, it had to be redone immediately. The other witness, an arequipeño named Flavio, thought that the baptism went smoothly, but Collin claimed that a single braid of the female baptizee's hair had remained unsubmerged, thus requiring rebaptism. Flavio, who was likely raised with a looser imaginary of "submersion" than Collin, was accused of overlooking a core doctrinal rule whereas, immediately after the rebaptism—when Flavio attempted to close the shutters in order to meet the official church's doctrinal demands of modesty—he was accused of inventing one. Either way, under Collin's White gaze, Flavio was an immature leader.

Reading Leaders

JASON: Do you find it pretty easy to discern the difference between a merely cultural LDS practice and the necessary, core basics of the gospel?

COLLIN: Most of my childhood, my dad was the bishop of our ward. He felt it was very important to follow the *Handbook*. But no more and no less. He always taught us, "don't try to push your interpretation of scripture or the *Handbook* onto someone else. If you wanna do it that way, that's fine, but don't force someone else to change just because you think that you can read between the lines better than they can."

Collin's roundabout answer was that he did find it easy to distinguish between the core and its superfluities. The core doctrine included the lines of text. The superfluous culture was between the lines. Collin considered his father's teaching enlightened and even progressive in comparison to what he perceived to be the sanctimonious teachings of the LDS corporation that employed him. However, from the perspective of linguistic anthropology, his father's teaching makes little sense. According to Peircean perspectival situatedness, a sign means nothing if it is disconnected from the one who writes it, the one who reads it, and the context of both (Rosa 2019). Written words have no objective meaning in and of themselves, meaning that *all* reading is reading between the lines (Kohn 2013).

The way Collin spoke of following *The Church Handbook of Instructions* was similar to the way in which the Holy Bible was interpreted in the nineteenth-century US before science and religion became incompatible categories (Easton-Flake 2020), namely, that there were two ways of reading it: straightforward (clearly correct) and not straightforward (clearly incorrect). Collin had the luxury of considering his reading of church manuals to be a straightforward reading only because he was brought up in the greater society that wrote those manuals. He assumed that it was his clear reading of unambiguous text that provided him access to its true meaning, when really it was his second nature understanding of the White logics that forged that meaning (Bonilla-Silva and Zuberi 2008).

During my study, the less thoroughly one had been socialized in US whiteness, the more carefully one had to decipher all text that came from Salt Lake City: the historical, cultural, metaphorical, administrative, spiritual, and shipping center of the church. Those whom the official church's leaders peripheralized through their central structure, even contemporary "Mormon Europeans" (Van Beek 2005) did not have the luxury of taking things at face value. They depended on leaders who dwelled in Zion's center for correct interpretation, which was precisely how centrality worked to shore up central church leaders' power, a power that Peruvians who wanted pioneer leadership status needed to tap.

Tapping that power was difficult because pioneer status recalled the leaders in the paradigmatic, Great Plains–crossing, Anglo Mormon origin myth, further solidifying Salt Lake City as the center, not Peru. Furthermore, that origin myth, along with most church text, was originally written in English, proficiency in which had become a quasi-official requirement for the Mormon category of leader the world over, even in wards where it was rarely spoken (Chen 2008). These complexities combined to make "non-Anglo leaders" an oxymoron in the church akin to "Chicano Mormon," an identity that historian Ignacio García unpacked in his memoir detailing how "Latino leaders [in the US were] constantly being asked to navigate a religious landscape that [was] often frustrating and confusing" (2015, 157) and how they preferred Spanish-language congregations in order to "keep from being overwhelmed by the whiteness of the Latter-day Saint gospel" (García 2020, 727).

However, for people like Collin who carried the non-oxymoronic label of "Anglo Mormon," navigating the power differentials embedded in the language of leadership to determine what really mattered was not confusing in the slightest.

I think the reason it is easier for my wife and I to recognize those differences, is because some of the things just don't matter. But some of them do.

For example, some Peruvian friends of ours here, their twelve-year-old son was being ordained as a deacon, and so the leaders came in and they were going to do it in priesthood meeting. And so, in came a [Peruvian] member of the bishopric. He said, "Ok, So-and-So, let's get up, we are going to ordain you as a deacon and give you the priesthood."

And I said, "Well, do you think we can invite his family here? Do you think maybe they would like to see that and have that experience?"

"Oh—oh—ok, that might be nice. We'll get his dad." . . .

Is it in the *Handbook*? No. It's not anything that *has* to be done, but I'd say that a really good cultural thing that we see in the United States is that these important milestones in our lives are family-shared events rather than just checking something off from a checklist.

Sometimes being able to decipher and distinguish what's cultural in the church from what's doctrinal is important, but we have to recognize when the cultural things do have an impact on the doctrinal and the spiritual and the way we feel.

Collin found an occasion in which breaking his father's command to stick to the church's handbook was justified. Suddenly, reading between the lines was all right. Suddenly—especially when nuclear family involvement was at stake—culture was good. This was an instantiation of what I call Nephite immunity (SL). Nephite immunity is the tendency of elites to think of their elite status as having been earned through their unique leadership capability of knowing when it is morally permissible to bend or break rules, not recognizing that such a capability stems solely from the fact that they—as elites already—made the rules. Nephite immunity is ubiquitous in colonial contexts wherein the providers of a new rule only have to obey it when it suits them (Robbins 2004). Since Anglo Mormons were the providers of the handbook but instead saw God as the provider, Nephite immunity functioned to both inoculate Anglo Mormons against "false culture" (Oaks 2012) and to automatically transform whatever leadership decisions they happened to make into gospel culture. Such automaticity enabled them to believe that the division between gospel culture and human tradition was obvious, that it somehow preexisted their decisions, and that adults who did not find it obvious were still in their "teenage years . . . of local ecclesiastical leadership" (Martins 2020, 422).

Such supposedly immature leadership included non-White Mormons, but it also apparently included White non-Mormons, like religious historian Laurie Maffly-Kipp (2020b) for whom it was also "not always obvious . . . where gospel culture end[ed], and national or familial traditions beg[an]" (150). Since the difference was obvious only to Anglo Mormons, only Anglo Mormons—or non-Anglo Mormons who had been sufficiently acculturated to Mormon Zion's categories—got to deem something either "gospel culture" or "false culture." Many Anglo and Peruvian Mormons in my study considered this ability to deem, which they called the "gift of discernment" (ML), to be the defining characteristic of leaders. Peruvian Mormons in my study considered that gift to be helpful in deciding which Anglo cultural norms to call divine and which to call humanmade. It helped them grapple with the sentiments behind a question that anthropologist of Mormonism David Knowlton asked: "Will Anglo-American culture be sacralized as part of the [Mormon] gospel, somewhat as Arabic culture has been in Islam?" (1996, 174).

What I perceived as the official church's increasing sacralization of US settler norms was ironic because the church's standardizing correlation movement of the 1960s that first packaged its manuals was actually designed to remove US culture from church doctrine in response to a growing global membership (Decoo 2015). Instead, it further embedded it (King 2019). An anonymous Mexican Mormon mother in 2015 expressed this succinctly: "When the leaders speak to us, they speak from the US reality" (qtd. in Kline 2020, 323).

Anglo Mormonism's category of leaders required US whiteness on top of gender and pioneer identity. The infusion of those three requirements into "leaders" is expressed in a *Book of Mormon* story—my inspiration for "Nephite immunity"—wherein a pale-skinned Nephite missionary, Ammon, was so persuasive that he succeeded in converting an entire kingdom of dark-skinned Lamanites and bringing them over to live on Nephite lands. Those Lamanites were so faithful to their new gospel that they took the commandment "do not kill" literally, a little too literally for Nephite tastes. When another group of Lamanites came to kill them, the Nephites were forced to do all the fighting on their behalf because they refused to defend themselves. In my reading of the story, Nephite military leaders then resorted to showing the pacifists a loophole in their vow to not kill; the strapping young boys of their second generation had not been born when their parents made the vow and, as such, could be led (by light-pigmented, male Nephites) to war.

Be they the Nephites of old or the Anglo Mormons in my "Taco Tuesday" gringo group, White people refused to recognize that their confidence in bending rules when a higher morality supposedly required it did not come by virtue of their superior leadership but simply by virtue of the fact that they were members of their worlds' hegemonic castes and, as such, got to define both the rules and the occasions that justified their exception (Agamben 1998). This Nephite immunity explained why an Anglo Mormon felt that a miniskirt during Sacrament Meeting could be overlooked while a Peruvian Mormon felt that it could not. It also explained why an Anglo Mormon felt that profanity on the temple site could be overlooked while a Peruvian Mormon felt that it could not. Finally, Nephite immunity explained why Anglo Mormons felt that they could bend the official church's modesty in dress standards by exposing semi-transparent baptismal clothing while Peruvian Mormons felt that they could not. Anglo Mormons suspected Peruvian Mormons who did not participate in justified rule-bending to be underdeveloped leaders when, in my perception, their only deficiency was in US settler culture. Regarding church leadership manuals that, if followed with common sense, were supposed to result in little modular Utah-Zions that belied locality and transcended the cultural categories of local leaders, Peruvians were damned if they followed the rules and damned if they did not.

The Leaders' Tools

In this chapter I focused on the regimes of power that blocked Peruvian Mormons from figuring as worthy, nonmachista, masculine pioneers and, therefore, as leaders. I delineated the factors that made it impossible for Peruvian Mormons to distinguish between culture and doctrine, and I argued that the Anglo-controlled church saw that impossibility not as proof that Mormon doctrine *was* cultural, but as proof that Peruvians were not capable of living "gospel culture" and, therefore, not capable of being leaders. One symptom of their infantilization of Peruvians was that central church leaders, instead of hiring an arequipeño Mormon, flew in an Anglo Mormon—Collin Daly's boss—to be the Arequipa temple construction site manager.

A White foreigner led the crowning achievement of local arequipeño Zion-building. Therefore, arequipeños became followers, not leaders. However, in the next chapter, I will discuss how arequipeño Mormons disrupted their official church's narrow categorization of leaders with their own ample category of government that radiated pioneer indigeneity. In chapter 2, Peruvian Mormons will demonstrate, much like Native survivors of American Indian boarding schools, that "no institution is total, no power is all seeing" (Lomawaima 1994, 164). They will do this by converting the Shining Path War into the origin story of Peruvian Mormon Indigenous government. Further, they will establish that origin story through the selfsame narrative devices appropriate to gospel culture that the early church's Anglo leaders used to exclude indigeneity from their origin story of the Mormon Pioneers.

CHAPTER 2

Government

> I think it has been easy for us to
> recognize what's cultural versus
> what's doctrinal because, big deal if
> they fold the sacrament tablecloth
> side to side or front to back. Right?
> —Collin

Stagnant Path

In the last chapter, we saw how gospel culture allowed Anglo Mormons like Collin to be completely honest when they claimed that there was an unambiguous distinction between the core gospel aspects of Mormonism that were vital, and its local cultural instantiations that were not a "big deal." The problem for the inclusivity of Zion occurred when there was a categorical distinction made between humans who could discern between gospel and culture, and humans who could not. This painted those who could not into the well-worn box labeled "unfit for self-government," the same box into which the US and other Western societies had, at one time or another, placed almost every nation-state in the Global South, including Peru. This chapter analyzes how Peruvian Mormons extricated themselves and their nation-state from that box and, in so doing, formed their own category of government as a group of autonomous leaders who did not merely represent Peru in a larger Anglo-controlled government, but who made Peruvian Mormonism into a government of Indigenous Peruvian pioneers.

Of course, according to social evolutionary theory, it was not merely a static box within which Peru was trapped, but a stage on an evolutionary teleology of development with the United States at the apex (Zea [1975] 2012). Collin saw this teleology as naturally mapped onto a chronological progression of years with some countries falling a quantifiable distance behind others. He saw Peru as so inherently fixed at a retrograde rung on that hierarchal chronology that he switched to Peru's dominant language, Spanish, in order to describe it.

A lot of my theories and analyses about Peru have to do with a roughly twenty-year period of um—just uh—it—estanque [stagnation]? Estancados [stuck]? Where everything in the country just kind of stopped because of the Shining Path.

And so, for example, you look at the growth of the church in Chile. It was slow, slow, slow, and then—eighties and nineties—it just *vroom*, it just went through the roof, right? The baptisms!

But now it's leveled off. Now, we [Peru] were slow, slow, slow, up until the late nineties. And then it took off. I look at that, and also the economy of the country, and I attribute a lot to the Shining Path.

If you have twenty years where nothing can happen, the Shining Path years, it's like you are building this momentum for those twenty years and when it is over, something is going to happen. And, man—the church growth!

You look at where church growth is and where economic growth in Peru is today versus Chile, and it's about twenty years behind. And that time period kind of coincides with that Shining Path stuff.

One of my [Anglo Mormon] bosses remembers staying the night in Lima at hotels and bombs going off all through the night, and gunfire. Kind of scary times.

At the end of this chapter, Barrio Periféricos members Delia and Salvador will refute Collin's Peruvian stagnation narrative with a counternarrative of Peruvian church and state government ascension. However, in order to expand the category of government, let us first look at what both the narrative and the counternarrative have in common: the "scary times" of the Path War, or, as the Runasimi speakers hardest hit by the war called it, "sasachakuy tiempo [difficult time]" (Theidon 2013, 3).

Indigenous Government

In the Anglo Mormon origin story, there were many scenes of similarly scary times. Stalwart frontier Anglo Mormons obtained their pioneer leadership capabilities by courageously pressing on through such times, the most oft depicted of which was the massacre at Hawn's Mill. Most Peruvian Mormons in my study saw films reenacting October 30, 1838, when the bloodthirsty Missouri militia slaughtered Mormons, including unarmed boys, in order to expel them from the state that, during my study, remained slated as the future site for the literal New Jerusalem from which Christ himself will rule at his Second Coming (Reeve 2015). Mormons often considered disasters like Hawn's Mill to be producers of the pain necessary for growth. Similar to the way a metallurgist uses a "refiner's fire" to burn impurities out of metal in order to enhance its desired properties, God burns those whom He loves in order to bring out their true potential.

Tribulations like Hawn's Mill and other Mormon expulsions spatially and discursively mingled Anglo Mormon colonizers with Indigenous peoples who were suffering Jacksonian removals. Both groups were seeking to reconstitute their fractured and displaced governments. Both groups had to pioneer those governments in new lands. Both groups considered themselves to be at war with enemies both tangible and intangible. Mormons would increasingly adopt the symbolic power of martial metaphors—which already saturated *The Book of Mormon*—to heighten the urgency of their responsibility to missionize the Indigenous people of Abya Yala.

Similar overlaps between pioneer indigeneity and pioneer coloniality refracted in the Shining Path guerrilla, which, like many socialist movements in Latin America, such as Chile's Allendismo, advertised its governmental reforms as pro-Indigenous even though many Peruvian societies that actually claimed indigeneity, similar to Chile's Mapuche (Bacigalupo 2016), disagreed with the Path's economic schemes that centered on "the production and promotion of a 'civilized' subject: the agricultural producer" (M. E. García 2021, 96).

Despite the fact that criollos were usually the ones behind Westernized socialist movements throughout Latin America, it would become the Indigenous victims of those movements whom the US would brand "communist rebels" or, post 9/11, "terrorists" in order to justify the ethnic cleansing that US-installed, neoliberal governments would subsequently carry out under the guise of restoring peace (Longley 2009). Peru's president, Alberto Fujimori, was no exception to that pattern. In an act that Collin considered a necessary evil, Fujimori had at least 35,000 highland Runasimi speakers killed and an unknown number of Indigenous people sterilized as retribution for the unrest that the middle-class, academic, non-Indigenous Shining Path leaders helped create (Peruvian Truth and Reconciliation Commission 2003).

This is not to imply that Runasimi speakers of all classes and genders did not exert both violent and nonviolent power in their families, village governments, and the nation in general as the true foundational governors and resisters of the Path unbeholden to settler socialist influences. It is also not to imply that speaking Runasimi naturally denoted peasant class status (Reinaga 2010). In fact, it was partially through the war itself that Peruvianness made Runasimi synonymous with Indigenous peasantry. Through a complex interplay of media spectacle and racialization—largely perpetrated by pituco anthropologists, journalists, and the criollo novelist Mario Vargas Llosa—the war was framed as a clash between two coexisting but irreconcilable Perus: "modern/civilized/coastal Peru, with Lima at its center, and the traditional/savage/archaic Peru, mapped onto the highland communities" (Theidon 2013, 10). In order to justify as collateral damage the killing of noncombatant speakers of non-Hispanic languages, Spanish-language Peruvian media reduced them, en masse, to docile and thus disposable Indigenous peasants lacking the agency sufficient to resist their puppet masters: criollo university professor Abimael Guzman and his native English-speaking, anthropologist colleague, Efraín Best. Guzman was jailed as the Path's leader (he died in 2021), but his imagined hordes of mindless indio minions—not leaders—were executed without trial.

> COLLIN: There is a [*Book of Mormon*] scripture, what did it say? I am paraphrasing, but it's something about dethroning a wicked king [Guzman] won't come without the shedding of much blood. And I just, I kind of parallel that to that Shining Path period and Mr. Fujimori. There was no way that they were going to get rid of the Shining Path passively.
>
> JASON: So, Fujimori was necessary to get rid of—
>
> COLLIN:—Yeah, and I hate—we hate to say that or anything because what he did was so—*ppsshhh*—wicked.

Collin credited Fujimori's genocide and his IMF-mandated neoliberalization with saving Peru from falling even further behind on his chronological teleology of government. When Collin posited that Peru fell twenty years behind Chile, which itself, as he explained to me on another occasion, fell twenty years behind the United States, he unwittingly exposed a fascinating mismatch within Zion's category of government: the reason that he gave for Peru's stagnation was the same reason that Peruvian Mormon leaders gave for Peru's ascension. During the twenty years of the anti-US, Maoist guerrilla movement—a time in which Collin claimed that "nothing happened"—Peruvian Mormons experienced the refiner's fire of their own Hawn's Mill and their own Zion's Camp. During this time of sacrifice and suffering when, for their own safety, all Anglo Mormon leaders and missionaries were removed from Peru, Peruvian Mormons not only proved that they were capable of self-government, but they became the Mormon Pioneers in their own right. What Collin considered to be the etiology of Peru's chronologically quantifiable underdevelopment some Peruvian Mormons considered to be one of Peruvian Mormonism's strongest claims to the throne of the Kingdom of God upon the Earth at the center of Zion's government.

Ascendant Path

Simón Balboa was one of many arequipeño Mormons in my study who renarrativized the scary times in Peru as an epoch of spiritual growth through suffering akin to that experienced by those pioneers who crossed the Great Plains and created a theocratic government in Utah that they called Zion. According to the gospel cultural norms forged in Zion, only pioneers could govern it. Therefore, Shining Path Mormon origin storytellers in my study, like Simón, often narratively reconfigured Peruvian Mormons into pioneers before converting their mobilizations into government.

Having moved on from the Path War's trauma to become a high-level church employee, Simón often traveled between Utah and major South American cities. In December 2017, I caught up with him for an interview in Utah, and so I began asking about Utah's own progress toward Zion status. He almost immediately shifted the topic to a discussion of Arequipa's pioneering of government.

JASON: What does Utah still need in order to truly become Zion?

SIMON: I think that here in Utah they had the blessing of receiving the gospel firsthand, and it was marvelous. The pioneers did an incredible job in these lands, but my impression is that, as the years have gone by, the younger generation has forgotten a bit of what the pioneer sacrifice meant. Us over there in Peru, we saw a little of what the pioneers saw here in the US when they started their new religion with all the opposition in Missouri.

Well, that same opposition was felt by us in Arequipa in the beginning. The Catholic priests would come and attack the first Mormons there. They took a procession with their Virgin to the first chapel built in Arequipa—Umacollo—and they threw rocks at us.

Then the Shining Path came in the eighties and nineties when I was a stake president. I received a threat letter where they gave me thirty days to get out, and if I didn't, they were going to kill me and my family. And they were also going to attack our chapels.

They did it, Jason. I was with my wife one day driving my car in Camaná [near Arequipa]. We passed by the chapel, and it exploded. Right where I worked. I was seeing all the dust from the roof that caved in and the glass.

In Arequipa, I am going to introduce you to the pioneer of Cusco, the father of one of the missionaries who died, murdered by the Path.

JASON: Did the Path have something specifically against the Mormon church?

SIMON: No, they were basically against all religions of foreign origin. They related the church to North American interests—Pizza Hut, McDonald's, and the Mormons . . .

At first, we had a lot of Catholic opposition, but with time, we had the communist opposition. Now the Catholics love us. There has been a change, and they have seen that we are not purely Yankees. We are a people of North American *origin*, yes, a very US religion, but it goes further than simply politics. It offers you a change of life.

We have won respect from the Catholics, and a little from the communists as well [laughs].

JASON: This is the history of the Peruvian pioneers!

SIMON: Yes, because, in 1992, [leaders at] the church [headquarters in Utah] decided to take out all North Americans from Peru, *all of them*—missionaries, the temple president, mission presidents, managers of organizations, everyone. In one day, Jason. In a single day, they got everyone out. From '92 to '96: Four years when we didn't have a single American. It was very traumatic for us to feel that from one day to the next, we were suddenly only Peruvians. . . .

"Now what are we going to do? Do we shut down and go away and forget about the church?"

And, you know what? A marvelous thing happened. With tears in our eyes we said, "No. Our American leaders and missionaries came. They taught us. They entrusted us with the truth. Now it is our turn."

And the fulltime missionaries, the Peruvians, didn't shut down the programs. We kept on teaching. The baptism numbers did not diminish. They maintained. A few years later we were 100 percent self-reliant with our own missionaries for the entire country.

That was a miracle.

The leaders, stake presidents, mission presidents—Latinos 100 percent.

What started out as an attack by the Adversary [Satan]—and it seemed it would destroy us and win the day—was converted into a blessing, and we were victorious.

We learned how to manage the Peruvian church without guidance from you guys [Anglo Mormons].

So, going back to your original question, what does Utah need? To remember the marvelous examples of the pioneers, just as we have learned from you guys.

Besieged by Catholics and communists, Peruvians suffered, and their suffering equated to that of the storied Anglo Mormons besieged by Missourians and the elements. In my estimation, this forged Simón himself into a pioneer leader whereas someone like me merely had "pioneer ancestry."

Simon's story recalls the title of Mexican Mormon historian Moroni Spencer Hernández de Olarte's (2018) dissertation, "If We Can Lead a Revolution, We Can Lead a Church." It details how some Mexican Mormons, many of whom had been Zapatista sympathizers during the Mexican Revolution, split from the Utah church in 1936. They began their own Mexican Mormon church because the Utah church continued to place them under Anglo leaders—under whiteness—even after they proved their capacity for self-government during Mexico's 1926 forced evacuation of Anglos. Though other Mexican Mormons remained loyal members of the Utah church, the Utah church did not reward even them with a modicum of self-government until it called a Mexican stake president to lead them in 1967, nearly ninety years after it had established its first mission in Mexico. Surely Mexican Mormon government had sufficiently "matured" decades earlier, leaving White supremacy as the only impetus for the delay in calling Mexicans to lead Mexico. Such a deprivation of Mexican self-determination meant that—as with its category of leaders—whiteness was a predominant requirement for the official church's category of government.

However, whiteness played an opposing role in Ayacucho, headquarters of the Shining Path guerrilla. I never personally visited Ayacucho, but it became an important place in the Shining Path Mormon origin story that my Peruvian Mormon study participants retold. According to anthropologist Kimberly Theidon (2013), many Ayacucho villagers considered Shining Path militants to be nonhumans because they wandered without ties to pacha. They also considered them to be light-pigmented foreigners. In the Ayacucho anti-Path worldview, in order for one to govern, one first had to be "people," and "one way people [were] made" (261) was "being of a place" (262). In Ayacucho during the scary times, a group had to be local—dark-pigmented—in order to fall into the category of "human" at all, much less "government."

Such a wariness of whiteness remained in post–Shining Path Peru. It left traces in Simón's Shining Path story and, therefore, in the Peruvian Mormon category of government that his story helped construct. As a result of his church-directed travels, Simón understood Latin American governmental weakness as being unjustly naturalized within Anglo culture. He knew that Anglo Mormon leaders pathologized Latin American self-government. Therefore, his continued fealty to those leaders only accentuated his bravery in having the gall to assert that Peruvian Mormons could form a strong government without White guides ("you guys").

Of course, in considering the Peruvian church's governmental success to be a miraculous, rather than expected result, Simón betrayed his belief that Peruvians were innately incapable of self-rule and could only overcome that by following Anglo leaders. Still, that glimpse into his internalized racism made Simón's offhand labeling of the first cusqueño to join the church as the "pioneer of Cusco," sound all the more radical. Throughout the interview, Simón used the honorable title of "pioneer" so freely in association with arequipeños and cusqueños that I felt liberated enough to try it out myself, daring to say, "Peruvian pioneers." Though a non-Mormon may see our interview as riddled with internalized paternalism, our use of "pioneer" in a context outside of the Anglo Mormon origin myth imbued our conversation with an anti-Utah-centrism that some faithful Anglo Mormons might have considered anti-Mormon. Albeit mildly, our conversation offered a version of government that was counterhegemonic. Within gospel culture's narrative norms, claiming that Peruvians were pioneers was tantamount to claiming that Latin Americans could govern themselves.

Our conversation also ran counter to the hegemony of the civilization-versus-indigeneity, "Two Perus" model created through the Path War. Simón's opposition to that model was evident in his unifying use of the identifier "Peruvians." Not once did he, or any of the other storytellers below, imply that only highland Peruvians were innately nonleaders. Quite the contrary. Though he essentialized Peruvians as deficient self-governors in comparison to "Americans," he constructed both coastal and highland Peruvians as one Peru combatting that deficiency in a united Peruvian church government.

His unifying construction partially stemmed from the way that Lamanite identity related to Peruvianness, building off Inca identity to fabricate a national and even hemispheric common ancestry. In my experience, most Peruvian Mormons cast all Latin Americans as Lamanites even if they had few or no ancestors autochthonous to Abya Yala. Therefore, Lamanite identity at its most capacious functioned in Peruvian Mormonism to unite criollos, mestizos, indios—and even the group that both the Two Perus discourse and the official church completely elided, negros—under one Lamanite government of pioneer indigeneity wherein whiteness was no longer paramount.

Governmental Rite

Another high-level church employee, Pedro Córdoba, connected the Shining Path narrative in an entirely different way to pioneer status and, therefore, to the Mormon category of government. Our interview took place in Utah in November 2017. I came to know Pedro because before the church hired him, he was the immigration lawyer whom many in La Familia would hire in order to bring more family members from Peru. He stated, "I was the pioneer who immigrated [from Peru] with my wife and two kids. We didn't immigrate to Utah looking for a better economic situation, we immigrated because of the Path. So, I had friends, people I knew in Utah, and I started working here, and that's that. I was the pioneer because then my parents came, my sisters."

The Path caused Pedro to pioneer the Córdoba familia in Utah. Calling himself a pioneer in the context of immigration was even more counterhegemonic than Simón's use of the word, given that US Mormons were more predominantly Republican than any other US religious group (Lipka 2016). The Republican party, at the time of the interview, was in control of the executive branch of the US government and was more blatantly anti-immigrant than it had been in decades. Yet, despite the risk of offending Anglo Mormonism, Pedro proudly wrapped around himself the holy pioneer banner, usually reserved for Anglo Mormons, in order to identify as a Mormon pioneer immigrant capable of self-government.

For others, such as Barrio Periféricos members Delia Zeballos and Salvador Suarez, speaking of how Peruvians took the reins of their own Mormon government during the Shining Path years was not as risky because they did not use the term "pioneer." This meant that they did not explicitly equate Peruvian ascension within Mormonism to the archetypal Mormon origin story of governing Utah's Zion.

Delia, a limeña (person from Lima) met Salvador, an arequipeño, during a missionary reunion for those who had served in the Peru, Lima, South Mission. They later wed. In relating the complex and nonlinear conjunction of stories below, Delia and Salvador did not make the lexical connection to pioneer status required for Zion's category of government, but they occupied the narrative role reserved for pioneer leaders in Mormon origin stories: the vanguard of a new self-governing religion coming into its own.

Even though the Shining Path origin stories of Peruvian Mormonism that my study participants told me were not stories that they felt comfortable telling to many other people in their ward families, they were still powerful expressions of what Peruvian Mormons imagined as possible regarding the revamping of the Anglo Mormon category of government. For example, in her storytelling, Delia exposed and subtly contested another hidden requirement, in addition to whiteness, of Anglo Zion's government category: masculinity. In other words, similar to the stories that Shining Path militants themselves told to Theidon, Delia and Salvador's Shining Path "stories convey values and meanings; they construct a new moral order" (Theidon 2013, 224). That order was one wherein Peruvians were leaders under their own government with its own required amounts of masculinity, pioneering, and indigeneity.

However, in order to fully appreciate their story, which revolved around their missions, one must first understand the Mormon mission as the principal acculturation ritual for reproducing gospel culture in the future leaders of Zion's government. For the Mormons in my study of all nationalities and genders, the mission was a sacred bootcamp. Before I allow Delia and Salvador to tell their stories, I will first explain how the Mormon mission functioned as the Army of God (ML) disciplining its cadets in the proper sanctification, gendering, classing, and policing of government as a category of Zion.

During the celebratory openings of their mission call e-mails, which came from the office of the Prophet himself, my teenage study participants discovered together with their families and ward families the exotic or familiar world cities that God had reserved specifically for their evangelizing efforts. I attended many of these e-mail opening celebrations, but I will focus on that of one missionary from my ward family in Barrio Periféricos, Gilberto, which I believe was emblematic of the processes that most male missionaries underwent.

Gilberto was twenty when he opened his mission call e-mail in June 2018. He had joined the church only two years earlier. He was the only Mormon in his family, so he did not grow up with the expectation that, as a male, he needed to prepare financially, physically, and spiritually to serve a fulltime mission, a service that the official church considered an obligation for all able bodied eighteen- to twenty-six-year-old male Saints during my study. That youthful window of time was the only one in Gilberto's lifespan within which he could serve a fulltime mission as a duty to God. He could serve one later as an elderly, retired, and married man together with his future spouse in a couples mission (ML), but that would not fulfill his youthful duty.

Shortly after joining the church, Gilberto moved from the highland town of Andahuaylas to the city of Arequipa in order to enroll in one of its dozen institutions of higher learning. One of Barrio Periféricos's many unmarried matriarchs—Ofelia, whom I will properly introduce in subsequent chapters—took him under her wing and was instrumental in convincing him of the eternal importance of his eighteen- to twenty-six-year-old window of missionizing duty. She persuaded him to take two years off of his studies and apply for a mission call. She also helped him navigate the application process, which involved worthiness interviews with Bishop Paucar, medical physicals, and a short questionnaire about language skills and previous travel experience that he e-mailed, through our stake president, to the central church offices in Salt Lake City.

With Bishop Paucar, Gilberto negotiated the percentage of his monthly mission fee that he would be able to contribute from his saved-up wages as the Runasimi Club advisor at the local university, the same university, incidentally, that employed Abimael Guzman before he initiated the Shining Path. Bishop Paucar agreed that the ward's mission fund, which was not supplemented with infusions from Salt Lake City, would loan Gilberto the remaining portion of his monthly mission fee.

When I arrived at our chapel's cultural hall for his e-mail-opening party, Gilberto was there alone in a thick green sweater and leather jacket struggling to connect his laptop to the ward's WiFi (the password of which was the same in every Mormon chapel in the world—Pioneer47—referring to 1847 when the Mormon Pioneers arrived in Utah). Soon, other ward family members trickled in, some with donations of Inca Kola, chips, popcorn, and other light snacks. The ward's current set of foreign missionaries also walked in. Elder Horsthauser was an Anglo Mormon from Idaho. Elder Wero was a Māori Mormon from New Zealand. The hall was abuzz with speculation. To which world mission would Gilberto be called to serve? Ofelia, in her role as his adoptive mother, began to write down people's guesses. The one who guessed correctly would get the entire bag of empanadas that Ofelia purchased on her bus ride over to the chapel.

She let me look at the list of guesses. Of the thirty guesses, eighteen were to one of Peru's dozen official, named missions, which had subdivided and become far more geographically specific since 1959 when a single mission, the Andes Mission, covered most of South America. Two guesses were to Mexico. Five were to Bolivia. The rest were to Paraguay, New Jersey, Utah, Chile, and Ecuador. Of the eighteen Peru guesses, eleven were to Cusco. Many Barrio Periféricos members seemed to think that because Gilberto was one of the only ward members who spoke Runasimi, he would be called to a Runasimi-speaking area like Cusco. They also assumed that since he was poor and, in the words of one member, "uncultivated," he would be called to somewhere in Peru, Bolivia, or Ecuador where he would, presumably, find it easy to coax other poor and uncultivated people into the waters of Mormon baptism.

As Gilberto opened his Gmail account, which was now projecting onto a portable screen, he looked like he was about to faint with anticipation. Ofelia had to click open the e-mail on his behalf. He was called to "the Spain, Madrid, South Mission" and was to report to Madrid's Missionary Training Center in two months' time.

Ward members were in shock. Much to Ofelia's consternation, some found it difficult to hide their jealousy and frankly, their racism. In so many words, my second councilor in the Super Quorum presidency, who was a returned missionary (ML: someone who had completed a full term of missionary service), asked me, "Why does this cholitito [little, tiny Indigenous boy] get called to Spain when I, who studied abroad at BYU and already spoke English even before my mission, had to serve in lame old Lima?"

As his question exemplified, returned missionaries often felt that they deserved more for their willingness to serve in the Lord's Army than they received. The mission had indeed trained them for high positions in Zion's Anglo-run, English-speaking government. Therefore, many resented not being quickly called into those positions after their missions. Returned missionary politics were further complicated by the stigmatization of males who were not returned missionaries. Saints who would have gladly accepted a mission call but who had simply missed its life stage window by becoming Mormon after age twenty-six were often lumped into the same stigmatized group as born-in-the-covenant Saints who had waywardly dodged their duty of missionary service as youth.

The second-class status of males who had not served missions—not to mention the third-class status of those who were dishonorably discharged from missions—contrasted drastically with the obeisance paid to returned missionaries. The male returned missionary was a revered category of person among all of my Mormon study participants. Its status was tantamount to that of "veteran" among my Anglo study participants. Just as US war veterans were asked to stand on the bleachers and be recognized at The Days of '47 Rodeo in Utah during my study, returned missionaries—myself included—were often asked to stand and be recognized whenever our ward's Sunday School manual reached a chapter about the duty that all Saints, not just fulltime missionaries, had in performing missionary work through sharing the gospel in small ways with coworkers, schoolmates, family, and friends.

The respect that Mormons paid to returned missionaries was also similar to the respect that followers of other religions paid to returned pilgrims, such as Muslims returned from Mecca. Yet, respect from coreligionists was only one of many qualities that made the Mormon mission a pilgrimage. From the opening of his e-mail assignment, the Mormon mission became both a pilgrimage to the holy house of Zion's government and a rite of passage toward a leadership position in that government for Gilberto. The founders of anthropological pilgrimage studies, Edith and Victor Turner, considered pilgrimages to sacred sites ritualistic and "liminal phenomena" (Turner [1967] 1979) in that they fostered "communitas," the sacred center lying between social structures. Pilgrimage was, among other things on the Turners' list, "movement from a mundane center to a sacred periphery which suddenly, transiently, becomes central for the individual, an *axis mundi* of his faith" (Turner and Turner [1978] 2011, 34). The central purpose of sending Gilberto to serve a mission in a place not of his choosing—a place peripheral to his experience—was to give him, not those missionized by him, an axis mundi of faith. Gilberto, as a missionary-pilgrim in Spain, would achieve "direct contact with the sacred" (Winkelman and Dubisch 2005, xxiii) "unmediated by holy church powers and representatives" (xxii).

In fact, one of God's mouthpieces, a member of the Twelve, tried to explain the lack of human mediation in the process whereby the Lord assigned fulltime Mormon missionaries (his audience for the following quotation) their own personal sacred place to missionize. "In those sessions when I . . . participate in deciding [which missionary] the Lord would call [to which mission] . . . I'll just tell you, no member of the Twelve called you. It was not a human choice. It was not a computer that did it. I'll just tell you that of all the experiences I've had of having the mind of the Lord made fairly clear—or *very* clear—nothing compares to the experience of those moments of missionaries being assigned" (Eyring 2011, min. 0:49).

What that modern-day apostle was saying was that Jesus Christ Himself selected the place where Gilberto was to go, meaning that Madrid was to become an intimately personal holy land for him. This divine selection process made the mission a pilgrimage for missionaries of all genders. However, the Mormon mission was also a textbook rite of passage as if lifted directly from the pages of Arnold Van Gennep's ([1908] 1961) book *The Rites of Passage* wherein "the liminal period" between "rites of separation" and "rites of incorporation" was coined (Shepherd and Shepherd 1998). Though the rite of passage aspect of the mission only adhered to males directly, it constructed the proper masculinity that delimited all Mormon categories—especially government—and, as such, affected all Mormons in my study regardless of gender.

Upon receiving his call, Gilberto reported to our puneño stake president on the date appointed in the e-mail. The stake president put Gilberto through a laying-on-of-hands ritual called the "setting apart," after which he remained apart from the World until being ritually released post mission. For the duration of his two-year apart time, he used a new name, Elder Cusurichi; he could not embrace members of the opposite sex; and his telecommunication with kin—including Ofelia—was severely restricted. His entire two-year mission to Madrid (which would have been 1.5 years had he been female) was liminoid in many of the ways Victor Turner (1979) outlined; Elder Cusurichi, a neophyte, was an empty vessel into which the doctrine of his religion was poured; if he did not "return with honor" after having completed his full enlistment period, then he would become a nonperson in his ward's society; he was at the complete mercy of his male mission president; and similar to the military, he and his companions would have nothing "to demarcate them structurally from their fellows" (234). While on his mission in and around Madrid, Elder Cusurichi had to stay with his assigned companion at all times except while using the restroom. His companionship pairing changed every few months at the direction of his mission president. Those changes often corresponded with displacements to a completely different zone, such as the Canary Islands, within his greater mission's territory.

Unlike Elder Cusurichi, most Peruvians in my study were called to serve missions within Peru. There, in addition to experiencing the lifeways of five different zones over the duration of their time as missionaries, they roomed, ate, lived, and worked with an average of five different companions from South America and five from Utah or surrounding states. The Anglo friends that immigration lawyer Pedro Córdoba mentioned having in Utah were his former mission companions who, having gone through the same rite of passage, became his blood-brothers as it were, soldiers from the same platoon. Companions received identical living stipends and dressed the same, though one companion be from ritzy Sundance, Utah, and the other be, as Pedro was, from an invasion in Lima without running water. Together they walked the same roads, knocked the same doors, taught the same lessons to those few willing to listen, experienced the same relief when a fellow Mormon would rescue them from the constant rejection of proselyting by giving them a "referral" to a non-Mormon friend who was interested in a free copy of *The Book of Mormon*, felt the same success when a dear investigator whom they had been teaching for months would finally fix a date for her baptism, and suffered the same disappointment when that investigator would get close to her baptismal date but suddenly recant because she could not bring herself to give up coffee, which was against the official church's health code. Experiencing the same emotional, spiritual, and material conditions while working sixteen-hour days with someone of a different background created a sense of equality within mission companionships. This temporarily equalizing aspect of the mission fostered an interclass communitas in a worldwide "supranational church" government (Knowlton 2008, 405) through the liminality of missionary work and the "homogeneity and comradeship" (Turner 1969, 82) it engendered.

However, in formulating Zion's future governors, the mission served an unintended purpose for the impressionable Peruvian young adults in my study. The mission sparked migration. Though migration was something that the central church no longer wanted, its missionary program could not help but motivate Peruvian returned missionaries to migrate to places where non-Peruvian categories of government reigned. This was because the mission introduced missionaries to "non-Peruvian worldviews on class, gender, and race" (Alcalde 2018, 66) that gave them an advantage in certain destinations over migrants without mission experience. The mission also motivated migration by granting missionaries a controlled "first experience in the embodiment of otherness" (46), showing them what it was like to live different lifestyles, including the lifestyles of social classes both higher and lower than the class within which they had been raised.

Unfortunately, though the mission often fostered class equality, it almost always reinforced national inequality. As a result of the "colonial mentality" (Stewart 2020, 177) inherent in the Mormon missionary structure of predominantly White foreigners sent to metaphorically mine "brown gold" (Bessire 2014, 96), the communitas that I observed in mission companionships consisting of Utahans and limeños, for example, was never created from an equitable fusion of Utahan and Peruvian versions of government. Utah's government always took precedence. For this reason, Peruvian Mormon returned missionaries often felt that the gospel culture to which their missions ritually acculturated them could only be implemented into true government in the space of Utah. Therefore, when Pedro returned from his mission, the shock of inequality from sudden reentry into his former rung on the Peruvian class hierarchy, combined with the violence of the Path, motivated him to immigrate to Utah wherein the bulk of his blood-brotherhood and cultural capital had, by then, coalesced. In his mind, only in Utah could he fully participate in Zion's government.

Peruvian Mormon Pachacuti

In counterpoint to Pedro's experience, when I heard Delia and Salvador recount their Shining Path pioneer narrative detailed below, I witnessed the process whereby Zion's government became dislodged from its implicit association with Utah, with Anglo Mormon pioneer stories, and with settler colonial gospel culture in order to coalesce around Peru. This governmental dislodging made way for the possibility of a new category of Mormon government injected with Peruvianness.

DELIA: When all the North American missionaries were evacuated, it was difficult for us Peruvian missionaries left behind because, you can imagine, I just had my zone-change to San Juan de Miraflores [in Lima]. Normally that zone had eighteen missionaries, but after the North Americans left, we only had ten. It was horrible because in our area we had to cover three wards all by ourselves.

There were a lot of baptisms though because the members learned how to help us.

It was a positive thing because, since they saw that we were only two missionaries for three wards, when we got home at night exhausted, we would always find slips of paper under our door. They were referrals filled out by the members with the contact information of their friends. This meant that the members had started to become more aware of missionary work. They were forced to step up.

In traditional Mormon pioneer storytelling—an aspect of gospel culture—not only did every cloud have a silver lining, but God deliberately created disasters in order to topple the next domino in His ultimately beneficent plan. In this pioneer spirit, Delia renarrativized the height of violence in Lima as "a positive thing." For Delia, the dramatic decrease in fulltime missionaries required the lay membership to become missionaries in their own neighborhoods, thus spreading the gospel in an even more effective fashion than if the North American missionaries had stayed.

This disrupted the prophesied role "Ephraim" (Europe) was supposed to play in sharing *The Book of Mormon* with "Manasseh" (Abya Yala). Thanks to the Path, Lamanites (descendants of Israel through Manasseh through Lehi through Laman) ended up occupying the pioneer place reserved for Anglo leaders in *Book of Mormon* prophecies of latter-day evangelizing. The predestined governed switched places with the predestined governors.

Of course, Delia was careful to not narrativize racial hierarchy-toppling or throne usurpation into her story, so she reinserted her White mission president into what she felt was his rightful place at the center of Peruvian Mormon government. "I won't say that we were anguished, but it was a little sad not to have a mission president. We went almost two months without a mission president. You felt like you didn't have parents. And that president, President Openshaw, he knew Peruvians very well. He was an amazing president."

Comparing the lack of one White male leader to the lack of both parents not only corroborated the mission as a coming-of-age time apart from parents, but it also conjured the Anglo church's foundational patriarchy within Mormonism's category of government. To Delia, the exaltation of fathers within familial and missiological governments felt apt, partially because of her indoctrination under an aspect of the mission rite called the "mission mom." Only married males were called to be mission presidents, but their wives were expected to offer emotional, medical, and culinary support to missionaries. In the case of the Openshaws, though Sister Openshaw fulfilled her motherly duties toward the neophytes equivalent to her husband's fatherly duties toward them, she was merely Sister Openshaw, not President Openshaw. This linguistically naturalized the subordination of motherhood to fatherhood in Delia's understanding of government. In fact, patriarchy was so naturalized for Delia that she did not mention Sister Openshaw in this version of her Path story at all. It was as if President Openshaw were both a mother and a father. As it was with US presidents and first ladies, his wife's governmental power adhered to only his governmental authority, not to her own.

Therefore, though Delia's Path story somewhat dislodged whiteness from government, it cemented patriarchy. This pattern of refurbishing Anglo Mormonism's category of government by fortifying some aspects while diminishing others continued throughout Delia and Salvador's narration.

> SALVADOR: Openshaw already knew Peru. He was working in the embassy when he was a stake president, and then they called him to be the mission president. Since he was associated with the United States' embassy, he got threats. And well, they took out all the Americans, even the temple president, all the temple workers: everyone, everyone, everyone.
>
> DELIA: Not a soul remained.
>
> SALVADOR: So, with them went practically all the leadership and the experience—because the Americans were the experience, the leadership—and they left.
>
> It was a difficult process, but in the long term it was beneficial because the local leaders learned. It marks the takeoff point of a new pachacuti in the church here in Peru and in Latin America.
>
> JASON: The church wasn't ruined after all.
>
> SALVADOR: No, no. On the contrary.
>
> DELIA: It grew.
>
> SALVADOR: It grew. The stakes multiplied.

Stakes were administrative units made of multiple wards. The name derived from biblical imaginings of Zion as a great tent that needed more stakes to fasten it to the earth as it expanded. Many difficult metrics had to be met for a Peruvian stake presidency with its twelve high councilors to replace an Anglo mission presidency in the governmental oversight of many geographically proximal congregations. As a result, the multiplication of stakes was a more reliable measurement of church membership growth than mere baptismal statistics, which often represented people who never returned to the chapel after their baptism.

In mentioning these metrics of real church growth, it was almost as if Salvador were directly rebutting Collin's theory of Peruvian stagnation that stemmed from the hegemonic theory of social evolution. In that sense, Salvador's discourse was threatening to the Anglo Mormon category of government, which was part of that hegemony. However, his discourse simultaneously bolstered White hegemony in portraying the removal of "Americans" as the true hardship that befell Peru during a time when tens of thousands of Runasimi-speaking villagers were murdering and being murdered. Still, his use of the Runasimi word "pachacuti" (PL) undermined Anglo hegemony yet again. For Salvador, neither the removal of Anglo Mormons nor the murders of Indigenous Peruvians merited the naming of a new historical pachacuti—an Andean "millennial understanding of time and space, in which one world dramatically ends and another begins" (Theidon 2013, 64), thus organizing time into a nonchronological, cyclical series of world-changing events. For Salvador, the Peruvian Mormon pachacuti did not begin when Anglo church leaders established the Andes Mission in Lima in 1959, nor did it begin when the "Americans" were removed in 1992. Rather, it began postremoval. That was the moment when Peruvian Mormons took the helm of their own religion, pioneered their own Zion, cultured their own gospel, and defined their own pioneer indigenous category of government.

Battle-Hardened Misioneras

In the case of the Path, the blessings that formed Peruvian Mormonism's own government did not stop at decreasing Utah's supremacy. They also decreased patriarchy.

Despite her aforementioned erasure of Sister Openshaw, the role that femininity played in Delia's mission rendered her official church's brand of patriarchy illegible within her new version of government.

> DELIA: As misioneras [female missionaries], for example, there were times when they would keep us in our rooms. "No, you can't go out for four days because of terrorism."
>
> You can only imagine with what gusto we'd finally leave our rooms! You'd leave determined to baptize half the world!
>
> So, we became misioneras aguerridas [battle-hardened female missionaries] with much more desire to proclaim the gospel, right?
>
> For example, it was amazing to us when we'd go to the zone meetings, and they'd give us the baptism statistics for each zone. We were surprised

because in Ayacucho, it was the most difficult place in all of Peru, but they always had the most baptisms.

Misioneras carried the kin title of "Sister" followed by their paternal surname. Misioneros (male missionaries), instead of carrying the gendered kin-equivalent title of "Brother," carried the biblical, hierarchical title of "Elder" (even in Spanish). Though sometimes seen as de facto leaders over nonmissionaries, even males, misioneras could not occupy any mission government positions—district leader, zone leader, and assistant to the president—all of which were open to misioneros. Also, because they did not hold the priesthood, misioneras did not even get the satisfaction of baptizing the people whom they lead to conversion. Furthermore, despite being misioneras aguerridas, they did not compute in their official church's gender category as warriors. Therefore, during the Path War, they were not sent to the most dangerous—ergo, the most missiologically successful—place: Ayacucho.

Those inequalities all stemmed from the social fact that, though female missionaries in my study underwent nearly all the aforementioned liminal rites, the mission was only considered a required rite of passage for males (McDannell 2020b). The mission, in which females participated just as actively as males, was somehow only "an important aspect of creating manhood" (Patterson 2020, 65). Genderblind discourses around the mission served to both naturalize the second-class status of femininity in supranational Mormonism and to mask the requirement of masculinity for the category of government. This happened because the mission functioned as a formal rite of passage only for impressionable Mormon males but was seen as being gender-neutral because females could technically also participate. Nation-state militaries did the same thing to national femininities, but at a larger, and thus even more invisible scale.

Such invisibility made Delia's simultaneously militaristic and feminine classification of misioneras as "aguerridas" into a subtle but powerful unmasking. In fact, the way in which Delia described the role of misioneras during the war, combined with the role of female leadership in the Shining Path government itself, created a conceptual instability that knocked government slightly further out from under the colonial construct of gender in Peruvian Mormonism.

This knock to hegemony was only slight because a former Mormon prophet, who was also a member of US President Dwight D. Eisenhower's cabinet, had the foresight to deliberately design the Mormon mission after the most successful invasive force in the world: the US military. One of the military's facets that translated especially well to the mission was the sexist equation: leaders are warriors and warriors are men (Gallango 2019). To tighten this equation, Anglo church leaders "cast missionary work in a biblical idiom already saturated in ancient patriarchal vocabularies" (Golding 2020, 171), to which they added hypermasculine, military metaphors. Yet, Peruvian society in general and Delia's experience of Peruvian Mormon society during the Path War in particular helped denaturalize that equation. Recall Abish from Delia's utterance at the beginning of chapter 1. In a society wherein only males were meant to be warriors and leaders, the police would not automatically suspect a female of terrorism. The Republic of Peru, therefore, may have been a society wherein females could be warriors and leaders too.

Flora Tristán, a Francoperuvian proto-feminist ethnographer of the 1830s, described how First Lady Francisca de Zubiaga de Gamarra—a field marshal and sharpshooter who led troops in battle—was the unofficial but acting president of Peru from 1829 to 1835. Tristán theorized that female dominance in Peruvian government was in fact so pronounced in comparison to France that it actually reversed European sexual dimorphism: "There is no place on the whole earth where women are more free and where they exercise more power than in Lima. They reign there exclusively. From them comes every impulse. The women from Lima absorb all for themselves the weak portion of energy that hot and intoxicating climate leaves upon the happy inhabitants. In Lima, the women are generally taller and of a more vigorous constitution than the men" (341, translation mine). Other scholars have shown that Peru was a nation wherein wartime women were seen more as heroes than victims (Tupac Amaru Bastidas 2011). It stands to reason, therefore, that Peru's Mormonism would have a differently gendered government category than Utah's Mormonism.

Within Peruvian Mormon government, it also stands to reason that indigeneity would intersect differently with gender. Delia exemplified that categorical intersection as a Lamanite misionera aguerrida fighting for spiritual lives during one of Abya Yala's most category-altering civil wars. Longstanding Indigenous Andean categories disintegrated during the Path War, not only because of the ways it upturned colonial, gendered combat roles—an estimated 40 percent of Path militants were women (Theidon 2013)—but also because of the ways in which the intimacy of the slaughter dissolved an important substance of Andean relatedness: the gaze. Hamlets fought among themselves. Informants betrayed their own neighbors to Shining Path militants, to the anti-Path vigilante peasant patrols, and to the national military death/rape squads. Path and anti-Path militant leaders were often women, thus placing female-coded bodies into contexts of male-coded violence. Husbands and wives killed other wives and husbands, disrupting the cosmic complementarity that made people human. Even nonhuman people, such as mountains, took sides. Gossip became deadly.

Postconflict, neighbors no longer had faces that could withstand gazes. Communities accustomed to establishing their own humanity by cultivating reciprocity with other humans, by appeasing nonhumans, and by avoiding anti-humans—such as the pale-skinned, fat-sucking monster pishtaco—"grew strange unto themselves" (Theidon 2013, 3). Instead of runakuna (human people), they became iskay uyukuna (two-faced people). People feared kin more than they feared pishtacos. No roles were reliable, much less gender and government roles.

While postwar reconciliation involved making each other properly gendered and raced again according to a newly forged Peruvianness—manipulated through another substance of Andean relatedness, cuisine (M. E. García 2021)—it mostly involved a more fundamental recalibration: making each other "people" again. Furthermore, in a *Book of Mormon*—esque form of mutability, there was a phenotypic aspect to this restoration. Path militants were thought to have identifying marks on their arms that—like the dark skin that Lamanites will purportedly lose when they become leaders again—the militants lost when they became human again.

As Delia and Salvador's Peruvian Mormon origin story demonstrated, Peruvian categories of personhood and perception were recalibrated, not simply among the Path and anti-Path strongholds of Ayacucho's hamlets wherein Theidon (2013) conducted her ethnography summarized above, but across Peru. This meant that the categories of Peruvian sainthood were also recalibrated, regendering gospel culture's category of government to a previously unthinkable extent: A Lamanite misionera became an aguerrida warrior-leader in her own pioneer story of Peruvian self-government.

"No Matter How Much of a President You Are"

Below, while Delia conceded the Peruvian Mormon social fact that masculinity and whiteness—embodied in the person of her mission president—still formed outsized portions of "government" among Peruvian Mormonism's categorical requirements, she also clarified what would no longer be tolerated despite the fulfillment of those two requirements. The following extended anecdote recounts the miraculous extraction of two Peruvian missionaries in Delia's cohort who ended up being drafted into the Peruvian military during their mission service.

> Elder Huamán committed an error. He didn't regularize his documentation before leaving for his mission, so when he got to Ayacucho, he had his companion, Elder Giraldo, and every day there would be draft raids.
> When it came time to see Elder Huamán's documents, the commanders saw an irregularity: "Since your documents are bad, which is your own fault, you are going to have to do military service. All right?"
> Obviously, the missionaries protested, "But, no way! Why? No!"
> Immediately they enlisted him.

And to his companion they said, "You can leave."

"No, I can't leave because we are companions, and they told me not to leave him."

"Ah, all right then. You get in there as well!"

And they enlisted him too. By the time the mission president was notified, the documentation was already entered, and they were soldiers.

When the mission president's assistants finally came, they found them with uniforms and shaved heads [laughs], and for two months they were serving their country, doing drills, everything.

But they were also preaching the gospel to many soldiers, and they had baptisms in there as well.

Something very special happened with all of this because President Openshaw was still there. I was assigned to Cusco at the time, and he traveled to Cusco very worried and told us, "Their two months of basic training are almost up. If we don't get them out of the army fast, they are going to enter the battlefield."

And since they were young men in Ayacucho itself, well, it was practically a death sentence. In those two months, the mission office in Lima did all kinds of paperwork, but they were always denied. It was terrible. And Giraldo wasn't about to abandon his companion [laughs].

So, when President Openshaw arrived in the Cusco zone, we had a kneeling prayer. "From this very moment. We are going to fast and we are going to pray," he said.

We prayed, and the blessing was given because with only one day to spare before they went into the infantry, the mission leaders from Lima arrived in Ayacucho. President Openshaw obviously couldn't go himself, being a North American. They couldn't find anyone to speak with, but suddenly a car pulls up right next to them and out walks one of the generals. Our mission area leader goes up to him: "We have a problem, people know us as the Mormons, and we have two missionaries"—

"What? What? You are the Mormons!? I had a Mormon friend, an excellent guy. I admire you people, you know that? I owe you a lot. Which young men are you're looking for?"

And the general himself signs them out. That same day, both missionaries were discharged.

So, when President Openshaw returned to Cusco, he said, "Our prayers were answered—cutting it a little too close for my taste—but the Lord got the missionaries out."

President Openshaw was the best. But one lesson to take from Peru, for example, is that Peruvians don't allow themselves to be had. No matter how much of a president you are, if you do something wrong, the people are going to stand up.

Peruvians demonstrated as much with Fujimori. They called together everyone from the four Suyos [a Runasimi word meaning the four districts of the Inca Empire] and all of Peru rose up against him, and Fujimori escaped [laughs], ran away with his tail between his legs because he was scared.

And that is what characterizes Peruvians, even more now that the terrorists did us so much harm.

Delia said, "no matter how much of a president you are" immediately after mentioning her Anglo mission president. This rhetorical proximity represented her least subtle critique of the Anglo Mormon version of the "government" category. I interpret her as basically saying, "Openshaw was lucky that he was a moral human being, because if he had not been, his maleness, his calling, his priesthood, and his foreignness would not have been sufficient to maintain his authority as a leader in a Peruvian Mormon government. Not anymore. Peruvians have their own authority now. Our authority is not derived from our being called by Anglos into static positions pre-infused with *their* power. It derives from the dynamic people power released when all four Suyos unite."

In using a Runasimi word, Delia indexed her indigeneity and her Peruvianness. Meanwhile, in the entire arc of her narrative encapsulated below, she used gospel culture's trial-by-fire westward pioneer trope to index her status as part of a Mormon government. Therefore, her narrative leadership and sainthood reverberated both pioneering and indigeneity.

And the terrorism lasted so long. Even before my mission. I remember the chapel was only like five blocks away from my house in Lima, and my dad would always say, "When you are on the street and you hear bombs, get against the wall. Don't run. Calm down."

It was a daily thing. When we went to youth activities at the chapel, suddenly: *Boom!* the bombs. But it was a special time because there were so many of us in the church's youth organization, and we all went together. As kids we'd say, "This is our generation's challenge. We are going to go to the chapel anyway."

And of that whole group of youth, all of us ended up going on missions, both women and men. These difficult things strengthened our testimony [sense of the church's veracity].

Nowadays the kids go to youth activities and there are no bombs or blackouts or dangers. Now it's just whining, "I don't want to go to the activity. I don't want to go to the chapel."

Or, "So early?!"

While for us, we practically risked our lives to go to the youth activities and to go to early-morning Seminary.

So, I think that all those obstacles helped us to value having a chapel, to value having people give of their time to teach us the lessons, to value having our religion.

Peruvian Self-Government

Where did the most baptisms take place? When and where were missionaries miraculously liberated from certain death? When did the highest percentage of youth complete their mission pilgrimage and rite of passage? If the answers to these questions include the times and places of the most intense violence, then nothing less than a truly "Mormon" pioneer story is afoot. In their continuous narrative, Delia and Salvador hit all the hallmarks of pioneer origin myth. Another of those marks, as both Simón and Collin also demonstrated, was the seamless conflation of Zion-building with state-building. For example, Delia went from talking about a mission president to talking about a national president without skipping a beat. This conflation of church and state formation happened in other venues as well. For example, Peruvian migrants who converted from Catholicism to Protestantism in Korea "talked about alcohol abuse, infidelity, and the worshipping of false idols as both evidence and causes of Peru's (and Latin America's) economic and social suffering" (Vogel 2020, 93).

In order for a story to be a Mormon pioneer narrative that lives up to gospel cultural norms, it must have the potential to scale out until it becomes the causal force behind all global advances. Mormons of many nationalities have told me that radio was invented so that the Mormon Tabernacle Choir would have a venue of distribution and that flight was invented so that missionaries could get to their missions. In Delia and Salvador's tale, the fate of Peru was inextricably tied to the fate of Peruvian Mormonism because the age of terrorism produced local leadership, which was something that they saw as naturally scarce in both the Peruvian church and the Peruvian state. This forging of government was what sparked my final question.

JASON: This all reminds me of how the future government of the church emerged from Zion's Camp. [Zion's Camp was an enterprise, mentioned in the beginning of chapter 1, whereby Joseph Smith led an army of Mormons against settlers in Missouri]. Do you think the Path War was like Peru's Zion's Camp? I mean, do you think that church government was run in more of a Peruvian style afterward?

SALVADOR: Yes.

JASON: In what way?

SALVADOR: Yes, the Peruvianness of the church was reinforced a lot during that time. Because it used to be the church of the gringos. It had that image. But once the terrorism happened, the Peruvians themselves, over time—because it was only in 2015 when they started sending North American missionaries again—the Peruvians started to finally take control of the church out of necessity. The idea that the church is of Jesus Christ was strengthened. It isn't a US religion, right? It is a restored, ancient religion.

Here Salvador openly contested US-centrism while subtly uplifting indigeneity in its stead. That he left unspoken the place wherein his religion was anciently practiced only made it ring louder to insider ears: pre-Hispanic Peru. Mormonism, as Salvador told me on many other occasions, was not merely a restored ancient religion, it was a restored pre-Inca religion. Salvador's subtext was that Mormonism was even more Peruvian than it was "American."

SALVADOR: That is why the church has grown so much in Peru. We are more than a half million Peruvians who are baptized, with four temples [announced, but only two actually constructed], so you can see the solidity of the church.

In the same time frame in which the church in Chile was established, the church has progressed a lot more in Peru. The church started much earlier in Chile; I think in 1920. In Peru it didn't start until 1960. So, in only sixty years the church has matured much more in Peru than it has in 100 years in Chile. And one of the factors is that the Americans left, and the Peruvians had to be the ones to hold up the church. Not that there weren't *many* mistakes.

DELIA: A lack of experience.

SALVADOR: Yes. As Peruvians, we are characterized for our lack of honesty. We aren't that honest. And that got reflected in the church, right? But that is also one of the proofs that the church is not led by men, rather it is led by the Lord, and He attends to His accounts, and He sees the way in which imperfect people like us can become perfect through the refinement of difficulties. And we have lived those difficulties. We have become part of that history.

DELIA: We have been attacked by terrorists.

"That history" referred to the history of the church writ large. The Path pioneer origin story was not simply a quaint local instantiation of an unmarked— meaning automatically Anglo—gospel culture that could be published in central church magazines as yet another heartwarming example of how the world's poor struggled bravely to achieve the skills of self-government that only Anglos possessed innately. The Path War was not simply Mormon Peru's Zion's Camp. It was the Mormon world's Zion's Camp. According to Salvador, it was a government-generating trial-by-fire equivalent to Zion's Camp or Hawn's

Mill and as such, it should have formed part of a canon of mythology globally relevant to the entire Mormon supranation just as Zion's Camp was expected to do. Put differently, if White supremacy were eliminated but the Zion's Camp story somehow remained applicable beyond Anglo society, then the Shining Path story would become just as applicable beyond Peruvian society. Both stories held enough pioneer indigeneity to become equally foundational to the global Mormon category of government.

Salvador concluded, "But, in the present day we can see the blessings of that, right? Because Peru is a more prosperous country. Certainly, we still have a lot more advancing to do, but compared to those decades, there is more economic capacity now. The church is more mature. So, the Lord has blessed these lands. Peru is going toward good paths now and that is all thanks to the faith of the members of the church." For Abimael Guzman and the vision of Peruvianness that he represented, the shining path to Peru's future was Marxism. For Salvador, the true path was Mormonism. For me, Mormon pioneer stories—in their strong association with evolutionary hierarchies, hegemonic notions of Western supremacy, capitalism, and Utah-centrism—seemed impossible to weave into the gospel culture of such a complex Peruvianness. Nevertheless, that was precisely what Simón, Pedro, Delia, and Salvador did. Salvador was somehow able to make a nod to the veracity that he perceived in North American supremacy while simultaneously and specifically reversing Collin's "twenty-years-behind-Chile" theory of Peruvian stagnation, all without betraying any sign of cognitive dissonance. For her part, Delia was somehow able to trouble the gendered aspect of the Anglo Mormon category of "government" and its similarity to the US category of "military" even after emerging from what was basically a 1.5-year ritualization of female inferiority. To these Peruvian Mormons, the same Shining Path pioneer story that, to me, seemed dizzyingly contradictory, made perfect sense within the Peruvian gospel culture that they pioneered by overcoming God-given adversity. Without disrupting Utah-centrism, they used Peruvian-style renarrativization (Vogel 2014) to ingeniously recenter Mormonism on Peru and prove that Peruvians were a self-governing body.

Path storytelling was not the only means through which Peruvians in my study made claims to gospel culture's coveted, pioneer titles of "leaders" and "government." In the next chapter, I explore other, more structurally profound ways through which this was done, ways that complicated the possibility of Peruvian Mormon categorical adaptation in a context of multivalent pioneer indigeneity. Refurbishing "leaders" and "government" opened a breech, allowing Peruvian Mormons to infiltrate the more ethereal Mormon category of legacy to the extent that their claims to indigeneity made them the aboriginal inhabitants of a Zion exclusive to pioneers.

CHAPTER 3

Legacy

And should we die before our journey's through,
Happy day! All is well!
We then are free from toil and sorrow, too;
With the just we shall dwell!
—"Come, Come Ye Saints" (Clayton 1985, 30)

Pioneer Legacy

The moral of both the pioneer, Anglo Mormon and the Shining Path, Peruvian Mormon origin stories was that God turned tribulations into blessings. This moral had the power to grant both stories a legacy within gospel culture. However, the Peruvian Mormon story needed to eliminate some requirements from the Mormon category of legacy in order to make room for Peruvians. This was because legacy was an unmarked term in gospel culture that really meant "pioneer legacy." As with most other categories of Mormon Zion, this ultimately meant US, White, male, pioneer legacy. Therefore, Peruvian, female, Lamanite-identifying Mormons had their legacy-building work cut out for them as they creatively wove their Peruvian origin stories into those of the Mormon Pioneers. This chapter explores their Peruvian Mormon legacy-weaving, specifically focusing on the complexly material loom made of death, dance, blood, darkness, and stone and on that loom's struggle with legacy's frayed threads of sacrifice, gender, race, and place.

Tribulations

"Legacy," on the lips of my study participants, connoted the importance of connecting ancestors to descendants and of keeping future families faithful to the official church despite tribulations. The ways in which my study participants lived legacy, however, were more complicated. They lived legacy as an interwoven mat of contradictions that deepened its connotations, enshrouding the term with a mysteriousness that captivated them in its indefinability. Disturbingly, at least one thread of Mormon legacy's convoluted interweave was necropolitical. It concealed the disregard for human life often correlated with the moral, "tribulations bring blessings," in Christian missionization. For example, among the Ayoreo of Paraguay whom a non-Mormon Christian group missionized in the late twentieth century, this moral translated into the "terrible irony . . . that missionaries had to first intensify or create the savage realities they aimed to alleviate and transcend. They thanked God when he 'opened doors' through devastating epidemics . . . [which they used] to stage demonstrations of the power of God's Grace [antibiotics] over satanic witch-craft" (Bessire 2014, 100).

In the Shining Path Mormon origin myth, the negligence of sending Peru-vian missionaries to the most dangerous area of Peru—Ayacucho—while extracting Anglo Mormons from the entire country paralleled the negligence concealed in the portion of the Anglo Mormon Great Plains–crossing history that—because of its heightened tribulation—came to symbolize the entire Anglo Mormon origin myth. That portion involved the Martin and Willie handcart disaster of 1856 wherein over 150 overland travelers from Illinois to Utah—most of whom were recently immigrated and baptized European Mormons—died in a snowstorm (Hein 2014).

This was the disaster that Mormon reenactors of the Trek explicitly depicted as they sang the above hymn during my study. It was the disaster that I reenacted together with Peruvian American Mormon teenage members of La Familia in 2007. The mythology of the disaster was well known among my Mormon study participants of all nationalities. However, few knew the context behind it. The context was that the Prophet Brigham Young could have easily prevented the disaster had he valued the lives of his new converts as much as he valued his own. Instead, he—the wealthiest man in Utah and a seer of future events—allowed those converts to come to Utah late in the year pushing their own handcarts when he could have facilitated their well-timed and well-provisioned travel as he had for those in his own ox-drawn party nearly a decade earlier.

In 2007, near the actual site of the disaster on the church's property in Martin's Cove, Wyoming, instead of hearing about its shocking preventability, the youth group that I was called to lead only heard about its faith-promoting potential. The elderly couple who told us the story to prepare us spiritually for our three-day handcart-pushing reenactment—Trek—had been called to serve a church historic site couples mission in Martin's Cove. They told the same story to thousands of Mormon youths each summer who lived within driving distance of the actual legacy-generating sites of Mormon legend instead of having to creatively reenact Trek upon other, less Mormonized ground. Accentuating the perfect pioneer setting, the mission couple had perfected the telling of the pioneer story so that the legacy-promoting, pioneer-forging blessings that came from the disaster outshone its morbid undertones. Even the frostbitten amputees who survived Martin's Cove to live in Utah's Zion reportedly privileged the moral, "tribulations bring blessings" over an equally fitting moral, "a stitch in time saves nine," which would have implicated Brigham Young's negligence (Hafen and Hafen [1960] 1992).

During my study, narrative privileging of legacy-promotion over life-protection also mirrored the Israelite privileging—in the biblical book of Exodus—of arduous Promised Land pioneering over inconvenient Indigenous Canaanite removal. This mirroring became complicated when Zion-building Anglo Mormons laid claim to both the pioneering and the indigeneity, but it became a paradox when Indigenous Mormons reappropriated the very form of indigeneity that Anglo Mormon settler colonists fabricated and, with it, built legacy (Taussig 1992). I hope to elucidate that paradox through the sentiments of my study participants as they commented on the interplay between lineage, responsibility, and faith that appeared to demarcate their cultural category of legacy.

A Chilean Mormon named Ignacio Monte had a particularly poignant experience involving the balance between legacy-promotion and life-protection. His thoughts on that experience exemplified the paradox of Mormon legacy relative to Peruvianness. He was the church's facilities manager in Lima on the day when all Anglo Mormons were evacuated from Peru because of the Shining Path guerrilla war. I interviewed him in October 2017 in Utah. I met Ignacio through our mutual connection to Pedro, La Familia's former immigration lawyer from the previous chapter.

> I think that a lot of people feel that Peruvians are very docile—and they are in certain ways—but they have a very strong spirit.
>
> Now, as to my experience being there, I was charged with sending home the bodies of two missionaries killed in the highlands. It got to the point when we had to understand that we were inside an independent power that was not controlled, which was the guerrilla, and we had to learn to coexist with that.
>
> So, there were rules that we had to follow in Ayacucho, right? We didn't send any gringos over there because the Shining Path was explicitly anti-US.
>
> Well, what did not occur to anybody was that—when we pass instructions on down to those below, one tends to think that everyone is going to understand what one is thinking, right? And the instruction was that no Americans should be sent there, but nobody ever said that a blond-haired, blue-eyed Peruvian would also run a risk, right?
>
> So, there was a Peruvian missionary with blond hair and blue eyes with his companion, and they were killed.
>
> Now, the terrible thing was to think, or to feel, that it could have been avoided, right?

But there it is.

Many times, in large organizations such as the church, instructions come down and the people on the ground, the ones who have to implement them, do not understand them or they see them in a different way. All they do is read the words, "no Americans over there."

And so, well, "Peruvians! Let's look for all the Peruvians!"

And Peruvians go.

One should have included the reason behind the instruction, right?— think it through a bit better.

Though Ignacio came dangerously close to implicating the cross-cultural insensitivity of the central church's "read between the lines" rule-bending expectation (mentioned in chapter 1) in the death of two Peruvian missionaries, he quickly recovered the blessings-through-tribulations moral, thus maintaining the legacy-promoting pioneer spirit that converted the Shining Path narrative into a Mormon pioneer origin story.

Then the instruction came that nobody who wasn't Peruvian should be in Peru at all. . . . All the Peruvians knew that now everything was in their charge. . . . As a result, the feeling in Peru now involves knowing what Peruvians are truly capable of.

Not so much that we don't need North Americans or that North Americans are not good. They are good.

The point is that, at what point do Latinos or, in this case, Peruvians, take responsibility for who they are? And they did it in a brilliant manner.

The question of who Peruvians are bespeaks their historic status as docile, colonized, Indigenous people in relation to their contemporary responsibilities as brilliant, self-governing Mormon pioneers. The fusion of antonymic repulsion and bipolar fascination that the potential amalgamation of those identities—pioneer indigeneity—produced in Ignacio was too unwieldy for him to fully narrativize. Thus, he omitted the blue-eyed missionary's companion's phenotype. As I later found out, the companion was a brown-skinned cusqueño with Mormon "pioneer ancestry." In this instance, "pioneer ancestry" does not mean "Anglo Mormon pioneer ancestry." Instead, it means that he was the son of "the pioneer of Cusco" (one of the first cusqueños to become Mormon) whom Simón mentioned in chapter 2. In Mormonism, those with pioneer ancestry were supposed to be light-pigmented, not dark-pigmented. Therefore, though both companions were equally dead, Ignacio privileged the more tragic, and thus more legacy-promoting of the deaths: the death of the whiter, and thus more pioneer-like body.

The other body, an Indigenous pioneer body, disturbed the monopoly that Anglo Mormonism had over pioneer indigeneity. That monopoly was implicit in the Anglo Mormon pioneer story structure, which Ignacio knew well, wherein Anglos anachronistically became the Salt Lake Valley's first inhabitants despite that valley's deep relationship with the Shoshone, Paiute, Timpanogos, Ute, and other nations since time immemorial. Tragically, the cusqueño missionary was guilty—from the Shining Path's perspective—because of his association with US Mormon pioneering. Yet, he was fit for the fatal risks of Ayacucho in the first place—from the US Mormon church's perspective—because of his skin tone's association with indigeneity. After all, it was not he who was sent to Ayacucho in error. The mistake was sending a blond. "Such a situation . . . highlights the differentiated meaning of citizenship in Peru, and even the differentiated value of human life" (Boesten 2010, 140) in the church.

In the previous chapter, I discussed how creations of pioneer identity played out as Shining Path stories contested Utah-centrism and settler coloniality. In this chapter, I focus on how other kinds of stories helped grant Peruvian Lamanites a pioneer life and legacy in a Zion framework that required sacrifice and death. In Anglo Mormonism, pioneer indigeneity was concocted as a form of "setter nativism" (Tuck and Yang 2012, 2) wherein pioneer, settler colonist identity and an ill-appropriated indigeneity combined in ways that only served to sharpen the colonist/indigenous dichotomy. However, when Peruvian Mormons seized control of Mormon legacy, they created alternate pioneer indigeneities that melded that dichotomy into something new. This chapter provides a glimpse into the new spacetimes and genealogical structures that allowed Peruvian Mormons to become the first inhabitants of holy places with multitemporal Mormon legacies.

Lamanite Legacy

Though some used their Shining Path experiences to forge a unique Mormon pioneer identity that elevated the Peruvian Zion closer to the storied Utah Zion, most Peruvian Mormons in my study had never heard the Shining Path Mormon origin story. Some were not yet born or not yet Mormon during the war. Others were too busy worrying about martial law to notice the evacuation of Anglo Mormon leadership. Pioneers like Delia tried to keep the story alive orally, but Peruvian Mormonism's daily, central focus on Utah-distributed texts considered globally relevant tended to eclipse local pioneer storytelling.

Yet, as I describe below, it was precisely through those Anglo-written texts that Peruvian Mormons formulated for themselves a pioneer Indigenous legacy. The Utah cadre of La Familia—over 150 Peruvian and Latin American Mormons and non-Mormons all living in or near Salsands, Utah, exemplified that formulation. Jacoba Arriátegui and Arcadio Costa gradually brought La Familia from a working-class section of Lima, Callao—"considered one of the most dangerous places in Peru" (M. E. García 2021, 146)—to New Jersey in the 1970s at Jacoba's insistence. Her decision was consistent with a pattern wherein "women spearheaded Peruvian emigration to the United States" (Paerregaard 2008, 230) between 1950 and 1980. Shortly after their arrival, Jacoba joined the church, and La Familia moved to northern Utah where, after Arcadio eventually joined, they became instrumental in pioneering Spanish-speaking Mormon branches within greater English-speaking stakes of Zion. They deliberately constructed those branches as "pan-ethnic [places] where they could better engage with a broadly Latinx heritage and cultural environment not found in white, Anglo US Church spaces" (Romanello 2020, 29).

Part of that construction included instituting celebrations of Indigenous legacy. Though the Costa family claimed to be "nonindigenous by culture" (De la Cadena 2000, 273), they were proud Lamanites, an identity that implied indigeneity by descent from textual, *Book of Mormon* peoples. In and around these celebrations, I observed how Lamanite identity allowed Latin Americans who were raised to consider "Indigenous" an insult akin to "uneducated" to consider it instead an opportunity to educate the insulter on indigeneity's textually verifiable, erudite, Israelite origins. As historian Elisa Eastwood Pulido (2020) concluded, "the Book of Mormon made indigenous Americans a kind of 'people of the book'" (29) rather than symbols of illiteracy. As a result of this destigmatization of indigeneity, even the few Latin American Mormons in my study who emphasized their European descent (mostly Uruguayans and Argentinians) sought a sort of pan-Latinx class solidarity in Lamanite identity, though they were loath to claim Lamanite genetics.

For detribalized Latin Americans of Indigenous descent who converted, or whose ancestors converted, into mestizos or US Latinx in order to ameliorate their stigmatization, Lamanite identity served an important purpose. It allowed them to retribalize themselves on their own terms with the aspects of indigeneity that they chose (Call 2021). This placed Lamanites, as it did chola marketers in Huaraz, Peru, "between the social categories of rural/urban, indigenous/mestizo" (Babb 2018, 100). Furthermore, Lamanite identity allowed Mormons to perform both spiritually and materially what Protestant identity allowed the Andeans in Kimberly Theidon's (2013) study to imagine only spiritually. It "allow[ed] them to imagine a Christian community that erased centuries as well as cultural and national differences and to script a world in which they as well as the Israelites travers[ed] the same landscape—a landscape of exodus, struggle and return" (90).

However, for Native Mormons who already had tribal inclusion—a few of whom participated in my study—Lamanite identity tended to be alienating. As Ute national citizen Lacee Harris (2021) asked in 1985, "Were those Lamanites my Indian people? My people were good, deeply spiritual, in tune with the rhythms of the earth and with their own needs. How could we be descended from a wicked people? How could I be a descendant of wickedness and still be good without repudiating the heritage that made it possible for me to accept Mormon goodness?" (92).

Those questions' feedback loop encapsulated the paradox of a Mormonism that pretended to rescue indigeneity from the very doctrine that determined its relationship to indigeneity: the doctrine of genocide (Hernández 2021). "Lamanite," in order to overcome this complexity, had to overflow mere identity. It had to become legacy. Jacoba, and others like her, built Lamanite identity into Peruvian Mormon legacy. Her way of showing pride in her identification with her salvaged Indigenous origins was to institute in Utah what neo-Indianists instituted in Cusco in the 1940s—folkloric dance (De la Cadena 2000). Jacoba's repertoire of Peruvian dance was specifically designed to replace the stereotype of the "melancholic, introverted peasant" with that of the "festive Indian . . . decked out in rich, multicolored wool clothing" (277, 285). Jacoba's children, and now her great-grandchildren, grew up dressing like ñustas (Inca princesses) and dancing "Valicha" (a cusqueño dance) on Mormon stages in cultural halls throughout Utah as part of Lamanite legacy celebrations alongside their Latin American and occasionally Polynesian and Diné counterparts, all bedecked in the regalia of what they understood to be authentic indigeneity (see figure 2).

Jacoba was part of a growing grassroots of "Spanish-speaking LDS Latinas who worked tirelessly to create fun activities and culturally based events that celebrated Latin American heritage for their children" as a bulwark against "the discrimination they faced" (Vega 2020, 602) across the United States. Such dedicated pioneering of recently refashioned cusqueña Indigenous dance, especially coming from a proud limeña like Jacoba who claimed to descend from but not inhabit indigeneity, spoke to indigeneity's multivalence and multitemporality in Andean constructions of legacy.

For example, in rural Bolivia, according to anthropologist Andrew Canessa's (2012) study, some of the very people thought of as the nation's most Indigenous often did not consider their own children to be Indigenous. In their view, since people were Indigenous by lifestyle, not blood-descent, if their children moved to the city—leaving the cycle of communal reciprocity that created their conception of Indigenous legacy—they were no longer Indigenous even though, from a genetic standpoint, they may have had 100 percent Aymara ancestry. Furthermore, the parents themselves were only Indigenous in Canessa's translation of the Aymara word for their identity, Jaqi. In their translation, they were simply human, meaning that indigeneity for them was a doubly vacuous concept.

Some upwardly mobile descendants of Jaqi went to great lengths to decrease the traits that they perceived to be the outward manifestations of indigeneity and its implied provinciality. However, anthropologist Ulla Berg (2015) found, in the case of Peru, that when this upward mobility led to US migration,

FIGURE 2. The anniversary celebration of Jacoba's Spanish-speaking ward in Salsands, Utah. After performing "Valicha," Peruvian ñustas (geometric hats, middle left) filmed their Colombian coreligionists' dance. October 2017. Photo credit: Jason Palmer.

Indigenous Peruvians suddenly felt free to exotify aspects of their indigeneity, discovering that, in US contexts that commodified ethnicity (Comaroff and Comaroff 2009), a certain Indianism could bolster rather than diminish their cosmopolitanism. Jacoba, in line with this phenomenon, made sure that everyone whom she constructed as Costa-kin in Utah (including me) learned to dance in cusqueño costumes, costumes that her siblings who remained in Callao, some of whom I interviewed, reportedly would "not be caught dead wearing."

Yet, as figure 2 demonstrates, there was a gender dynamic to the "everyone" whom Jacoba taught to dance Lamanite legacy. Jacoba's 2017 dance production included mostly women, and women tended to keep their costumes on throughout the night while the few men with dancing parts took theirs off immediately. As with the commodification of indigeneity in the tourist industry in anthropologist Florence Babb's (2018) field site of Vicos, Peru, "women, notably through their use of dress and language, once again [were] shown to be the principal signifiers of traditional culture, the indigenous, and the 'Other'" (186). Indeed, Marisol De la Cadena (1995) famously observed that women near Cusco were thought of as more Indigenous than men. During her fieldwork in the nineties, it was advantageous for Indigenous men to become mestizo to avoid discrimination since they were the ones who had to interact more with mestizo society, particularly through mandatory military service. Though De la Cadena (2008) later noted that being Indigenous had gained new political traction in Peru that exceeded the category of ethnicity and that men were once again retaining their indigeneity, I noticed that, in the late 2010s in Latina Mormon Utah, Lamanite legacy was enacted by females more than males.

Conversely, when our puneño stake president in Arequipa, Peru, organized folkloric dance competitions in which Barrio Periféricos members participated (including myself) in 2018, men and women danced and dressed up in equal numbers. As far as I observed, there were no men or women in the entire stake who dressed indigenously in any aspects of their lives outside of these church-sponsored dances. At the competitions, the regalia was not considered an expression of personal indigeneity tied to the locality from whence both the dancer and the dance hailed. Rather, the regalia was simply part of the pre-packaged dance ensemble, forming a "jungle-coast-mountains" national folk legacy open to all Peruvian ethnicities. Most of the dances in our arequipeño stake were coded as either autochthonous to the Amazon or the Andes, but the criollo dance of "La Marinera" always made a requisite appearance as did a few dances of Afroperuvian origin, though the stake included neither criollo nor Afroperuvian members. From my perspective, which Bishop Paucar will demonstrate below to have been faulty, nothing in the dances tied them to Lamanite identity or to any evocation of indigeneity as being part of an ancient legacy. Rather, the indigeneity expressed in our stake's dance competitions in Arequipa seemed contemporary. The oldest reference that I could gather came from a dance that interpreted the plot of *Blood Festival*, the 1941 ethnographic novel by a Peruvian national hero, criollo anthropologist José María Arguedas.

On the other hand, in the Latina-led dances of Utah, ties to ancient Indigenous legacy and to Lamanite solidarity were explicit, not only in the commentary of invariably male emcees (whose speeches females invariably wrote), but in the invitation of male Diné hoop dancers and male Samoan Fa'ataupati dancers. Traveling from distant Utah wards, those non-Spanish-speaking dancers' presence at the Spanish-speaking Pioneer Trail ward celebrations could only have been explained—and, in fact, was explained over the mic—as stemming from a shared, pan-hemispheric Lamanite legacy.

Why did it seem to fall to women to keep that legacy alive? Why did that legacy require more buttressing in Utah than in Peru? I think the answers inhered to the social fact that Spanish-speaking wards in Utah were refuges from Anglo Mormon society (Romanello 2020), and that males, naturalized as leaders, had to leave those refuges in order to deal with their Anglo Mormon stake leaders—the Leaders—more often than females. Meanwhile, in Arequipa, Mormon wards were refuges from an Andean Catholicism coded as pejoratively Indigenous. Many arequipeño Mormons understood Andean Catholicism as including the degraded practices for which Lamanites were cursed with dark skin in the first place, thus becoming a race. Many non-Mormons who sought to become or already were arequipeños netos—an already complexly Indigenous and Catholic identity—were concerned with downplaying the "Andean" and accentuating the "Catholic." They desired to de-Indianize both their religion and themselves.

Mormonism fast-tracked that desire. When arequipeños netos were Mormon, their Lamanite identity was the culmination of their de-Indianization because Lamanites were predestined to become White in Mormon prophecy. However, Lamanite identity was also the culmination of their retribalization. This seeming contradiction worked because arequipeño Lamanites were retribalized only into the "decent" aspects of Indigenous legacy as these became acceptable—and commercialized—within Peruvianness.

Therefore, Lamanite identity allowed arequipeño Mormons to be simultaneously more proudly Indigenous and less pejoratively indio than arequipeño Catholics. Through their interreligious competition to purge themselves of the "indecent" aspects of indigeneity, both arequipeño Mormons and arequipeño Catholics built Indigenous legacies in direct contrast to the lifeways of Indigenous migrants to Arequipa whom they actively stigmatized, racialized, and marginalized in their daily interactions. To explore that apparent hypocrisy, vital to understanding Peruvian Mormon legacy, I provide the following anecdote of my involvement with our ward family's dance troupe. As the Super Quorum president of Barrio Periféricos, I was expected to participate, and recruit my quorum members to participate, in the stake's folkloric dance competition against other wards. I was surprised at how seriously our ward took the competitive aspect of the dance festival. Bishop Paucar, determined to finally win that year (2018), hired a non-Mormon dance coach who fitted us with rented costumes and taught us the steps. The only aspect of the attire that we were expected to buy for ourselves was the footwear that went with most Peruvian folkloric dances coded as Indigenous as opposed to criollo or Afroperuvian: ojotas. Ojotas were sandals made of recycled tires that people throughout the Andes whom mestizos insulted as "indios" wore in their everyday lives. People who, usually out of necessity, wore ojotas in their everyday lives did not usually wear them on special occasions like dances.

Nobody in our dance troupe wore ojotas in their everyday lives, but they all had their own pair that they used exclusively for the dances that required them to dress "indio." When I took my 6'2" self to Arequipa's central market seeking US men's size-12 ojotas, I received more than a few strange looks. But I was ultimately successful.

Before each of our exhausting rehearsals, our dance coach taught us the meaning behind what we were dancing, which was basically an interpretive demonstration of the Andean Catholic cargo festival called yunza. Cargo festivals were common throughout Latin America during my study. They often consisted of a male and female couple (be it a husband and wife or a grandmother and grandson) who were in "charge" (cargo) of funding and organizing an expensive festival to honor their town's patron saint or to represent a hometown organization during Carnavales (a merrymaking extravaganza of relaxed norms anticipating the austerity of Lent). Townsfolk, including diasporic townsfolk and their descendants living abroad, would lighten the immense financial burden of the sponsoring couple by contributing gifts to the festival. In Arequipa, those gifts usually consisted of cases of beer. The patron saint aspect of the festivals, as our dance coach taught us, represented only a thin veneer of Catholicism atop ancient ceremonies of ritual drunkenness, some of which may have come from Africa. These ritual giveaway parties were meant to lubricate the tellurian cycle between human and nonhuman people so that wealth never concentrated in the hands of a few. In the case of the specific cargo festival called yunza, the symbol of wealth distribution was the chopping down of a tree laden with gifts. Similar to a piñata, but for adults, when the tree fell, all would rush to grab a blanket, pot, balloon full of cash, or box of diapers from its fallen branches.

After weeks of practicing our non-alcoholic, child-friendly representation of the yunza through Barrio Periféricos's wholesome recreational dance, a Peruvian Catholic friend invited me to attend a real yunza. Though yunzas were usually associated with Carnavales rather than patron saints, this one was convened so that Indigenous migrants from the highland town of Lari living in the city of Arequipa could honor their patron saint eight days after she was celebrated in Lari itself. I wore my ojotas. My friend thought that was hilarious, but some of his friends, who probably wore ojotas to work cultivating the fields of pitucos every day, seemed to think that I was making light of their poverty. My friend smoothed things over, explaining that I was just a stupid gringo with no malicious intent. He lent me a woven sash and traditional Lari tassels so that my Patagonia-brand hiking vestments would come closer to matching the intricate festival costumes of Lari. Among hundreds of traditionally clad attendees, I was the only one with ojotas. We danced in the dirt around growing, then diminishing beer crate pyramids, occasionally giving the tree of gifts a chop with an axe. At 3:30 a.m., the tree finally fell. I was told that the person who was drunk enough to give the culminating chop had to sponsor the next year's yunza.

At rehearsal the very next night in the well-lit outdoor basketball court of Barrio Periféricos's Utah-built chapel, Bishop Paucar, a tireless dancer, asked me why my ojotas were dirty. I told him, proudly, that I had danced at an actual yunza. He stopped dancing. All twelve of the people in our dance troupe, six male and six female, stopped dancing. Our non-Mormon dance coach paused the music on his Bluetooth speaker. Something similar to the following conversation ensued, observed by all:

PAUCAR: Do you mean that you actually went to one of those drunken circuses?

JASON: There was a lot of drinking going on, but it wasn't a circus. I don't know, I guess I thought it would be anthropologically interesting to compare an authentic yunza with our sanitized simulation of one and our tiny papier-mâché excuse for a tree.

PAUCAR: Is that what you think this is? A simulation!? Look, Brother, you've got it backwards. We're the ones who are authentic, and it's probably good that the professor [dance coach] hears this because the whole purpose of this dance contest is to share the gospel. Sometimes we forget that we are the ones, those of us who are Lamanites, who know the true origins of the yunza. Sure, the professor is right about it being pre-Inca and not Catholic, but think about it, Brother, who were the pre-Incas? Where does a tree appear in *The Book of Mormon*?

JASON: Lehi's dream?

PAUCAR: Exactly. Just so the professor knows, Lehi was an Israelite, and he was the first human to arrive in Peru with his family. He had a dream where he saw a tree full of excellent fruit. His first thought was to gift that fruit to his family.

Think about it.

That is what the yunza is all about, spreading the fruit of the tree of life to the human family. It's not a coincidence that both Lehi's dream and the yunza are about a tree full of gifts. In fact, all the dances of originales [Indigenous peoples] that we will see at this contest have their roots in *The Book of Mormon*.

The sort of people with whom you danced last night, sure they are originales, sure they come from traditional villages, but they have corrupted the yunza. Our dance restores it.

Bishop Paucar felt himself to be part of a restored Indigenous tribe, the Lamanites. His tribe, unlike the tribe of the Lari villagers, carried on indigeneity's authentic legacy. Bishop Paucar's own mother was a monolingual Runasimi speaker who wore ojotas as she sold ceviche in Cusco's main market. Yet, he did not consider his connection to her to be the true source of his indigeneity. Instead, he believed that the Mormon prophet Lehi, Laman's father, was his indigeneity's true source. His knowledge of Lehi allowed him to repudiate many aspects of his Indigenous upbringing without feeling the guilt of betraying his people. In fact, from his perspective, he was rescuing his people from their corruption of Indigenous legacy.

However, unlike his Spanish-speaking counterparts in Utah, Bishop Paucar spent much of his time at church surrounding himself with people who already accepted Lamanite legacy as the one true Indigenous legacy. Thus, Lamanite identity filled arequipeño Mormons like Bishop Paucar with an Indigenous legacy that went relatively uncontested, unmentioned, and unquestioned in their wards and stakes. He might have never mentioned it at all had I not brought my dirty ojotas to practice that day. For arequipeño Mormons, therefore, the authenticity of Lamanite identity was so obvious that it went without saying. From their perspective, one would have to be blind to not see the connection between the yunza tree and Lehi's tree.

For my ward family members in Barrio Periféricos, Lamanite legacy required little awareness and, therefore, minimal buttressing. For Latinx Mormons in Utah, on the other hand, Lamanite legacy was hotly contested. In having to constantly broker with Anglo Mormons, Latino Mormon leaders in Utah perceived in their racist comportment and commentary that the official church found Lamanite identity increasingly embarrassing. Some Latino leaders in Utah reported to me that Anglo leaders had both implicitly and explicitly transmitted to them the official church's shame over having fomented Lamanite identity to begin with when it first began missionizing Latin America. Meanwhile, most Peruvian leaders in Arequipa had little to no contact with Anglo leaders, so they did not realize that Lamanite legacy was under threat in the official church. Conversely, most Peruvian leaders in Utah, who were mostly men, had to deal with Anglo leaders continually. Therefore, while Utah Latino Mormons in my experience almost invariably understood themselves as genetically descending from Abya Yala's original people—the Lamanites—they did not dare accentuate the Lamanite aspect of their sainthoods very often. Instead, they left it to Latinas to innovate a regenerative Lamanite culture and to safeguard a Lamanite legacy. That such a legacy required safeguarding also stemmed from the cruel irony that even as indigeneity was becoming less stigmatized in both Peru and Utah, its Lamanite variant was becoming increasingly untenable in Anglo Mormonism's striving toward a postracial United States. This partially explained why, at the folkloric festivals that I attended, Lamanite legacy was carefully cultivated among LDS Peruvian women in Utah but taken for granted to the point of being considered unremarkable among Peruvian Mormons of all genders in Peru.

"Just Like the Original"

Though Indigenous performance was an important ingredient of Costa family legacy in Utah, La Familia's legacy was also constructed through an iterative blend of genealogy, temple-sealing, and missionization. The last endeavor was what motivated Jacoba and Arcadio, as an elderly couple in 2009, to serve a two-year mission in the Peruvian Amazon where, as our conversation will demonstrate, they pioneered Mormon pioneer legacy-building itself. During a campout of La Familia in Utah in July 2015, I convened a focus group around the campfire. The circle included the following adults: Arcadio, Jacoba, Hector (their son), Carolina (Arcadio's cousin), and Nilda (Jacoba's half-sister). Arcadio quickly shot down the premise of my focus question—"What is it like to be a Peruvian Mormon in Utah?"—declaring that it was no different than being any other "kind of Mormon." He then posed his own question:

ARCADIO: We have done the pioneer Trek in Wyoming, but I am going to tell you something. I travel to South America. If here in Utah we do the pioneer marches and we go to the plains where the pioneers crossed, and we feel that spirit of so many people who died there, then why in South America do they not teach that? Why don't they even bother to do what my wife and I did on the mission [in Puerto Maldonado, Peru]?

We talked to the members, and they, themselves, made their own handcarts; they, themselves went out with their kids up here on their shoulders to walk and walk under a sun that was about 120 degrees, and the people were crying.

We would stop, and the bishop would cry reading *Our Legacy*, reading from stop to stop the whole history. He said, "We had never heard. We had never had a pioneer march. This is new for us." . . .

It seems like a lie, but I'm telling you: those people cried something fierce. Seriously! The bishop? Oh man! Cried himself an ever-loving river! He felt the spirit of so much sacrifice! . . .

And we got all the four wards together and every single one of us marched together.

NILDA: You mean that they didn't teach it over there before you got there?

ARCADIO: No, because—

NILDA:—Why didn't they teach it?

. . .

CAROLINA: Because maybe they tell themselves that it's something that only the Americans do—

ARCADIO:—It is the history of the church! And so why don't they put it into practice in other places? Why only in the United States?

CAROLINA: Yeah, that's wrong [to not do Trek reenactments outside of the US] because those reenactments are from the church. It was from the pioneer journey that the church was formed.

. . .

HECTOR: Part of the reason is that, where are they going to walk? That land in Wyoming is owned by the church, and I understand that Martin's Cove and all that is the church's property.

ARCADIO: Well, yes, but that doesn't—I mean, there are places to walk over there in Peru. My point is that—as a teaching, as a teaching that they might feel—

JACOBA:—Look! [all side-conversations cease]

All we did was a little thing . . .

I brought prairie dresses for the sisters and also shirts and White-people pants for the brothers. And for everyone—hats and bonnets. I bought forty hats. And that is how we planned it . . . I supposed that only the mothers and the fathers would come.

No! The whole family came, with little kids and newborns. With everything. Just like the original. Walking on the earth.

. . .

ARCADIO: The thing I want, Nephew [Jason], is sincerely just one thing: How can we expect to get a testimony? How can we expect that testimony to grow only through stories? Only stories, even if they are true. Only storytelling.

If the people participate, if the people feel a little bit of thirst, a little bit of hunger, a little bit of fatigue, they will simply say, "How did those pioneers do it?"

"The pioneers could have only done it with the help of God," was the answer to Arcadio's question. Unfortunately, this meant to me—one who knew the Ute side of the story—that God was on the side of my ancestors, the settler colonists, as they destroyed Indigenous nations. It was mimetically nauseating to imagine people who identified with those nations dressing up like my great-great-grandparents and reenacting what, to me, seemed like their own oppression. For me, and for many other settler colonists, the dialectical boundary between indigeneity and coloniality needed to remain stark (Bacigalupo 2016). Making it porous was revolting. However, revulsion was far from La Familia's reaction to Jacoba and Arcadio's pioneering of the Anglo Mormon origin story among Peru's Indigenous Amazonians. For La Familia, the handcart was a symbol of perseverance, not genocide. Arcadio, someone who danced his Indigenous ancestry upon Mormon stages, wanted me to understand that what might have seemed like a story that belonged only to those of Anglo Mormon Pioneer ancestry was actually a legacy that belonged just as deeply to him.

Legacy's Components

The manual that Arcadio mentioned, *Our Heritage: A Brief History of The Church of Jesus Christ of Latter-day Saints*—translated into Spanish as *Nuestro Legado* or "Our Legacy"—claimed to be a history but functioned as an origin myth in that its purpose was not to state historically verifiable facts but to bolster one of legacy's key ingredients: faith. Mormon faith required sacrifice. Joseph Smith (1844) believed that "a religion that does not require the sacrifice of all things, never has the power sufficient to produce the faith necessary unto life" (69). He also felt that "we should covenant to sacrifice all that we possess, even our own lives, if necessary, in sustaining and defending the Kingdom of God" (Mormons in Transition [1990] 2011, 9), a sentiment that I often observed my Spanish-speaking study participants ritualize inside the Ogden, Utah, temple as part of a ceremony called the Endowment (ML).

Faith's need for sacrifice required that the Martin's Cove handcart disaster stand in for all overland crossings in the archetypal Mormon origin myth even though, historically, only 5 percent of Mormons who came overland to Utah did so by handcart (Reeve 2018). Only the most death-defying aspect of the history made it into the myth. Trek reenactments thus transformed Martin's Cove into a material "space of death" (Taussig 1984). Similar to Ayacucho during the Shining Path War, in that "space of death, the signified and the signifier [came] unhinged . . . order [was] disrupted, and the surplus meaning unleashed [gave] rise to tremendous portent" (Theidon 2013, 15). It was this portent that, though sparked through simulation rather than massacre, unleashed tears in Jacoba and Arcadio's bishop during the Trek that they staged in Puerto Maldonado. Death built his faith.

Anglo Mormon church leaders were very aware of the evangelizing opportunities—and the agricultural metaphors—that spaces of death provided, which was partially why they often sent missionaries to "glean" the mission "field" in the immediate wake of military "harvests." Since Anglo leaders knew that the rampant death in Ayacucho would likely create a "world in which the bewildering loss of context resulted in subjects radically unmoored from the moral limits that tethered life to some sense of predictability" (Theidon 2013, 64), they sent missionaries there to tether the untethered to the Mormon faith. Precisely because they disrupted order, spaces of death opened spaces of sacredness. The church's Anglo leaders could then sanitize those sacred spaces into places of holy order, places of Mormon legacy.

But to fill spaces with sufficient death, mythologies had to be manicured. Therefore, it was necessary to trim from Mormon mythology the statistic that, based on US death rates at the time, making the nineteenth-century journey to Utah only increased one's chances of death by 1 percent (Reeve 2018). If included, that statistic would not only sap the myth's power by decreasing the quantity of death, but it would also risk raising a question of death's quality: By what percentage was the chance of death increased for those whose lands the pioneers crossed and usurped?

That question, and the decades of massacre it evokes, would awkwardly demonstrate how whiteness trumped faith in the creation of pioneer legacy. After all, there was a very specific quality of death required to produce settler legacy: Indigenous death (Gilio-Whitaker 2019). That was why the Shining Path War was rarely depicted as a national tragedy in Peru (Manrique 2003). Peru styled itself a settler state, and the vast majority of those who died in the war were coded in Peruvian national media as Indigenous: the very people whose death hastened settler triumph. The official church demonstrated its ultimate allegiance to the settler project's doctrine of genocide during the Shining Path War because it only found it necessary to ask Indigenous-looking Peruvians, not Anglos, to sacrifice "even [their] own lives" to missionize Ayacucho. Yet, as Ignacio made clear in what he left out of his fable of the blond Peruvian, while Indigenous deaths made settler legacy materially possible, they threatened its moral justification. They had to be edited from origin stories along with excessive settler survival. Paradoxically, settler death satisfied a sacrificial mythos of pioneer legacy for which only Indigenous death could create space.

If I tend to belabor this anti-Indigenous aspect of the Anglo Mormon category of legacy, it is because, as historian Waziyatawin (2012) wrote, "colonization ought to be one of the most easily recognized forms of oppression in the world, but it is not" (172). In fact, during my study, colonization was celebrated in an official Utah state holiday called "Pioneer Day." The power of the Anglo Mormon origin myth to produce celebration from oppression derived from its diligent obfuscation of a key historical pachacuti. That pachacuti was the transformation in northwestern Abya Yala when humans, living for centuries alongside the Spanish doctrine of slavery (Reséndez 2016), suddenly also lived, in 1847—the very year celebrated annually in Salt Lake City's Days of '47 Parade—under the US doctrine of genocide. Legacy, therefore, in both the Anglo Mormon and the Peruvian Mormon versions of the category, was not simply about life and death in my study. It was about pioneer life and Indigenous death.

Gendering Legacy

Exaggerating settler death to achieve faith and erasing Indigenous life to achieve whiteness were not, however, the only processes of legacy found in the Anglo Mormon origin story. As gender studies scholar Sara Patterson (2020) described, "The LDS community had at its disposal countless stories that lifted up Mormon pioneers as the epitome of American masculinity" (69). Therefore, while it was complicated for Peruvian Mormon men to dislodge the whiteness requirement from the category of legacy, it was doubly complicated—under a lens of intersectionality (Crenshaw 1991)—for Peruvian Mormon women to dislodge the masculinity requirement. For example, at one point in the official Trek reenactment of the Martin and Willie handcart disaster at Martin's Cove, Wyoming, in which I participated as a chaperone for three Peruvian American Mormon teens in La Familia years before this project began, the males in our party were to leave the procession of handcarts and watch as the females, alone, struggled to push the carts up the course's steepest hill. Dubbed "The Women's March," this stage of the journey was meant to reenact the moment in 1847 when the men left to support US imperialism in its conquest of Mexico and usher in the aforementioned age of genocide.

In that night's testimony meeting around the campfire, emotions remained muted as the female teens expressed the faith that they garnered through their sacrifice of physical exertion. However, tears streamed freely from both male and female teens as they described what the whole production was ultimately choreographed to privilege, the male sacrifice. Forced to stand idly by while women performed men's work, men sacrificed their holy gender role as providers. In other words, though the feminine sacrifice was, as in the days it reenacted (Bowman 2020), more extreme than the masculine sacrifice, it was only temporarily pedestalized as a prop for masculinity's ultimate enthronement on the stage of pioneer legacy. Similar to the way that Peruvians in the last chapter characterized the lack of Anglos as the true hardship that befell Peru during the Shining Path War, Trek characterized the lack of males as the true hardship that befell the Mormon wagon trains during the Mexican American War. Once again, this placed femininity and indigeneity into a category that was "supported by similar myths about both groups: that they [were] by nature passive . . . [and] dependent" (Babb 2018, 79).

Placing Legacy

Judging from the Anglo Mormon origin myth's geographical structure, another important ingredient for the category of legacy—on top of faith, death, and masculinity—was Utah-centeredness. Since Utah was the destination of the origin narrative, and since, according to anthropologists Sylvia Yanagisako and Carol Delaney ([1994] 2013), "the explanatory schemes upon which identity was based have been shown to rest not on the bedrock of fact but suspended in narratives of origin" (1), Utah landscapes needed to be embedded into the identities of all who sought a Mormon pioneer legacy. However, what happened when people were not physically in, or did not biologically descend from those born in "the sites where these stories and identities [made] sense?" (2).

That was a question that the all-Anglo, all-male, stake-level organizers of our Spanish-speaking ward's participation in "Trek 2007" never asked themselves because they never had to. On all previous occasions in which our stake leaders in Ogden, Utah, organized Treks in Wyoming, they did so for five English-speaking wards. The year that my spouse Elvira and I were called to chaperone our ward's Spanish-speaking youth on Trek was also our stake's first year of having a sixth ward that happened to be Spanish-speaking. As our Anglo stake president condescendingly put it in a planning meeting that I attended, it was his stake's "first year of having the blessing of dealing with our brothers, the Hispanics."

Traditionally, each youth was supposed to trek on behalf of a personal ancestor who was, preferably, an actual Mormon plains-crosser. That ancestor was to be researched, and his or her name was to be stitched or painted onto the various, intensely gendered, pioneer-era crafts and clothing fabricated over that year's preparations for Trek. The stake president, in his paternalistic beneficence, made a special provision for our "Hispanic" youth that accentuated their deficiency in pioneer ancestry, diminished the richness of their Indigenous ancestry, and precluded the mere mention of their Black ancestry. Instead of encouraging them to research and walk on behalf of one of their own ancestors, or at least on behalf of one of the few dozen Black and Indigenous Mormons who made the plains-crossing journey according to the historical record, the stake president's activities director assigned each Spanish-speaking youth the name of a random Anglo who died at Martin's Cove. Needless to say, this not-so-subtle privileging of Anglo pioneering over Black and Indigenous pioneering tainted the experience. Our Spanish-speaking youth, three of whom were our Peruvian American nieces and nephews in La Familia, were not allowed to reenact their origin story in a way that made sense to them. They were not allowed to trek for their own ancestors because their ancestors had pioneered legacies that were not considered Mormon.

The Mormon origin story made sense to our stake's Anglo youth because it granted them the autochthonous, Utahan identity that they needed in order to see themselves as the colonized, not the colonizers (P. J. Deloria 1999). Black and Indigenous Mormons were actors in the plains-crossing history, but the myth culminated in the arrival of only Anglos to a space devoid of lives that they considered human. Therefore, the myth was designed to only make sense among the descendants of those Anglos who had to rationalize their continual colonization of that space. The myth made colonization itself into a legacy worth trekking for.

Yet, Arcadio's theory that pioneer sacrifice had to be enacted, not just retold, broadened the myth's applicability. It was not merely that people needed to reenact the historical sacrifice in order to believe that it really happened to Anglos in a specific spot. Rather, as people performed the myth, it took on a new existence as a personal legacy to which they attached their own bodies, sweat, and tears. In other words, legacy required sacrifices, but sacrifices could be made in any space—not just Utah—and at any time—not just 1847.

What Will Our Sacrifice Be?

If space was sacralized into Zion through the secretions of sacrifice left on the land, and if people who made those secretions were pioneers, then arequipeño Mormons could be pioneers and create legacy too. At least, that was Barrio Periféricos member Ofelia Dominguez's opinion. I met her in my first week of preliminary research in Arequipa in 2016. She was baptized Mormon in 2001 but was born and raised Catholic in Arequipa. Her dream was to visit Utah.

In July 2016, I asked her how she would feel once the Arequipa temple was completed. She responded that, though it would become the temple of her home city, she would retain an even more special feeling toward the Lima temple because of the financial sacrifice entailed in taking time off work, the gastronomic sacrifice of having to eat subpar (non-arequipeño) food, and the physical sacrifice of the spine-numbing, thirty-two-hour, roundtrip bus. "Though it may be true that we don't have to travel with our handcarts like the pioneers," she stated, "we still sacrifice a lot to get to Lima and to work in that temple. I think that there will still be a sacrifice with the new, Arequipa temple, but it won't be *such* a huge sacrifice like the one that our ancient pioneers made. Right? Maybe the sacrifice that we have to do now, or rather—the duty that is ours now, is to accelerate the construction of the temple by doing our genealogy, the vicarious work for our dead."

Ofelia not only considered herself part of the "our" who got to have ancient pioneer ancestry, but also part of the Arequipa temple's legacy. She believed that her sacrifice of time spent in researching her ancestors directly accelerated the construction of the temple wherein those ancestors would later be sealed to her in rituals necessary for both her salvation and theirs.

At the time of the above utterance, the temple project had stopped entirely. Ofelia's claim, common among arequipeño Mormons at the time, was that the construction delay stemmed not from the church's legal hurdles in developing its chosen temple site—which included 3,000-year-old Yarabaya terracing that Peru's Ministry of Culture designated an intangible patrimony—but from a lack of enough local ancestor data to make the temple worth building.

Needing to imbue the temple with pioneer legacy rather than Indigenous legacy, the Anglos in charge of its construction, including Collin from chapter 1, went to great lengths to deter locals from sacrificing their time and talents on the actual construction (Palmer and Knowlton 2020). But Ofelia found a workaround. She knew that, within the exclusive walls of dedicated Mormon temples, ancestor names written on tiny papers became proxies for the spirit bodies of individual ancestors who had to be ritually sealed to their living descendants in order to complete forever families. If the temple ran out of ancestor names, no "vicarious work for our dead" could be conducted, and temple work would halt.

Ofelia saw the lack of known, named, and digitized arequipeño ancestors as a call to sacrifice that she could channel into the production of legacy. I watched over the next few years as genealogy—largely through Catholic baptismal record digitizing marathons that led to thousands of typed papers-cum-proxies for the individualized dead—became a way for Barrio Periféricos members to materially participate in temple construction. In a contradictory cycle, novice genealogists accumulated legacy under Arequipa's ground. In the process, they recruited ancestral pacha in the fight against Peru's Ministry of Culture, which blocked the construction of a foreign edifice atop the agricultural earthworks that Ofelia's pre-Inca ancestors built.

Owning Legacy

Ofelia's ancestors, who hailed from autochthonous Andean villages, channeled the pre-Utah aspect of Mormonism's origin story—Lamanite identity—in ways that pushed the limits of Yanagisako and Delaney's ([1994] 2013) affirmation that "origin myths, precisely because they hook individual identities to ontological realities, are not substitutable" (3). Peruvians achieving pioneer legacy through Lamanite identity did not substitute old stories for new ones, and they did not discriminate between modern Anglo and ancient Israelite versions of pioneering. Theirs was a multitemporal, generative amalgamation of legacy. During my study, modern Lamanites' adoption of that amalgamated legacy sparked migrations that led to a new demographic reality in Utah: most Anglo Mormons were, at long last, living alongside authentic Lamanites as Latin American Mormon immigrants continued to arrive through the networks laid by their overlapping ecclesiastical and familial memberships. Along with folkloric dances like Jacoba's, those immigrants brought with them their own traditions of *Book of Mormon* theatrics, such as the annual Christmas song and dance ensemble, Luz de las Naciones (Light of the Nations), which— increasingly coopted by the official church—was performed in Salt Lake City's Temple Square by select members of Utah's Spanish-speaking wards, including my spouse Elvira, throughout my study. It often portrayed Aztec and Maya civilizations in relation to a popular *Book of Mormon* interpretation wherein Jesus, also known as Quetzalcoatl, visited Mesoamerica.

Such "Indigenous" extravaganzas competed with the Anglo Mormon settler colonists' longstanding tradition of appropriating *Book of Mormon* conceptions of indigeneity into pageantry (C. C. Smith 2015). Over multiple summers starting in 2014, I observed Anglo Mormon pageanters in Manti, Utah, use brownface and headdresses to reenact scenes from *The Book of Mormon* such as that involving "Samuel the Lamanite," one of the book's few righteous Lamanites. These well-attended outdoor Mormon Miracle pageants represented "the settler-colonial sublime, art that conceals and obscures the erasure and appropriation of specific Indigenous people and practices" (M. E. García 2021, 63). Interestingly, in 2019, the Prophet discontinued the Manti pageant. Perhaps its flamboyant anti-indigeneity was making his church unmarketable in a nation-state suddenly disturbed by its slaveholder statuary. However, the reason for his cancelation was not as important as his assumed authority to cancel. Only one who claimed exclusive ownership of the pageant—and the legacies behind it—could cancel it. The problem for Anglo church leaders was that they were no longer the sole stakeholders of pioneer Indigenous legacies.

Indigenous Blood

Pascuala Cusicanchi (Pasi) held stakes as well. Pasi joined the church in her hometown of Cusco and served a mission in the same place that I did—La Paz, Bolivia. Pasi identified proudly as a Lamanite, and her words demonstrated how stories created legacies that would not be discontinued no matter how embarrassing they became to Anglo church leaders who helped create them. Pasi mirrored many Peruvian Mormons who changed not only their identity, but their biological lineages through those legacies. She also exemplified many unmarried Mormons whose partial motive for traveling to Utah was to find a Mormon spouse so as to catapult Mormon legacy across generations. I met Pasi in Utah at a Mormon Comic-Con of sorts called the Sunstone Symposium. She was staffing a booth for a nonprofit poverty relief organization created by Spanish-speaking Anglo Mormon University of Utah professors. I went on to occupy a small position within that NGO, and Pasi became my supervisor for our humanitarian work in Cusco. Through that work, I had the opportunity of visiting Pasi in both Utah and Cusco on multiple occasions. The following excerpt came from an interview in August 2015 in the spacious living room of her former mission companion's home near Salt Lake City where she lived during her year-long stay in Utah.

> JASON: Since you've been in Utah, have you learned a lot about the pioneers who crossed the plains and arrived here?
>
> PASI: In Peru, I knew about the sacrifice, the essence of it all, right? . . . But it was here in Utah where I finally could feel the true sacrifice [crying].
>
> It wasn't easy at all. I mean, how could they have done those things? To go through hunger? To go through illnesses, the loss of family members and children, and keep going forward?
>
> And it is here in Utah where I finally appreciate where I am from. I realize that I am part of the history of *The Book of Mormon*. Or *my* ancestors are.
>
> They are the chosen ones, and over time maybe they rejected the Lord, and they didn't pay attention to the commandments. Well, they still maintain that position, but it is you guys who are the pioneers who have defended *The Book of Mormon* with cape and sword and given your lives for that book, and for that history that belongs not to your ancestors but to mine.

In going to Utah, Pasi recovered her ancestors' story and with it, a piece of pioneer Indigenous legacy. Pasi took her body to Utah, and Utah converted its very genetics through stories both colonial and ancient. This was in line with Arcadio's theory of performance versus storytelling, and it was what made Lamanite identity into an indelibly material, rather than merely spiritual legacy. As Pierre Bourdieu (1990) wrote, "The body believes in what it plays at. . . . It does not represent what it performs, it does not memorize the past, it enacts the past, bringing it back to life. What is 'learned by the body' is not something that one has, like knowledge that can be brandished, but something that one is" (73).

In Utah, Pasi conjured the magic of mimesis (Taussig 1992), releasing a power that removed the boundary between indigeneity and coloniality in her very flesh, allowing her to become an Indigenous, Mormon pioneer descendant. In so doing, she destroyed the indigeneity versus coloniality dichotomy: her claims to Zion now predated Anglo Mormon pioneering by millennia.

Furthermore, her "new" ancestors were characters from Utah's holy text, and so Anglo Mormons validated them more than her own people did. Therefore, her ties to the land of Cusco—a *Book of Mormon* setting as we shall see in the next chapter—fortified her now ancient ties to the land of Utah.

> JASON: Upon coming to Utah, you said that you valued yourself as a Lamanite even more than you did during your own mission where, I imagine, you must have been talking about *The Book of Mormon* every day.
>
> PASI: It was different. Well, over there in Bolivia, being in the mission, I always had identified as—maybe I didn't know the word "Lamanite," or I didn't understand it well, but yes, I have always identified as a descendant of the Inca . . .
>
> I have a surname that is unique in my country, and they say it is Inca and, I mean, how can I put this? I identified already, but it was being here in Utah where I came to appreciate more *The Book of Mormon* and my part in this chosen people. I understood well how the Lord had so much patience with my ancestors [laughing].

Utah, a place more distant from her Inca past than Bolivia, was the very place where her indigeneity became complete through her co-ownership of Mormon stories. If Anglo Mormons owned those stories because their ancestors sacrificed their lives for them, Pasi owned them doubly. Not only were their ancestors her ancestors, too, because they were the Utah pioneer heroes of her religion's modern origin story, but blood from its more ancient origin story—*The Book of Mormon*—ran in her veins. Her indigeneity became multivalent under those spatiotemporal shifts because she did not replace the legacy of the Inca with the legacy of the Lamanites, she fused them into a nuanced legacy of pioneer indigeneity that secured a part for herself among a storied, chosen people. Furthermore, since "our sovereignty flows directly from our origin story" (Valandra 2019, 73) Pasi's ownership of story granted her a legacy of self-determination in Zion, not merely of tokenized representation.

A year after the above interview, during a visit that I paid to Pasi at her home in Cusco, I wrote the following fieldnote:

> Pasi said, "In Utah they talk so much about a language that they do not know, and I have blood from the people who speak it." She often referred to herself as the Inca Princess while in Utah. Her White friend knew how interested she was in ancestry and gifted her a DNA test kit through the church's family history website. It came back showing that Pasi was "93 percent Indigenous," which she said is really rare for South Americans. She seemed very proud of it. She used the phrase, "sangre indígena" [Indigenous blood].

The notion that indigeneity could be expressed as a percentage seemed normal in places, such as the United States, where biological kinship was naturalized as the only nonfictional type of kinship. It also seemed normal in places where biologists had constructed DNA into scientific proof that "blood" was not only a symbol of relatedness but that it contained the actual stuff of relatedness. In the United States, "under the blood quantum regime, one's Indianness progressively decline[d] in accordance with a 'biological' calculus" (Wolfe 2006, 400). Cusco, Pasi's place of residence during most of my study, also operated within a US-influenced version of that regime during the late 2010s. However, Inca governance tactics from the early 1430s influenced Cusco's understanding of blood's connection to relatedness as well. Though what might be termed a "royal blood quantum" inhered to related-ness among the Inca, I got the sense among newly baptized Mormons in both the high-elevation Andean city of Cusco and the mid-elevation Andean city of Arequipa (about a ten-hour bus ride away from each other) that the transmission of relatedness through "blood" was not something that they took for granted (Arguedas [1941] 2011). As other anthropologists have also noted, people throughout the Andes seemed to use food (Weismantel 1995), drink (C. Allen 2014), and land (Canessa 2012) as idioms of kinship trans-mission just as often as "blood," and when they did use "blood," it was not as synonymous with DNA as it tended to be among my Anglo Mormon study participants. In fact, when Peruvian Mormons in Arequipa spoke of blood-forged relatedness, they often alluded to the iron (or lack thereof) in the blood rather than the DNA. Therefore, as someone for whom the conflation of genetics and blood was not totally naturalized, when Pasi said "Indigenous blood," she was not indexing the essential, genotypic fact of her Inca body, a fact constructed to symbolize both patriotic Peruvianness and backwards antimodernity through the complexly nonphenotypic racialization of Peruvian indigeneities (De la Cadena 2000). Instead, Pasi was indexing "the blood-infused but more-than-biological relationship" (Tallbear 2013, 59) between herself and her Lamanite tribe.

Pasi's cusqueña indigeneity strengthened her pioneer legacy just as her pioneering strengthened her Indigenous legacy. Receiving a Lamanite transfusion into her already Indigenous blood allowed Pasi access to an alloyed legacy, a legacy of pioneer indigeneity. Adding Mormon pioneering to her Indigenous legacy rescued that word—Indigenous—from Peru's tired racist regimes and infused it with pride. Bathed in the light of her newly alloyed legacy, Runasimi—the preferred language of her parents—became an honorable *Book of Mormon* language instead of a nationally stigmatized one. Furthermore, the possibility that Pasi's own parents spoke a *Book of Mormon* language plugged her into a status in the destination place of her religion's origin story—Utah—that seemed to surpass even the carefully indigenized status of Anglo Mormons' pioneer legacies. Judging from Anglo Mormonism's pageantry and hymns, many Anglo Mormons wanted desperately to be Indigenous. Yet, they could not compete with Pasi, the Inca Princess. At 93 percent, Pasi was even more genetically Indigenous than the few Anglo Mormons with a verifiable "Indian princess grandmother" (V. Deloria 1969, 3), let alone the many who merely had an "Indian-grandmother complex" (4).

However, for the arequipeña Ofelia, who had never been to Utah, there exuded a holiness to the sacrificial secretions of legacy left there that gave Anglo Mormons a pioneer indigeneity difficult to surpass. I asked Ofelia if there was a difference between the Salt Lake temple and the Lima temple.

> Just a little while ago, I was in the Lima temple, and you can feel it. It is like they say, a little piece of heaven in the temple.
>
> But when one sees the temple of Salt Lake, one remembers all of the things that the pioneers went through to build it. I know that there is a more special feeling toward that temple because there was a lot of suffering.
>
> Not like now, where we'll just say, "Okay, the temple is going to be built in Arequipa."
>
> "Yes, cool! Call the construction company!"
>
> The machinery comes, the workers come, and they start to build. There are aerosols and special machines that can paint in the blink of an eye.
>
> On the other hand, back in those days, according to what I've seen in videos and what I've read in *Our Legacy*, they suffered a lot on the Salt Lake City temple.
>
> It has a history, so there is a more special feeling toward it, toward the hands that carved in it the words: "Holiness to the Lord."

Dark Dancing

Ofelia felt that the sacrifices in the literal building of Utah's Zion were greater than in her local Zion and that the legacy from those sacrifices, rather than being transferable to Arequipa, was deposited into the autochthonous granite that remained pristine in the Salt Lake City temple walls. Pasi, on the other hand, thought of that pioneer legacy as somehow transmittable through generations and, as such, corruptible over time. She said, "What I have observed here [in Utah] . . . is the fact that there are many people that have been blessed, maybe not so much because of their own faithfulness, but because of the faithfulness of the pioneers. The Bible says—and I have felt it with the people—that the Lord blesses unto the fourth generation. I have seen many of my Anglo friends receive a lot of blessings even though they weren't being faithful to many commandments. Instead, they had ancestors who were faithful."

At first, Pasi was hesitant to speak too openly about those unfaithful descendants of the unmarked "pioneers" because she knew that I was one. Therefore, she changed the subject to the unfaithfulness of "her people" who attended her Spanish-speaking ward in Utah.

> They are not very faithful in keeping the commandments. For example, there are many brothers and sisters who work on Sundays. I think that the Sabbath day is sacred and that should be the same here, in China, or in Conchinchina. . . . I don't know if I'm being Pharisaical or not, but I make the effort to actually keep that commandment, and many of my brothers and sisters around here do not.
>
> That is unfortunate because this group that is here in Utah is a small branch that has descended from the Lamanites.
>
> Well, as such, their righteousness should be up to the level of the pioneers. But that is still not happening. . . .
>
> And I shouldn't say this of my people who are here in Utah without including the fact that the descendants of the pioneers are also *not* worthy representatives of their ancestors' legacy, sorry to say.

On the one hand, according to Pasi's dichotomous usage of the words "Lamanite" and "pioneer," her people were not pioneers. Her people were Lamanites. Only my people were pioneers. On the other hand, Pasi was a pioneer stakeholder in *The Book of Mormon* because, once accepted, it immediately became the story of her people, the story that was appropriated from her people to provide the faith necessary to start a new civilization in Utah, a civilization that periodically purchased its White privilege by oppressing her people (Reeve 2015). She lauded that appropriation as necessary to formulate a pioneer Indigenous legacy, but when she went to Utah hoping to find her people living by that legacy, she saw its moral discarded. Her people of promise, those who, as *The Book of Mormon* prophesied, would build the New Jerusalem, were living unworthily in the very place of their legacy's genesis.

JASON: And what do we lack, we who are descendants of the pioneers?
PASI: You know what? The pioneers are dead.

The pioneers have lived and ended their lives in poverty. Many have risen above and have gotten businesses and from them come the legacies of many rich Mormons [laughs].

But one must recognize that this comes through the blessings of the Lord from the promises that He made to the pioneers because of *their* sacrifices. He blessed their generations. And it is calculated up until the fourth generation approximately that descendants remain faithful. But not after that. . . .

Many people who have a lot of money have drifted from the Lord. They live off of customs.

It's like me. I was a Catholic girl, and I had my Catholic customs. So, for me it was very normal to do certain things that were just a part of my life.

So, you guys just so happen to have the true customs, but you do them for the same reasons that I did my false Catholic customs. You don't do them with heart. Instead, you simply follow what you are taught without questioning it. And when you don't do it with heart, you start seeing things as so natural that you start thinking, "Hey, if my neighbor has a stake-level calling, but he does something that's not right, I'll do it too because it must be right if he does it."

As a result of the fungibility that caused the biospiritual transmission of legacy through blood to lose viability after four generations, Pasi was able to construct herself as inhabiting an even more legitimate pioneer Indigenous legacy than those with Anglo pioneer ancestry. In this way, Pasi's simultaneous resistance and loyalty to colonializing narrative forms such as *Our Legacy* was similar to Dakota linguist Ella Deloria's resistance and loyalty to the Holy Bible. Like Deloria, Pasi "developed a shrewd ability to encode strategies of dissidence within Euroamerican narrative forms" (S. Gardner 2009, viii). Not only was Pasi more Indigenous than Anglo Mormon "settler nativists" (Tuck and Yang 2012) and "pretendians" (Tallbear 2021b), but she was more of a pioneer than they were because she did things out of choice—heart—rather than custom. She was alive and pioneering the church in the present, and where were the Mormon Pioneers? The pioneers were dead. Since Pasi saw sacrifice as a necessary aspect of legacy, she viewed generational Mormonism's logical tendency to lessen the need for sacrifice as a dilution of legacy. This made her, as a first-generation Mormon, more of pioneer than me, a fifth-generation Mormon, even though I was supposedly the one with the pioneer ancestry and, as such, the one with authority to define Mormon indigeneities, stories, and legacies.

Recorded below, Pasi provided a poignant instantiation of her theory that the early Anglo Mormon pioneer sacrifices were losing their legacy-building power among the current generation. The example that she chose of pioneer legacy-betrayal required a motif that she acquired from *The Book of Mormon.* That motif equated indigeneity with darkness and darkness with evil. She depicted a Mormon dance as dangerous because it involved the very aspects of her indigeneity that she was told to purge in order to forge the alloyed pioneer indigeneity necessary for a legacy in Zion.

There is a danger in this: Many Mormons in Latin America or that aren't from Utah, even Europeans, they think that everything that is said and done in Utah is okay. Right? But it isn't.

It isn't.

Here's a little detail: Maybe I'm just being really nitpicky about this, but when I got baptized at age twenty-four, I had already lived my youth and everything, so I knew what the World was like and fully understood that joining the church meant giving that up. But upon arriving here [to Utah] they invited me to this Hispanic church youth party, and I went, and it seemed to me—I said, "This dance is just like one from the World. How is it possible that the Leaders are permitting this?"

And the youth were all happy with disco lights in the *dark* and everything, and I was like—"the only thing it lacks is cigarettes and alcohol!"

It was the same.

And so, I didn't—I—I honestly did not go in. I didn't feel at all comfortable there. I didn't feel right about that, that if one decides to take on other kinds of customs—and I had made the decision to go for different kinds of customs—well, I wasn't about to return to the same old ones, right?

My Peruvian friend, he called me up after: "Pasi, why did you leave?"

I told him, "I'm sorry, but it doesn't seem right to me. I felt so uncomfortable that I just turned and left."

"I'm sorry," he apologized. "Pasi," he tells me, "Look, it shocked me too the first time, and well, later I started going back with friends, and I'm over there a lot, and we don't do anything bad."

And I say, "I know, but"—

And he told me, "The parties that the Americans put on are worse, Pasi."

And I'm like, "*members*?!"

"Yes," he tells me.

And I say, "Wow. Well, I hope to go to none of those [laughs]." Sincerely!

The dance confirmed for Pasi what she was beginning to see as the twofaced aspect of Anglo Mormonism's category of legacy. This two-facedness recalls the Nephite immunity mentioned in chapter 1 but conjures a more insidious application and a deeper hypocrisy. As Pasi began to realize that Anglo Mormons had a legacy of justifying unrighteousness, she found herself in a double bind. If she went along with her coreligionists, her pioneering sacrifice of leaving her customs behind would be in vain. Yet, by not participating in those dances she discarded an opportunity to fulfill her principal reason for coming to Utah in the first place—finding a Mormon spouse and thereby perpetuating a new and more honest legacy.

The very scene that might have resulted in her future forever family patterned itself instead after the World that she had sacrificed so much to leave in her past. The fact that Pasi chose to point to a church-sponsored dance as an example of pioneer corruption lacking only alcohol to make it completely sinfull was significant given her mention of customs (costumbres). In the colonial Andes, the phrase "usos y costumbres" (uses and customs) was a catchall term for anything that the Catholic "pioneers" assigned to the realm of pre-Hispanic, Indigenous religion (Arguedas [1966] 1975), a realm that they actively linked to the underworld (Durán 1967), the dark, and—as such—the devil (O. Harris 2006). During my study, Catholics in Cusco called the people who practiced that pre-Catholic religion "costumbristas" though, in the minds of cusqueño Mormons, syncretic Andean Catholicism itself was fused with an occult costumbrismo imagined as rife with alcohol and diabolical dances, such as the yunza.

The Book of Mormon fomented those imaginings. It reflected US anti-indigenous and anti-Catholic discourses by constantly describing Native people and the "traditions of their fathers" as "loathsome" (J. Smith 1830, 528) and by repeatedly comparing the Catholic Church, in some interpretations, to a whore. For many Peruvian Mormons, Catholicism was too Indigenous, excessive indigeneity was dangerous, and the dancefloor spawned Indigenous Catholic excess and corruptibility. Fear of this corruptibility was why our stake presidency in Arequipa tried to make sure that the folkloric dances chosen for competition were vibrant, contemporary, and not associated with Andean ancestors in any direct way. When I asked Peruvians in my study which of the Andean Catholic costumbres they abandoned to become Mormons, they almost always referred to drunken dancing in the dark. Even if they were not really into that, and Pasi was not, it was the first thing that came to mind because of its tight association with their new religion's image of ancestral loathsomeness.

Pasi surely felt a mimetic version of that loathing as she stared into the two-facedness of Mormon legacy: Anglo Mormon dances rumored to be even "worse" than the devilish dance that she witnessed wherein Latinx Lamanites, in the cradle of *The Book of Mormon*, appeared to go back to the old, tellurian customs.

Templar Stones

Pasi chose to repudiate yet another custom imagined as part of that pre-His-panic, Andean world, one that was contradictorily both central and inimical to her conception of Zion's legacy: the idea that Earth could be sacred. Yet, Pasi parted ways slightly with Ofelia in that regard. A year after my above conversation with Ofelia, she found another way to sacrifice for her temple that was more direct than individuating and digitizing her ancestral collectivity (thus sanitizing it, sealing it, and making herself safely—rather than danger-ously—Indigenous). Through a series of miracles, she succeeded in finagling her way into becoming one of four adults to have the sacrificial privilege of blistering their hands with pickaxes as they, and the small group of youth that they chaperoned, prepared the Arequipa temple construction site—atop the previously intangible Yarabaya earthworks—for the groundbreaking cer-emony's seating arrangements and awnings. In March 2017, I interrupted her recounting of that experience through WhatsApp to ask a question about her relationship to the plot of land that her church's Anglo leaders had chosen—and legally conquered—for her temple.

> JASON: I wanted to ask you a question. You said that you went many times to the temple plot before, right? So, did you ever end up collecting a little bottle of earth from there like you told me that you wanted to?
> OFELIA: Yes, but I only ended up bringing back a stone.
> JASON: Oh, even better.
> OFELIA: I have here the little stone. It is among my collection of little stones that I have. So, I have a stone that stays there and that, well—When I went with my Seminary students, I told them that we could each take one: one stone from the temple to have it as a memento of something that was part of the land.
>
> So, I have a stone that I took right from that spot. A little piece of earth. That is what I have.
>
> And well—Where were we?

She did not want to dwell on this topic because she knew that I was assign-ing meaning to her rock collecting (see figure 3) that she did not believe existed. She did not consider her templar stone to be a "subjective object" (Santos-Granero 2009, 9) a sacred Andean huaca (animate stone), or a symbol of her Andean-Mormon syncretism. Yet, she did keep it on her display of mementos, which looked strikingly like an altar.

Denying that her stone had sacred power fit with what Theidon (2013) understood "as 'floating charisma' [wherein] the transformative power of faith is no longer 'fixed' in religious images or moored to the landscape" (92). In cosmologies of floating charisma, if the sacred did not transcend the dark

FIGURE 3. Ofelia's Seminary students taking a selfie with the Arequipa temple construction and Yarabaya terracing one year after their stone-collecting. April 2018. Photo credit: Jason Palmer.

earth, then it became like darkness at a dance in that it risked turning diabolical (i.e., Catholic, i.e., Indigenous). Many of my Peruvian coreligionists felt a sense of danger associated with the emplaced sacred, which was why they almost always reacted defensively when I asked them if they thought that Utah was a sacred place. They wanted to make sure that I knew that they knew that the sacred could not be placed and that their journey to Utah, despite Utah's centrality in their origin myths, identities, and legacies, could not be compared to a pilgrimage.

> PASI: Maybe I read about Utah in the books and saw the images, but to tell the truth, I never really had the all-out desire to come here. . . . In reality, it just wasn't my objective.
>
> JASON: But it was for other Mormons in Cusco?
>
> PASI: Yes, they manifested as much.
>
> JASON: And what reasons did they give for wanting to come to Utah?
>
> PASI: Well, it's just that they always say, "Wow, the temple is over there, and it is the symbol of the Lord." And so of course they have the desire to know that place because of the sacrifice that it implied.

JASON: But you never had—

PASI:—I looked at it, and I respected it, and I always said, well, "the house of the Lord can be wherever."

JASON: Like in Lima?

PASI: Yes, close to where I live.

Here, Pasi implicitly criticized those with vestiges of a sited concept of sacredness and even went so far as to trouble the sacredness of one of the few earthly localizations that Mormons were doctrinally allowed to associate with the sacred: the temple. When she claimed that "the house of the Lord can be wherever," she liberated the Mormon origin story from its Utah-centrism by liberating it from place entirely. Pasi's pioneer Indigenous legacy thus became appropriately Zion-like in that it was paradoxically both bound to and free from both Salt Lake City and Cusco, past and present.

Ofelia, on the other hand, planted legacy into her arequipeño home. With her little stone from the temple grounds, she made herself part of pioneer Indigenous legacy. Referring to her stone as one of the "little details" that cumulated into "legacy," she stated in May 2017,

> We should work to leave a legacy for our kids, to leave these legacies [pointing to her stone collection], and may these little details cultivate in our generations the desire to leave those little details as a legacy because they are going to have them as treasures for themselves.
>
> That is what I have also learned in the church. So that maybe if I happened to go over there to the temple lot and I found something, well, I grab it, even if it be only a little stone. And I'd say, "Here. Look. This is it. This is what I brought from that place."

She went on to say that she took that rock from the temple site so that she could tell her "future generation": "I went to the land of the temple when it was not yet built, and this is the evidence, and this is what it was like before being. Before the temple was constructed."

The sacredness of the stone lay not it its housing of ancestral spirits, such as the spirit of her Runasimi-speaking grandmother whose llama bell sat near the temple stone in Ofelia's display of mementos, but in its encapsulation of herself in connection to her future kin, a kin for whom she will be the pioneer hero. She did not admit that the stone itself was sacred, but for her descendants it will be. It will prove that she was on that local spot of Earth before an Anglo Mormon prophet proclaimed it holy. That spot, extracted from the site and injected into the stone, became latent sacred place. It made Ofelia into "the prior" (Povinelli 2011). The stone was a piece of pioneer Indigenous legacy that belonged to her and made her into the link that connected a disorderly, pre-Inca plot of land to a future chapter in the ongoing story of Mormonism in Peru that her grandchildren will read as "our legacy." In this way, links to pacha and unsacred stones lent yet another valence to the category of legacy, designating Ofelia as one of the first on the land of an arequipeño Zion.

Almost Pioneers

In the same WhatsApp conversation that I had with Ofelia in March 2017, she told me how church officials at the Arequipa temple groundbreaking ceremony employed the word "pioneer" in a way entirely new to me at the time.

JASON: I have never heard anyone use that word outside of the context of the famous pioneers who arrived in Utah.

OFELIA: Me either, Brother. I have also never heard that, *ever*. Right?

And it gets me very emotional that the authorities would have made that gesture toward the elderly brothers and sisters here in Arequipa by calling them "pioneers," right?

And truthfully, I feel an enormous gratitude for everything that was done that day, for the words that they spoke to the pioneers, calling them up one by one to make their shovelful of earth with the golden shovels.

And to wait for them.

Another thing that filled me with emotion was that on Friday, while I was working there clearing the grounds to set up the chairs for the event, I started thinking, "Wow, to think that now I have something to leave behind for my generations," right?

To be able to tell them that I was here working, that I was here present for the first shovelful of earth. So, it will be something that they will always remember and that they will pass from generation to generation.

And then came the immense emotion that I felt upon knowing that I was clearing the ground so that the temple where my daughter will be sealed [married] can be built [crying]—

And not only the sealing of my daughter, but it also came to my mind that my generations were going to make sacred covenants there in that temple.

I saw the legacy that I was going to be able to leave my future and past generations so that they might say of me, "my great-great-grandmother or my great-great-granddaughter, she helped."

Witnessing the Leaders recognize her own people for the first time as characters in a legacy-generating, pioneer story sparked a vision wherein Ofelia became the cosmic bridge between her ancestors and her descendants. Despite the modular business structure centered in Salt Lake City that only allowed Anglo Mormons like Collin's boss and those he hired to work on the temple's tangible materiality, Ofelia was one of a handful of arequipeño Mormons who managed to physically labor on its earthy preconstruction. Achieving that opportunity required intense lobbying, skill, and divine intervention because having "a local" make her hometown temple part of her legacy was opposed to the church's blueprints, which I leafed through during one of my many visits to the temple construction site. The sheer out-of-placeness of the Arequipa temple, like the Salt Lake City temple before it, was deliberately engineered to inspire holy visions of "settler society transplanted, created anew on expropriated lands" (Kerns 2021, 99). For Anglo church leaders, making a temple holy required taming the wild. This required ordering and, as anthropologist Mary Douglas (1966) observed, "ordering involves rejecting inappropriate elements" (44). There was nothing more inappropriate to the settler colonial project of temple-building than the indigeneity and locality that Ofelia embodied. Therefore, dashing many arequipeña's hopes, the Twelve—using holy order to squelch the impromptu sacred—did not even allow local Relief Societies to knit white doilies for the temple's altars, something that they had traditionally allowed in other Latin American temple construction projects but that had apparently, according to Collin's boss, "gotten out of hand" (Palmer and Knowlton 2020, 406).

Yet, while others were denied the opportunity to deposit pioneer sacrifices materially into the temple, Ofelia got to shovel rocks so that the universal Mormon folding chairs—cherished symbols of the church's global modularity (Inouye 2015)—could be set up for the groundbreaking dignitaries, including the Catholic archbishop of Arequipa. Through her sacrifice in "clearing the grounds" and the resulting stone in her collection, she will become the link to unite her dead with her as-yet-unborn, two previously estranged halves of her legacy's saga. Turning linear time upside-down in the place of Zion's culmination—the holy temple—she sutured Zion's splintering of space and time and became the Mormon Pioneer for both her Yarabaya great-great-grandmother and her Lamanite great-great-grandchild. Her pioneer Indigenous legacy appeared complete.

• • •

I had the privilege of visiting an elderly married couple recognized as pioneers in the Arequipa temple groundbreaking ceremony. Baptized in 1960, Ronal Escobar and Leticia López were among the first few hundred Peruvians in the world to be Mormons. Though they did not have much to say about the Shining Path tribulations, they did admit having suffered "almost pioneer" tribulations of their own. On the day of our interview in March 2018, their home was decorated with depictions of White Jesus preaching among ancient Mesoamerican White people exactly as it had been decorated forty years prior when Young Single Adult (ML) Mormons would gather in their living room for wholesome recreation. One of those youths was a newly baptized Simón

Balboa, the same arequipeño who used the term "pioneer" in reference to Peruvians in his Shining Path story in chapter 2. Now a high-level church employee, he was likely the one behind the relinquishing of the title "pioneer" at the groundbreaking ceremony and of its surprising conferral upon those not of Anglo pioneer ancestry.

As they were among the first Mormons in Arequipa—heroes in its own origin narrative—I will give them the last word on what it meant for Mormon legacy, through both pioneering and indigenizing, to transfer from Utahans to arequipeños. Notice from the very beginning of the interview excerpt how Ronal immediately converted my question about Utah into one about Arequipa.

JASON: What image do you have of Utah?

RONAL: I think of the history that we have of the church growth with Joseph Smith the Prophet, and so much persecution that they didn't know how to escape it, and here in Arequipa we've also had persecution.

The newspapers warred against us. They were always picking at our prohibition against alcohol. I remember in the very first days, when I was baptized, the membership started to grow, and we would travel to thermal pools for baptisms.

The press would follow us. One time at a kiosk, a man with a bottle of beer and a cup stood next to a member who happened to be drinking soda out of a bottle. They snapped a photo. In the newspaper the next day, the headline read:

"There They Are, These Are the Mormons!"

"Supposedly these Mormons don't drink. But look what we saw!"

What didn't they say about us? Uy! They would even say that in our chapels we had many rooms where men would hook up with women. All lies. The Catholic priests would wait for us on the corner, throng around us, and say, "Where is that book?"

And they would snatch our *Books of Mormon* away, "These must be burned. These are worthless."

But the Catholics are more accepting now.

LETICIA: Even my niece has accepted. She hasn't accepted baptism yet, but one can still hope. When my mother died, my niece had never before seen how members who have gone through the Endowment in the temple were buried. . . . It impacted her to see that a man and a woman who are sealed in the temple go to the tomb in their ceremonial robes.

And ever since then, my niece—hopefully, hopefully, we are—

RONAL:—We are waiting for the Arequipa temple open house so that she can go.[2]

And for us as well, it has been a surprise, what with the groundbreaking and all that. Elder Balboa came here with another brother—

LETICIA: I knew Elder Balboa from when he was a young man.

RONAL: Yes, just a little guy. They asked us this and that, just like you are asking us. Then, two or three days go by, and we get an invitation to go to the groundbreaking because they knew that I was almost the pioneer of the church, right?

LETICIA: And they told us not to take anything, not even a camera, so we didn't. And this sister went, and she gifted us this photograph.

Brother, I didn't even know she had taken it!

RONAL: It is nice to remember. When we entered the awning, they were going to start the session for the ceremonial shoveling. We sat up front, and they told us, "Please, this is where the authorities are going to sit, so sit a little further back."

So, we sat in the back.

Suddenly—we didn't know this was going to happen—but suddenly they called to us through the *microphone!*

We were *the first ones* to shovel the earth!

We did it, and there's the photo. [The framed photo was displayed atop one of Leticia's hand-knit white doilies of the sort that she would have liked to have been allowed to donate to the temple.]

LETICIA: Yep, right there. Those shovels were heavy. . . . My husband was looking at me wondering, "How did she even lift such a tremendous shovel?"

And in front of everyone they announced, "They were the first members of the church."

JASON: How did it feel to be recognized as pioneers?

RONAL: Uy, that was a privilege.

LETICIA: Yes, because we had never even so much as imagined it. We are faithful only because we have faith.

We weren't trying to be pioneers.

We fulfill all things only because that is what we learned. It has cost a lot, but here we are, year after year.

JASON: Do you compare yourselves to the pioneers who arrived in Utah? Because that word, "pioneer," I had always only heard it associated with them.

RONAL: Well, they suffered a lot more.

JASON: You think so?

LETICIA: You know what, Elder [Jason]? When I heard the history of the pioneers and how they were persecuted and had to go to Lago Salado [Salt Lake] to look for a site where nobody would harm them, and how they found an inhospitable site and had to fight to be able to live there, and how they couldn't even—it wasn't exactly a Garden of Eden, in fact *everything* was inhospitable, and how they suffered, I started crying.

Such strength?!

Because there is not a single human who could have the strength that they showed.

And some leader told me that they were chosen, already preordained in the pre-Earth life to be able to do that.

So, thinking about my own experience that I told you before, I wonder, when I listened to that voice at the foot of my bed before I was a member, and it told me in a very harsh voice—not a small, soft voice—it said, "So, that's what you are? Just like an animal? All you do is eat and sleep?!"

I woke up, Elder, like you have no idea!

I went to the Catholic church first, but then the Mormon missionaries came to get us out and bring us to the right path [laughing].

JASON: Do you mean that, like those who arrived in Utah, you were also preordained to be pioneers?

RONAL: Exactly. That is how it is.

JASON: Pioneers from Arequipa. And like you said, you've had to suffer too.

RONAL: No, no, no. Not that much.

LETICIA: From what?

JASON: Well, it's been difficult to build the church here.

LETICIA: Yes, it has cost us a lot, but now we have been born spiritually and we must fight for our spiritual life. Like they say, "We have spiritual ears and spiritual eyes."

And I'd ask, "but what do you mean?"

In the *thousands* of classes that I have had during all my time in Sunday School and other special places, like the General Conferences, I now know what that means.

I wanted Ronal and Leticia to proclaim their rightful ownership of Mormon legacy. They refused. Perhaps they were being humble, perhaps they did not want to offend me, one of "pioneer stock," or perhaps they sensed that claiming pioneer identity was somewhat sacrilegious given that Mormonism's Utah origin story centered Anglo pioneer legacy rather than Lamanite pioneer legacy. However, though not quite sure if they had suffered enough to be true pioneers and keepers of legacy, Ronal and Leticia liked the idea of having been ordained in a pre-Earth life to become such. I can say that, during my visits to their home, I felt that I was in the presence of pioneers in every portentous sense of legacy's semiotics, including the pioneer Indigenous semiotics made even more complicated by Ronald and Letica's light skin tone and upstanding racial status as arequipeños netos.

Whether it be through reenactments of settler death in order to obscure Indigenous death during Great Plains trekking simulations in the Peruvian Amazon, through restoring the true meaning of the yunza, through the intertwining of origin stories and blood lineages to create multivalent indigeneities that eschewed the inner world's darkness, through the encapsulation of pioneer indigeneity in stone, or through simply living in daily faith among a growing fellowship of Saints, Peruvians like Jacoba, Arcadio, Pasi, Ofelia, Ronal, and Leticia seemed to have fulfilled their official church's categorical requirements for legacy. However, they may have also dangerously exceeded those requirements. Sensing this, they all kept their comments saintly, not after the manner of confident first inhabitants of Zion—full citizens who could afford to exert ownership over its legacy—but after the manner of almost citizens trying hard not to offend so as to, one day, belong. After all, despite her otherwise counterhegemonic remarks in our interview, even Pasi always used "pioneer" synonymously with Anglo Mormon. Furthermore, according to Ronal—who died before the Arequipa temple had the open house that he was earnestly awaiting—even after six decades of arduous Mormon legacy-building, he was still only "almost the pioneer."

In the next chapter, I follow this "almost" as it related to why Peruvian sacred stories did not become globally relevant, holy histories in the Mormon supranation. The answer derived from the status of Peruvian sacred places, from the fallen status of the Indigenous bodies associated with such places, from the status of sacredness itself in comparison to holiness, and from the contradiction behind how one of Leticia's most "special places" could be a conference that she had never physically attended. These intersections of holy sites and sacred bodies drilled into the more obscure veins of pioneer indigeneity that bled at the rendezvous of Peruvianness and Zion.

CHAPTER 4

Holiness

> You're going to write this in your book:
> "My crazy Uncle Celso was standing at the edge
> of Sacsayhuaman in Cusco, looking out upon
> the city below, overcome with emotion, feeling
> the Peruvian joy of being at the center of Peru
> for the first time. Like a key in its slot, just fitting.
> Finally fitting. Even though he'd never been to
> Cusco before in his life because as a Peruvian
> he couldn't afford to travel, now, as a powerful
> American, he can. The Peruvian is finally home!"
> —Celso

"Burying Everything Original"

Unlike Sofi from the introduction, Celso was one of the siblings in La Familia who also got to count as a sibling in the United States. On that evening in 2016 when he grabbed my digital recorder and began pontificating on the palimpsestic cusqueño sunset we were witnessing, Celso had recently become a US citizen and was touring Cusco with his siblings so that they could give their US-born children a taste of Peruvianness at its mythical source. He continued,

> Cue the fake tears, the sobs of exultation. Zoom out. Camera left. Wide-angle shot pans out slowly and you see my silhouette with Cusco in the background.
> One for your book cover. Don't say I never gave you anything, Nephew.
> That's my classic sarcasm, of course, but seriously, Nephew, the reason sarcasm occurs to me is that—I mean, sure there is beauty, and, yeah, I feel it.
> But there is also destruction.
> Looking out upon Cusco as you and I are doing now, I feel the beauty. I mean, who wouldn't? As they say, it is like the navel of the earth, especially for Peruvians.
> Here, I feel my Peruvianness, but I also feel the destruction of the Spanish Conquest.

Maybe that's what Peruvianness is: destruction and beauty, Spaniard and Inca, the conquerors and the conquered.

Maybe that's why we have a complex as Peruvians. I don't know if it is an inferiority or a superiority complex, but we have a complex.

They always taught us growing up that Francisco Pizarro was a hero, that having the Spaniards conquer us was a good thing. But here you can see for yourself on this skyline that it wasn't. Look at all the Catholic temples burying everything original!

But, why do I say "conquered us" as if I'm 100 percent Inca? I could just as easily say, "we conquered them." How do I know how much of a Spaniard I am versus how much of an Inca or Moche or Wari or even African?

Try to imagine what this city would look like had the Spanish never conquered it. It would be rad [bacán]. I really would be overcome with emotion. Then, it wouldn't be sarcasm. You'd really get your book cover shot. No fake tears or anything.

But looking out over Cusco without this mess [desmadre] of Catholic temples, would I feel Peruvianness? No, because what is Peruvianness if it is not the mix of both destruction and beauty? And that is palpable in the very brick in Cusco: Spanish atop Inca.

You know the refrain that says, "You aren't a Peruvian if you don't have either Inca or Mandinka [a West African people]?" Well, that means we Peruvians are all mixed in some way: Blacks, Incas, and Spaniards. We don't know what we are, so we have a complex.

Well, here in Cusco, that complex is in the very brick, in the stone. The Spanish forced Blacks to build with stones hewn by Incas. The complex that we Peruvians have is solidified here in the ground, which is why Peruvianness emanates from this place. That is why I wanted my daughter to come here. She needs to feel the reality of her roots.

And it is beautiful. Why? Because of what we don't see. Do you see a McDonald's? No. Do you see a Walmart? No. A Bed Bath and Beyond? God no! And guess what, Nephew? Don't tell your aunt I said this, but guess what else you don't see? And thank God that you don't see it: a Mormon temple.

Celso never mentioned the word holiness in his entire hourlong tirade about Cusco's skyline, but he mentioned temples. The temple was the central symbol of Zion's category of holiness during my study. However, the key to holiness was not the temple, but centrality itself. Central power helped states "to secure their legitimacy, to naturalize their authority, and to represent themselves as superior to, and encompassing of, other institutions and centers of power" (Ferguson and Gupta 2002, 982). The Mormon church's proliferation around its Utah center had similar effects. One of these effects allowed the arequipeña pioneer from the previous chapter, Leticia, to speak of the official church's

General Conference as her "special place" even though she had never been to Salt Lake City where it always convened. Instead of her traveling there, Salt Lake City came to her. The bright images on her darkened chapel's projection screen semiannually transformed her local arequipeña periphery into a virtual center, meaning that her locality only got to mutate into a holy, "special place" when it was bathed in the magic of Lago Salado (Salt Lake City) and enveloped in the strains of its Mormon Tabernacle Choir.

A more unexpected effect of the official church's Utah-centeredness was that it provoked in Celso, a Peruvian Mormon, disgust at the idea of a Mormon temple in Cusco, his center of Peruvianness. In Celso's perspective, placing a Mormon layer atop the Spanish-Black-Inca fusion would have given Peruvians an even deeper "complex." However, the crux of Celso's comedic monologue lay in the uncomfortable parallels he drew between coloniality and holiness. Colonizing land and making land holy seemed to Celso to come at the same cost: "burying everything original." By "original," I think that he meant both creative and Indigenous. What might this dousing of originality and burial of indigeneity mean for the holy space-making endeavors of resourceful Lamanite pioneers with claims to indigeneity?

Holiness versus Sacredness

Celso was the only Peruvian Mormon in my study who admitted that he joined the church for pragmatic reasons. Most other Peruvians in my study, especially in La Familia, became Mormons because of dreams, visions, or other supernatural events that called them to be Saints. Celso was never called. Instead, finding himself and his young nuclear family in a predominantly Mormon neighborhood in Utah wherein LDS church membership appeared to be the key to youth summer camps, neighborhood potlucks, stable employment, and even true acceptance into the Utah bounds of La Familia as policed by Jacoba, he got baptized with an "if you can't beat them, join them" attitude.

Most other Peruvian Mormons in my study would have been overjoyed to see a Mormon temple added to Cusco's skyline. Therefore, Celso's disparagement of that possibility surprised me. I felt that it represented a rebellion deeper than mere nonconformity to official church norms. Hidden within Celso's somewhat parodic musings lay his conflation of Spanish colonization with Utah Mormonization. Such a conflation presaged Peruvian reconfigurations of Anglo Mormonism's category of holiness, reconfigurations that required recognizing Mormonism's core motives as being the same ones that defined settler colonialism itself. "Settler colonialism is not only about the negative possibilities of destruction. Settler colonialism is also a spiritual and socio-political perversion that redefines destruction as a necessary evil. It's a process of sanctifying destruction itself" (Zahzah 2022, 45). I believe that Celso feared a Mormon temple in Cusco because it would symbolize the center of Mormonism destructively overtaking the center of a Peruvianness already based on destruction. A Mormon temple in Cusco would foreshadow, in Celso's mind wherein Mormonization and colonization were conflated, the creation of a false consciousness wherein the center of Peruvians' oppression became the center of their sainthood. Celso told me on other occasions that such a false consciousness partially explained why Peruvian Mormons felt a drive to migrate to Utah, the holy place of which Mormon holy temples in other places were but mirrors. In Celso's understanding, they migrated to Utah to become whole. In my understanding, the etymological twin of whole is holy.

Ever since Celso's immigration to Utah in 2000, not a year went by without the Utah arrival of another already-Mormon member of La Familia to which he belonged. The Peruvian Mormon migration to Utah buttressed his hypothesis that Peruvians were a brainwashed people drawn to whichever holy metropole happened to have colonized them more powerfully. Seeing a Mormon temple in Cusco would confirm Celso's ultimate fear about the depths to which his people's "complex" had sunk them. In his mind, such a sight would certify his people as a "colonized people," one that philosopher Frantz Fanon ([1952] 1994) uncharitably defined as "every people in whose soul an inferiority complex has been created by the death and burial of its local cultural originality" (18).

Yet, at the same time, Celso felt that the Peruvian "inferiority complex" was itself Peruvianness, something that was beautiful precisely because of its contradictions. During my study, Mormon Peruvianness was like Mormon holiness in that it both required and rejected colonization. In this chapter, I explore such parallels and contradictions by analyzing how some Indigenous pioneers disrupted the core-periphery structure that their Utah-centric church imposed upon them. I argue that, without decentering Utah, they centered their Utah-based religion around Peru's land by staking their own Peruvian claims to Mormon sacred geographies and holy historiographies. Through this centering of Peru, Indigenous pioneers depolarized the binary pairs carefully ensconced within the apparent "wholeness" of the Anglo Mormon category "holiness." Unveiled, those pairs affixed sacred to Peruvian and holy to Mormon.

To further Peruvian Mormonism's work in breaking down the unitary façade of Anglo Mormon holiness, I have not been using the terms "sacred" and "holy" as synonymously as the Anglo-controlled church would like throughout this book. Using sacred and holy as synonyms helps the official church keep its true synonym for holiness invisible. Using holy and sacred as synonyms cements the above pairs—"sacred Peruvian" versus "holy Mormon"—to their separate poles while appearing to mix them freely. Therefore, I employ a construct that I learned in Cusco designed to expose the true purpose of Anglo Mormon holiness by contrasting it to sacredness. While attending Cusco's folkloric performances with Celso and his US-born teenage daughter, one of which took place in front of a Catholic church built atop an Inca observatory at Coricancha, I asked cast members if they thought Cusco was holy. One pointed to the Catholic church and said, "That's holy." He then pointed to the Inca construction underneath it and said, "but that's sacred. Holy and sacred: they are not the same word."

One aspect of the tension between those two apparent synonyms that was applicable to the official church's core-periphery structure was that the holy imposed from above while the sacred seeped up from below. During my study, Mormons of many nationalities differentiated between holy and sacred, albeit less consciously than cusqueño non-Mormons. Though official church publications used the terms synonymously, lay members generally used "holy" (ML) to mean orderly, imposed, rote, controlled, whole, universal, and divine. Conversely, they use "sacred" (ML) to mean secret, creative, insurgent, volatile, material, personal, and spiritual. In Celso's understanding, the place where the holy and the sacred met on Cusco's ground became a new third entity that exceeded both holiness and sacredness while adhering to both coloniality and indigeneity. He called that entity Peruvianness. As I explained in the introduction, I call it "pioneer indigeneity."

The pioneer indigeneity dialectic does not map onto the holy-versus-sacred dialectic as if to reaffirm coloniality as holy and indigeneity as sacred. Instead, it exposes the holiness hidden within what Anglo and Peruvian Mormons in my study categorized as sacred even as it exposes the sacredness hidden within what they categorized as holy.

Ultimately, in contexts of US and European coloniality seen through Cusco's holy-versus-sacred dialectic, pioneer indigeneity exposes the Anglo Mormon category of "holiness" as synonymous not with sacredness, but with "whiteness." This chapter is, therefore, an investigation of the categorical conflation of holiness with whiteness and how Peruvian Mormons decoupled the two by making ancient, non-White Peru central to Mormon holiness rather than peripheral. In this investigation, I will first discuss how the Anglo-controlled church's power to define holiness increased through history-making in US Mormonism. I will then extend the discussion to Andean Mormonism, demonstrating how multiple valences of time and space created pioneer indigeneities capable of deeming places holy without the permission of whiteness. I will demonstrate how indigeneity went about spreading holiness over places that whiteness had relegated to a second-class sacredness. Finally, and throughout, I will analyze the threat that non-White holiness posed to Zion's order.

Public Holy Land

Historian of religion Ernest Renan ([1882] 2018) stated that "historical error is an essential factor in the creation of a nation" (251) and, I would add, in the creation of a religion. Quests to make the United States the holy center of the world and to maintain Utah as the holy center of the church used the same tactic: they elevated certain origin myths to the high category of "history." The US origin myth was elevated to a height so lofty that it naturalized the justification of US territorial conquests even in the minds of its most anti-imperial citizens. As a result, in US mythology, only overseas conquests counted as evil imperialism. This construction of "imperialism" as only that which illegitimately transgresses the bounds of natural oceanography created the narrative contrast necessary for the conquest and colonization of Native nations within the continent to count as something other than imperialism. Replacing Native nationhood with US empire counted as benign, natural expansion and even as predestined, holy pioneering.

To showcase the naturalization of US holiness and the "American" identity that it created by weaponizing history, I will use the words that an anti-imperial, antiracist, Anglo paleontologist spoke at an anti-Trump rally that I attended in 2017 on the steps of the Salt Lake City capitol building:

> The . . . National Monument . . . preserves a record of three ancient cultures that stretches back 14,000 years. It preserves records of modern tribes and of Mormon pioneers. . . . [It] is one of the last landscapes in our country that remains undeveloped and untouched by the hands of humans, and we need to preserve places like this . . . because in them we find hope for . . . humans, for us who need these lands as a reminder of our heritage and a way to reconnect with our humanity.
>
> Unlike most other countries in the world, America had the vision and the generosity to preserve large areas of land purely for their own sake, for future generations. . . . This, this, our public land system is what makes this country great. . . .
>
> Trump . . . and a few politicians are trying to destroy this, and it is time we call this what it is, an enormous land grab to take these lands, *our* lands, all of our lands away from the American public and to turn them over to private interests. . . .
>
> All you have to do is go east of the Rocky Mountains to see what a landscape tied up in private and state ownership looks like. That is why millions of people from there come here to renew their connection with our country.

Elevating the US origin myth of decolonization to the level of "history" allowed for this kind of discourse wherein each individual "American" got to fulfill her own personal Manifest Destiny to procure her own "connection to our country." This settler-scientist's use of the word "our" was especially disturbing given the active presence at the rally of diplomats from the Ute, Shoshone, Paiute, Goshute, Ute Mountain Ute, Hopi, Zuni, and Navajo nations. Yet, she had to say "our" in reference to the land now known as Utah because that "our" was what allowed the United States to deny that it was a settler state. "Our" was what allowed the United States to think of itself as having already decolonized. "Our" was what allowed US land-use to be "generous" and not genocidal. Most importantly, "our" was also what allowed "public land" to become a racial codeword (Woodson 2019) in Utah that did not allow Indigenous people to be fully human. The paleontologist betrayed that code by saying that the monument represented 14,000 years of continuous habitation in the same breath in which she said that it was "untouched by the hands of humans."

Humans did a lot of touching of that land in those 14,000 years, but her acceptance of the US origin myth affected whom she was allowed to count as human because it affected what she was allowed to count as "touching" the land. In this way, "settler state conservation policies stem from 'protecting' slivers of nature by killing and removing Indigenous peoples from the land to create nature reserves, national and state parks, and 'public lands'" (Red Nation 2021, 27). Declaring a site "public land," therefore, was the secular equivalent of declaring a site holy. In settler logics, both actions required Indigenous subordination (Bitsoi 2017).

If US origin myths accepted as history did not allow Indigenous presence to count as human habitation, there was no way that they were going to allow hackneyed Indigenous sacredness to count as holiness. The main purpose of the anti-Trump rally was to block his boundary reduction of Bears Ears National Monument, yet even Trump conceded the point that Bears Ears was a sacred space for Native people. What neither he nor his liberal settler opponents could comprehend was the possibility that Bears Ears was a holy place for Native people tantamount to what the Salt Lake temple was for Mormons.

Even though "our American Indian myths and hero stories [were] perhaps, in themselves, quite as credible as those of the Hebrews of old" (Eastman 2003, 5), Anglo settlers could not conceive of Indigenous holiness because holiness invoked permanence, like text on a page from the biblical Book of Hebrews, not like voices in oral history. For settlers, orality was to sacred was to savages as literacy was to holy was to civilization (Mignolo 2003). That was why Jerusalem, the place biblically promised to Jewish settlers, was the Holy Land. That was also why Bears Ears, the space that some Native people told stories about, was merely a sacred site. If sacred and holy sounded synonymous to the paleontologist, she could have tried flipping that script and listening to the strangeness of calling Jerusalem "the Sacred Land," and of calling Bears

Ears "a Native holy site." Capitalizing on the revolutionary potential of that strangeness, Oglala Lakota water protector Bill Means deliberately flipped the settler script when he wrote in *Landback Magazine*, "the Black Hills is our Jerusalem" (2022, 39). Indeed, in anthropologist Ella Cara Deloria's (1988) work of ethnographic fiction, *Waterlily*, she never used the word "sacred" to refer to Dakota ritual sites and life-giving, nonhuman relatives. They were always "holy." For example, "water was holy" (206). Part of the colonizers' work of displacing Native people, therefore, was to discursively separate them from the holy and lexically enclose them within the sacred. In settler society, settlers captured the holy and left Native people with the sacred. Ergo, the holy held more value than the sacred in colonized places (Padilla 2013).

What might happen to the valorization of the sacred and the holy in a pioneer indigenous society run by Lamanites? Peruvian Mormons provided me with an imaginary for that scenario, which I will discuss below, but first, more analysis of the settler imaginary is necessary for sufficient contrast.

Settlers at the 2017 anti-Trump rally imagined Indigenous people as creating ephemeral stories, not land-impacting, cosmopolitan histories, even though Indigenous civilizations permanently engineered the ecologies of Abya Yala through vast, systematic, international, and transoceanic networks and earthworks thousands of years before Christopher Columbus (Weatherford 1987). Furthermore, even though Indigenous people made up only 5 percent of the world population in the late 2010s, they continued to play the central role of stewards over 80 percent of the world's biodiverse land (Deranger 2018). Yet, US colonial mythologies, whether conservative or progressive, elided Indigenous centrality, and Mormon prophecies had similar effects on those whom Anglo church leaders sought to peripheralize in order to divest them of the power to "touch" land in ways that made it holy (Brooks 2018).

In the 1850s, the Prophet Brigham Young commanded settler-missionaries to different parts of the West in order to subdue it and its Native inhabitants (Farmer 2008). Colonization was part of making the Great Basin Desert "blossom as the rose" (J. Smith et al. 1835, 192). Yet, it was also part of making the desert's Native inhabitants "blossom as the rose" (Peterson 1981, 5). Using the same botanical analogy for the people of the desert as they did for the desert itself in those two separate prophecies, Anglo church leaders acknowledged that what continued during the late 2010s to be the US legal notion of Indigenous peoples (Saito 2015) was also the divine notion: they were part of sacred nature, not holy civilization, and therefore their presence did not count as human habitation. Since they did not inhabit, they did not make holy.

Both Peruvians and Anglos emphasized this when they told me the Anglo Mormon origin story. They highlighted the hand of God in the story by saying that not only was the Salt Lake Valley uninhabited when the Mormons arrived, but that it was uninhabitable. After 14,000 years of the valley being uninhabitable, it was only made habitable in 1847. Furthermore, during that vast timespan, it never became habitable for the many Indigenous nations living therein. It only became habitable for Anglos. Therefore, in making it habitable, the Anglo Mormon origin myth made Salt Lake City holy. In making it holy, the myth made it non-Indigenous.

In this way, the Anglo Mormon origin myth partially concurred with Supreme Court Justice William Johnson's (1831) definition of Native people as "wandering hordes, held together only by ties of blood and habit" (27). This pathologizing verdict depicted Indigenous people as floating over a land that they were not tied to in any significant way, "only by ties of blood." In this extreme mindset, land for Native people was neither sacred nor holy. Yet, blood was also where the US and Mormon peripheralizations of indigeneity parted ways. In Mormonism, "ties of blood" would never be prefaced with "only." Ties of blood, especially ones that went back to Israel, were holy.

Holy Order of the Sun God

Mormon doctrines regarding Indigenous holiness were both legitimating and pathologizing. *The Book of Mormon* connected contemporary Native people to the Israelite subtribe of Manasseh through his descendant Laman. Andean Laman-*ites'* eventual acceptance of *The Book of Mormon* as both a holy text and as a factual pre-Hispanic history of their Judeo-Christian ancestors was part of a cyclical multitemporality that simultaneously anteceded, paralleled, and postdated the rise of the Inca.

The first Peruvian to achieve the designation of "author," Inca Garcilaso de la Vega, wrote of the Inca accession to power as having a badly needed civilizing effect on the "pre-Inca." Per Garcilaso ([1609] 2009), the sacred Inca veneration of the sun brought Andeans closer to a teleological apex of religious evolution that only required Spanish Catholicism to crown with holiness. In other words, the sun was sacred, but only the Son was holy. About 340 years after Garcilaso published his 1609 account, neo-Indianist cusqueños in the Catholic republic of Peru drew on his books to reconstruct sun god veneration as an identity-building, tourism-promoting, holy-making festival called the Inti Raymi. This festival dared infuse Indigenous holiness into a site, Sacsayhuaman, that existed before the Catholic Church's holy-deeming authority. In other words, it made holy and official what Garcilaso confined to the sacred and emergent. The sun's holiness now rivaled the Son's.

It was held every June 24 in Cusco (see figure 4), and Peruvian Mormons born in Utah—including Celso's daughters, nieces, and nephews—would often attend because their Peruvian Mormon parents wanted them to feel both the holiness and the sacredness of their Peruvianness. As mentioned,

FIGURE 4. The Inti Raymi. June 2016. Photo credit: Jason Palmer.

I accompanied some of them in 2016. My postfestival conversation with another Peruvian Mormon, Pasi, at her home in Cusco provided me another window into holiness. I witnessed how the holy-deeming authority of Incas, Spaniards, and US Mormons bled together to form a unique spacetime that granted Peruvian Mormonism's complex form of indigeneity—pioneer indigeneity—power to break apart and mix the segregated pairs polarized under the false unity of Anglo Mormon holiness. Such a decoupling produced new permutations—such as Indigenous holiness—without necessarily eliminating the stereotypical pairs, such as Indigenous sacredness.

The elaborate Inti Raymi theatrics included a scene in Cusco's main public square wherein an actor dressed to represent an Inca emperor granted the contemporary president of Peru authority to rule, thus flipping the script about the source of holy order and blurring the boundary between the secular and the sacred. Purportedly, the occasion that I witnessed was the first time since President Fujimori in 1991 (De la Cadena 2000, 175) that a sitting president, in this case, Pedro Pablo Kuczynski (PPK), deigned to participate in the ceremony. I asked Pasi about the significance of PPK's presence. She said that she thought it was very significant because "PPK is of the tribe of Ephraim, and we are from Manasseh. As little as a few years ago Peruvians wouldn't have been able to accept a White, former US citizen as our president, but the previous president, Ollanta Humala, who is Native, has run our country into the ground. Since the scripture says, 'My children, the Lamanites, will be carried on the shoulders of Ephraim,' we need someone from the tribe of Ephraim to lift us up, to continue lifting Peru out of darkness until it is fulfilled that the Lamanites blossom in the desert."

By "tribe of Ephraim," Pasi meant "White people." It would be easy to read Pasi's words and assume that she had internalized both the Mormon pathologizing of Lamanites as savages and the US pathologizing of Peru as unfit for self-government. Words like Pasi's were why Celso feared that his fellow Peruvian Mormons were brainwashed. They were why critical anthropologists (Baca 2008) and decolonization activists (Newcomb 2019) rightly decried Mormonism's attempt to replace people's rich, accurate oral histories with a demeaning, anachronistic, textual perversion of them invented by Joseph Smith. From the view of Native studies, *The Book of Mormon* did to Indigenous cosmology what elite Peruvian chef Virgilio Martínez did to Indigenous gastronomy. Like Martínez, Smith granted Abya Yala's landscapes "long histories of authentic Indigenous tradition that only he [could] recover and reproduce" (M. E. García 2021, 68). In this view, rather than restore the sacred, Smith caged it.

However, Pasi and bold Lamanites like her not only freed the sacred from Smith's cage, but they also pioneer indigenized it into holiness. They did this through two forms of "epistemological disobedience" (Mignolo 2009, title) that I call "trans-temporality" (SL) and "tele-territoriality" (SL).

Trans-temporality

Different human societies manipulate different categories in order to fit new information into what they already know. Societies that use trans-temporality manipulate time. Trans-temporality is simply the cultural ability to adapt time to allow for new information. Societies that think of time as permanently following a sequential line of past, present, and future often consider transtemporality a transgression. Sometimes they call it anachronism. Sometimes they call it fatalism. Within trans-temporality, what non-Mormon historians recognize as Joseph Smith's settler anachronism can become instead part of the cyclicity of time that Andean philosophers consider integral to their historiography (Mallku Bwillcawaman 2015). Trans-temporality thwarts the construction of a binary, essential difference between holy, ordered Western time and fluid, sacred, Andean time. It also recognizes that the practice of incorporating new additions into myths that Western academics often considered to be set in the immutable past was a practice long held in Abya Yala. For many Andeans in my study, the past was ever present as if it were visible and ahead. In fact, in Aymara, "the word for past, *nayra*, is the same for eyes" (Canessa 2012, 33).

Per ethnographer Sabine MacCormack (1991), the Andean notion that the past lay ahead led to a tradition of quickly incorporating pachacuti from the present into existing myths of the primordium. As Tzvetan Todorov (1984) found in Central America during the destruction of Montezuma's empire, the people would integrate a new event "into a network of natural, social, and supernatural relations, in which the event thereby [lost] its singularity: it [was] somehow domesticated, absorbed into an order of already existing beliefs" (74).

When Christians came to the Andes in the sixteenth century, Andeans saw them "as fundamentally different from Andeans, as belonging to a separate epoch" (MacCormack 1991, 145). Therefore, the Andean myth of the First Age changed into one about an enmity between Andeans and Christians in which the Christians were all expelled. "The Augustinian missionaries, however, interpreted the myth . . . differently. They believed that the Christians of that earlier Andean epoch were proof that, long ago, the gospel had been preached in the Andes by one of Christ's apostles" (145). That notion eventually spread to Europe through Spanish chroniclers and was in the religious revivalist ether that saw Joseph Smith publish his account of Christ in pre-Hispanic America (Bushman 2007).

People like Pasi changed their biological lineage—their "ties of blood"— through that account. The trans-temporal conflation of pre-Inca, Inca, Spanish, and Mormon timelines allowed Pasi to adopt *The Book of Mormon* seamlessly into her connection with the past as if it were always part of her and as if it were ahead of her. *The Book of Mormon* was a tool of racialization meant to subalternize people like Pasi and confine them to an unruly, dark sacredness. Pasi used trans-temporality to appropriate that tool and transform it instead into a device that "nurture[d] Indigenous theological possibilities" (Hernández 2021, 4) and temporalized them as "holiness." Pasi, therefore, joined other Indigenous Mormons (Aikau 2012) in disrupting the academic argument that because institutions like Mormonism were never Indigenous, they could not be decolonized (Tuck and Yang 2012).

Pasi, as a proud Lamanite, went back in time and made Mormonism Indigenous in the first place. In so doing, she did not erase whiteness from her category of holiness—Brown Manasseh still needed White Ephraim—but she infused White holiness with indigeneity.

Tele-territoriality

Instead of manipulating time in order to incorporate new information into what is known, tele-territoriality manipulates space to transport one land's categories to another land. This is important because the new conceptualizations that Peruvian Mormons like Pasi created imbued not only the temporal aspects of their indigeneity with holiness, but also the spatial aspects. Many

Andeans in my study, like Pasi, had a "sited identity" (Thomas 2002, 372) or a group sense of self as tied up with a physical territory. The way for Pasi and Lamanites like her to acquire a sited identity that could tie into both Utah and Peru to make both equally holy was opened once they transgressed linear time. Put differently, once they were connected to pre-Hispanic, Mormon ancestors through a Utah-distributed book, Peruvian Mormons were free to expand the sites of their identities to include Utah in the holiness that they already granted to Peru.

This holiness teleported across territory, uniting Peru with Utah into a single holy site. It was as if a conduit connected them, perforating the Earth's molten mantle much like the sacred tunnels that connected Lake Titicaca—the Inca's holy site of emergence—to the ocean. Such tele-territoriality was what provided Pasi a greater connection to her newly acquired Mormon ancestors while she was physically in Utah than while she was in Peru where they were buried. It was not that Utah was more holy than Peru, it was that, through tele-territoriality, Peru's holiness transported to Utah along with Pasi's body. Pasi seemed to understand that Peru, and specifically Cusco, lent Utah its holiness through Lamanites like her.

Tele-territoriality reversed the General Conference phenomenon whereby Utah biannually shone its holiness to a deficient periphery. Tele-territoriality melded the core with the periphery. While Pasi was in Utah, Peru's holiness was coterminous with Utah's. They were the same place. They were whole. For a cusqueño Mormon named Moisés whom I interviewed in Utah in August 2016, tele-territoriality was powerful enough to allow him to move holiness not only through earth, but also through kinship, even to non-Mormon Lamanites.

JASON: Do you feel any connection between *The Book of Mormon* and your own ancestors?

MOISES: A lot of Navajos come to where I work, and the sounds that Navajo has don't exist in English but do exist in Runasimi. And I love to see Native American people because they remind me of my own family members. Their faces [rostros] are so similar to those of my grandparents, to those of my cousins. Once I met a young man on the bus in Salt Lake City who looked so much like my cousin that I spoke to him. I asked him in English, "Do you speak Spanish?"

And he told me, "No, I'm Native American."

And when he said that, I shut up, but I felt very strongly the connection between him and me, that despite us not knowing each other before, I still felt that—generations ago—we were part of the same single family.

We have the same traces, the same blood, and even the same sounds used for speech.

JASON: I mean, but the question was whether you—

MOISES:—Well, those things are what make me feel a connection to *The Book of Mormon* because it tells us that we all came from the same single family that got subdivided.

Today we can see that the remnants of those tribes and cities are the Navajo, the Utes, the Aztecs, the Mayas, and the Incas. But all of them are exactly the same.

Tele-territoriality tied Moisés—an Indigenous person from Cusco—to the Indigenous people of Utah by transfusing blood from *The Book of Mormon* into both his veins and theirs. In using blood to erase tribal and nation-state borders, tele-territoriality spilled the contents of holiness and mixed its polarized vocabularies. After all, blood and borderlessness were polar opposites within the hidden binaries of Anglo Mormon "holiness." Blood belonged to holy ordered place because it set the quantifiable, genetic boundaries of ancestral membership vital for temple sealings. Borderlessness belonged to sacred wild space because it honored boundless, shifting forms of relatedness that could not be pinned down long enough to be sealed.

As with most of the tools of pioneer indigeneity, tele-territoriality was contradictory. It contradictorily promoted both a constructivist borderlessness and an essentialist blood. It promoted borderlessness by making Abya Yala's indigeneity whole (holy) again. It demographically de-minoritized both Native Americans and Latinx people by combining them with the diverse masses of Latin America to form one "hemispheric Indigenous identity" (Thayne 2019, 331) that made Anglos the true hemispheric minority. Yet, tele-territoriality also promoted the Anglos' kin idiom—blood—as the substance of true, verifiable relatedness. As it did so, it reduced the symbolic importance of food as the substance of relatedness for many Andeans (Krögel 2010). Blood, as an idiom of official (holy) kin solidification in Anglo Mormonism, did not carry as much weight for non-Mormon Andeans in my study as it did for their purported ancestor, Father Lehi, whose Zion-bound blood was powerful enough to create a New Jerusalem. For many non-Mormon Andeans, food was more central and more sacred than blood to the mechanism—pacha—that cycled substance between people and places, making holy both their relatedness and their land (C. Allen 2014). However, for Moisés—as an Andean Mormon— blood overpowered food as a kin idiom.

Lamanite tele-territoriality's arithmetic was not meant to decolonize Mormonism because many of its attributes canceled each other out. It transgressed both colonial pioneering and Indigenous decolonial activism in equal measures. However, it also broke the rules of arithmetic altogether, reversed all cancelations, and powerfully channeled Peru's Indigenous holiness into settler Utah and vice versa. Lamanites in my study wrenched indigeneity away from stereotypes of the static, quaint "sacred" used to minoritize Native people.

Then, they took that dislodged indigeneity and placed it instead at the holy extreme of the holy-versus-sacred dynamo that structured holiness as a category of Peruvian Mormonism. For Moisés, tele-territoriality's use of blood, a kin concept with relatively little significance in his native Andes, connected him to his Andean ancestors—*The Book of Mormon*'s heroes—making him feel a border-eliding kinship to Utah where the blood-descendants of those heroes—the Navajo—dwelled. Pioneer indigeneity's tool of tele-territoriality filled his relationships and, by extension, his territories with holiness, thus centering both Peru and Utah in his cosmovision.

The Book of Mormon, Peru

However, was not Utah already sufficiently central within Moisés's category of holiness? During my study, I assumed that the tendency of Lamanite epistemological disobedience to center Peru without bothering to decenter Utah would only bolster the holy church's hegemony. Yet, my assumption depended on a linear time that supposed Anglo Mormonism would react *after* Lamanite disobedience. In reality, Lamanite metaphysics tapped time and territory at both ends of that sequence such that the stronger the central church's holy grip, the more that Lamanites were able to coopt its holiness and transfuse it into Peru. In fact, multitemporal holiness in Peru accumulated to the point when *The Book of Mormon* began to take place in Peru in the minds of many Peruvian Mormons. Peru became a *Book of Mormon* historic site. And for many reasons, all ironic, the Anglo leaders in Salt Lake City did not like it. It was not so much that Anglo church leaders could not abide the holy historical discovery that Peru was a *Book of Mormon* setting, it was that they could not compute the phrase "Indigenous historical discovery" at all. The Doctrine of Discovery, issued by the Holy See, sheathed holiness through the centuries with so much whiteness that Anglo church leaders saw Indigenous discovery as an oxymoron. Lamanites did not discover. Lamanites did not deem holy.

Therefore, because *The Book of Mormon* was the keystone—the holiest center—of Mormonism, the Anglo Mormons who controlled its printing and distribution deliberately peripheralized the very places where its story was set along with the people who inhabited those places. Peruvian ownership of *Book of Mormon* stories and Peruvian contributions to *Book of Mormon* scholarship went unrecognized because "whites, be they Nephites, Puritans, or Mormon pioneers, control[ed] the means of the production of history. . . . Oral histories, if they survive[d], [were] deemed folktales, family lore, and given a second-class status as reliable archival sources" (Mueller 2017, 54–55).

Nevertheless, now that Pasi and Moisés were Lamanites in a biological, territorial, and multitemporal sense, they, and other Lamanites, ignored their central church's peripheralizing schemes and took control over the narrative history of pre-Hispanic Christianity in Abya Yala that their membership in the church made possible. Pasi, for example, posited that people who came from traditional villages around South America recognized truth in *The Book of Mormon* because "they still have their oral legends, and they correspond to *The Book of Mormon* story." In her work with a Utah-based NGO, she went to Paraguay to help pregnant mothers who had gone directly from their pre-Christian lifeways into Mormonism. In June 2016, she told me that their entire group converted to the church at once because they were listening to *The Book of Mormon* and said something to the effect of, "This is our history written down. How did you guys know about this? Where did you get this book!?" They were almost accusing the missionaries of stealing it from them. Therefore, according to Pasi, they knew it to be a true history because it matched their oral history almost exactly. She told me that the reason Paraguay's legends matched *The Book of Mormon* was that Paraguay's Indigenous people originally came from Bolivia and that the visit of Jesus as mentioned in the book happened around Lake Titicaca on Bolivia's border with Peru. Apparently, Jesus walked on Lake Titicaca's water.

Basilio Corimayta, a Peruvian from a small town near Arequipa who had lived in Utah since 1983, had a similar experience to the Paraguayans when he first read *The Book of Mormon* in Lima. He knew that it was true right away because "there was a *ton* of coincidence, too much coincidence to not be true." In one of my many interviews with Basilio, who, like me, married into La Familia, I asked him what some of those coincidences were. He said that in Machu Picchu, there was a place called Intihuatana. "It looks like a sundial, and it is the place where the Inca king tied the sun in the sky for thirty-six hours so that the people could finish building Cusco." That night without darkness matched the cosmic sign of Christ's birth that Abya Yala received, according to Basilio's interpretation of *The Book of Mormon*.

Those ethnoarchaeological proofs of *The Book of Mormon*'s historicity were part of a narrative that was increasingly at odds with the official church which, ironically, desired to distance itself from the idea that *The Book of Mormon* was a history of Abya Yala with a verifiable geography and holy places that still existed. The Anglo church sought that distance because the racist paternalism implicit in Lamanite identity was clashing with the colorblindness that church leaders were beginning to embrace. For the official church, Lamanites became "impossible subjects" (Ngai 2004, title): people "who cannot be and a problem that cannot be solved" (5). Lamanite identity—the very identity that Anglo church leaders helped create—became a public relations problem, something to be mitigated and, if possible, ignored until it followed the noble savage and disappeared into the wilderness.

True Lamanites, however, as owners of *The Book of Mormon*, were not disappearing. They were adding details to the story, connecting the end of the written narrative to what they saw in the ruins of civilizations around them during my study, thus infusing those places with holiness. Erudite Lamanites across the Andes even established an official academic association and fully fledged school of thought called the LDS South Americanist School of Book of Mormon Geography. The first of this school's eight tenets, as stipulated in its private Facebook group, was "that the genesis of the history and geography of *The Book of Mormon* had its origins in South America" and then slowly spread north as the narrative of the book progressed through the centuries. Of course, because the powerful association of whiteness with holiness affected the Anglo academy just as much as it affected the Anglo church, no members of this school were invited to contribute to Oxford University Press's edited volume *Americanist Approaches to "The Book of Mormon"* (Fenton and Hickman 2019).

I found that South American Lamanites who had never heard of the official South Americanist school of thought tended to arrive at its tenets independently. As Jacoba told me in September 2017 in Salsands, Utah:

> I brought my kids over here [to the United States from Peru] when they were very little. They didn't know Peru. But little by little, I am taking them back and teaching them what Peru is and what the ruins are. Three years ago, I took Hector, my son. We went to Trujillo, and he just stood there agape, looking.
>
> "Mamá," he said. "This is [the *Book of Mormon* city of] Zarahemla."
>
> "Zarahemla?" I asked.
>
> "What did Zarahemla look like, Mamá? It was a walled city, and what was the width of the walls, Mamá? Because it describes them right there in *The Book [of Mormon]*," he said. They were almost one meter thick, and the city was right next to the sea.
>
> "This is it," he tells me. "Here you have the ruins of Zarahemla. Look at the precise height of the parapets that are just so. And look at how they were described as terminating vertically one by one. It is all here." . . .
>
> So, I go about teaching my kids little by little, and every time I go to Peru, I take one with me, or some grandkids, and I go about teaching them the story of *The Book of Mormon*.
>
> "Here it is." I tell them:
>
> "Look."

Her husband, Arcadio, was sitting close to us trying to watch Univision's coverage of Puerto Rico's Hurricane Irma during this interview, but he could not contain himself and chimed in,

> ARCADIO: I had a book. It tells of Incas named Viracocha and Pachacutec. Their god tells them, "Here my god was sitting."

The god, what did they call him? He had a name, and with His finger he drew many worlds—and that is a book that is not Mormon—and it says that those many worlds were His.

So, what is it that *The Book of Mormon* teaches us?

JASON: That God made many worlds before this one?

ARCADIO: Of course. So, how did this Inca know that God had many worlds? It must be that when the Lord came here to the Americas, He arrived over there [in Peru] and not here [in North America]. . . . So, after that, it says that four brothers arrived.

JASON: Meaning Lehi's sons: Nephi, Sam, Laman, and Lemuel?

ARCADIO: Yep, but they call them "The Four Brothers Ayar" in their Quechua language, see?

JASON: Then why do the artists of Book of Mormon scenes never depict Peru?

JACOBA: Because they only know what it's like close around here . . . they haven't exactly studied Peru. They can't even imagine the grandeur that exists in Peru. They can't fathom it. Because if they went, they would remember the descriptions of Zarahemla.

. . .

ARCADIO: And in Machu Picchu, we saw with our own eyes the—

JACOBA:—the baptismal fonts. But Arcadio, where was it that we saw the tree from Lehi's dream carved onto the mountain just like the Nazca lines?

Jacoba's return trips to Peru were "acts of self-fabrication" (García 2021, 128). They refabricated homeland into holy land. Moreover, they refabricated her into a natural-born citizen of that land: a Native of Zion. As she saw her homeland with new eyes—such as Hector's, attuned to *Book of Mormon* architecture—she constructed a new sainthood for herself, one made of adobe brick and Inca-hewn stone. Those new eyes and that new sainthood gave Jacoba ultimate authority to speak on the subject of *Book of Mormon* archaeology. Therefore, Jacoba and Arcadio's discussion was not speculation.

They were sure that some of *The Book of Mormon*'s events happened in Peru. However, Arcadio and Jacoba were not White. Their surety did not count as official church knowledge. As such, the following 2018 statement from the church—one of the few times that an official church publication used the word "Lamanite" since 1999 to implicate contemporary people—was a direct affront to their authority as Indigenous people of the Peruvian Holy Land: "Just as the history of the northern ten tribes of Israel after their exile in Assyria is a matter of speculation rather than knowledge, the history of the Lamanites after the close of the *Book of Mormon* record is a matter of speculation. The Church . . . does not take a position on the specific geography of *The Book of Mormon* or claim a complete knowledge about the origins of any specific modern group in the Americas" (Church n.d., para.9).

The problem with that declaration's parsing of the terms "speculation" and "knowledge" was that for the Anglo church and other settler institutions, such as "the sciences," White people's speculation *was* knowledge. Conversely, "Indigenous peoples [were] viewed as exceedingly 'spiritual,' and dominant scientific traditions . . . tend[ed] to denigrate Indigenous understandings of the world as beliefs rather than knowledges" (Tallbear 2021a, para. 1).

White, male artists got to speculate all they wanted. Those speculations were elevated to knowledge when their muscular Christianity, masculinist, racializing illustrations of Mesoamerica (J. K. Allen 2020)—and not counter-hegemonic paintings by female artists, such as Minerva Teichert (Campbell 2020)—were the only ones included in the print edition of *The Book of Mormon* to which my study participants had access. These illustrations, since they were only of Mesoamerican settings, were easily adopted into what was known among Anglo Mormon archeologists as the limited geography hypothesis. This hypothesis was that *The Book of Mormon* told of a very small group among an already-populated continent. It went against the hemispheric hypothesis, which was that the book explained how the entire Western Hemisphere and Pacific Islands were populated. Limited geography not only contradicted what most of my Peruvian Mormon study participants knew to be true about their own sainthoods, it directly opposed what their Anglo leaders told them was true.

For example, the arequipeña pioneer Leticia from chapter 3 remembered attending a regional conference in Lima in 1968 at which an Anglo member of the Twelve visiting from Salt Lake City stated that Peruvian Mormons (then numbering only 8,000) biologically descended from the Inca. He then made a declaration that I was able to find in former mission president Dale Christensen's (1995) account of the official church's missiology in Peru. He declared that the Inca biologically descended from Lehi who "landed on or near the coasts of Peru" (112), making "the land of Peru . . . one of the most important lands in all the history and development of the people of *The Book of Mormon*" (112). Later, that selfsame member of the Twelve along with his brethren in the church's top leadership sided with a minority of Anglo Mormon archaeologists and geneticists against the hemispheric theory and in favor of a limited geography theory that they eventually narrowed down to either Meso-america or North America (Duffy 2008). In so doing they betrayed hundreds of thousands of South American Lamanites with deep existential stakes in the hemispheric theory. Their willingness to betray Lamanites when confronted with scientific evidence demonstrates that within "power and resource imbal-ances, in which some peoples' ideas and knowledge are made to matter more than others, genetic markers and populations named and ordered by scientists play key roles in the history that has come to matter" (Tallbear 2013, 7).

Story versus History

Most of my Peruvian Mormon study participants in Peru and Utah were almost completely unaware or uninterested in those theoretical contests and disavowals. They were too busy filling out *The Book of Mormon*'s lost details and searching out its holy places. In so doing, they gracefully sidestepped the question of how they could conscionably belong to a church that excluded Peru, and by extension Peruvians, from holiness. They were too interested in making Peru holy, using their official church's own tactics, that they genuinely did not notice that they were working against their church leaders' deliberate exclusion of them from holiness. This represented a novel instantiation of anthropologist Rudi Colloredo-Mansfeld's (2009) concept of "vernacular statecraft" (89) that he learned from Indigenous politicians in Ecuador. Among Peruvian Mormons, it became vernacular saintcraft: using the official church's tools to adapt sainthoods to local conditions in ways that those sainthoods did not know were prohibited.

As I will soon demonstrate however, some Peruvian Mormons did know that those tools were prohibited, and they used them anyway. Still, whether deliberate or inadvertent, Peruvian sainthoods remained vernacular because they never achieved official recognition from the holy church. Peruvians got sacred story, but that did not count as holy history. "LDS history [was] measured in handcarts, prairie skirts, and a determined self-sufficiency" (Maffly-Kipp 2020b, 143) not in parapets, stone fonts, and Indigenous cities. As such, there was a gap between Indigenous story and "official"—meaning holy, meaning White—history.

Recently, however, central church leaders seemed to be trying to close that gap. Part of their attempted mending had to do with Mormonism's foundational penchant for record keeping and bringing history up to the present time. Perhaps regretting that this had almost always only meant the history of Anglo Mormons, the church corporation, in 2015, created a new subdepartment of paid positions—the Office of the General Manager of South American Church History. The aforementioned arequipeño Mormon Simón Balboa, a Shining Path survivor who identified strongly as a biological descendant of Laman, was among the first employees of that department. His job as assistant to the general manager (an Anglo Mormon) put him in the center of the tension between what his White supervisor and other White gatekeepers would accept as globally relevant, holy Mormon history and the sacred oral histories that he heard from "local" Mormons in Peru. In an interview in December 2017, he told me about the two lines of authority through which his writing had to pass before being accepted as history: "First, I give it to the Area Presidency who look at the doctrinal aspect, just so that we aren't talking about the Three Nephites . . . none of that stuff, and then the other line is through the *Church*

History Department [English]. They have to see if the dates are correct, the places, the people, all that information."

The Three Nephites were fodder for much Mormon folklore because when Jesus visited Abya Yala, He promised them that they would stay on the Earth until His Second Coming. During my study, the Three Nephites were sometimes used to explain why certain congregations in Latin America claimed to have already been Mormon before the first Mormon missionaries arrived, implying that the Three Nephites got to them first. Simón, however, was not allowed to share those types of stories or to tie the Nephite visitations to specific places. In fact, Anglo church leaders did not allow him to publish stories that would imbue any specific place in South America with the holiness reserved for privileged North American church historic sites, such as Martin's Cove, Wyoming. Many of those US holy sites were the private property of the church corporation, and if the unspoken US legal maxim held true that whiteness was a prerequisite for property (C. I. Harris 1993), it was no wonder that Anglo church leaders could not allow for stories with the slightest bit of non-White, territorial holiness. Even though the Three Nephites were imagined as White, as were the Anglo prophets to whom Simón will refer below, the sheer Latin American placement of the stories was enough to associate them with non-whiteness and thus disqualify them from inclusion into holiness, into history.

Simón continued, "I interviewed the pioneer of Cusco who now lives in Arequipa. Men like him tell me that President Kimball came to Cusco determined to close it [as a mission district], and then he had a vision wherein Nephi asked him not to close Cusco, and so he didn't. Today Cusco has two stakes. It is its own mission. To me that is amazing, but when I presented that to the History Department in Salt Lake City, they accepted it, but they don't want me to publish it. That gives me sadness."

As a church employee and a loyal church member, he was not willing to elaborate on that sadness, but I felt that it had something to do with a disconnect between the reason that Anglo church leaders told him that they could not accept those stories and what he felt, deep down, to be the real reason. That reason elicited an antonym of holiness: alienation. However, I will examine that later. For now, Simón remained upbeat:

> The Lamanites are all over South America in different tribes. They maintain their culture, but the ones who maintain their culture the most are the Otavalo in Ecuador.
>
> Have you seen how they do their long hair, their clothing? Impactful. Among them there is a tradition:
>
> When the first otavaleño got to know the church, he declared that when the American missionaries like you came and taught him of *The Book of Mormon*, he said, casually, "Oh, I knew about that already."

"Yes, but how did you know if we are the first ones?"

He said, "I had a dream, and a man came who looked exactly like him," pointing to the cover of the book. *The Book of Mormon*, Jason, used to have the depiction of Moroni on it. He said, "This man told me in a dream that you guys would come."

Moroni's peremptory visit centered indigeneity by relegating to the periphery the male Anglo missionaries' holy roles as knowledge sharers and White saviors. The otavaleño pioneer did not need the White missionaries. His knowledge came directly from the book's holy source: Moroni, the same Indigenous (albeit White) man who told Joseph Smith about the book in the first place.

Such a decoupling of whiteness from holiness was offensive, at least to two Anglo church employees, Richard Turley and Clinton Christensen. Their 2019 book sanctified one Anglo male's three-month visit to South America as "a turning point for Latter-day Saints on that continent" (viii). Since these historians may very well have been among the gatekeepers blocking Simón's efforts to center indigeneity in official Mormon historiography and holiness, the structure of their own book is a window into Anglo holiness's true categorical requirements. Almost every page and photograph of the book was formatted both vertically and horizontally to visually center an Anglo male's name, an Anglo male's face, or simply an Anglo male's white clothing in contrast to his dark, South American surroundings. In the authors' graphic categorization, South American history could only be holy if South Americans remained its backdrop, not its protagonists.

Lamanite Epistemology

In his unpublishable Ecuador manuscript, Simón sabotaged Anglo Mormon "holiness" in ways more profound than simply centering indigeneity. The otavaleño's nonplussed reaction to the fulfilment of his vision—"Oh, I knew about that already"—reflected the commonplaceness of such manifestations in Lamanite constructions of holiness. His nonchalance in the face of the supernatural matched the way most Latin Americans in my experience discovered the church's veracity, and it contrasted sharply with Anglo Mormon ways of knowing that the central church was what it claimed to be, the only organization on the planet with God's authority to conduct His holy business.

In general, Anglos knew through scarcely decipherable feelings, similar to those that caused them to shed a tear during a touching film, whereas Latin Americans knew through intense dreams, visions, otherworldly voices, physical visitations, and coincidences that seemed inexplicable without divine causation. As to the latter manifestation of holiness, a member of my ward family in Barrio Periféricos provided an example. Her name was Rosa. She was an unmarried mother who owned a soccer jersey sewing business in Arequipa's historic downtown. She had three male employees who periodically interrupted our interview to solicit her expertise. She identified as a Lamanite. I recorded my June 2018 conversation with her as we sat among sewing machines and scraps of fabric. I asked her how she became a member of the church.

Church wasn't what I needed. And no matter what church I went to—like my brother's church, what was it called? The Church of the Living Water?—it didn't sit right with me. . . .

But one morning when I was reading the Bible . . . there was something strange, Brother, because when I started to read . . . I started to feel that it wasn't me who was reading, instead it was someone else who was reading to me. . . .

I heard the voice of the Lord, and I, in that moment, finally broke into tears, Brother. . . .

Then He asked me if I loved Him. [crying]. . . .

I answered Him with all of my love, "yes!" [long pause, recovering from emotion].

That is how it happened, dear Brother.

I told Him, "Lord, I love You, but where should I go?"

That is what I asked Him.

"Where do You want me to go if You want me to go somewhere?"

That is how I talked to Him.

"If I go with my mom to the Catholic church, I don't feel right. Where do You want me to go? But Lord," I said, "Lord, today I'll make You a proposal: the first person that You send to the door of my house and the first one who knocks on my door, I will ask him what church he goes to. And if he goes to the Catholic church, then so will I, and I will be forever faithful. I will show You how much I love You. And if it is my brother, oh well, I'll go to his church. Even though I don't like it, I'll go."

And that is the proposal I made, Brother. And so, I waited for someone to knock. So much uncertainty! Who will be the first one to knock?! My brother was going to come at 4:00 on the dot supposedly, so "Ay, please let 4:00 never come!"

But nobody knocked. And it was 4:00.

Suddenly—a knock! And my brother is extremely punctual. "Wow, it must be my brother. Ay, what have I done!?"

But when I open the door, it was the missionaries! Brother, when I saw them, I didn't think, "Oh no, anyone but them!" Instead, I felt an *immense* joy that welled up from I don't understand where. Only then did I remember that Mormon missionaries even existed. I told them, "I am waiting for you."

Rosa's coincidence, which was strikingly similar to the 1901 conversion story of Mexican Mormon luminary Margarito Bautista (Pulido 2020) to whom I will refer below, was impossible to ignore because it was large. Many of my Anglo Mormon study participants, on the other hand, explained their foundation of belief as an accumulation of feelings that were small. Such a powerful size contrast at the level of knowledge represented another flipping of the script or "great reversal" (Thayne 2019, 326) within "Zionist . . . power relationships" (326) regarding holiness, this time in ways that filled some Anglo Mormons with jealousy. A common Anglo thought process, which I often perceived in my Anglo mission companions' reactions in Bolivia to our baptizees' conversions to Mormonism from 1998 to 2000, can be put to words: "If holiness is whiteness, how could God possibly give unto a non-White Lamanite a larger manifestation of His holy power than the one that He gave unto me, an Anglo? Either the Lamanite must by lying, or the manifestation must have come from Satan." Ethnographer Jennifer Huss Basquiat (2004) recorded similar reactions to Haitian Mormon conversion stories among Anglo missionaries in Haiti.

However, Anglos—ever the capitalists—did not take lying down what they perceived to be a zero-sum power struggle for the hording of Heavenly Father's limited holiness. Since they controlled what got written in holy text, they used propaganda to combat God's diminishing of their exclusive right to holiness, a diminishing that happened when He granted too great a portion of that holiness to Lamanites. They textually demonized as "too sacred" all ways of knowing other than those that came through the "still and small . . . voice of The Spirit" (Packer 1991, para. 6), which they took great pains in their speeches, hymnals, and manuals to clarify as "never" (para. 7) a literal voice despite its undeniable literalness throughout *The Book of Mormon*. "These very delicate, fine spiritual communications are not seen with our eyes nor heard with our ears; it is a voice that one feels more than hears" (para. 1). That God Himself was disobedient to that epistemology when He spoke audibly and mundanely to Simón's Lamanite informants perturbed the Anglo church to the extent that it could not trust Simón's Lamanite ears and eyes to recognize proper holiness in history.

In sum, Anglo church leaders racialized Lamanites at every level, even at the phenomenological level of metaphysical holiness. If Lamanites could not be allowed to know more and more deeply than Anglos, they certainly could not be allowed to inhabit the very places mentioned in *The Book of Mormon* where Jesus Christ Himself spoke—audibly and in person—to their ancestors.

SIMON: These experiences, I have them, I have gathered them up, and I have sent them to Salt Lake City, of course. But when I wanted to put them into the Ecuador book, they told me, "no."

Another time, in Cusco, Elder Boyd K. Packer [of the Twelve] said, "Lehi himself taught from here and Moroni was right here in Cusco."

So, in the Peru book, I published that Packer spoke in Cusco, but I did not publish what he said in Cusco [laughing].

JASON: And why do you think that they don't want those things in the book?

SIMON: I think that we lack more—you should know, Jason, that if I have here a single point in space, many lines will pass through it. I need to provide Salt Lake City with more points so that only one line passes through all of them.

Anglo church leaders wanted all histories to match. They wanted sameness. Yet, Simón wanted to include a different history because "different histories explain different things, and it is only the tyranny of scholastic logic that wants to pin people down to one version of experience—to one seamlessly coherent narrative" (Theidon 2013, 214). But there was more to it than that.

If it truly were the case that church headquarters simply needed more points of triangulation before categorizing sacred stories as holy histories, and if Anglo church leaders truly thought that human eyes and ears almost never perceived divine physicality, they would not have published in their new series, *Saints*, the following extravagant story from 1829 in Fayette, New York, witnessed by a single person, Mary Whitmer. "One day . . . she saw a gray-haired man. . . . His sudden appearance frightened her, but as he approached, he spoke to her in a kind voice that set her at ease. 'My name is Moroni.' . . . The old man vanished a moment later, leaving Mary alone" (Church 2018, 70–71).

How did the story of old man Moroni make it into the church's officially published history for distribution to its members all over the world, while a story with the slightest Mormon validation of Andean locality did not even make it into the official history of the church in Peru? That the church's publication committee was somewhat woke to the racist implications of that contradiction and to the whiteness/history versus indigeneity/story trope of the US academy was evident in the first two words of the subtitle of *Saints*. It was no longer "*The History*," as it was in the previous version, *Our Legacy*. Now it was, "*The Story*." The publishing committee's excitement to display its wokeness was also evident in Mary Whitmer's gender. The committee knew that the early Anglo church had been guilty of relegating women into the same pole of holiness to which it relegated indigeneity: the sacred, savage, hysterical pole. Yet, as with all colonial organizations (Quijano 2019), the church's publishing committee only elevated female voices if Indigenous ones could thereby be silenced (Niumeitolu 2019). Therefore, the rest of *Saint*'s subtitle unmasked the official church's regnant coloniality. It was not, *Saints: The Story of The Church in the US*, it was simply, *Saints: The Story of The Church*.

If the official church did not have a core-to-periphery structure designed to erase indigeneity, then it would not be able to get away with marking one story as that of Peru while leaving another as simply "the story." This characteristic of statelike entities to set up a periphery in order to have a center from whence to consolidate power makes the center not only a point that the periphery orbits around, but a pinnacle that towers vertically over it. Within that pinnacle—or temple—"The 'higher up' officials are, the broader the geographical range of their peregrinations, and the more encompassing their optics on the domain of state activity and its relation to what is merely 'local'" (Ferguson and Gupta 2002, 987). This allows those in the center to feel that they are not local, but global, making their history everybody's history.

Under that delusion, the story of Mary Whitmer was to be holiness-promoting for Mormons the world over because she apparently had no sacred cultural trappings to indicate her locality. In reality, however, she had plenty of cultural trappings, the foremost of which was masked because of its own supposedly universal holiness: her literacy. Her story was written down for an objective, dispassionate understanding. Indigenous stories, on the other hand, were told to ears and eyes accustomed to the messy sacred, not the properly holy. Yet, her literacy further masked the true linchpin of her situated story's ability to become knowledge in the Mormon supranation: her whiteness. Since "in early Mormon history, literacy signifies whiteness and worthiness, when a Mormon historical subject becomes a writerly self, he or she also becomes—figuratively, and the Latter-day Saints believed, perhaps even literally—a white self" (Mueller 2017, 59).

Whiteness and holiness were synonymous not only in early Mormon history, but also in recent Anglo Mormon historiography. Such was exemplified in BYU professor F. Lamond Tullis's (2018) account of the 1915 execution of a hacienda-administrating Mormon branch president and his Otomí-speaking first councilor in Hidalgo, Mexico, at the hands of Zapatistas. The branch presidency's martyrdom was the mere backdrop of Tullis's overarching argument: the early Hidalgo Saints who were "strong" (143) enough to resist the schismatic wiles of "Margarito Bautista's apostate group" (156) hellbent on "confusing people" (106) with Lamanite-power ideology were only those who "did indeed pull themselves up by their bootstraps" (138), "learned English" (143), and allowed the Anglo-controlled church's acculturation schools to indoctrinate their children to "one of the seminal achievements of humankind" (131), literacy. The corollary to his argument was that those Mexican Mormons who later joined the anti-imperialist schismatic movement called the Third Convention (Gómez Páez 2004) were too lazy to put in the work required to de-Indianize themselves. In conclusion, Tullis vilified those who appropriated Lamanite cursedness, flipped its script, and began their own brazen order of Lamanite holiness separate from the Anglo church. However, what

Tullis saw as apostasy, Mexican Lamanite Margarito Bautista and his recent biographer Elisa Pulido (2020) saw as a restauration of the Lamanite holiness from whence the LDS church itself had apostatized. Reminiscent of Simón's publishing struggles, one of the Salt Lake City church's main acts of apostasy according to Bautista was its 1935 refusal to publish his history of Mormonism in pre-Hispanic Mexico, which promoted "an indigenous re-centering of the world" (3). In order to bring that world to fruition, Bautista built the New Jerusalem in Ozumba, Mexico, without authorization from the Utah church. The resulting Lamanite religion, the Kingdom of God in Its Fullness (Murphy 1997), remains a thriving Mexican Mormon commune to this day.

Holy Disavowals

Given the past and contemporary states of Mormon history publishing, Simón's struggle became clear. His problem was not his insufficiently validated stories. His problem was his nonwhiteness. The mere fact that he wanted to include such stories indicated to the official church's press that he did not embrace White epistemologies enough to be trusted. The height of irony was that, in *The Book of Mormon*, the ancient Nephite's church press neglected to include "Samuel the Lamanite's" prophecies for precisely the same reason: his nonwhiteness (Hernández 2021). Only after Christ Himself chastised them for their racism did they go back into their records and restore Samuel's story. However, another of Simón's specific epistemological disobediences was perhaps more serious than his nonwhiteness: he gave importance to miracles that tied *The Book of Mormon* to Peru. In so doing, Simón gave too much holiness to locality. Whiteness thought of itself as global. Peru, on the other hand, was local. Stories validating the holiness of the Andes were too dangerously local and unstable to promote the kind of spirituality necessary for holiness to remain synonymous with whiteness. Therefore, they were not published.

I continued my line of questioning with Simón because he kept giving me hints that, since he could not publish these stories, I should.

JASON: When I served in Bolivia as a missionary, *many* people told me about how President Kimball said that Tiwanaku was a *Book of Mormon* temple. They said that he translated the runes on the Gate of the Sun.

SIMON: The local people have it.

I have been in the Gate of the Sun. In fact, it was all ready to go in the Bolivia book, but when we presented it to them, they told me, "It all looks good, but this bit about the translation from President Kimball, take that out" [laughs].

Well, the truth is that there exist many, *many* declarations from prophets, from apostles . . . nevertheless, we need to provide more, to continue the work of investigation. . . .

In Cusco there is an amazing temple: Coricancha. When I was an Area Seventy . . . part of my assignment was to travel with members of the Twelve who would come to Cusco because every time they go to Peru, they always want to visit Cusco, right?

In the temple of Coricancha they have the sun room, the moon room, and the stars room.

Well, each apostle whom I have accompanied there, I can testify for myself that they said, "These are—these three rooms are—and it could be the temple of Nephi that *The Book of Mormon* speaks of."

I have heard those opinions, those feelings from them.

Elder Nelson said, "We are in a sacred place."

And Elder Scott was very explicit about Coricancha being the selfsame [mismísimo] temple of Nephi.

This is all to say that the brethren have always expressed themselves very clearly in those moments because they felt something very special.

That same Elder Nelson who walked through the three rooms in Coricancha—rooms that astronomically aligned directly with the three rooms in contemporary Mormon temples representing the three degrees of heaven—became the Prophet not three weeks after my interview with Simón. President Nelson now had full authority to deem Coricancha holy or to at least allow Simón to publish the Twelve's "feelings" about it. Yet, during my study, he did neither. I imagined Simón's cognitive dissonance. He knew that though President Nelson knew that Coricancha was a *Book of Mormon* holy site, the Prophet deliberately hid that knowledge from the global membership just as he continued to hide President Kimball's declaration about Tiwanaku (Caspary Moreno 2021). Not only did the Prophet refuse to validate places in Peru with his official stamp of holiness, but he increasingly refused to even mention the Lamanite identity that made holy both those places and that stamp.

This evolution away from historic *Book of Mormon* places and contemporary *Book of Mormon* people is evident in the recorded dedicatory prayers of modern Latin American temples, of which there were thirty-nine by 2021. The dedication of each temple was the moment when it became officially holy, the moment when unholy people could no longer enter. What was said in the dedicatory prayer, therefore, became a metric of what counted as site-specific holiness at that time. To foreground the divorce of Lamanite identity from official holiness to which I referred in my final question to Simón below, I will now contrast the two dedicatory prayers that official church leaders had uttered in Peru by the time of the interview.

In the 1986 dedication of Peru's first temple (Lima)—South America's third—soon-to-be Prophet—Gordon Hinckley declared, in English: "We are particularly mindful this day of the sons and daughters of Lehi. . . . They have walked in darkness and in servitude. Now . . . the shackles of darkness are falling from their eyes as they embrace the truths of Thy great work. Surely, Father Lehi has wept with sorrow over his posterity. Surely, he weeps today with gladness" (1986, para. 4).

That prayer explicitly connected contemporary Peruvians to Father Lehi, and, by implication, to his son Laman. It also indirectly reminded Peruvian Mormons well versed in *The Book of Mormon* that Lehi was light-pigmented and that though Laman had fallen from whiteness, his descendants, the Lamanites—which most Peruvians Mormons understood to be themselves— could be restored through the Lima temple to Lehi's original level of whiteness. Hinkley performed that subtle reminder through his phrase "shackles of darkness are falling from their eyes," which is almost a direct quotation of a *Book of Mormon* prophecy about the Lamanites in the last days: "Their scales of darkness shall begin to fall from their eyes; and many generations shall not pass away among them, save they shall be a white and a delightsome people" (J. Smith 1830, 117). In his dedicatory prayer, Hinkley was basically saying that having an Anglo-built and controlled temple in Peru was bringing Peruvians one step closer to becoming White like himself and like their ancestor Lehi.

Understandably, a church that was thriving in the Global South during the 2010s would want to distance itself from such racist connections. It would, therefore, be tempted to cloak, if not entirely eschew, further talk of Lamanites in its 2015 dedication of Peru's second Mormon temple, Trujillo: "We pray for all in this land . . . Hasten the miracle of conversion among these great and good people. We thank Thee for the sacred record of Lehi, Nephi and Jacob, Alma and Mosiah, Benjamin, and Mormon, and of Moroni" (Uchtdorf 2015, para. 3).

This last prayer mentioned all the ingredients for Lamanite identity—a distinct people, a distinct land, and the Prophet Lehi—but it did not make an explicit connection between them. This ingenious tactic allowed the listeners to make their own connections. However, the speaker seemed to make a last-minute change to obscure the kin connection between his listeners and Lehi even more. Perhaps fearing that mentioning only Lehi would lead too obviously to Laman, he followed up that namedrop with a stumbling litany of seven other ancient *Book of Mormon* prophets and four repetitions of the word "and." That was one of the signs of embarrassment about which I was thinking when I asked Simón the final question:

JASON: Do you think that there is now less emphasis placed on the descendants of the Lamanites? I don't know if it is embarrassment—

SIMON:—Yes, what is happening is that the term, "Lamanite" in the last ten years *could* be seen as a pejorative term. Some members feel very identified, like me, that we have Lamanite blood, but others interpret it as "Indigenous," as a form of discrimination. So maybe that is why the Twelve are being a bit prudent in not mentioning "Lamanite" anymore.

Whether motivated by embarrassment or prudence, the Anglo church repudiated the importance that it traditionally assigned to the stories that Simón co-owned and coauthored as a proud Lamanite. Church leaders' changed stance toward Lamanite identity from one of paternalistic pride to one of shame coincided with an evolution in their official conceptualization of kinship. Their stance toward Lamanites showed them moving ever closer to alignment with essentialist US kin logics wherein what was felt as real kinship was whatever geneticists decided it to be. In fact, one of the most prominent US "fathers" of genetic genealogy was Anglo Mormon and Utah billionaire James LeVoy Sorenson (Tallbear 2013). For many Saints, DNA became holier than the words of Anglo prophets in tracing Lamanite "blood."

Therefore, after DNA evidence came out in 2002 that there were no Israelite genes among isolated Amerindian groups (Murphy 2003), the official church, having legal ownership of *The Book of Mormon*, changed its actual text. In 1981, the introduction to the book had read, "After thousands of years, all were destroyed except the Lamanites, and they are the principal ancestors of the American Indians" (qtd. in Fletcher Stack 2007). This was already a slightly watered-down version of Simón's theory, which was not that Lamanites were merely "the principal ancestors" to the Amerindians, but that they were the sole ancestors. However, in 2007, in direct reaction to mounting DNA evidence, that line was qualified even more to read, "they are *among* the ancestors of the American Indians" (J. Smith [1830] 2013a, vii, emphasis mine). The single word "among" seemed insignificant. In fact, most of my Peruvian Mormon study participants did not know about its addition to their holy text. Nevertheless, the word "among" diluted their descent from Israel and demonstrated the official church's capitulation to a US-centric notion of essentialist relatedness that had outsourced its kinship system to geneticists. Moreover, the addition of the word "among" demonstrated that authority over history's holiness could be weaponized to disrupt identity. Since Simón did not have authority, he became partially alienated from the power over his own identity. The pain of this alienation increased in intensity as he realized its true impetus: the White supremacy encased in his own religion's category of holiness.

Lamanite stories imbued places in Peru with sacred power. However, sacred place was risky for the church's Anglo leaders, not only because some modernist Christianities taught that the sacred had transcended the fallen Earth (Cannell 2006) and all of its rock sundials and fonts, but because when the sacred embedded into place, it grew beyond the holy church's control. For that reason, Lamanites like Simón were dangerous.

Sacred Slippages

The defensive tactics of those who feared Simón are exposed within pioneer indigeneity's holy-versus-sacred dialectic. To elucidate that dialectic further, I turn to the holy-atop-sacred palimpsest that was Arequipa and the surrounding Andes. Hiking in the 14,000-feet-above-sea-level hills around Arequipa, I would often come across rock piles called "apachetas" in Runasimi. These sometimes housed the ancestors of the pre-Christian age. Other times, they morphed into Catholic saint shrines like the ones at which my Peruvian Catholic friends prayed during our pilgrimage to the Virgin of Chapi, Arequipa's principal protector. At the beginning of our hike through the desert, one of them placed a stone into her purse. This was to represent her sins, which, miles later, she deposited at a giant, thirty-foot-high apacheta [mound of stones]. That apacheta was sacred and unofficial. However, the Catholic church nearby, which commemorated the site of an apparition of the Virgin Mary, was holy.

Some specific saint shrines in the Andes were both sacred (belonging to the pre-Christian ancestors of the inner world) and holy (belonging to the upper world of the Christian God). These saint shrines were called miracles, and each had a specific function such as potato fertility or llama protection. "Saints as miracles are intensely localized, identified not just with the place, but with the very soil and landscape . . . part of the efficacy of the miracle derives from stuff picked up off the ground—earth, stones, sheep droppings—which are talismans of whatever it is people desire. They take these objects home with them and make offerings to them" (O. Harris 2006, 57).

Stone was sacred in this cosmology because stone was from whence an "intensely localized" risky power that could be for both good and evil emanated. This bipolarity of the sacred was why Ofelia did not want me to read sacredness into her stone-collecting at the holy temple construction site mentioned in chapter 3. There was danger in it, which was how, as many of my Mormon study participants said, something could be too sacred. Tellingly, I never heard Mormons say that something was too holy.

Directly under many Andean saint statues, such as the Virgin of the Undermining in Oruro, Bolivia, there were deep tunnels dug into the mountain where people could make coca leaf offerings to strikingly different statues. These statues were faithful to pre-Hispanic archetypes of holy iconography, but they appeared to contemporary Christians—aesthetically influenced as they had been by centuries of deliberate demonological degradations of Indigenous holy imagery (De Mello e Souza and Robinson 1997)—to be devils. This demotion of the holy to the sacred and concomitant relegation of the sacred to the satanic was an extreme example of what holy colonial orders strove to do when the "intensely localized" nature of Indigenous places threatened their authority.

Jesus was resurrected, exited His dark, situated tomb, transcended the fallen city of Jerusalem, and ascended into the exalted, holy heavens. As He rose from sacred to holy, He rose from local to global. As Jesus's role in this nexus of Christian spacetime emblematized, the holy transcended locality in Christianity. If it had not done so, it might have remained sacred. And if it had remained sacred, it might have become diabolical.

I witnessed "local" humans, for whom their locality's significance exceeded the sacred-versus-holy binary entirely, slip into the official church's category of diabolical through that same logic. This slippage happened a little too easily and a little too often during my study for me to ignore the possibility that the holy church conflated sacred materiality with spiritual danger for precisely that purpose: to demonize indigeneity.

Wild Tongues

Joseph Smith was a man with his own connection to sacred stone. He used seer stones, some of which may have been pilfered Seneca grave goods (Murphy 2018), to translate a pre-Hispanic, Native text into English. Doing so might have given him a unique understanding of the connection that local, Indigenous kinways—and tongues—had to sited sacredness and holiness in upstate New York as well as a unique understanding of the danger that connection represented to his growing authority.

However, the contemporary church's portrayal of Joseph Smith's efforts to tamp down the effervescent sacred in his fledgling settler colonist religion strategically eliminated the connection to indigeneity altogether. The committee that wrote *Saints* claimed that "some of the Saints in Kirtland took their beliefs to wild extremes, reveling in what they took to be gifts of the Spirit [such as speaking in tongues]. . . . Others believed the Holy Ghost made them slide or scoot across the ground" (Church 2018, 112). What the committee failed to mention was that the scooting was to pantomime sailing across the river into Indian Territory to preach to the Lamanites and that the glossolalia was supposed to be speaking in Indigenous languages. As historian Max Perry Mueller (2017) clarified, "Smith used this outburst of religious fervor to differentiate between true religious experience and dangerous enthusiasm. In May 1831, Smith revealed that white converts were not expected to act more like Indians. Instead, in the restored church, the Indians were expected to act more like white Saints" (75).

Smith chastised his early flock of Anglo Saints for mistaking the sudden, rapturous ability to speak Potawatomi as a gift from the Holy Ghost. Thus, those Anglo Saints began to believe that speaking in tongues was excessive, chaotic, and too sacred. The church that Smith wanted to restore was Christ's church, and that was to be a church of holy order. Therefore, some Anglo

Saints were shocked when, one day at Smith's dinner table, a new member of their nascent organization named Brigham Young prayed in tongues. Their shock increased when, instead of chastising him, Smith praised him. According to the *Saints* writing committee, Smith praised him because "what Brigham did was different" (Church 2018, 163). He did not speak in the Indigenous tongue of what *The Book of Mormon* considered a fallen race of humanity. For Smith, Brigham's glossolalia was edifying, not degrading, and if something edified it was of God. "Edifying to whom?" was not a valid question because if something was edifying to a powerful light-pigmented person, it became holiness for everyone. That evening, Brigham Young prayed in the language that Adam spoke in the garden of Eden. It was the original, generic human language that connected all humanity precisely because it was not specific to an uncontrollably sacred site or to a specific Indigenous people who had an ungodly attachment to place and "a language that corresponded to a way of life" (Anzaldúa [1987] 2012, 77).

Therefore, from its earliest days, the official church carefully built a version of indigeneity against which it defined holiness. That holiness, the source of its power, would diminish if Indigenous "sacred" places were allowed to become central axes in the Holy Land of Zion.

As philosopher Gloria Anzaldúa ([1987] 2012) lamented, "*de-tongued. We are those of deficient Spanish. We* are your linguistic nightmare, your linguistic aberration, your linguistic *racial mixing*, the subject of your *mocking*. Because we speak with tongues of fire, we are culturally crucified. Racially, culturally, and linguistically *we are orphans*—we speak an orphan tongue" (80, translation mine). Far from speaking the tongue of Adam, Lamanites in my study spoke some of the most stigmatized tongues in the history of the United States. The presence in Utah of people who identified as Lamanites and who openly spoke an untamed, "wild tongue" (75)—such as variants of Spanish mixed with English, Runasimi, Nahuatl, Kichua, and K'iche—was, for many Anglo Mormons, an uncomfortable reminder of Indigenous existence, which "contradict[ed] the myth of settler society. The continued presence of Native people signifie[d] the incompleteness of the settler project" (Red Nation, 2021, 52) in Utah.

Indigenous presence was also an uncomfortable reminder of holy connections to specific places for my Anglo Mormon study participants. Their discomfort stemmed from whiteness's need to maintain the illusion of placelessness. "One aspect of whiteness . . . is its ability to seem perspectiveless or transparent. Whites do not see themselves as having a race but as being, simply, people. They do not believe that they think and reason from a white viewpoint but from a universally valid one—'the truth'—what everybody knows" (Delgado and Stefancic 2017, 91–92).

For the official church, Latin Americans were too embarrassingly placeable and sacred to be fully part of the body of the Saints during my study because the imaginary for that body was White and, as such, placeless and holy. It was the body of Christ, which was a pale skinned, blue-eyed, hypermasculine body. However, the church's Anglo leaders symbolically concealed Jesus's skin tone. They sought to eliminate it from the rods and cones of their parishioners through the magic of whiteness in a process that Fanon ([1952] 1994) called epidermalization. Per political scientist Kwame Ture (1990), White supremacy took epidermalization "to such ludicrous heights that it paint[ed] Jesus Christ white even though he never put his foot in Europe" (min. 41:40). White Jesus could have as anachronistic a phenotype as possible for the son of a Middle Easterner with ties to Africa, and it would remain unremarkable because White Jesus was imagined as placeless, and, as such, raceless. He, like the holy along with Him, transcended both place and race. He was just the generic Jesus, not the White Jesus. Everyone could relate to Him.

The deeply unquestioned naturalization of Jesus as an Anglo man struck me as I spent time in the homes of Barrio Periféricos members wherein I was the only Anglo man. As I was getting ready to conclude my time in Arequipa, I visited Darjart, the man who was called to replace me as the Super Quorum president. I needed to give him the quorum member roster that Ofelia had helped me color code into groups: active, inactive (ML), and extremely inactive. He was an artist. He showed me a painting that he had recently completed of some children in our ward sitting at the feet of Jesus (see figure 5). He told me that he used Elder Horsthauser as the model for Jesus. I asked him why he had chosen a cleanshaven, eighteen-year-old, Anglo male missionary as his model for a bearded, thirty-year-old, Middle Eastern carpenter. He looked confused. It was as if the sheer audacity of my question were denaturalizing the whiteness of Jesus in his mind. I did not record our conversation, but I jotted down the basic thrust of his reply:

> I guess I never thought about it. I mean, I could have used my neighbor who actually has a really nice Jesus beard. But he's also extremely dark and has the most classic Inca face you've ever seen. But yeah, I guess—Why couldn't Jesus look like an Inca? Right? I mean, if he can look like an Anglo-Saxon, he can look like anyone.
>
> But, if I painted Jesus in any way other than as a gringo, his race would become the focus of the painting, and I want the focus to be on the children. If I gave him an Inca face, it would become divisive and political here in Peru. It just wouldn't go over well—especially at church.

Indeed, evangelical Christians considered a particular Black Jesus spreading through US-based social media at the time as precisely that: a reverse-racist

FIGURE 5. The man who became the Super Quorum president after I left Arequipa painted this portrait of two young arequipeño Mormons. The model that he used for White Jesus was a male Anglo missionary from Utah. July 2018. Art credit: Darjart (pseudonym).

political statement. Christians of many races on those social media threads seemed to feel that Black Jesus grounded Jesus to Africa and, as such, "to what wa[s] merely 'local'" (Ferguson and Gupta 2002, 987). Their discourse implied that the proper Jesus needed to be White because His whiteness was what made Him globally relevant.

What about a Lamanite Jesus, or, for that matter, a Lamanite Saint? The sheer presence in Utah of Lamanites who dared call themselves Saints disrupted the illusion created by whiteness that everyone was the same. It disrupted the illusion that all lives mattered to official church leaders (Shange 2019b). In fact, as Anglo member of the Twelve Jeffrey Holland told a group of Native people (including many Navajo Nation citizens) in 1997, the increasing Lamanite presence in Utah demanded that Saints no longer "emphasize racial, or cultural distinctions, including Lamanite or tribal distinctions, in the Church. We are moving to that millennial day where we are all Latter-day Saints and there are no more -ites among us" (*Church News* 1997, para. 4).

In that statement, Holland's settler hubris prescribed a better form of indigeneity than that practiced by actual Indigenous Mormons. They did not get to be Indigenous in their own ways, but only in the ways that he permitted. Laman-ites had to de-"ite" and detribalize if they were to follow the desires of the Leaders. They had to conform to what political scientist Silvia Rivera Cusicanqui (2007) called "the authorized Indian" (4, translation mine). In the context of Peru's gastronomic boom led by criollo chef Gastón Acurio, the authorized Indian referred to the type who was "expected (and 'trained') to be clean and docile, and to reflect Peruvian . . . diversity—Acurio's beautiful fusion—in appropriate ways" (M. E. García 2021,102).

Among my Anglo Mormon study participants, tokenizing diverse skin tones and fetishizing diverse foodstuffs was appropriate. Among all Mormons, according to Holland, holding on to diverse identities, such as those that ended with -ite, was inappropriate. As it was in Acurio's vision for Peru, so it was in Holland's vision for the global church. All had to unite under one "whole" (holy) identity, an identity dictated by whiteness (holiness). Holland's presumptuous vision was nearly identical to Acurio's in both its whiteness and its masculinity. It exemplified how the construction of what constituted an ideal LDS indigeneity had always been managed ultimately by settlers just as "the construction of what constitute[d] an ideal LDS femininity ha[d] always been managed ultimately by men" (Hoyt 2020, 55).

As a case in point, I provide below a digitally recorded conversation that I had in August 2017, in English, with a young, male, Peruvian American BYU student about the former name of his dance troupe, Lamanite Generation.

JASON: Why do you think they changed the name?
JORGE: So, the reason I was told was 'cause when President Hinkley came out and said, "there's no -ites among us," that talk, it was kind of one of those things.

  We're just like, "Okay. Well, there's no -ites among us so we can't say we're Lamanite Generation."

  You know, like, this is a group——it's a group for everyone to enjoy, not just the Lamanites or the Lamanite People.

  For everyone.

  So, yeah. They ended up calling it "Living Legends."

The dance troupe comprised Pacific Islander, Native, and Latinx youth who traced their ancestries back to Laman and depicted them through drums and bodily movement to audiences all over the world. It changed its name from Lamanite Generation to Living Legends in 1991 (Spotted Elk 2019). "This situation is often a result of a direct effort to assimilate Latino adults and youth away from their [Spanish-speaking] congregations and toward a 'colorblind, fully equal' future with little diversity and no messiness" (I. M. García 2020, 740). During my study, I witnessed Living Legends diminish diversity even as it deployed multiculturalism in a way that "easily [became] another colonial tool for managing non-White bodies and spaces" (G. E. García 2021, 97). Within Living Legends, "folkloric belonging [could] be celebrated, as long as subjects [knew] their place in the colonial-capitalist order" (98). The troupe's name change was a microcosm of the categorical tension within holiness reflected in battles over Mormon history ownership and holy site designation because in the eyes of central church leaders, Jorge was no longer a proud purveyor of his own Lamanite history. He was simply a disembodied crystallization of generic legend. And, as White Jesus taught, "generic" was racial code for "White."

Peruvian Mormons' place-based stories were extracted, homogenized, and danced into a legend that mostly benefited whiteness by seeming to represent everyone. Living Legends' dancers were "called on to perform an authentic difference in exchange for the good feelings of the nation" (Povinelli 2002, 6). Living Legends thus represented "the familiar false universalism of liberal humanism . . . that . . . enable[d] multiple exclusions, erasures, and forms of violence" (M. E. García 2021, 96). Behind its façade of universal representation and greater inclusiveness, the name change relegated ever-shifting, contemporary indigeneities into a static, legendary past of sacredness where they needed to remain if Anglo Utah was to keep united—as if it were a single category—its centrality, its whiteness, and its holiness.

Though the Twelve could euphemize the disposal of Lamanites and otherites by calling it a unifying effort, it was simply a classic colonial tactic: peripheralizing one group to make another holy. No sooner had Peruvian Mormons recovered the true story of their forefathers than their church's leaders tried to take it away. Pasi, Moisés, Basilio, Jacoba, Arcadio, Simón, and Jorge were stakeholders in *The Book of Mormon*, the story that helped create Utah. However, when they went there hoping to heal the spatiotemporal distance from their history and its holy places, they found their identity either mocked as an antimodern false consciousness or feared as an unholy manifestation of Indigenous sacredness.

Lamanite Threat

The White supremacy that proclaimed US sites holier than Peruvian sites created in some of my Peruvian study participants an unarticulatable sadness. Part of that sadness radiated from the same colonial hypocrisy that Pasi felt at the dark dance, the Nephite immunity that warped the nucleus of all of Anglo Mormonism's categories. Another part radiated from alienation, the opposite of wholeness.

According to Fanon, Black Martinicans subconsciously felt a draw to migrate to their colonial metropole of France in order to heal a similar sort of alienation. They wanted to reunite with the Martinican wealth that flowed to France as a way of healing their relatedness to the place from whence that wealth was stolen. They wanted to restore wholeness with the stolen fruit of their labor. Anthropologists of pilgrimage understood similar migratory quests for wholeness as quests for holiness (Dubisch 2005), which was why Fanon ([1952] 1994) used the religious word "Tabernacle" (19, capitalized in the original) to describe what he thought Paris represented for Black Martinicans.

A thirst for holiness also explained why the historic Mormon Tabernacle in Salt Lake City's Temple Square was often the first stop for Peruvian Mormons immigrating to Utah during my study. Many even synchronized their migrations to coincide with the church's General Conference, convened near Temple Square, where they could hear in person what they grew up hearing only through satellite broadcast—the Mormon Tabernacle Choir.

Aaron was a case in point. He was a Mormon from Arequipa who had sporadic, informal employment in Utah. He acquired a ten-year tourist visa to the United States, which—unlike most Peruvians in my study—he was (at first) careful to not overstay. Technically this meant that he had to make sure that he left the United States every six months. In practice, however—especially during the Trump administration—it meant that he had to leave every few weeks so as to make his travel behavior seem "touristy." Like the profiling to which Peruvian migrants to South Korea had to submit (Vogel 2020), any US customs airport official had the authority to invalidate his visa if his sequence of passport stamps did not seem touristy enough or if his persona simply did not gibe with the official's fickle archetype of "tourist." As Aaron explained to me in an interview in Utah in August 2017, his visa was almost not enough for his second entry into the United States.

> When President Donald Trump got in, everyone was talking about how they weren't going to let people into [the United States]. Well, I wanted to go to the General Conference again, so I went to talk to the Arequipa mission president. I told him that I wanted to go, but I was afraid because customs gave me problems the previous time.
>
> This time, I was not going to take any chances: I was going to bring General Conference tickets, plus I was going to renew my temple-recommend.
>
> The [Anglo] mission president called his stake president in Salt Lake, and he sent him two tickets through WhatsApp. I printed them in Arequipa.
>
> I got off the plane and arrived in Los Angeles on the 24th of March, and the official tells me, "And you? What is your purpose for coming?"
>
> And I tell him, "I come for the General Conference of the Church of Jesus Christ of Latter-day Saints."

"Ah, you are Mormon?"

"Yes."

"Eh, your temple-recommend?" He asked me for it, and I had it in my wallet, right?

"Here it is." *Bam.*

He looked at it and everything and said, "What day is the conference?" And I said, "it is the 4th and 5th of April."

"And your invitation?"

"Here it is." *Bam.*

He looked at it, and he told me, "Okay, looks good, welcome to the United States." *Bam!* "Your stamp."

And I entered. And they didn't give me many problems or anything. . . . So that is what I value because I felt as if the Lord were telling me through His spirit that I should renew my temple-recommend and that I should take conference tickets with me.

Instead of giving him problems, the official gatekeeper of US border sovereignty let Aaron enter. Anthropologist Ulla Berg (2015) studied the phenomenon that had previously given Aaron problems: embassy and customs officials did not see Andean bodies as being cosmopolitan enough to make sense as travelers or to "successfully pass as tourists" (Vogel 2020, 37). She demonstrated that when "Andean" did not compute in a White person's mind as "tourist," it was because colonial regimes of power were at play, the same regimes that did not translate Simón's stories as histories or Peru's sacred spaces as holy places. Aaron's body was too Indigenous and, therefore, suspect in an area such as an airport, which was the epitome of placelessness. Berg explored the lengths that Peruvians took to change their bodies and textual backgrounds to look placeless. The only way to look truly placeless in the United States, however, was to look White, and since Aaron did not look White, he had to find another way to tie himself to whiteness. The visa was scarcely enough, but his tickets to the Mormon Tabernacle Choir—a choir that helped solidify the United States as the global center of White religiosity on the world's stage (Mueller 2017, 228)—had an explosively magical effect: "*Bam!*"

That both Aaron and his customs official would have tacitly understood the symbolic power of the Tabernacle only made sense in a context wherein whiteness had almost completely merged with holiness. Mormon Zion was that context and, though it was Indigenous, it was also colonial. Mormonism's coloniality explained why every one of Zion's categories in my study—including leaders, government, legacy, and holiness—became a "concrete instrument of action upon the Other" (Todorov 1984, 123) rather than a medium of exchange among fellow citizens. As a result of that violence, a symbolic relationship existed in the Zions of my field sites between traveling to the metropole in order to become whole (holy) and traveling in order to become White. Fanon ([1952] 1994) stated, "For the black man there is only one destiny. And it is white" (10). He claimed that for Black Martinicans, the center of oppression—Paris—was also the center of holiness, the Tabernacle.

Where was the destined center for Peruvian Mormon migrants who had been inculcated within national whitening projects (Roberts 2013), prophecies of literal skin color lightening (Kimball 1960), and the Utah-centric story of the church (Decoo 2013)? Many Peruvian Mormons made Peru the center. The Leaders, largely Anglo males, erroneously perceived the centering of Peru as a decentering of Utah. They felt threatened. That imagined threat was quantifiably amplified by their carefully curated church statistics which showed that Spanish-speaking wards in Utah had become "the main source of growth in the US church" (Romanello 2021, 3). The threat was simultaneously visually amplified by the corporal specter of White extinction reflected in the transgressive invasion of "peripheral" bodies into Anglo Mormonism's historic "core." Anglos' mimetic revulsion toward the Lamanites' melding of holiness's previously polarized categorical binaries—core-versus-periphery—may have simply been another instantiation of "the Latino threat" narrative (Chavez 2013, title) that affected the racialization of Latin American bodies in the greater United States regardless of Mormonism. However, as the Peruvians in this chapter demonstrated, narrative itself, through tele-territoriality and trans-temporality, held immense generative power over sited holiness. That power deepened the Lamanite threat narrative, making it even more paradoxical than the Latino one. Story reached in and rewired ancestries through multitemporalities that undermined sacred space and embedded in holy place. Peruvian Mormons created sacred holiness regardless of whiteness, and that stirred a defensiveness within the order that—because it was holy—was more complex than mere xenophobia.

Despite ecclesiastical edicts debunking Lamanite solidarity in the name of global unity, Peruvian Mormon history developed a powerfully unique, sited, holy sainthood—pioneer indigeneity—against which the Utah-centric church needed to fortify. After all, the Lamanites (a remnant of Jacob) were the chosen people of the Lord. The Lord Himself promised that if White people (Gentiles) did not repent, "my people who are a remnant of Jacob shall be among the Gentiles, yea, in the midst of them as a . . . young lion among the flocks of sheep, who, if he go through, both treadeth down and teareth in pieces, and none can deliver" (J. Smith 1830, 500).

As He did in *Book of Mormon* times, the Lord threatened in that scripture to use Lamanites in modern times as His chosen people. Ethnographer Stanley Thayne's (2019) study participant, an elderly Catawba Mormon woman, interpreted that scripture as meaning that "He is going to call us all together, and we're going to take our land back" (324). In the settler interpretation, however, "chosen" did not imply that God chose Indigenous Mormons to rule the New Jerusalem; rather, it implied that He chose them as a foil to create the necessity for rule. He chose Lamanites as a tool to violently awaken complacent White people to their destiny as the "governing prior": the rightful leaders and caretakers of both the Holy Land and the public land, and the only ones meant to be full citizens of Zion with the power to deem cities holy.

As Peruvian Mormons simultaneously contested and perpetuated that White destiny—vital to whiteness's grip on holiness—they contended with more of Zion's categories: (5) future, (6) marriage, and (7) independence. Those revolved around the nucleus of forever familia.

PART II

Forever Familia

CHAPTER 5

Future

[A] sensibility of living in the future
tense . . . posits fulfillment always in the
future, almost but not yet within reach.
—Samuli Schielke, *Egypt in the Future
Tense* (2015, 125)

Outside of Forever

Like the future, the Mormon city of Zion always lay just beyond the present horizon during my study. This was especially true of the Peruvian Mormon Zion, an entity that did not yet unambiguously count in Anglo Mormonism as having leaders, government, legacy, or holiness. Since many Peruvian Mormons found those categories too difficult to refit to their diverse dimensions, they saved their energy for a categorical retooling more central to their daily lives. This involved a refurbishing that became increasingly intense as their central church leaders eliminated peripheral concerns—such as pageants, archaeology, and Israelite tribal distinctions—in order to double down on a single concept that its publishing department popularized as "forever family."

Forever family sounded positive, but many of my Peruvian and Anglo study participants framed it in the negative: individual humans could not form parts of whole families in the next world without the rites that could not be performed outside of holy temples in this world. Refracted through forever family discourse, the conflation of whiteness, holiness, and wholeness discussed in chapter 4 reached its zenith in the temple. Without Mormon temples—all of which were saturated with white-pigmented symbology—there could be no familial wholeness, holiness, or whiteness. As an Anglo member of the Twelve stated in a General Conference in 1996,

> I wish to speak to all those who would like to know about eternal families and about families being forever. . . . While our individual salvation is based on our individual obedience, . . . we are each an important and integral part of a family, and the highest blessings can be received only within an eternal

family. When families are functioning as designed by God, the relationships found therein are the most valued of mortality. . . . If we return home alone to our Heavenly Father, we will be asked, "Where is the rest of the family?" (Hales 1996, para. 1,19)

Having to face Heavenly Father's deficit-based question made the future world a scary proposition for the members of Barrio Periféricos in Arequipa, most of whom did not find themselves "within an eternal family . . . as designed by God." To meet the definition of forever family, one requirement was that Mormons with children be ritually linked to an unbroken vertical chain of heteronormative, temple-sealed, conjugal relationships including their own and that of their parents. Unmarried parents could not be eternally bound to their own children. That rule alone bared from forever family status upwards of 70 percent of Barrio Periféricos' familias, many of which were forged through generations of unmarried motherhood. Therefore, most Barrio Periféricos members hoped that the new temple in their home city of Arequipa would get them closer to a Peruvian Mormon version of forever family status.

However, they were hesitant to shoot for the Anglo Mormon version of that dyadic term, "forever family," because they felt that the category of relatedness for the "family" half of its dyad was not translatable and, as such, too far out of reach. I honor that sentiment by keeping "familia" in Spanish. In other words, compared with the "family" half, participants felt that they had a better chance of fulfilling the requirements of the "forever" half. The problem was that the requirements of "forever" involved deep categories subsumed under the core cultural category of time. One of those deep categories was "future." For their familias to even begin to count in a future temporality called "forever," the Peruvian Mormons in my study had to reconfigure the Anglo Mormon category of "future" itself. This chapter focuses on Peruvian Mormons and non-Mormons as they theorized with future and reworked it.

Peruvians were not always aware of how they were actively recategorizing future so as to claim belonging in both Zion and, as I describe in my discussion of tourist visas below, the United States. However, the recategorization of future rose to the level of awareness in moments of categorical collision, such as when Peruvian future clashed with Anglo future. In those moments, Peruvian Mormons realized that only by temporally fitting themselves into the distant category of future could they rewire it with familia into the right relations of a new Peruvian Mormon category. I call that possible category "forever familia."

The Lamanite Future

I noticed a pervasive attitude among Zion builders in Peru and Utah, both Anglo and Peruvian. This attitude held that, where Lamanites were concerned,

Zion could only come to fruition in the next generation. In Arequipa in 2018, I told Bishop Paucar of my visit to a ward in Cusco a few years prior. After Sacrament Meeting, that ward's bishop announced an informational meeting for those who wanted to serve missions as retired married couples. That bishop encouraged members to attend the meeting by saying, "If all of our kids are eighteen or above, we should go on missions with our spouses. Most couple-missionaries are from North America, but we Latinos can go as well, especially from Cusco."

I asked Bishop Paucar what he thought of that. In his answer, he sounded resigned to what he considered the sad reality that such a thing was only wishful thinking in Peru. He harbored no illusions that he and his spouse would one day be able to be like Anglo Mormons and just up and leave their kids, cousins, nephews, elderly parents, and future grandkids, all of whom would be living in increasing, not decreasing, interdependence with them when their youngest reached eighteen. Meanwhile, as Bishop Paucar was telling me this, bishops of Anglo Mormon congregations in Utah were probably busy announcing recreational activities specially designed for empty nesters (AL). Many empty nesters in Utah were older couples who had already served multiple couples missions and whose children and grandchildren had moved away to form their own, distantly dwelling nuclear families. Empty nester activities were not necessary in Barrio Periféricos because most nests were overflowing. Bishop Paucar knew that this situation had to change in order for Peruvian familias to fully fit the Anglo Mormon category of forever family necessary for full citizenship in Zion. He also knew that such a revolution of kinship—a shift from pacha interdependence to nuclear family independence—would not be achievable in his generation.

Yet, he had high hopes for his kids. Born into an *almost* forever family, they would surely become the generation that would do fully forever family things like serve one mission as youth and another as older couples. According to Bishop Paucar, his generation and its backward kinways that fostered too much dependency would have to be eliminated before concepts like retirement, empty nesters, couples missions, and other indicators of a mature Zion could coalesce in Peru among Lamanites like him.

The Prophet Spencer Kimball prophesied that the future day of such a maturation would be called "the day of the Lamanite" (Maxwell 1985, 6). In 1947, he designated it as a day that was still only "about to dawn" (6) despite the Prophet Brigham Young's imposition, one century earlier, of Utah's Zion upon those whom he considered Lamanites (Hendrix-Komoto and Stuart 2020, 30). By 2017, another seventy years had passed, and the vast majority of Mormons with whom I spoke, Peruvian or otherwise, believed that "the day of the Lamanite"—when Lamanites would "blossom as the rose" (J. Smith et al. 1835, 192)—had still "almost, *but not quite*" (Bhabha 1984, 127) dawned.

For many, a sign of that dawn's impending arrival—and a sign that at least some Lamanite families had finally caught up to forever within the Anglo's category of future—would have been the calling of a Latino to the Twelve, a quorum that had consisted of Anglo males since the church's founding.

Such was the topic of hallway conversation after a conference speech that I gave at a university in Utah in April 2016. I invited Leopoldo Tellez to come hear me speak. I had met Leopoldo during a presentation that he gave the day prior at historian Fernando Gómez Páez's nearby Museum of Mexican Mormon History. Katari, a young Bolivian Mormon whom I had never met before, was also in the audience. In my speech, I mentioned the persistent homogenization of the Twelve. The Twelve had three vacancies for much of the previous year, which generated significant speculation among Latinx Mormons as to whether a Latino would finally join its ranks. Instead, six months before my presentation, central church leaders—true to form—filled all three slots with Anglo Utahans.

After the conference, Katari was interested in talking to me about the predominance of Anglos in the Twelve. We chatted about how unfortunate it was that, of all the Latinos in the church, not one was called to be an apostle. His theory was that central church leaders were terrified that Latinos would take control, that a takeover was looming, and that Latin America would become their institution's center rather than its periphery. He said something to the effect of, "Why not move the headquarters to a more central place between North and South America, closer to the concentration of members, like Ecuador or something? It is obvious that the church is afraid to give up power. They have a history of never wanting to cede authority to new groups."

I wanted to enlighten Katari on the Mexican Third Convention, which I had only just learned about the day prior at Leopoldo's presentation, wherein Mexican Mormons seceded from the Utah church because of similar critiques. I was just about to encourage him to go find Leopoldo, who owned many of the Third Convention's materials, including their magazine, *Sendero Lamanita* (Lamanite Path), but I suddenly noticed that Leopoldo himself was standing behind us, overhearing our entire conversation. We turned to him, but instead of extolling the Mexican Mormon rebellion against Anglo Mormonism—of which his own parents formed part—Leopoldo stated his hypothesis that "we Latinos aren't ready for authority."

Katari was beside himself with indignation: "How can you say that out of four million Latinx Mormons, '*we*' aren't ready!?"

Leopoldo proceeded to outline his bona fides as a former mission president in Latin America, demonstrating his firsthand knowledge that Latin Americans were not ready to "speak before presidents and kings," his prerequisite for taking the reins of the church. Katari was horrified: "And what do you think we're all doing down there in Latin America, shearing llamas? There are hundreds of Latino Mormons who could speak before presidents and kings far better than the apostles that we have now."

Leopoldo countered, "Who, then? Tell me one Latino whom you think could be an apostle."

Katari: "You could, Leopoldo, with all that experience."

Later, Katari and I had dinner in the university's food court and talked for another two hours. He believed, or hoped, that Leopoldo's thought process stemmed from his being a "White Latino" who could pass as completely Anglo if he desired. Katari wanted to believe that opinions like Leopoldo's were only possible among light-pigmented Latin Americans. However, in my experience, Katari was the outlier, not Leopoldo. Leopoldo's sentiment reflected that of most of my Latin American Mormon interviewees regardless of skin pigmentation: "Whites will raise us up like children, and one day, we 'shall blossom as the rose.' But we're not ready yet."

That sentiment formulated the day of the Lamanite as a future day when Latin Americans would finally fit the Anglo Mormon category of forever family—rather than their own category of forever familia—to the extent that they would inhabit a Zion future. In historian Ignacio García's (2020) estimation, "Latino Saints, no doubt, will one day sit in the highest councils of the LDS Church . . . but only after much grafting and assimilating. . . . Their sense of 'righteousness' rests on their ability to look (or act) like their white counterparts" (732, 739). In the 1850s of President Young, in the 1950s of President Kimball, and in the 2020s of President Nelson, finally arriving at a blossomed future meant being sufficiently White. Understanding this, it was no surprise to me or Katari that when God finally did call the first Latino to the Twelve in 2018, he was a White, Brazilian, multinational corporate business administrator.

Indeed, whiteness had shrouded the day of the Lamanite since its first imaginings. Upon arriving to Utah in 1847, the Prophet Brigham Young attempted to hasten Lamanite fruition by destroying the bilateral Ute family and grafting its remnants into the patrilineal Mormon family (Bennion 2012). Through killing and assimilation, he replaced Indigenous fathers and husbands with Anglo fathers and husbands in the hope that the resulting next generation would no longer be Indigenous (Cannon 2018). In Young's view, Lamanites could only blossom by leaving their Indigenous category of relatedness behind. However, Young's forced shifting of Lamanite kinways to produce Lamanite blossoming did not pan out mostly because "the idea that one could become distanced from indigeneity by having a non-Indian father was completely invalid to most Indigenous Nations" (Marley 2018, para. 7). The descendants of many of those settler-fathered Indigenous children remained strongly identified Utes—albeit also strongly identified Mormons—well into the future (L. A. Harris 2021).

Unfortunately for the "shall blossom" (J. Smith et al. 1835, 192) prophecy, such Indigenous resilience meant that Utah's Lamanites had still not blossomed because they had not lost their Native nationhoods. Yet, maintaining the future tense of "shall blossom" was precisely the point of the prophecy. *The Book of Mormon* functioned as one of the many justifications of settler colonialism found in US Indianist novels, place names, military operations, movies, missiles, helicopters, and mascots wherein "histories of Native peoples [were] recruited to give the country a taste of exotic authenticity" (M. E. García 2021, 16). If Lamanites were to actually leave their indigeneity behind and blossom into whiteness, then settler Mormons would have one less group from which to choose for the appropriation of indigeneity required to justify their presence upon Indigenous land. At the same time, the "shall blossom" prophecy "celebrated the Native until that day, always lodged in the distant future, when the Native could speak for himself" (M. E. García 2021, 90). Adopting Native people into settler society in order to have them actually blossom—fully fit the category of a "self" who can speak rather than an "other" who is spoken to—was never part of settler adoption fantasies. "These fantasies can mean the adoption of Indigenous practices and knowledge, but more, refer to those narratives in the settler colonial imagination in which the Native (understanding that he is becoming extinct) hands over his land, his claim to the land, his very Indian-ness to the settler for safe-keeping. This is a fantasy that is invested in a settler futurity and dependent on the foreclosure of an Indigenous futurity" (Tuck and Yang 2012, 14).

Lamanites will eventually fit the category of forever family, they will eventually fit the unmarked construction of "Mormon," they will eventually become an "us" (Boxer 2015, 149) in Zion, but central church leaders designed that "eventually" to never actually arrive. This is because "the logic of the blossoming must be internally consistent with the principles of erasing Indigenous people from stolen land and must uphold deflection of complicity in that theft. Therefore, the blossoming must be consistent with a logic of Latter-day Saint whiteness. It must be controlled, policed, and intelligible only by the power centers of Mormonism" (Benally 2017, 77). Tellingly, the only textual reference to Lamanites "already blossoming" (Christensen 1995, 168) that I could find came not from an Anglo Mormon, but from a 1984 quotation from José Sousa, a Peruvian Mormon pioneer.

As a result of Young's selective genocide and Kimball's perpetual futurizing, both the past space and future time of Utah were symbolically cleared of nonwhiteness. Paradoxically, this meant that, for those non-White Peruvian Mormons who strove in the present for the whiteness required to fully embody the category of forever family, Utah was the place, and the future was the time.

No Future in Peru

"There is no future in Peru." I often heard that spatiotemporal refrain from both Mormon and non-Mormon Peruvians in Utah and Peru and learned that it was indexical of at least three sentiments. In the rest of this chapter, I will focus on the first two. The first sentiment was the notion, similar to Young's, that the current generation needed to be sacrificed for the future of the next. Through that lens, the refrain could be interpreted, "there is no future for my kids in Peru, so I am going to sacrifice my current successful career and good relations there in order to immigrate with my kids to the United States."

Mido and his spouse Carol harbored that vision more resolutely than most of my study participants. They were the only non-Mormons in our large kin network—La Familia—in Salsands, Utah. They were also among the only ones who had an "Entry Without Inspection" (EWI) into the United States rather than a visa overstay. This meant that their illegality was more visceral and less socially acceptable, which affected their theorization of future in the United States. I interviewed Mido and his two twenty-something daughters Luzi and Sofia in their solidly middle-class Utah home on a Friday evening in August 2016.

Though both still lived with their parents, Luzi had a master's degree in biochemistry and worked for Novartis. Sofia was a certified nurse. Both had come a long way since their harrowing walk across the Sonora Desert that brought them to the United States in 2000 at the ages of nine and five respectively and that caused them to be selectively mute for two years. Carol was not present during the interview because she was working the night shift at the Skyline Select food factory that employed twelve of La Familia's members, including me, during my 2017 fieldwork in Utah.

Mido and Carol lived with their daughters as a nuclear family, but they were only a few blocks away from Mido's sister Lorna and his brother Rito, each in their own nuclear family homes. In fact, they were only a few minutes' drive from dozens of other nuclear nodes on La Familia's geographically compact Utah network. However, their physical proximity to the network did not mean full connectivity until a few months before the interview. The status of both their religion and their mode of US arrival placed them not only in "the shadows" (Castañeda 2019, 214) of Utah society, but also beyond the knowledge of most of La Familia.

La Familia was a complex conglomeration stemming from one matriarch, Mamá Marina (Palmer 2022), her three male romantic partners, and their own multiple female partners spread throughout the entire racialized geography of Peru. These relationships produced an estimated thirty-six siblings and half-siblings (a non-Peruvian categorical distinction) throughout the middle of the twentieth century. Jacoba devoted decades of her life to investigating those thirty-six siblings and their progeny. She felt that she was filled with the Mormon spirit of genealogy and that it obligated her to do that research. Furthermore, she reported being guided by the actual spirits of dead ancestors whom she witnessed posthumously writing data onto their own photographs. After actively sleuthing, contacting, and converting many of those siblings and their descendants to Mormonism, she brought them to Utah and constructed them into La Familia. However, even Jacoba had not met Mido and Carol until Mamá Marina's Utah funeral in 2016. To this day, Jacoba tries unsuccessfully to build them into Saints and temple-seal them into La Familia (Palmer 2023).

This complexity made La Familia a "mixed-status immigrant family" (Castañeda 2019) in more ways than simply immigration legality. Though Carol, Mido, Luzi, and Sofia all shared the same legal status—itself a complex gray area called 245(i)—their EWI status and devout Catholicism multiplied La Familia's multiplanar statuses across spectrums of class, race, power, and—as concerns this chapter—"future" in Utah society.

Mido began the interview explaining to me what their lives were like in Peru before his sister Lorna, then a recent convert to Mormonism, helped them see that what they had in Peru did not count as future.

> I was already married back in Peru, and I would converse with Lorna over the phone. She told me about the possibility of us coming here [to Utah]. Carol is a nurse. She worked in Peru as a nurse, and I worked in the administration of a clinic, almost the best clinic in all of Peru. I made pretty good money, and Carol as well.
>
> But what ended up happening? Well, we had good jobs, everything was going well for us, but then—it was all rooted in the fact that—we saw the *option* of coming over here, and Lorna would say, "Why don't you all come over here? You could work here."
>
> And so, we began to see that, and to start looking into coming here. And everyone in La Familia was in Utah because all of them came directly to Utah.

I asked more specifically about how Lorna convinced them that their future was in Utah. He told me that they all grew up in the northern coastal fishing village of Malabrigo, Peru, but that Lorna, from an early age, saw her future elsewhere:

> She finished high school, and one day she just up and says to my mom, "Mamá, I'm going to Lima to study."
> "But, Hija!"
> I mean, they didn't know where she was going to stay in Lima, but she went anyway and studied at the Peruvian Institute of Business Administration.

Lorna was really smart and since she liked to take risks, she didn't like to just stay in one place, she ended up becoming the chief financial officer in a large public clinic. At one point, they actually gave her a raise. [Lorna was also baptized Mormon during this time.]

And not one month after they gave her that raise, Lorna quit the clinic. They asked her, "But why? Why quit? We've given you a raise."

"I'm quitting because if I don't, I'm not going to be able to follow my plan."

Well, her plan was to come here to the United States, so she quit and came here to Utah [in 1993 with a borrowed passport and a falsified visa. At first, she stayed with Jacoba and Arcadio].

She was working. She got married [to an Anglo Mormon]. And it was like she saw that one could accomplish something here [in Utah], that one could progress, that one could—how do you say it?—leave behind what one may have been before, that we could become a little more than what we were in Peru.

And well, she cared about us a lot, the way siblings love each other, so if she was doing well, then of course she'd want her siblings, her family to do well too. So, she started to send help to my mom, to help her siblings, to help us.

When she came to visit once, she brought a computer, something that in Peru almost nobody had. I mean *nobody* had one.

Minus the clandestine border crossing and his nuclear family's precarious newness to Peru's professional class, Mido's experience was typical of middle-aged, Peruvian professionals in the early 2000s who migrated to the United States without legal permission to work in that he had a familial network that not only facilitated his arrival but also motivated it "with seductive fragments of life in the United States" (Sabogal 2005, 118). What set Mido apart from many of his contemporaries was that he did not originally have a "general hopelessness about the future" (118). Since he had personally experienced significant upward mobility without leaving Peru, hopelessness had to be taught, and he was not an amenable student.

You know what, though? Before Lorna came here [to the United States], I never once thought about coming over here. And even then, I never told Lorna that we would come because, in reality, we were doing fine.

But one day Carol tells me—it was all Carol's fault, in reality, because she tells me, "Mido, if your sister is telling us to go over there [to Utah], why don't we go? Maybe things will go even better for us."

And for Carol, it would be even more painful to go because at least I had my sister's house to go to [in Utah]. Plus, Rito was already here. My oldest sister, Nilda, was already here. But Carol didn't have a single family member here. She still doesn't, even now, right?

She doesn't have anyone, and they miss each other, for example, on important dates: Christmas, birthdays, all those things, right? And even now she is still crying, always.

Because it is painful to separate from La Familia.

It is painful.

But anyway, I didn't have Lorna's mindset that I wanted to come here [to Utah]. It was as if Lorna slowly inserted the idea into my head, and not just *my* head: Carol's.

Because if Lorna had only put it into my head, then Carol would have planted herself [in Peru] and never come here.

Lorna stuck the idea into Carol.

Of course, when we would chat through the computer that she brought us, Lorna would praise the US, and then Carol would encourage me.

Finally, Carol says, "Mido, why don't you find out how much you'd get for severance pay if you were to quit your job?"

"What for?" I'd tell her.

Finally: "All right, fine, if you insist."

Lorna had found her future in Utah. In fact, she found an Anglo Mormon man and was sealed for time and all eternity in the Salt Lake City temple. As a Mormon, she had achieved what counted as a futurized, nuclear, forever family. Therefore, it was only natural that, as a Peruvian, she would want to amplify that family into a forever familia by including her brother, Mido. However, as difficult as it was to convince Mido that there was no future for him in Peru, it was even more difficult to persuade him that his future was in the United States. He would not be seduced by the Pilgrims' city on the hill that bathed both the United States and Utah in Zion's light (Adams 1932). His ultimate refusal to accept the American Dream alluded to below remained tied to his refusal, despite two decades of constant familial and neighborhood pressure, to accept Mormonism. Why then did he acquiesce to migrating to Utah?

What eventually tipped the scales, enabling him to sacrifice his career and enabling Carol to sacrifice both her career and her familia, was the realization that there was no future for their daughters in Peru. Finding a future for them would require self-abnegation.

We wanted them to study. I mean, maybe a lot of people come here [to the United States] because of the American Dream, which is to make money, to have things. But Carol and I have another mentality.

We came for them to study, and if on the way we could get money, commodities, and things that we wouldn't have in Peru, that's fine, a bonus, but our priority was that they study.

That was why, when we arrived here, we started to work, work, work, work.

We worked so much that I had three jobs [fry cook, night janitor, and factory line-worker] and Carol had two [night janitor and factory line-worker]. Only recently, this year, did I finally quit one of those jobs, because in reality, we are tired after sixteen years of this. But thanks to that sacrifice, now the *whole world* in Peru is so proud of Luzi and Sofia.

Everyone is all, "I have my sister, my niece, my daughter, my granddaughter, in the United States."

You know what, it may have been painful, and it was very, very hard, but I don't regret having come here.

Originally, we were interested in studying English, but then we just stopped going. Why? Because the priority was these two [our daughters]. We had already lived. Our time was already up. It was them, them, and nobody but them. That is why Carol would say, "We've already lived. They haven't. Their lives are ahead."

And so that is why we discontinued English classes.

In reality, if I would have known, or if I would have had the possibility of coming as a younger man, I would have done it.

After sixteen years of packaging pumpkin pies for twelve hours a day at Skyline Select followed by another four hours of vacuuming at JCPenney's, Carol still identified strongly as a nurse. She even got a tattoo of a heartrate monitor on her shoulder. For his part, Mido went from being a top clinic's top accountant to being the low man on the McDonald's hierarchy. Still, they were grateful for having left Peru. In fact, Mido wished that he could have been shown earlier that the future was not in Peru. If his Mormon sister had only given him a glimpse of that when he was younger, then he might have had "future" himself rather than only providing it for his daughters.

Future versus Festival

Mido's narrative explains why, for many Peruvians, it was important to transmit the message of futurity to the next generation early on. Once kids saw "future," they would catch the ambition necessary to grab it. While in Utah in 2017, I had the opportunity to follow alongside an arequipeña woman named Luz Berta whose mission during her one-week stay in the United States was exactly that: to show her fifteen-year-old daughter the future. How I ended up being the one selecting which aspects of that future to show her as I drove her and her daughter, Alicia, all over my home state requires explanation.

On my first trip to Arequipa in the summer of 2016, I walked out of my hostel on the morning of the first day to see two strikingly dissimilar young men walking away from me on the sidewalk. One was six-foot four and blond, the other was five-foot two and had black hair. Both were dressed for soccer. Their mismatch reminded me of something that Ray, my Peruvian brother-in-law, once told me. When he was a missionary in Lima, his mission president, an Anglo Utahan, would deliberately assign mission companionships based on attention-grabbing contrasts. He would pair the tallest with the shortest, the lightest with the darkest, the fattest with the skinniest, and he would even play on surnames—Elder Snow with Elder White.

As I suspected, the young men were Mormon missionaries. I introduced myself as a returned missionary and was immediately on the team, both for soccer and, later, for proselyting. I told them that I was interested in arequipeño Mormons with connections to Utah, and the first person whom they took me to visit was an unmarried mother, Ofelia. Her daughter, Shannon, had visited Utah the year prior as part of a Peruvian dance troupe organized by a non-Mormon Peruvian dance professor who actively recruited Mormons because, since the Festival of Global Dance in Utah was organized by Mormons, he thought Mormons would have better chances at getting visas. He was right on that occasion, in 2015, and the Peruvian Mormon dancers had a month-long adventure dancing in folkloric festivals and visiting Mormon temples across Utah and Idaho.

Shannon was serving her mission in Paraguay while I was in Arequipa on that occasion, so I could not speak to her about her Utah experience. However, I kept in touch with Ofelia almost weekly over WhatsApp for the next year. She told me that the dance professor was organizing another trip to Utah and that this time she was going to be in on it rather than simply sending her daughter. She kept me up to date on the preparations and let me know the ulterior motives of the dancers.

Almost none of them cared much about folkloric dance. All they wanted were visas, and many of them, Ofelia included, wanted to fulfil their dreams of visiting Utah. Not all were Mormons this time around. Ofelia had heard that her Catholic friend, Luz Berta, wanted to give Alicia a trip for her fifteenth birthday instead of a quinceañera (coming-of-age party), so she told her about the dance troupe as a surefire way to get a US visa. Luz Berta, her eleven-year-old son Timoteo, and Alicia signed up. I too signed up on the Utah end as a host family. It was going to be the perfect opportunity for me to experience Utah through the eyes of someone who idolized it like Ofelia.

Like in 2015, they all went to the US embassy in Lima in their dance troupe costumes. This was 2017, however, and the Trump-era visa rules had changed. In 2015, the whole troupe of thirty dancers and musicians were interviewed as a group through a single conversation between the embassy official and the dance professor. The official gave them a seemingly random assortment of visas; some got ten-year tourist visas (including Aaron from chapter 4), others got three-month "performing entertainer" visas (including Shannon). This time, 2017, each individual participant was interviewed separately. Only eleven of the thirty walked away with visas. Ofelia was not one of them, but Luz Berta, Alicia, and Timoteo were. As a result of the low numbers, Peru was not represented in the Festival of Global Dance that year. However, I was still willing to be a host, and thanks to our mutual connection to Ofelia, I was Luz Berta's only contact in the United States.

She and her kids stayed in our rented apartment in Salsands, Utah, for five days and I drove them everywhere that they wanted to go, including the small Peruvian Independence Day celebrations in Salt Lake City where we happened to run into my brother-in-law Ray's spouse's sister Alba. While I was interviewing random Peruvians next to the Inka Kola and salchipapa vendors, Alba and Luz Berta chatted. I found out later that Alba had promised to give Luz Berta the inside scoop on navigating visa overstays and other immigration possibilities. They made an appointment to meet at Alba's house near Salsands. I drove them to it and was allowed to stay and record. The conversation below was between Luz Berta and Alba, one of the few born-in-the-covenant, adult Peruvian Mormons in my study. Alba hailed from a staunchly Mormon familia in the mid-Andean city of Chachapoyas, Peru. Alicia and Timoteo were also present in the room, listening.

LUZ BERTA: As you know, Peru doesn't give much of a future. My husband is a police officer, and he only makes 1,000 soles [Peru's currency] a month. Most professionals that graduate from the university will make 1,500 soles in the best of jobs, and maybe if it is the absolute best, 1,800 [about 600 USD]. And that isn't enough. And we are talking here about good professional jobs like nurses. That's why I'm looking into this because I'd like my daughter to have a future—

ALBA:—Let me be frank, when I came, I didn't even know if I was going to stay, I didn't have it planned out like that. But from the moment that I touched the ground in this city [near Salsands, Utah], I fell in love. I loved it, and I was actually thinking the same exact thing as you.

I said, "I want something better, even if it only be for my children."

Over there in Peru, they weren't going to achieve something like this. Plus, I was coming out of a divorce. I had all the responsibility for my kids. And that is something that causes one to start considering many things. I ended up earning in a single hour in Utah what I would earn in Peru in a whole day.

LUZ BERTA: To tell the truth, I would love to stay in Utah and work and all of that, but how? I came because there was a festival and I wanted to somehow give my daughter a trip. I don't make much, but I did it so that they might know, that they might see things from another point of view. I want them to see, to have ambition, and that they study and see another reality. It isn't for me.

ALBA: Look at me, kids, I'm telling you. Your mama is a good mother in the sense that she is giving you opportunities that you have to realize most youth do not have.

LUZ BERTA: Exactly, not many people of my same status would give something like this.

ALBA: The only thing I know is that God prepares the path for all people. I did the same thing for my kids; I paid their trip to Cancun, even as a divorced woman living in Peru. It was something completely beyond my possibilities because when I promised them the trip, I didn't have a single sol in my pocket. I spent a ton of money. One went one year, and the other went the next as their graduation trip.

I wasn't able to throw a party for my daughter's fifteenth birthday, and she desired it with all her heart. I myself didn't have one.

And it's not as if I were saying, "Since I didn't have one, you don't need one either."

It's that if one looks coldly at things, parties are irrelevant. You know why? Because all the money that you spend is not going to make every single person happy. The people who are happy are the people who would accompany you regardless of whether you have only a glass of water to share or a huge party to share.

And that is what I did with my daughter. With a couple of her best friends, we went out, we ate, we had fun, and that's it. If it were possible, fantastic, who wouldn't want a super quinceañera and all that? But look, if they had me choose between the two, I would have preferred my future.

Alba offered a choice between a single party and the entire future. The party represented a past associated with expensive Latin American festivals that, despite their emotional warmth, provided happiness that was both fleeting and grossly incommensurate to the expense. Within Alba's capitalist calculus, others' happiness—a form of social capital—needed to be bought for the lowest amount of economic capital possible (Bourdieu 1994). Why spend a whole quinceañera on the same amount of social capital that a glass of water could buy?

Alba's other option for her daughter was the future itself, which she represented as a trip to Cancun. The trip provided a glimpse into a temporalization associated with individual, nuclear family advancement, something that under "cold" consideration Alba found more lasting. For both Luz Berta and Alba, "future" inhered to material quantities that could accumulate and be preserved.

Some places and activities contained future, others did not. Activities that granted individual gain harnessed future. Activities that redistributed wealth let future slip away. Many Latin Americans were making similar associations, and researchers connected those to the rise of Latin American Protestantism (Dow and Sandstrom 2001).

In syncretic Latin American Catholicism's cargo system, it could eventually become a couple's turn to provide their town a lavish patron saint festival—such as a yunza—just as it could become their turn, if they had a daughter, to provide her an expensive coming-out party. Within Protestantism's ideology of unilinear upward mobility, such sponsorships and parties, including the kin relationships forged therein through indebtedness and godparenthood, were seen as financially ruinous. Such parties functioned to cycle the conjugal couple's entire life savings back into the continuation of community customs and relatedness. Capitalism, on the other hand, dictated that "any eventual surplus . . . be invested for future maximalization" (Schielke 2015, 126).

During my study, Latin Americans who desired such maximalization often saw Protestantism as a way to eschew a circular past concerned with distributing wealth and step onto an inclined plane of futurity concerned with accumulating it. They began to consider that "the surplus that any functioning economy produce[d] [could] no longer be expended in an annual feast. It [had to] be invested for future growth, and the worry about that future growth [was] a powerful emotional foundation for the ethos of scarcity" (Schielke 2015, 22). The way that both Alba and Luz Berta spoke of the future materialized it as if it were a substance, and a scarce one at that. Future, in their narrativization, was an element that flowed in large or small quantities depending on one's moral worthiness and geographical location. Some anthropologists claim that human kinship is based on shared substances, be they foodstuffs, DNA, territories, or legal documents (Carsten 2000). If that is the case, and if "future" was as much a substance for Peruvians as a temporalization, perhaps future was one of the shared substances that created Peruvian Mormon relatedness. Perhaps future was the substance of forever familia. That would explain why Peruvian Mormons like Alba sometimes found it easier than Peruvian Catholics like Luz Berta to decide to emigrate from Peru. Since, in many Peruvian mindsets, a sufficient amount of the substance called "future" could only be obtained abroad, making the choice to emigrate was relatively easy for Peruvian Mormons who had an extra motivation for obtaining that substance: inhabiting Zion as forever familias.

Participants in quinceañeras, yunzas, and other cargo festivals during my study became kin to each other and to their localities as the immense annual cost of the festivals reabsorbed itself into the cycle of substance-sharing and mutual indebtedness. Conversely, for Alba, that cosmovision of collectivity and of a future contiguous with the past lacked a directional linearity capable of thrusting future families onto higher rungs than past families. Alba sought a new cosmovision wherein her work and wages, instead of cycling right back into the Earth and being "closed off," as she stated below, would—like holiness—transcend the Earth. From that elevated vantage, her babies would be able to see "beyond their noses" and inhabit a future that she was constructing into one of their existential needs, right along with food and shelter.

ALBA: And what your mama says is true, being able to go abroad gives you another vision, and that is what I told my kids, "I am paying for this trip because . . . I want you to see that there is a world beyond your noses."

And that is something that very few of us ever see. We close ourselves off, and that is what your mama wants to avoid for you. She is teaching you that there is a world beyond your noses.

For my kids, it was their first trip abroad, and it was to Cancun, Mexico. They had a great time. Woohoo!

But it is the same thing that your mama is doing for you now. I am not saying that you should know the purpose of this trip in this precise moment—you will discover that on the path—all I'm saying is that you get a goal, a vision of what you want.

You are getting to know another world. This world here is beautiful, nice.

Here, there is much future going forward.

I'm telling you something that they told me, "If you come, come as a family."

And that is what I'd recommend to you.

If, for whatever reason, you all decide to stay here, stay as a family, come with your husband, come as a family. Don't just send your daughter here to study.

Future by Any Means

Alba might have gone on to say more about Utah—a space of substantial temporal flow with "much future going forward"—but at that point we took the conversation outside into her garden. As we walked, Luz Berta quickly whispered to me, "Turn off your stupid recorder." She thought it was keeping Alba from spilling the deep, extralegal immigration secrets that she promised to tell her. Luz Berta, who held a bachelor's degree in anthropology, did not know that I had recorded an interview with Alba before and that she had absolutely no qualms about revealing to me her "illegal" status and her opinions about the multiple ways of getting around it. The secret that Alba wanted to share had nothing to do with an expedient way to procure a student visa for Alicia, which was all that seemed to interest Luz Berta.

Alba's secret was that coming to the United States by any means necessary, even swimming across the border, was part of "the path" to the future. Legality and illegality had no bearing on the "right" way to come. The right way to come, according to Alba, was to come either as an already US/Mormon-defined nuclear family, or to come in order to complete such a family—a forever family—which Alba saw as both superior to and antithetical to Peruvian familia, a form of kinship that was stuck in the alcohol-rife, financially wasteful past.

Achieving a forever family through migration to Utah was precisely what Alba herself had done. When I interviewed her only two years prior, she had been in Utah for less than a year and was single. Now she was married to a Mexican American Mormon named Abel who, unlike her first husband in Peru who was an inactive Mormon, was worthy to marry her in the temple. This meant that she could finally be temple-sealed—as she was in 2018—to her two adult children for eternity. It also meant that when Alba discussed a future for her children, she alluded to something infinitely more significant than what Luz Berta and Mido, both Catholics, could fathom. Alba's invocation of "future" evoked a forever future. Since, in hindsight, coming to Utah was necessary to complete her own forever family—a family that could now remain together after death—she assumed that the same would be true for Luz Berta. Why else would the Lord bring Luz Berta to Utah through such a convoluted set of circumstances if not for the purpose of making her Mormon and, in so doing, offering her the ritual opportunity to futurize her family?

As Craig Christensen, a General Authority Seventy of the church (one rank under the Twelve), remarked on a postcard that missionaries distributed to homes throughout Utah County: "Make no mistake, the Lord is gathering his elect to Utah. They think they are coming for employment. They think they are coming to be near family and friends. They think they are coming for an education. Some don't really know why they are coming here. But the reality is that the Lord is gathering His elect to Utah, and He expects the Saints to welcome them, embrace them and share the Gospel with them." Christensen's narrativization was similar to the renarrativization of a Peruvian Protestant in Korea regarding his countrymen's migratory motivations: "They had a vision, Korea. And what was their vision? Save money! But what did they find? They did not find what they asked for. They found something else. They found the vision God had for them" (qtd. in Vogel 2020, 95). Likewise, Alba's immigration secret was that Luz Berta needed to think bigger than simply giving Alicia a taste of US futurity: Luz Berta needed to convert their week-long trip into a permanent immigration to Utah. In Alba's imagination, Utah was the only site of forever familial futurity since there was "no future in Peru." In the excerpt below, Alba emphasized that seeking forever family futurity made all things sacrificed seem frivolous, be they the comfort of legality or even what "familia" used to mean back in Peru. Letting her anthropological sensibilities get the better of her, once Luz Berta herself caught on to Alba's missiological motives, she insisted that I turn my recorder back on in Alba's garden.

ALBA: First of all, I would never marry for papers, but I have been to singles events and dances in the church where the women are like vipers ready to bite into anyone who is an American citizen, even an old man with a cane who can barely walk. They'll marry for papers in a heartbeat.

There is this thing where a woman with a husband in her country will get married to a US citizen here with the idea of divorcing him once she is a citizen and then petitioning her real husband with a fiancé visa. But now Immigration caught onto it, and that just makes it harder for people like me and Abel who get married for love.

Abel's father crossed the border at age fourteen and was deported thirteen times. Eventually he married, but they never became citizens. But, thanks to them, Abel was born here and so he understands both cultures.

He helps me to not be so sentimental about being here looking for the future instead of being home in Peru. He gets me to forget about visiting my mom in Peru and to stop mommying my kids. I didn't talk to him for a whole month at first when he told me that they needed to get out of our house and find their own place to stay, but then I understood. It dawned on me. He's right. The Americans are right.

That is why we Latinos don't progress because we are too sentimental about family things when what we have to do is look only to the future and go forward.

That is the good thing about this country, that we learn to make the hard decisions to leave family so that we can cut ties that stop us from progressing into the future.

Peru has no future.

You will be getting a different future for your kids in the United States, whereas if they stay in Peru, they will not have any kind of future.

LUZ BERTA: But if you are illegal, you can't go back to visit Peru ever.

ALBA: People who are here for years are just fine being illegal, no problems.

The police aren't out to get you like people told me they were. That is from envy because sometimes fellow Latinos don't want you to succeed here. They want you to live in fear, so they tell you, "The police will take away all your stuff and send you back."

So, I lived in fear until I looked out the window and saw the police waving at me and saying, "have a nice day," and it was totally normal.

The people who get deported, it is their fault for hanging out with the wrong kinds of friends.

That said, the government knows all about us. They know where we eat—those of us who came with passports—and they track us everywhere.

So, they know full well that we overstay visas, and they could kick us out, but why don't they? Because we do jobs nobody wants to do.

Alba's stance on Immigration and Customs Enforcement (ICE) baffled migration scholar Susan Bibler Coutin when she read an early version of this manuscript. Given her decades long anthropological work with undocumented—and undocumentable—migrants and deportees who lived in a stymied futurity that she called the "space of nonexistence" (2003, 27), she wondered how Alba could be so cavalier, blaming deportees for their own deportation. While some of anthropologist Elena Sabogal's (2005) study participants with very little time in the United States had similarly blasé attitudes, saying things like, "as long as you respect the laws . . . don't drive drunk . . . you can live happily in the shadows" (124, translation mine), they tended to change their tune after realizing that ICE would find any pretext necessary to deport even the most law-abiding, middle-class migrants. What then explained Alba's complex claims regarding the happily illegal future that she wanted Luz Berta to hope for in Utah?

Before attempting an answer, I must make a declaration. After years of attending Spanish-speaking wards in Utah, visiting members of my ward in ICE detention, and picking up my "Hispanic Troop" Boy Scouts from school because their parents, mostly mothers, had been detained after yet another ICE raid—I can confidently claim that Alba's downplaying of illegalized futurity was disingenuous. Utah's ICE was not tempered by Utah's famous White niceness—quite the contrary (Low 2009). In Utah, as elsewhere in the United States, "deportation regimes [were] profoundly efficient in provoking fear through a combination of targeting a few people while fostering an enduring sense of danger and fragile existence" (Castañeda 2019, 217), even for US citizens, increasing numbers of whom depended upon undocumented family members during the late 2010s. The close-knit, confessional sharing inherent to Mormon wards and the fact that ICE accepted anonymous tips compounded this future of fear in Utah. "The fear of denunciation, that someone [would] report their parents or siblings to authorities, [was] ever-present" (217), especially since members of Spanish-speaking wards constantly had in their midst Anglo overseers from stake or mission leadership councils ostensibly there to teach English or otherwise "support our Hispanic brothers and sisters," as one of those overseers told me. Coreligionists could become ICE informants in places where, as one Mexican Mormon migrant noted, "white members were really loving until they found out I didn't have papers" (qtd. in Romanello 2020, 17).

Furthermore, the church controlled the Utah state government. Not only were most members of that government also members of the church and loyal to its top leaders, but those leaders also had various ways of directly and indirectly letting Utah lawmakers know the Prophet's wishes and stances on specific bills. Despite central church leaders' public overtures toward tolerance of immigration, despite their strategic media campaign to welcome those few whom the US awarded "refugee" status (which rarely included Latin Americans), and despite their army of Spanish-speaking returned missionaries in every level of government who knew intimately the conditions that Latin American migrants were fleeing, Utah immigration policy ensured fearful futures for the peoples it racialized, minoritized, and illegalized (Romanello 2021).

Visa: Tangible Future

Alba's claim that being illegal was "just fine" downplayed the suffering of her fellow undocumented coreligionists even as it contested the hegemonic Anglo Mormon category of "future." Though faithful to a religion that foreordained the United States as the future world hegemon within a holy text proclaiming that God Himself established the US Constitution (J. Smith 1844, 373), Alba did not consider her original transgression of US border sovereignty—a visa overstay—to be morally wrong.

That apparent contradiction derived from an important ontological fact within the Peruvian Mormonism of my study: the visa was a miracle. In the parlance of Erica Vogel's (2020) Peruvian Protestant study participants in Korea, it was a "*respuesta*, or personal message from God, that . . . migration . . . was predestined" (92). The visa was the ticket to "future" for my study participants. It was the documentary manifestation of destiny.

Since "it [was] virtually impossible for low-income racialized Peruvians . . . to obtain a foreign visa via official means" (Berg 2015, 73), when they did obtain one—even if a large portion of the process included unofficial means of their own fabrication (recall Sofi's marriage to Rafa)—they invariably considered the visa a sign from God. Dozens of Peruvian Mormons told me visa stories that, as in novelistic depictions (Desai 2006; Recacoechea 2007), they usually narrativized in the stark terms of spiritual destiny, of final judgment, of hell (not achieving the visa during the first five attempts), or of heaven (*Bam*, your stamp!).

Despite all the fraud that they had to commit in order to prove documentarily and bodily that they had such strong financial, linguistic, geographic, academic, and ancestral ties to Peru's light-pigmented upper-class that they had no use for a tourist visa outside of genuine tourism, it was always God Himself who ultimately gave them the very visa that they planned on overstaying illegally. Consider the following narrative composites that I have collected over two decades in La Familia:

> God prompted me to show up to the embassy for my interview on the precise day when officials were in an uncharacteristically good mood.
> God sent the requisite "bad cop" official to the restroom at the precise moment when my number was called to the next window.

God caused my temple-recommend to slip out of my billfold in front of the only official who happened to be Mormon.

God temporarily gave my female interviewer the gift of discernment (ML) usually reserved for male bishops so that she would perceive that, though I was, of course, planning to overstay my visa, my heart was pure and that I would be an asset to her nation.

These small miracle stories told and retold throughout the Peruvian Mormon immigrant diaspora combined into a symbol so portentous that it exceeded the holiness of US immigration law: the tourist visa was an irrefutable sign that God wanted it to be overstayed. This was even the case back before biometrics (circa 2002) when visas could be obtained by completely circumventing the US embassy, as was the case with Lorna, meaning that even if a professional criminal physically created the visa from scratch, it was still from Heavenly Father.

Peruvian Mormons would quibble about the scriptural provenance of Coricancha and Tiwanaku, but the US visa—as the least ambiguous signifier in Peruvian Mormonism—had but one interpretation: divinely sanctified future.

Illegality and Meritocracy

The ease with which Alba justified her own illegality within a settler state that her church's top leaders sanctified above all, save the temple, did not baffle me in the slightest because I was raised with the contradiction that it reflected. It was the same contradiction that Pasi felt at the dark dance and that Simón refused to verbalize regarding the church's history department. It was a contradiction at the heart of a question that those Peruvians in my study who feared opening history books depicting their church's violence against Indigenous people dared not ask but always sensed: If Anglo Mormonism could justify a small atrocity from the past—a dark dance or a holy site deletion—what could it justify in the future?

The answer was that Mormonism had a well-documented history, not merely confined to Brigham Young, of being able to rationally and theologically justify absolutely anything (Krakauer 2004). Justifying a visa overstay was nothing in comparison to justifying genocide. In fact, as late as 2010 at the church's university, BYU, genocide remained so academically justified that it was only after intense lobbying and personal risk that Cayuga and Diné student Eva Bighorse (2021) was able to simply "generate dialogue among BYU students that genocide [was] not the Lord's will" (114).

The Mormon skill of rationalization even had a name in Utah, "lying for the Lord." Lying for the Lord was a form of "theocratic ethics" (Quinn 1994, 112) that was coined during Utah's polygynous era of federal prosecution. Like many Anglo Utah Mormons, I curated a photograph of my great-great-grandfather proudly dressed in a black-and-white striped jailhouse jumpsuit (Chamberlain and Chamberlain 2009). My polygynous ancestors lived in illegality. They presented one face to the feds and another to their church. This chiseled into Utah's very topography the two-facedness that Pasi perceived at the dance. My ancestors had to become twofaced in order that their socially unacceptable families could have a forever.

Since Mormonism's past was forged in happy illegality and weaned on twisted theocratic ethics, Alba's victim-shaming discourse on deportation in Utah made a twisted sort of sense. It was a way of projecting a uniquely Mormon form of illegality into the future. Her blaming of deportees instead of deportation echoed the sentiments of most Latin American Mormon migrants to whom I spoke, documented or not. They almost never admitted that their futures were in any way restricted by their undocumented status. They projected the full burden of their abject status in US society onto the faultiness of their own individual choices, whether these included slacking off in ESL class or hanging out with the wrong friends. I believe that their mindset stemmed from one of the morals of *The Book of Mormon*. That moral stated that if one was not prospering in the land, one was not being righteous enough. Invisible oppressive systems that allowed unrighteous people to prosper at the expense of righteous people could not exist in Mormon cosmology. Upward progression was a clear, unobstructed path toward the future. There was no inequity on that path. Once humans found it, they all started at the same place on it, and all that remained was their individual choice to follow it.

Future Return

However, though unobstructed, straight, and narrow, there were distractions near the path that tempted humans away from their future.

ALBA: And I could go back and visit my mom now. I mean, I have the papers, but I can't because my husband got sick and how am I going to leave him?

I know that is a gringo way of thinking that is kind of severe.

I mean, not visiting your mother when you *can*!? When you have *papers*!?

But I am learning that is the right way to be, because we get too sentimental as Latinas, it's what keeps our country behind, backward. Anyway, it is great to live in the US, and you live a new life where you can actually have a future.

In critiquing the idea of return, Alba's discourse highlighted the ways in which, for lower-class migrants, "future" was synonymous both with entry into the middle-class and entry into the United States. Returning to Peru was tantamount to returning to where one started on Peru's class hierarchy. Returning benefited anthropologist Cristina Alcalde's (2018) upper-class Peruvian study participants because they started high. Only in Lima could they enjoy all the privileges of their class, such as walled segregation from other classes, club memberships, and domestic servants. Therefore, they often returned to Peru permanently. The upwardly mobile Peruvian migrants in my study, on the other hand, had much to lose by returning permanently and even much to risk by returning for a visit. They often saw return to Peru as traveling back through time to a backward past. While those in La Familia with the financial and legal means enjoyed short, sporadic visits to Peru, they usually balked at the prospect of returning permanently. Instead of requiring Peruvian earth, as "future" did for Andean Catholics like Luz Berta, La Familia's Mormon future transcended it.

LUZ BERTA: But I'm already married, and we have no family here at all. We'd be illegal forever and never be able to travel back to Peru even to visit.

ALBA: Look, that is true, but that is part of coming here. There is a reason that here in Utah people get married really young. They focus so much on their future family because that is what life is all about in our church.

You leave your mother and father and cleave to your husband and future kids. And so, they come back from their missions at twenty-one and look for young women to marry—and sometimes it is too young, and I don't agree with that either, like sixteen- or seventeen-year-old girls.

But that is the mindset that you have to get into when you come here: you are forming a future family, not holding on to your past family.

So, come illegally if you have to, but come as a family—you, your husband, and kids—and you will have to work hard, and you will have to live in bad places at first and with people whom you don't like, but you will be willing to do all that, to live illegally, because it will give a future for your kids.

In this conversation, Alba and Luz Berta began talking past each other. Instead of addressing Luz Berta's concern about not being able to go back to Peru, Alba focused on why she should not need to. Peru as a place was conflated with kinship for both of them, but Luz Berta had developed no tripartite spatiotemporal division in her concept of "familia" that could conceive of kin divisions mapping perfectly onto past, present, and future places. Luz Berta did not segregate family into past family and future family.

In Luz Berta and Alba's native Andes, there was a concept of future, but it did not imply a sense of unilinear progression *toward* anything, much less toward the discrete subdivisions of family that Alba denoted "past family" and "future family." The future of the Andean cycle—pacha—that included as "familia" all humans and nonhumans within reach of its reciprocity seemed opposed to Alba's category of "future." In fact, an Indigenous organization in North America, the Red Nation (2021) branded multinational corporations like Alba's church "enemies of the Earth and the greatest danger to our future" (143). Under that lens, Indigenous futures and Mormon futures appeared to be mutually exclusive.

Peru Time

For Peruvian Lamanites to count as Mormons with "future," they had to confront that mutual exclusivity and its aphoristic concretization: "there is no future in Peru." As the words of Mido, Luz Berta, and Alba demonstrated, the first facet of that refrain called for the sacrifice of one generation so that the future of the next might arrive unhindered by backward-thinking parents and untied to places that recalled a mother-visiting, "sentimental," antifuture past.

That one of those places was Peru opens the second facet of the refrain. Anciently, there was no concept of "future" in Peru remotely commensurable to what that word denotes in contemporary English (Mallku Bwillcawaman 2015). The entire history of time itself followed a different trajectory in Peru than it followed in the territory that incubated Mormonism. As a result, in the late 2010s in Peru, time and its discrete domain labeled "future" flowed differently than they did in the United States. Uncoincidentally, Peruvian time corresponded to the stage pejoratively labeled "third world" in Collin's globalization teleology. Such a ranked, temporal worlding of countries—not to be confused with the third world as an anti-imperialist solidarity (Prashad 2008)—was widely accepted among Mormons in my study. For example, a young Mormon couple from Idaho that I interviewed in Arequipa told me that their goal had long been to live in Peru for three months, and that—like training for a marathon—they had deliberately worked up the ability to live in Peru, in their estimation "a third-world country," by first living in Mexico, "a second-world country."

Sociologist E. P. Thompson (1967) explored the way that notions of time became inextricably associated with the technological stages up that evolutionary hierarchy of worlds from gathering to hunting, to horticulture, to agriculture, to mercantilism, to industrialism, to Fordism, and finally to the supposed apex of human evolution—mature capitalism. Human bodies habituated to the uppermost of those stages had internalized arbitrary units of time as the natural units of work. They worked to "spend" a monetized amount of time rather than to complete a set task. "Puritanism, in its marriage of convenience with industrial capitalism, was the agent which converted men to new valuations of time; which taught children even in their infancy to improve each shining hour; and which saturated men's minds with the equation, time is money" (95).

Mormonism, as part of a globally proliferating Protestantism that was affecting Peruvians in Korea as much as Peruvians in Utah, both spiritualized and racialized that equation. For example, anthropologist of Korea Vogel (2020) expressed one of her Peruvian Protestant study participants' feelings on remittances. From his perspective, "no amount of money would ever be enough for his [Catholic] family unless he successfully converted them into people who knew how to value it correctly" (78). Many Mormons in my study, as time-disciplined modern Puritans who had mastered the highest levels of US neoliberal capitalism (Ong 2003), harbored sentiments similar to those of Peruvian Protestants in Korea. They tended to see people whose lives were more integrated with tides, solstices, and alpaca sheering cycles—that is, people with lives disciplined to tasks rather than to clocks—as wasteful, lacking urgency, and as sloppily participating in "alternate bouts of intense labor" (Thompson 1967, 73) and in unplanned, inordinately prolonged—and often drunken—idleness. Such people held valuations of money—and, therefore, future—that were incorrect in the eyes of both Protestants and Mormons.

I admit, as the most time disciplined Mormon in my study, Peruvian future was crazy making for me. While living in Arequipa, we enrolled our daughters in an all-girls, public—and therefore, Catholic—school. In the United States, we were accustomed to receiving a detailed academic calendar of the entire year in advance, complete with days off and "early-outs." This allowed us to plan short family trips. In Arequipa, we had no such luxury. On many occasions we did not even find out about a school holiday until the day before it happened. For example, Good Friday was a national holiday in Peru, yet for the life of us we could not get the school principal to let us know whether or not that fact implied a holiday from Catholic school. The other parents, who were up in arms about almost everything else that the principal decided, did not seem to care at all that nobody knew if the day after tomorrow was to be a school day or not. In fact, in the WhatsApp parent group, a parent posted the following on the morning of Good Friday: "Quick question, is there school today?" It turned out that there was.

Not planning for the future, even the immediate future, was more socially acceptable in Peru than it was in the United States. For an example affecting the national economy, one day, the Peruvian president PPK decided that if Peru won its qualifying match to enter the 2018 World Cup, the next day would be a national day off from work. Peru won. Unfortunately, the holiday did not apply to Peruvians in the diaspora with whom I had to work at the Skyline Select factory in Utah the next day. While on the pumpkin pie line, I could not help wondering how the factories in Peru would survive an entire day of global capitalism without labor. Under such temporalities, it was no wonder that for those Peruvians in my study who sought "future," the very word had a weak association with Peru and a strong association with the United States.

It was significant that my daughters' school was the setting wherein a lack of concern for the future was taught by example because, along with the US church, the US school was one of the principal institutions used to inculcate time thrift. Thompson (1967) noted that the writer of an anonymous list of grievances against British idleness in 1772 "saw education as a training in the 'habit of industry'; by the time the child reached six or seven it should become 'habituated, not to say naturalized to Labour and Fatigue'" (84). Indeed, the aspect of the Church Education System (CES) that Peruvian Mormons seemed to cherish most was its inculcation of puritanical time thrift, something that they did not imbibe during the non-Mormon aspect of their regular school day. In Barrio Periféricos, the most talked-about of the CES's many programs was Seminary (ML). CES designed Seminary to be concurrent with the four years of US-style high school, and each year's curriculum focused on one of Mormonism's four canonical books. In Utah, most public high schools and junior highs had a church-owned, dedicated Seminary building across from their campuses. Seminary for those students was incorporated as just another period of their regular school schedule and was designated as "released time" on their transcripts. Seminary teachers in Utah were CES employees and were usually paid a higher salary than their secular high school teaching counterparts next door. In Peru (and most places outside of Utah) on the other hand, Seminary teaching was an unpaid ward calling like any other, and lessons were held early in the morning before regular school started, usually in the home of the teacher.

Seminary seniors were often asked to stand before their congregations and "bear testimony" of their Seminary experiences to motivate incoming freshmen. I witnessed many such testimonies in Barrio Periféricos, and they almost always skipped over what was learned in Seminary in order to elaborate on the character-building aspects of waking up early enough to attend it. The typical testimony began with a comical description of the lethargy that made attendance impossible in the beginning. This was made even more comical to my Anglophone ears by the Peruvian enunciation of the verb "madrugar," which I translated as "to unfortunately have to wake up early." The testimony would then shift to the hateful tactics to which parents resorted, usually involving ice water, in order that students might develop the austere habitus of early rising. Finally, testimonies unanimously ended with expressions of gratitude, not for what was taught in Seminary, but for its unlocking of a brand-new time of day, a time that promised to forever provide an edge over sleeping competitors in the battle for entry into a time-disciplined future of scarcity.

Ofelia was a Seminary teacher in Barrio Periféricos. When one of her potential students convinced his mother, Nailah, that he really could not madrugar, the subordination of gospel curriculum to early rising was made explicit.

Ever since last year, Nailah was pestering me saying, "Sister, I want you to teach [Seminary] in the afternoon."

I consulted with the supervisor [a called position], and the supervisor consulted with the brother who is in charge of Seminary in all of Arequipa [a CES paid position].

He declared that afternoon Seminary was prohibited because the youth must learn to sacrifice, to get up early.

So, last year, I told Nailah that, but she didn't give up. She just started teaching her son Seminary in the afternoons without consulting with the supervisor or anyone.

One day, another mother approached the supervisor to ask for the registration forms for her daughter and she says, "My daughter is going to take night Seminary."

"But, Sister, there is no night teacher."

"Isn't Sister Nailah teaching it?"

And so, the supervisor got angry and accused Nailah of attributing to herself the calling of Seminary teacher.

Nailah basically called herself, and that is why the supervisor is constantly checking on that class because as soon as other youth who lived near Nailah found out about it, they were like, "Oh yeah, it's in the afternoon?! We don't have to madrugar anymore?! We're there!"

Now she has a decent-sized group, like six students. So, we're going to see what happens with that group. How will they end up? Nobody knows.

Even though Nailah's students were receiving the same Utah-designed, manual-driven education as Ofelia's own Seminary students, Ofelia worried about how the time difference would affect their future. Mormon Seminary taught in the afternoon might not have been enough to counteract the relatively time-undisciplined education that students received during the rest of their day in arequipeño schools. It certainly would not have been enough to prepare students to compete with the intense future-centrism of the Utah-style education embodied in the eighteen- to twenty-year-old Anglo missionaries for whom Ofelia cooked every day and with whom her Seminary students would soon be paired when they went on their own missions.

Chronological Failure

As an embodiment of Utah education myself, I could not understand why, on the eve of Carnavales season, nobody, not even the Arequipa tourist office, could tell me on exactly which calendar dates it fell. "Just walk around the city pretty much every weekend in February, maybe March, and you'll probably run into Carnavales." I soon realized that spontaneity was precisely the point of arequipeño Carnavales. Annual Carnavales, pre-Lent Andean Catholic festivals based on the lunar, rather than on the Western calendar, were a reprieve from the otherwise constant tension, not only with the West's discipline of religious penance and asceticism (amplified during Lent), but with the West's discipline of incessant future planning. To schedule Carnavales on one's Franklin Day Planner (patented by a Utah Mormon) would be to profane that rest. Taking such a reprieve from the clock-conscious, future-centric competition of Western modernity was badly needed in Peru because many Peruvians, particularly Peruvian Mormons, were constantly berating themselves over what they perceived to be their chronological failures. They felt that those failures were part of what kept "future" out of Peru.

Unfortunately for Peruvians who sought to be full Mormons—Mormons with the proper category of future—chronological failures became moral failures as they realized that Zion time and Peruvian time did not coincide. Zion was a place of forever families, but Peru was a space of familias with no forever. This was not only because a linear, discretely bounded future had a weak discursive and ancestral association with Peru, but also because, as previously discussed, the future was always only for the next generation.

Paradoxically, those who had no future in Peru—the Lamanites—were also those perpetually stuck in the future. Mormon prophecy confined Lamanites to the future just as the US media did to the non-Mormon counterpart of the Lamanite—the Latinx. As anthropologist Jonathan Rosa (2019) explored, "these media portrayals emerge as part of a deceptive social tense in which today's Latinx marginalization is legitimated by a figured egalitarian future. *Latinidad* . . . is more than 500 years in the making, yet always just on the demographic horizon. How is it that a population whose origins in many ways predate the very European histories in relation to which 'America' is conventionally imagined, could be framed as a demographic whose value lies only in some figured future?" (15).

Likewise, in Anglo Mormon categorizations, Lamanites always "shall blossom" but never "are blossoming," and certainly never "have blossomed." Peruvian Mormons' perceived chronological failures in their battle to achieve at least the future category of forever family—a battle that often involved migration to Utah—solidified their unblossomed present, third-world past, and antifuture forever. In the next chapter, I will follow one of these chronological failures—unpunctuality—before delving into the third facet of why "there is no future in Peru," which cuts closer to the more sensitive half of the forever familia concept, namely: familia.

CHAPTER 6

Marriage

While I am in my early years,
I'll prepare most carefully,
So I can marry in God's temple for eternity.
Fam'lies can be together forever
Through Heav'nly Father's plan.
I always want to be with my own family,
And the Lord has shown me how I can.
—"Families Can Be Together Forever"
(R. M. Gardner 1985, 300)

Eternal Punctuality

During my study, Peruvian bodies were relegated to an always-future time, often distant from Peruvian places, making Peruvian Mormons perpetually late to their own Zion. Those not born in Mormon homes did not have the opportunity of singing the above Anglo Mormon hymn in their "early years." For many, discovering Mormonism and being baptized after prime marriage-able age meant that they did not find out until it was too late that marriage was the key to a cosmologically physical place known as the Celestial Kingdom, the highest of Mormon heavens. This chapter follows unmarried Mormons as they made up for lost time on the unidirectional, narrow track progressing toward a forever family future-time in a forever family future-place.

Unmarried Peruvian Mormons sometimes felt guilty, not only because they were always already late to forever family, but also because they came to see themselves as the embodiment of an existential unpunctuality. This unpunctual existence—the condition of being slightly off schedule according to proper, Utah-defined time—informed discourses of lateness in Peruvian Mormonism involving both the most macrolevel scales of eternal life stages and the most mundane aspects of daily reality.

The official church's focus on punctuality and marriage contrasted so significantly with the way time worked in Peru that official church manual-driven activities and meetings in Peruvian Mormon chapels became concrete demonstrations of how getting married on time, getting to church activities on time, and getting units of money in direct proportion to discrete units of time were all fundamentally part of the same overarching achievement. That achievement involved escape from a cyclical reciprocity that privileged place, and entry onto an eternal progression (ML) that privileged time.

This chapter is about the category of marriage in Zion's forever family–engineering platform. However, it is also about the larger temporal regimes of eternal progression under which punctuality discourses became inextricable from marriage in Mormonism. This inextricability of linear time from nuclear family caused Peruvian Mormonism's place-based forever familia to distinguish itself from Anglo Mormonism's time-based forever family.

There was no more direct way for me to witness the Mormon nexus of time and family that was marriage than to attend Barrio Periféricos's weekly Sunday School meetings. Our Sunday School teacher was Delia, the same misionera aguerrida from chapter 2. One Sunday in 2018, she gave a lesson on punctuality that, at first, had nothing to do with marriage. However, she later clarified that her lesson's punctuality category had the same temporal structure as Mormonism's marriage category.

> If I say, "what is the point of arriving early if everyone else is going to be late?" the message that I am giving myself is, "Delia, you are not in the wrong. Relax. All is well in Zion. Eat, drink, and be merry. You don't do it because you are a bad person, but simply because it is true; nobody arrives on time."
>
> So, I give myself a message of mediocrity. I don't do it all the way.
>
> I am becoming a mediocre person because I am not giving of my fullness.
>
> For example, when I went to a Relief Society activity that was for humanitarian aid, they had indicated a specific hour, 7:30. I was there at 7:25, and I waited. 7:30 came, and nobody was there.
>
> 7:40?
>
> Not a soul.
>
> Finally, the main organizer arrived, and I said, "Ay, Sister, I was scared that I was in the wrong place. What time is it going to start?"
>
> "Truthfully, the time was at 8:00, but we told everyone 7:30 because you have to tell them that it's a half hour before it really is."
>
> And I said, "But, Sister, we are His church! If this were just a social club I might agree, but, Sister, with all due respect, I tell you: We are the true church. We can never give a time that is not what it claims to be, especially you as our leader. Sister, for me it is a very grave offense when someone says, 'Tell them to be there at 7:30 so that we can start at 8:00,' I consider that abysmally insulting."

Right here in this church manual it is teaching us that time is valuable. We have to respect it, and we have to respect the time of other people. We can't go around convinced that such behavior is not wrong because if we convince ourselves that what we are doing is not wrong, we are just feeding the mediocrity.

We are not giving of our fullness.

We saw in the last class that the fullness of abundance was the abundance of the gospel, right?

So, it is the same thing. It is very important that we teach our kids about this punctuality stuff, our loved ones. Why? Because unpunctuality is a—_____ [pauses deliberately for someone to fill in the blank. Nobody does]—*deficiency!*

It limits us terribly. But we are going to work on it, and we are going to work with our families first, okay?

Also, we are a very unpunctual ward, terribly unpunctual. So, we need to help our leaders, help our members to know that when they set a time, that time is the time.

So, if something in the Relief Society is at 6:00, I don't care if the chapel is completely locked and barred, I am going to be there at exactly 6:00 standing outside the gates like an idiot. And why will I do that? Like my son says, "Why are you standing out there, Mamá, if the chapel is closed?"

And obviously, if we get there on time for any event, the chapel is always closed, right? I just tell him, "Alberto, through my way of living, I must change whatever the other members think."

And it works.

It is not easy when you have a family because you might have all the desire in the world to be punctual, but if your family doesn't do it, it becomes more difficult for you.

But we have to just be there insisting and insisting and insisting and someday, at some future moment, your kids will be earlier than anyone.

Including only the punctuality section of Delia's greater lecture on the importance of maximizing our short time on this Earth may seem like a strange way to begin a chapter on singleness and marriage. Being late to an important life stage event, such as marriage, and being late to a Relief Society meeting might seem like two incommensurable scales of unpunctuality. However, for Delia and the larger antimediocrity discourses that she espoused, being perpetually single and being perpetually late both required the same sort of self-deception regarding what was and was not "wrong."

For many Mormons in my study, being a single adult was wrong. It was a state of deficiency just like unpunctuality. Delia posited that if we wanted to be excellent, full, complete people, we had to subscribe to a punishing future tense that did not forgive even a half hour's lateness, let alone lateness to the vital rite of passage that was Mormon temple marriage. We needed to feel bad about everything that we did that was not in lockstep with that tense (Rifkin 2017). Even though she knew that time in Peru did not work as it did in her Utah-produced manual, she tried to be the change that she wanted to see in her local stake of Zion. Therefore, she was at church on time "like an idiot" when nobody but her son—and, presumably, God—was there to see her.

By focusing on this, Delia "illustrated a particular *mujerista* [womanist] feminine logic" (Vega 2020, 604) that celebrated the quotidian aspects of faithful life over which women had control: getting their families to church and pressuring male leaders to start church on time. Another facet of mujerista theology that Delia, and most of my Peruvian female study participants, unwittingly emulated—which may relate to the likelihood that both mujerista theology and its masculine counterpart, liberation theology, started in Peru (Isasi-Diaz 1996)—was the elevation of marital "domesticity to a pillar of virtue" (Vega 2020, 605). Delia's motivational, mujerista discourse heightened my awareness of something that many in the putatively secular United States had forgotten; both puritanical time-discipline and the version of capitalism that it enabled were religious things (Delaney 2004). The problem for Peruvian strivings toward familia futurity was that the religious domaining of time made lateness a sin, not merely a "deficiency," and people with certain sins—such as the sin of thinking that single adulthood was "not wrong"—were not likely to "marry in God's temple for eternity" as the epigraphic hymn demanded. Such a conjunction of lateness with the eternal welfare of the soul placed many Peruvian Mormon single adults outside of the category of family and outside of Zion's gates.

Sectorizing Time and Family

In Delia's lesson, she masterfully pieced together the Sunday School manual, another church manual called *Starting and Growing My Own Business* (2017) from the church's *Self-Reliance Initiative*, the church's document called "The Family" (mentioned in chapter 1), and—mostly—her own extemporaneous thoughts. After her monologue on punctuality, she began extolling nuclear marriage as the unit of capitalist production and reproduction. She stated that the male-headed conjugal couple's home needed to reflect a strict gender hierarchy and no more than two cohabiting generations (parents and children) lest it devolve into a rhizomatic caretaking network and means of equal wealth distribution. One message of Delia's lesson seemed to be that nonnuclear familia structures with conglomeration models of marriage portended dangerous communism. For Delia, danger pervaded pacha and other communal familial models common among her Sunday School students (and her own relatives) wherein marriage was the melding of two or more existing familial complexes. She depicted such familias as straying from the righteous foundations affixed to individuation models of marriage. In sum, her lesson made clear that for Peruvian Mormons to properly move away from a pacha kin model founded in place-based, collective reciprocity, their movement toward the individuation of nuclear family units had to coincide with the adoption of an individuated time. Forever family required a time that was separate from place and relatedness. It required a time that was futurized and self-reliant.

In her punctuality monologue, Delia described such a futurized time as difficult, even idiotic to try to adopt in Peru. This difficulty was a real one because Peru was part of the place formerly known as Abya Yala, which had a meaning that was progressive but not conjugated into the future tense (Mallku Bwillcawaman 2015). The Indigenous rights activists of the Andes who used "Abya Yala" (Earth in the blossoming) as a placename for the so-called "Americas" wished to restore with that placename a sense of time as tied to locality, or, more accurately, as indistinguishable from place. They called that sense "pacha," a concept that Western ethnographers mistakenly translated as merely "Earth." Pacha, however, "does not suppose the separation of time and space, pacha is the conjunction of both at the same time. It is more than that, it is also order. Consequently, if pacha has the connotation of cosmos, it speaks of an interrelated cosmos, intimately interdependent on different elements. Therefore, pacha should be understood as home, within which everything and everyone belongs to one family under one roof" (81).

The official church's project of separating time from Earth, of further cutting time up into sectors of past/present/future, and finally, of disciplining individuals to be "on time" as dictated by numbered minutes and generations was all inextricable from its simultaneous project of cutting up families into nuclear units destined to live under separate roofs. Conversely, pacha encapsulated interdependence. However, interdependence did not imply a negation of futurity. The Andean ontology that pacha was conglomerated familial coresidence lay askance, but not completely opposed to the Mormon ontology that future was family.

Socially Engineered Retornadas

Crossing Andean and Mormon notions of time and family probe the categorical mismatch of "marriage" in Zion and connect to the third level of meaning for the refrain, "there is no future in Peru." This meaning sprouted from the fact that Peruvian Mormons in my study could rarely be on time. Not only did many of them suffer, along with Peruvianness itself, from what Delia considered a profoundly pathological unpunctuality, and not only were they, like Bishop Paucar, often two to three generations behind Utah Mormons, but they had also often just missed, or feared that they might soon miss, a vital Mormon life-stage deadline. Both male and female unmarried Mormons in Peru for whom the unwritten Mormon marriageability deadlines were fast approaching basically had no family—and thus no future—in Peru.

They had no family because no matter how many aunts, uncles, brothers, sisters, godchildren, comadres (mothers of godchildren), godparents, and cousins they had and with whom they lived "under one roof," they lacked the principal ingredient of the primordial and newly traditional Mormon family—a spouse.

They had no future because their future was in Utah. Utah was where they had the highest statistical probability of finding their only path to a fully celestial and "blossomed" futurity—a Mormon spouse. This calculus was the result of two equally important facts, one doctrinal and the other demographic. The doctrinal fact was that a Mormon had to marry another Mormon—religious endogamy—in order to be temple-sealed during life and inherit the Celestial Kingdom in the afterlife. The demographic fact was that the highest concentration of marriageable Mormons in the world during my study was to be found in Utah.

Pasi, the dance abstainer from chapter 3, was one of many single Peruvian Mormons whom I encountered during this project who, in their late twenties and early thirties, were pushing the chronological boundaries of Mormon marriageability that Sunday School lessons on time-thrift and scarcity, such as Delia's, helped draw. Pasi was one of many single Peruvian Mormons who found that optimal marriage partners were harder to find in Peru than in Utah. Pasi gave three main reasons for her mate-finding difficulties in Peru, none of which had to do with an inequality in the population ratio of Mormon women to Mormon men.

The first reason was that many ward families in Peru did too good a job at being families. By this she meant that, in being shelters from the rest of Peruvian society—which did not necessarily persecute Mormons, but simply held to customs that were against Mormon worthiness standards—Peruvian ward families spent so much time eating, partying, and worshiping "under one roof" that they fostered a feeling of siblingship. Often, that feeling became so strong that it provoked the incest taboo. In other words, when Pasi attended well-lit, ward-sponsored dances in Cusco where she would interact with many marriageable Mormon males, she would often understand those males to be her brothers in a sense too literal to allow for marriage. She felt the demands of familial exogamy—marrying outside one's family group—even more keenly than the importance of religious endogamy. In English-speaking wards in Utah, on the other hand, members were not quite as tight knit. Utah's Anglo Mormons did not spend nearly as much time at ward activities as their

Peruvian counterparts, so marriage matches made within the same ward family were more common (though often still felt as slightly incestuous).

The second reason that Pasi used to explain why it was more difficult for her to find a mate in Peru than in Utah had to do with the franchise model of Mormon Zion. The model stipulated that wards in Peru be mapped the same as wards in Utah despite an important difference between the two places: Peruvians tended to live in giant familial complexes and Utahans tended to split off and form distally dwelling nuclear units. Part of the franchise model dictated that ward families should be small enough for everyone to know everyone else. This meant that wards would occasionally split and be remapped, keeping each ward to about 150 active members. The effect on the ground in Peru of this Utah ward-mapping practice was that some Peruvian wards consisted of only a few familial complexes because those were all that was necessary to bring the ward's numbers up to 150 members. This meant that Peruvian ward families often literally mapped onto preexisting Peruvian familias. The Abedul family in Barrio Periféricos was one such family. For young Fabio Abedul, transplanting the Utah ward-mapping practice to Peru meant that when he attended his ward dances, most of the dance partners available to him in his age cohort were his actual cousins, aunts, nieces, and sisters, not to mention his sisters in Christ.

Mormons in both Peru and Utah were expected to join the ward family assigned to their place of residence. They were not allowed to simply choose among any of the wards in their cities, but Mormons in Peru often did so anyway for the purpose of finding someone to marry who was not already "familia." Others, like Pasi, went further. They immigrated to Utah.

The third reason that Pasi thought her husband search would be easier in Utah than in Peru was that male returned missionaries, or retornados in Peru—its most eligible bachelors in Pasi's mind—found female returned missionaries (retornadas) like Pasi to be counterintuitively less desirable as marriage partners than females who had not served missions. As this third reason is more complex than the first two, it provides a unique contemplation of the category of marriage that I will allow Pasi's words below to prepare.

From her ancestral home in Cusco, Pasi was the regional supervisor (an unpaid position) over the entirety of South America for a humanitarian-aid foundation that Anglo Mormons in Utah kickstarted. At the time of our only digitally recorded interview in 2015, she had been in Utah for almost a year. This meant that she was about to overstay the extra six-month extension of her original tourist visa that the foundation had helped her acquire years prior. I did not prompt the following utterance from that Utah interview with any questions about marriage or migration, yet that was the import and subtext of each of Pasi's sentences.

Two years ago, I came here to Utah for one week with the foundation to raise funds for the children, and from that I obtained my tourist visa. So, when I went back to Cusco after that week, I said, "Well, I have the visa."

And, as they always say, "take advantage of it!"

And I'm like, "how am I supposed to take advantage of it?"

But I said to myself, "there must be a reason I have it."

So—right?

"I'll have to see."

And I don't know if you've noticed that retornadas in my country are always—it is difficult for them to get married. All the people I know here in Utah who are retornadas have their families already [meaning, they have been married already]. They get married after their missions.

So, I said, "Wow, over in Utah they actually appreciate retornadas."

But they don't in Peru. The Peruvian guys always say, "Oh, you retornadas are so obsessed with the mission rules. I don't want to be forced into daily morning scripture study like during the mission."

What idiocy! I mean, I think that is just an excuse to not make the decision—.

But as I was saying—I think that—that drives a lot of it—and so—having the visa and thinking about my whole life—well, "I am going to use this visa to see how things go for me over there."

Pasi chose her language and silences carefully. Her declared reason for being in Utah was to change her tourist visa to a student visa so that she could study in BYU's English as a second language program. Yet, she had an ulterior motive for migrating to Utah that she suspected that I would surmise because of a key that she had already given me, one that she knew any Mormon would understand—her age at baptism, which was beyond the age of prime marriageability. When I did not seem to use that key to decode her migration story as being largely a husband-search, she gave me another clue—her retornada status. When I still refused to connect the dots and ask directly about her marital motivations for being in Utah, she got confused and felt it would be less awkward to simply preempt my inevitable question: "I arrived here [in Utah] with the hope—well—that—This is the truth— I'll say it again—Upon figuring that I didn't have any progress in my city, I mean—I felt that I wasn't progressing spiritually, both personally and in my profession, and like, let's say—basically—since marriage wasn't happening for me in Cusco, I came here to Utah."

Pasi was baptized Mormon at the age of twenty-four. This meant that she was not on time for certain age-specific life stages that were vital for full Zion citizenship. Foremost among those was marriage. During my study, the ideal female age for Mormon marriage was nineteen for reasons I will soon discuss.

In Pasi's new Mormon lexicon, marriage was the only way for someone older than age eighteen—an "adult" in Anglo Mormonism—to count as a member of a family. Pasi demonstrated that lexicon in her usage of "family" during the interview to mean only the sort of family that one forges upon marriage, not the sort into which one is born. "Family," in the linguistic norms of Pasi's Peruvian Mormon congregation, no longer connoted one's parents and siblings after one became an "adult." In other words, "family," especially when spoken in reference to Mormon matrimonial futures, was an unmarked term among many of my study participants that meant "nuclear family," which further meant a monogamously married heterosexual couple cohabiting only with its biological or legally adopted children. Therefore, when Pasi became a Mormon as an unmarried twenty-four-year-old, it was as if she became an orphan even though she was living pacha relatedness with a multitude of hermanos and other kin. She lost her linguistic status as a member of her parents' family when she became a member of her ward family. In sum, though twenty-four was a highly normative age to be single among non-Mormons in Cusco, upon crossing over into the timeline of Mormonism, Pasi found herself already dangerously late to the matrimonial future required for her to become a family member ever again. Her sudden orphanhood combined with her sudden unpunctuality to heighten the urgency between the lines of the interview transcript wherein she equated her matrimonial future to "progressing spiritually."

Pasi's new Mormon timeline was not only more fast-paced than her Cusco timeline, but it was also more strictly gendered. Both of those aspects were partially due to the church's understanding of unmarried missionary work as the supreme classroom for proper masculinity equivalent to married motherhood, the key classroom for proper femininity (Moslener 2020). To ensure that young females who wished to be missionaries ended up having time in their reproductive life spans to also be wed mothers, the church's top leaders socially engineered different minimum mission ages and service times based on gender. From 1830 to 1898, females could not serve missions at all. In 1951 the minimum female missionary age changed from twenty-one to twenty-three, and then back to twenty-one again in 1964 where it remained until 2012 (Golding 2020). During that time span, the male minimum age was always set at least two years younger than the female age. During my study, males could serve two-year missions at age eighteen, but females had to wait until age nineteen, and they could only serve 1.5-year missions. The extra year gave females more time to find a marriage option so that they would not choose the mission option. Marrying before turning nineteen was not unusual for Mormon women because Mormon men who returned from their missions as early as age twenty were looking for a mate younger than themselves for the same reason that they were looking for a mate without mission experience.

They were the ones—according to "The Family"—who, "by divine design, preside[d] over their families in love and righteousness" (First Presidency 1995, para. 7). Wives did not preside. Therefore, husbands needed to be more experienced in the sort of righteousness for which the mission served as a bootcamp.

Ironically, Pasi's entry into the one Mormon life-stage for which she was not late—the mission—reduced her marriageability even more than her age. The cut-off age for serving a mission was twenty-six. Pasi had only been a Mormon for one year when she enlisted as a missionary. Perhaps she chose a mission because she perceived the unspoken social fact that returned missionaries were more fully "Mormon." However, another social fact to which she was less privy at the time involved the gendered distinction between retornada and retornado. If men did not complete the full two years of their missionary rite of passage, they remained in a state of perpetual liminality in Zion, making them the least eligible bachelors (Shunn 2015). This was not the case for Mormon women in my study. Completed or not, their missionary service literally did not count. For example, at one of the many statistics-reporting meetings that I attended as the Super Quorum president in Barrio Periféricos, the stake president had each of his seven bishops, including Bishop Paucar, shout out the number of youths currently serving missions from each of the seven wards under the stake president's jurisdiction in order to calculate each ward's algorithmic self-reliance. Missionary numbers were indicators of what the central church called "self-reliance" because the Lord promised "blessings" (a complex interplay between spiritual and economic benefits) to nuclear families that sacrificed their sons to church missionary service in other parts of Peru or the world. Tabulating the sum of those individual families' sacrifices and combining it with other metrics of family-level self-reliance equaled each ward's gross self-reliance on the bottom line of the stake president's progress reports to Salt Lake City.

Bishop Paucar yelled out, "four," which I knew included one male missionary and three female missionaries. Other bishops yelled out higher numbers, the highest being eleven. The numbers that the bishops were shouting out seemed exaggerated to the stake president until he realized what was wrong. He playfully chided, "Nice try, guys, but stop inflating your numbers with misioneras. You know that sisters don't count toward the missionary metric."

For females, neither statistical nor social inclusion was increased through missionary work. Returned from her mission at age 26.5, not only was Pasi even later for marriage than before, but she was now a stigmatized retornada. Retornadas were stigmatized because their most eligible potential mates, retornados, often saw them as too capable of leadership to fit the subservient role of a nurturing wife that "The Family" prescribed. Also, since the mission was considered an obligation for males but only an option for females, females who chose the mission were sometimes assumed to have done so only because they had no options for marriage (Radke and Cropper-Rampton 2005). In practice, this meant that a retornada was often plagued by the unasked question that she assumed was on every Mormon's tongue, "What was so wrong with you that no retornado wanted to marry you before you turned nineteen?"

Marriage and the Making of a Person

This is all to say that at age twenty-six, Pasi was well beyond Anglo Mormonism's ideal age of marriageability. Furthermore, as a retornada who daily promoted the forever family on her mission to Bolivia, she was more aware than ever of the relationship that this timeline had to full Mormon personhood and goddesshood. Part of the forever family propaganda was that in order to become true Saints in this life and gods in the next, humans had to be married. For various historical reasons involving the defense of polygyny (Bennion 2004), the transferring of polygynous zeal to monogamy, and the defense of monogamy during the culture wars of the 1960s, Mormons in my project granted an outsized importance to marriage and motherhood relative to greater Christianity (McDannell 2020b). However, that Pasi's message would not have sounded entirely foreign to Bolivians brings up an important and obvious point: Mormons did not have a monopoly on the idea that marriage was vital to personhood.

In this discussion of what Pasi had to overcome in order to achieve inclusion in an Andean Zion and of what her struggle revealed about the diverse categorizations labeled "marriage" across Peruvian and Anglo Mormonisms, it is important to consider Andean expectations of marriage along with Mormon ones. Marriage was an important part of personhood in the Andes in general, but it meant something different than it did to Anglo Mormons because the deeper category of "gender" itself meant something different. Throughout this book, my utilization of generalized Andean examples risks essentializing Andeans. To mitigate this, I must clarify that there was no such thing as an Andean culture and that British anthropologist Andrew Canessa's (2012) Jaqi study participants in Bolivia were never analogues to a mystical past of ungendered complementarity. Just because they lived in rural areas and because Canessa coded them as "Indigenous" did not mean that Jaqi lived as they always had. However, because of geographical proximity, it stands to reason that Pasi's urban cusqueña life shared some elements of a prior symbolic repertoire with Jaqi society that her life did not share with Anglo Utah Mormon society.

Therefore, a glimpse at the world through the eyes of Canessa's anthropologized (which is to say, fictionalized) Jaqi study participants during the time of his fieldwork (which is to say, they have since changed) might elucidate some important differences and similarities, small as they were, between greater Anglo and greater Andean gender expectations. This contrast might, in turn, provide a sense of the categorical rewiring of "marriage" in which unmarried

Andean Mormons like Pasi had to engage during my fieldwork, the late 2010s, in order to exist as both Andeans and Mormons.

For Jaqi people, rather than being part of one's primordial essential nature, the aspect of personhood that Anglo Mormons would have called "gender" was constructed. What Mormons would have considered a human infant, Jaqi people saw as a genderless pile of raw materials with certain happenstance characteristics, such as the beginnings of a penis, that could have been molded into what, one day, might have become one of two binaries, the combination of which made a full human (Canessa 2012). Philosophically, those binaries formed part of a larger system of complementarity which sustained "that no being or happening exist[ed] monodically, rather it always ha[d] its compliment" (Mallku Bwillcawaman 2015, 70).

Among Jaqi people, if a "male" was desired, the umbilical cord of the proto male would be cut longer to help with penis growth. This idea that even phenotypic sex needed assistance in Bolivia was in line with anthropologist Elizabeth Roberts's (2012) study of in-vitro fertilization (IVF) clinics in Ecuador wherein "nature [wa]s not seen as a fixed object, waiting to be discovered by people . . . instead it [wa]s experienced as malleable, shaped through interactions with people who exist[ed] in relation to the material biological world" (xxiv). "Where people do not see genitals as the root explanation of gender, it is interesting to note that genital development is dependent, at least partly, on human intervention" (Canessa 2012, 127).

In this interdependent construction of gender/sex, maleness was not seen as superior to femaleness. Theoretically, but definitely not in practice, there was complete parity between the two poles that formed part of the greater tent of complementarity and ayllu kept taut through the tension between ayni and tinku (reciprocity and alienation). What made a person was the combination of the two poles in marriage. In fact, the word for marriage in Aymara, jaqichasiña, means "the making of a person." Jaqi people in Canessa's view did not enter the other world complete without their opposing pole, so if a male died unmarried, he was buried with a hen, and a female with a rooster (Canessa 2012). This "unity and fight of contraries" (Mallku Bwillcawaman 2015, 222), represented in contemporary rooster and hen burials, was found painted on ancient ceramic art all over the Andes. Since rooster and hen burials balanced the polarity, there was little societal anxiousness and pressure to marry before death. Pressure to marry was anathema because society was centered around good relations—pacha—that belied individuality and identity. This ethos of oneness regarding life-stage events was also felt among Dakota people according to anthropologist Ella Cara Deloria (1988). Speaking of the Beloved Child rite, she wrote that "the majority lived and died content without its coming to them personally" (76). They were instructed that if the ceremony happened to one in their age cohort, it was happening to them all because "'you are all one,' they were told" (75). Likewise, among Jaqi people, as long as enough marriage was happening in the ayllu to produce the humans vital to its cycle, it did not matter that marriage was not happening for a specific individual. In other words, the unmarried state of individuals in the ayllu did not place their eternal lives at stake in the same way that being unmarried did to individuals in Zion.

Another result of the collective relations among Jaqi people was that birth from a woman did not make a person more related to that woman than the person was to the ayllu as a whole through pacha (Cannessa 2012). As such, Jaqi people did not descend from individuals at all, much less individuals with discoverable lineages that needed to be urgently digitized and linked in Mormon temples in order to become legitimated as forever families. For example, in a Peruvian highland village called Carhuahuran, as Kimberly Theidon (2013) documented, there existed affection between kin, but it was not considered natural. Children had to be deliberately taught how to make their mothers love them. The mother-child relationship in Carhuahuran resembled the fiancé relationship in Anglo Mormon courtship in that it had to be cultivated. It could not be taken for granted.

Some of the categorizations of marriage in Canessa's and Theidon's field sites likely influenced Pasi. Therefore, incorporating Mormonism's lineage directionality and time sensitivity into her understanding of marriage likely represented a challenge of categorical reconfiguration for her. Such a reconfiguration was material, rather than simply symbolic, because it involved her Utah immigration. Her involvement with Utah heightened the challenge of marital reconfiguration for her because Utah was from whence the "unidimensional LDS woman [wa]s broadcasted as the LDS female *par excellence*" (Hoyt 2020, 54). Pasi, and others like her, "as women, and as women living outside of the U.S., . . . are given an ideal to strive for that is based upon a femininity that is largely unattainable. This potentially keeps other ways of knowing and doing the feminine inaccessible, unofficial, and even unacceptable. In short, any femininity that isn't aligned with the dominant North American model of ideal LDS femininity is irregular, or other" (54).

The principal unspoken ideal of that broadcasted, LDS femininity did not simply involve eventual marriage as did for Jaqi people. Rather, it involved early marriage. In sum, the Anglo Mormon archetype of early marriage merged with the stigmatization of her age and retornada status to heighten Pasi's danger of being stuck in perpetual non-sainthood. Her civil status, a status that she had not considered an important part of her femininity before she was baptized Mormon, was now causing her to reevaluate her entire life.

Extremely Single (Never Quite) Adults

Recall the ontological fact of the visa as a miracle, the cardkey to the future. In the interview, when Pasi said, "having the visa and thinking about my whole life," she was interpreting that miracle in the only way that it could be interpreted in Peruvian Mormonism. She was basically saying, "Maybe God gave me this visa because He has a husband waiting for me *now* in Utah, the only place where proper femininity is practiced and where even retornadas are marriageable."

The visa, as miracles tend to do, came in the nick of time. Back from her mission, Pasi went from not relating to others in terms of civil status to suddenly being halfway on a spectrum between soltera (single) and what Peruvian Mormon singles jokingly denoted "solteraza" (extremely single). Incidentally, that joke was the motif of a talent night that I attended in the stage-equipped cultural hall of Barrio Periféricos's chapel in 2018. Mormon talent acts in Arequipa tended to consist of either lip-syncing to popular music or lampooning aspects of gospel culture. Since the Jóvenes Adultos Solteros (JAS) (ML: Young Single Adults) organization was in charge of emceeing the event, satirizing the Mormon pressure to get married became the night's comedic focus. The JAS representatives adopted hilariously realistic radio-announcer voices to introduce each skit from an offstage mic. If a fellow JAS member happened to be in the next act, the emcee would say something akin to the following statement that I caught on film: "And finally—for all you ladies in the room—singing the part of Daddy Yankee, we have none other than the soltero, the solterísimo, the *solterazo*—Kenny! [applause]. Oh, and Kenny, your girlfriend called into the station with an urgent message for you: She does not love you."

"Kenny, she does not love you," became the running joke of the night. Unfortunately, in the lives of many of the Peruvian Mormon singles in my study, the tongue-in-cheek designation of solterazo became less funny and more serious as they approached their thirty-first birthdays, because that was the age at which they graduated from the official organization for "youth" ages eighteen to thirty, JAS, to another organization for singles simply called Adultos Solteros (AS) (ML: Single Adults). In Peru, AS was the singles' organization for (never quite) adults ages thirty-one to death. Just as Jaqi people were not complete until they were married, there was a sense in Peruvian Mormonism that singles were not adults in the full, unmarked sense of the term. Rather, they were "single" adults. If one was female and belonged to AS, one was—no longer jokingly—a solterona (spinster).

AS represented another life stage at which being single carried gendered repercussions. Unlike English, Spanish technically has a male equivalent to spinster—solterón. However, "solterón," like "bachelor," can carry a positive connotation evoking freedom while its female counterpart cannot. In both English and Spanish, the connotation behind "spinster" had no male equivalent that approximated its negativity during my study. This provides linguistic evidence that, in both the United States and Peru, being single was more socially and economically dangerous for females than it was for males. In

Mormon Zion, however, since marriage was technically as vital for godhood as it was for godesshood, thirty-one-year-old unmarried males existed closer to their female counterparts in spiritual precarity than they did in social precarity.

Peru did not have the Mormon population to warrant organizing entire congregations around age and civil status demarcations, but Utah did. The ageist structures of these singles wards (AML) in Utah represented one of Katari's biggest criticisms of Utah Mormonism. This came to the fore during our aforementioned conversation in the food court of a university in Utah where he studied. Katari was a twenty-six-year-old Bolivian male. He told me that he wanted the church to fess up to the social engineering that it was doing regarding marriage. He wanted to write a paper about how putting singles into wards based on ages with cut-offs was especially damaging to women. He told me about a twenty-seven-year-old woman in his own eighteen-to-thirty ward in Utah. Only six males in her ward were older than she was and, as such, they were the only guys who could have possibly asked her out according to the norms of Utah singles wards, which required the male to be older than the female in a courtship. But, instead of asking her out, they would only ask the "fresh meat": the new college freshmen moving into the neighborhoods near the university every semester.

I asked Katari, "But once she hits thirty-one, she will be transferred to the thirty-one-to-forty-five ward, so won't she suddenly become the hot item herself?"

He answered, "Yes, but that's not a good thing. Thirty-one-to-forty-five wards are full of men who have one thing in common: no women wanted them for some reason—and, more often than not, it was a good reason."

The bishops of singles wards were not selected from the men within the ward as bishops usually were. Instead, they tended to be older, married men called from nearby family ward (the opposite of singles wards) to leave their ward families behind and serve on special assignment as bishops in singles wards. A singles ward bishop would be expected to attend church with his wife in order to exemplify the marital futurity that his unmarried parishioners needed. Katari told me what he called "horror stories" about bishops of eighteen-to-thirty wards who were so obsessed with the kick-out-at-thirty-one rule that they would actually break up couples—the whole point of the singles ward—by announcing to the man, sometimes at his ward-sponsored, thirty-first birthday/farewell party, that he had to leave his girlfriend behind in the eighteen-to-thirty ward and join the thirty-one-to-forty-five ward. Katari told me about one thirty-one-year-old guy who actually had to be escorted out of Sacrament Meeting because he refused to leave. I did not ask Katari if the man's banishment from his girlfriend's ward resulted in their breakup, but Katari's stories spoke volumes about how obsessed the Leaders were with micromanaging the marriages of young people.

What affected Katari the most was how his religion's ageist structures pressured so many to marry young that the pool of marriageable women was almost completely depleted for twenty-six-year-olds like him. To illustrate how the pressure to marry became toxic within AS organizations and how that hampered recategorizations of "marriage," thus inhibiting ampler figurations of forever family (such as forever familia), I will now describe a few meetings that I attended with members of Pasi's ward in Cusco. The experiences below happened one year after my recorded, Utah interview with her.

Pasi was back in Cusco and still single after her yearlong sojourn in Utah, which everyone in her cusqueño ward family knew about. She invited me to what she told me was a "Family Home Evening" for the "youth" of her cusqueño ward in which she was assigned to give the lesson. Family Home Evening, also called Family Night was an initiative that the church started in 1965 (Stanton 2020)—complete with a globally homogenizing manual—wherein nuclear families were supposed to sacrifice social, professional, and even ecclesiastical affairs one night a week, preferably Monday, in order to spend time together singing, studying scriptures, and, most of all—as "The Family" states—having "wholesome recreational activities" (First Presidency 1995, para. 7). In Utah this became a consumerist extravaganza. Not only did most movie theaters, bowling alleys, and "fun zones" advertise Monday Family Night specials, but LDS bookstores, such as the church-owned Deseret Book, sold all kinds of *Book of Mormon*—themed Family Night games and supplies. These included the starkly raced, hypermasculinized action figures of Ammon (a Nephite) and Samuel the Lamanite, which, among other items from Deseret Book, Peruvian Mormons in Peru often requested that I bring back from my trips to Utah as there were no branches of Deseret Book in Peru.

One popular Deseret Book item that I saw on the walls of many Peruvian Mormons in Utah was a pegboard whereupon the hand-painted names of family members were cycled weekly through Family Night's different roles. Any visitor to the home during the week would see that it was Tatiana's turn to say the opening prayer, Mamá's turn to decide on the activity, Junior's turn to give the lesson, and Papá's turn to provide the refreshments. Family Night, therefore, not only gave Utah businesses a chance to demonstrate their Mormon-friendliness, but it also gave Mormon families a material way (home décor) to show off their dedication to achieving the only social grouping—the nuclear family—that was legible in Anglo Mormonism as "family."

Peruvians in Peru—who were often the sole Mormons in their familias—sometimes banded together for Family Night in groupings that, on every other night, did not get to count as families by Anglo Mormonism's standards. On the occasion documented below (June 2016), since Pasi said "youth," I assumed that she was taking about some sort of combined Family Night for her ward's Young Men/Young Women organization for children and teens ages eleven to seventeen. However, that seemed strange to me because, if it really were a night for the whole family, it would not have been exclusive to children and teens. Since we got to the chapel in Cusco on time (7:00) for Family Night, we had time to talk before it actually started. Pasi kept saying things like, "a lot of the youth my age want to go to Utah." She was thirty-one, so not exactly a "youth" in my mind. Suddenly, it was 7:30 and the activity was going to start. That was when I saw the group of "youth" that she was talking about and finally put two and two together. The Family Night was to be a combined JAS and AS activity (mostly AS) and not a Young Men/Young Women activity, which was why calling it "Family Home Evening" made sense to Pasi. The idea was that single adults, being single, did not have families with which to do a Family Home Evening. Even though most cusqueño single Mormons lived under the same roof with large extended families, some of which were Mormon familial conglomerations that were matrilocal and that provided the ward with the lion's share of its membership, those nonnuclear networks somehow did not count as "Family" for "Home Evening" purposes and so singles had to combine into a little "AS family."

During the rest of the night, the AS members kept calling our group, "we, as youth," even though I was thirty-eight, and I was sure that some of them were older than me. I did not consider myself a "youth" and I wondered why they did. Racism called Black men "boys." Sexism called women "girls." Had the adults in Pasi's AS family internalized Mormonism's stigmatization of singleness to the extent that they would call themselves "youth" until they were married?

In the front of the classroom stood two men: the ward AS president, Riqui (single), and a member of the ward's bishopric assigned to oversee AS, Brother Lobón (married). They called the single man by his first name and the married one by the formal Brother-plus-surname. They were both approximately the same age. There were four men and six women in the room. They immediately asked me how old I was and if I were married to see if I belonged in their group. I did not, but they said that I could join anyway, just that once.

We were supposed to break the ice, so Riqui had everyone relate their "funniest comi." I was not the only person who did not know what he meant by "comi," so he translated it as, "what is your hobby that is funny?" I was surprised at how childish the ensuing anecdotes sounded to me. Was I just buying into the suggestibility of the idea that this was a meeting of "youth," or was it that considering themselves to be youth really made them see the world in a more childlike way? Riqui said that he glimpsed a fat lad on the bus sit on a piece of gum. As the lad got off the bus, the huge strand of gum strung between his backside and the seat all the way out the door. In Pasi's "comi," she tried to joke about Utah's mythical status as a Mormon mate-finding mecca, but what she ended up saying was simply: "The number of AS that we have here in Cusco is nothing. In Utah, there are 400 in one group, lots of spouses to choose from."

At that, there was an awkward silence. Everyone seemed to be thinking, "with those odds and after an entire year in Utah, why is she still single?"

After Pasi's lesson, it was time for the recreational activity. I had been to dozens of similar Family Nights among Peruvians and had always found them enjoyable. However, this was my first time going to an AS activity. Even though we played many of the same classic Latin American Mormon games that I had come to tolerate, if not love—getting straight-faced opponents to laugh by acting like a poor cat or donning thick gloves and unwrapping a chocolate bar with a spoon until someone else rolled a six—this time it all seemed degradingly silly. We played a nonedible version of the chocolate game until almost 10:00, and when we finally had to stop, the woman who supplied the dice from her purse—which she told me that she always had at the ready in case a game was afoot—seemed inordinately dejected. I could not help feeling that the AS meeting was like an AA (Alcoholics Anonymous) meeting. It was as if singleness were a disease: "Hi, my name is Pasi, and I am single."

A month later, I was back in Cusco attending Pasi's ward's Sunday School, which took place after Sacrament Meeting. Her ward had a segregated Sunday School class just for AS. Brother Lobón let me attend despite my married status. During Sunday School, we sat around the table with seven other single adults, a few in their sixties. AS President Riqui started the lesson by saying that whenever people pressured him to get married, he would tell them, "Why do you care if I get married?" He told us how the female missionary pair currently assigned to the ward (one Anglo, one Peruvian, both fifteen years younger than him) were trying to convince him to consider the many eligible ladies in the ward by using the biblical argument that "it is not good that the man should be alone" (Genesis 2:18). He countered with his own argument: he wanted to find a wife who understood the true meaning of "The Word of Wisdom" (ML: the Mormon health code). He then said, "I start with that little anecdote to segue into the topic of today's lesson: The Word of Wisdom."

After the lesson, the stake-level AS representative came in to promote the Cusco-wide AS convention, complete with a dance, a "fireside" (interactive motivational speech), and a sightseeing trip to Moray. She asked everyone how much of the 50-sol fee they would pay her right then, but almost nobody was planning on going. Riqui himself was not going because he had to visit his mom. The representative was aghast, "But you are the leader! You have to go!" Meanwhile, another woman was WhatsApp-ing AS members in other wards throughout Cusco. None could attend.

Those two meetings—the AS Family Home Evening and the AS Sunday School—helped me pinpoint a few aspects of the category of marriage in Zion that were contested between Anglo and Peruvian Mormonism. One of those aspects had to do with the Anglo Mormon idea that husband-wife love was superior to parent-child love. The other had to do with Anglo Mormonism's future-centric understanding that one's future spouse was out there waiting and that it was one's responsibility to love that person in the present enough to find her or him as soon as possible. Both of those aspects of marriage were ritualized in the penultimate, and most strikingly gendered ceremony that Mormons carried out in their temples during my study. The ceremony was called the Endowment. It involved theatrically ritualizing the biblical Adam and Eve human origin story, and it made clear that the proper Mormon husband was to be a middleman between his wife and God. He was to be the symbolic liaison tasked with bringing his wife into Heavenly Father's celestial presence. During the participant vocalization aspect of the Endowment, even unmarried women had to covenant out loud in unison to obey their husband. For an unmarried woman, the Endowment gave a future man whom she did not yet know power over her access to the divine.

Regarding Pasi's categorization of marriage vis-à-vis the proper amount of love that she should have been feeling toward her future spouse and the impetus that love was supposed to produce in motivating her to attend the activities necessary to find him, the AS meetings draw attention to the contradiction that AS represented: AS members invariably resented the Mormon social pressure to marry, yet they reproduced that pressure among themselves and perhaps even internalized its infantilization. One reason for this was that single adults, like Riqui, were themselves called to lead AS. Riqui's biggest stressor was convincing people to attend spouse-finding activities over which his own son-mother relationship took precedence. In Peru, where it was more socially acceptable than in Utah to use fear tactics and guilt trips to get people to comply, threatening to label someone inactive if they did not attend an activity was common during my study. Her ward family often labeled Pasi inactive, not because she did not sacrifice countless hours each week to church-related activities, but because she did not usually attend the AS ones.

Assigning her to teach the lesson for that Family Night was merely a ploy to procure her attendance. AS activities, by their very AS nature, always had a single objective—matchmaking. All AS members knew this and most AS members resented it. Yet, when Pasi did not attend AS activities, she was not only in danger of being labeled inactive—a designation that a bishop could use to rescind her temple-recommend—but she was also in danger of failing to prioritize her love toward a future unknown husband whom she would have to marry in that temple, a future husband to whom she had already ritualized her obedience and subservience inside that temple. Since being single meant being never quite a Saint, the mate-finding mechanisms of AS were potential keys to Pasi's ultimate sainthood. At the same time, since being single meant being never quite adult and never quite family, the automatic age- and gender-based identity that came with AS membership marked Pasi as a perpetually orphaned youth excluded from mature, forever family homemaking in Zion.

"To What Should a Daughter of God Aspire?"

AS was an especially sore subject for the person who contributed most to my research, arequipeña Mormon Ofelia Dominguez. As an unmarried mother, Ofelia should have had an extra motivation to find a husband above and beyond Pasi's motivation. Not only was getting sealed in the temple to a husband an unwritten requirement for full, unstigmatized Zion citizenship in Barrio Periféricos where Ofelia served in many callings, and not only was a husband a written requirement for goddesshood, but having a Mormon husband was the only way that Ofelia could be temple-sealed for eternity to the person whom she loved the most: her daughter. Daughters could be sealed to mothers in the temple, but only as appendages to the temple-sealed nuclear couple bond. In Anglo Mormonism—the Mormonism that wielded the most power over temple sealing rules and categorizations of marriage—mother-to-daughter love was dangerous and could even become pathological. It became pathological if it distracted single mothers from the love that needed to be driving them: love toward a future husband.

Ofelia's navigation of the love-pathologizing that happened in her AS organization opens a window into the inner workings of the Anglo Mormon marriage category. Those workings demonstrate that Delia's punctuality lesson's capitalistic, scarcity-fearing versions of time and love structured the nucleus of the marriage category. To accentuate Ofelia's negative opinion of AS, however, she first described the pathologizing that happened in the Relief Society, the church's organization for all women over the age of eighteen, single or married. By the time of our thirty-third recorded interview (February 2018), I had apparently asked Ofelia every question under the sun except one.

> OFELIA: Well, the question that you have yet to ask me is, "When are you getting married?" Because everyone else in the world has asked me that question, absolutely everyone, and you are the only one who hasn't, and that is why I trust you [laughs].
>
> JASON: Well, you have told me about the stress of being single in the church. My mom is single as well, and I know it is difficult for her because a lot of the church's messaging has to do with—
>
> OFELIA:—with the family, yes. And there are a lot of sisters who utilize that in order to scorn the single sisters. But I loved the speech that President Thomas S. Monson gave, I don't remember in what year, but it is etched into my memory.

Speaking directly to the single mothers, he told us that we had done a good job with our children. He admired us for being alone and for bringing up our children alone.

He said, "The promises of the Lord are fulfilled for all who stay firm and faithful. If you haven't been married in this life, the Lord will give you a husband in the next, so don't worry. Don't get desperate. Live tranquilly."

And to the single sisters who don't have kids, he said the same thing, "If you haven't had the opportunity, the Lord will give you the opportunity over there."

And one time during Relief Society class, a sister was trying to offend me on this topic because she had some kind of problem with me, so she started saying, "Only the sealed are going to enter into the kingdom of God. Only people with husbands are going to have eternal families. Some single sisters think that just because they sent their kid on a mission, they're fine."

I was the only one in the room who had a child currently on a mission, so I got angry and said to myself, "This sister is going to pay for what she just said" [laughing].

Vengeance!

So, I let her finish. And she looked straight at me, "Any opinions?"

"Yes, I have one. Sister, you are mistaken," I told her.

She said, "How am I mistaken? The manual specifically states"—

—"The manual can say whatever it wants to say," I told her.

I wasn't the only one she was offending, there were plenty of other single sisters there as well, and they didn't dare speak up, but since it was a personal attack on me, I said, "This is what President Thomas S. Monson, our prophet, has said: 'All promises will be fulfilled.' If the Lord has promised eternal life unto all those who are faithful, then we are also included. You aren't guaranteed an eternal family just because you got sealed in some temple. I don't care if you are sealed to them, if you don't work with them, they aren't going to be with you in the eternities. The promises are only for those who remain faithful."

And she just stood there. And, of course, the other sisters started to jump in, "Ofelia is right!"

But that is what keeps me at peace, and my patriarchal blessing also says it, I mean, my blessing is really short, but in one of its few lines it says that I shouldn't worry about obtaining my eternal partner in this time because if I were to worry about it, I would have a lot of problems and even get sick.

And so, whenever someone would ask me, "Hey, why don't you get married already?"

I would say, "Well, yeah, I guess you're right."

But then I would remember my patriarchal blessing, and I'd remember that speech, and I'd say, "I shouldn't worry anymore. If the Lord doesn't want to give me a partner during this time, why get desperate?"

One of the things I've always said is, "I know who I am."

And I have always repeated that to my daughter, "You know who you are, right? So, who are you?"

"I am a daughter of God."

"Remember that always, and how should a daughter of God behave? To what should a daughter of God aspire?"

So, I repeated that over and over and over to her. And I say it to myself as well.

I am a daughter of God.

Just because He hasn't seen fit to give me a partner in this time doesn't mean that I'm going to get desperate and settle for, in quotation marks, "cualquier cosa" [whatever comes along].

I'm not going to get desperate and say, "All right, the next man I find: *Bam!*" Right? Because first I have to see if he is going to help me grow.

Ofelia was able to navigate the impersonal pressure to marry in her manual-driven, bureaucratic religion only because of her personal relationship to God. Many Mormons in my study had received a written "patriarchal blessing" thought to be personal scripture from the Lord Himself through His mouth-piece, a local, stake-level leader called a "patriarch." The patriarchal blessing was a personal scripture so sacred that it was not to be read by anyone but the person whose future it foretold. With that material blessing in her arsenal along with a memorized speech by the living prophet of her Heavenly Father directed specifically to her as an unmarried mother, she was able to withstand the onslaught of demeaning depersonalization that would have had her marry cualquier cosa. She was able to broaden her perspective into a pacha-like union of time and space, such that "this time" came to mean, "my time on this Earth," and "over there"—a seemingly spatial reference—became "my time in the next life." In this sense, Ofelia exemplified anthropologist Savannah Shange's (2019b) observation that "the temporal is a zone of opportunity for subaltern subversion" (89). Ofelia subverted the church manual's fixed timelines that labeled her singleness late. She raided the marriage category and appropriated its desperate future tense, retooling it into a tranquil future tense.

The subaltern identity and premature dismissal of a church leader who dared "demonstrate the many kinds of families within the church" (Maffly-Kipp 2020a, 21) rather than celebrate only "the 'traditional' family" (21) contextu-alizes the danger that Ofelia's temporalizations posed to the Anglo church's fragile category of marriage. Her name was Chieko Okazaki, and she was called to the General Relief Society presidency in the early 1990s, the highest global presidency to which a female could be called in the church. In the same year that the male leadership, without consulting Okazaki, released "The Family," she spoke out very subtly against that document at General Conference. Her speech was about expansive relationality, constructed siblingship, and the dark side of "traditional family." Her speech was provocatively entitled "A Living Network" (1995). That title represented a possible redefinition of family that ran counter to the official definition in "The Family": a static unit. Though she was not excommunicated for her subversive recategorization of family, she was released from her high leadership position soon after.

Ofelia did not speak from a space of institutional power as did Monson or Okazaki; instead, she acted from a place of domestic power. This made her a mujerista theologian in the sense that she challenged "theological understandings, church teachings, and religious practices that oppress Latina women, that are not life-giving, and therefore, cannot be theologically correct" (Isai-Dias 1996, 1). In Ofelia's eternal perspective, a perspective that her Mormonism informed, existential lateness was not theologically correct. In the perspective of the Anglo male-written Relief Society's manuals, however, terrestrial tardiness to familial sealing ceremonies in stone temples carried over into a lateness that was everlasting. Those manuals almost seemed patterned after US Reconstruction era freedman's handbooks wherein the physical whip of slavery was replaced with the textual "emphasis on self-discipline and policing. The whip was not to be abandoned; rather it was to be internalized" (Hartman 1997, 140). Perhaps recognizing such grotesque vestiges in her church's manuals, Ofelia quite sacrilegiously interjected that "the manual can say wherever it wants to say," implying that whatever it wanted to say was not going to affect her self-worth.

Manuals written by male church bureaucrats in Utah could say what they would to the general masses of female membership. However, Heavenly Father knew who Ofelia was as an individual—as a daughter, no less—and He could help her circumvent His nuclear family dogma, a dogma that He knew could have psychosomatic effects ("and even get sick"). However, circumventing her official church's limiting dogma of familial scarcity was no easy task, even for Ofelia. This was because the increasingly patriarchal, bureaucratic structures of her church overlapped complexly, placing her fellow Saints at strategic counterpoints in order to harness their creativity to further the US colonial project.

Proper Amounts and Recipients of Love

Ofelia's church leaders sorted her attributes into diverse taxa based on the impersonal demographics of age, gender, and civil status. Though she chose to be a member of the church, that came with overlapping memberships in other suborganizations that her biology and her Mormon life-stage lateness chose for her. One of those organizations was AS.

OFELIA: The stake AS representative from our ward, Florencia, messaged me, "Hey, there is going to be a party and you must participate."

"No," I tell her. "I'm sorry, but my daughter is arriving from her mission, and I have to prepare her homecoming celebration," I very politely replied. . . .

But she kept on bugging me and started to really get under my skin.

So, she says, "You will come to realize that you must go to this party because you must find a husband."

That was when I lost it! I was beyond bothered, and I said, "In the first place, I know who I am. I'm not going to go out and grab cualquier cosa. If you are so desperate to marry yourself off, go get married for all I care. But not me!"

And she's all, "But why are you so cruel with me? Why do you respond like that?"

"Because I am telling you that I can't go. Nevertheless, you keep insisting."

"But it's that, can't you see? You are going to miss the train. Your years are flying by."

[Laughs] I tell her, "But I'm not desperate. Flo, if the Lord doesn't want to give me a husband here, that is okay."

"But it's that you don't even try!"

"The Lord knows my heart, and He knows what I'm thinking. He knows that I'm doing my part, and so who are you to tell me that I'm not?"

Ofelia's problem mirrored Pasi's problem of never being on time for the Mormon future tense. Yet, Ofelia had an additional problem: loving her daughter too much for the Mormon forever family. Not only was Ofelia single, but she was also a single mother. According to Florencia, her future husband was out there, yet she did not love him enough to look for him. Instead, she loved her daughter. Florencia, herself under immense pressure to marry, accused Ofelia of using her daughter's homecoming preparations as an excuse for not going to the AS activity, an activity that represented the last train to the future.

Florencia's train analogy was spot-on. There was no better metaphor for linear, schedule-driven time across empty space with an infinite potential of possible destination points that all lay ahead. Each station along the unilinear track held the possibility of somewhere better in the future. The cold, iron rail represented Mormon time. In fact, the *Book of Mormon* prophet Lehi had a dream wherein he had to hold fast to an "iron rod," which led him in a straight line through the mists of darkness toward the tree of life. Eating of the tree's fruit brought to his mind the epiphany of forever family in the first place.

In like manner, for many Peruvians living near Peru's Cerro de Pasco mine, the company town's iron rails became the central arteries of life, "encoding the dreams of individuals and societies by representing the possibility of being modern and having a future" (Berg 2015, 57). Ulla Berg's study participants in her ethnographic work near the mine—which, incidentally, was founded by an Anglo Mormon—could not fathom why she would want to rent an apartment far from the busy highway connecting the community to the capital. Berg found that community residents felt a recharging sense of possibility emanating from the road, a sense that it would lead to something. "This 'something,' the never-ending sense that there had to be something ahead, something better and more exciting, is the condition of modernity itself" (57).

If this is the case, Mormonism, unlike Catholicism, is a modern cosmology. In Catholicism, humans fell (thanks to the sin of Eve), and their goal is basically recuperative—to get back to the paradisiacal state from whence they started. In Mormonism, humans are embryonic gods who (thanks to the foresight of Eve) will surpass the state from whence they started and continue to "salir adelante" (get ahead in life) in an eternal upward progression toward "something better."

Florencia was genuinely worried about Ofelia because if her love for her daughter caused her to miss the train, she would lose her chance for the conjugal love that was required for that eternal progression. Yet, ironically, Ofelia was the one who cared about finding conjugal love. Florencia thought of marriage as simply a hoop that she needed to jump through to make it into the highest of Mormon heavens, the Celestial Kingdom: the only station on the track with train connections leading infinitely upward. For that, any temple-worthy Mormon man would do. Ofelia was the one with the audacity to desire an actual affinity for the man she might marry (Palmer 2020). She also had the audacity to go against Delia's punctuality lesson and say, "all is well" in the present. Ofelia was convinced that her singleness was "not wrong" despite Delia's defamation of such thinking as "feeding the mediocrity."

According to many in her ward (including Delia), Ofelia was on track to the medium heaven, the Terrestrial Kingdom. Making it into the highest heaven—what Mormons called "exaltation" as opposed to mere, mediocre "salvation"—required being sealed to one's spouse in an earthly temple either during this life or, by proxy, after death. In this cosmovision, the importance of love paled in comparison to the importance of ticking a box on a checklist of hierarchized, one-time rites or "ordinances," the culmination of which was temple marriage. As the Prophet President Nelson declared in 2019 in what many US Mormon feminists dubbed the "Sad Heaven" speech,

Love songs perpetuate a false hope that love is all you need if you want to be together forever. And some erroneously believe that the Resurrection of Jesus Christ provides a promise that all people will be with their loved ones after death.

In truth, the Savior Himself has made it abundantly clear that while His Resurrection assures that every person who ever lived will indeed be resurrected and live forever, much more is required if we want to have the high privilege of exaltation. Salvation is an individual matter, but exaltation is a family matter. (Nelson 2019, 89)

This contrasted sharply with the speech Ofelia referenced from President Nelson's predecessor, Thomas Monson. Per President Nelson, we will all live forever, but only the exalted will live together forever. When President Nelson said "family," he was referring to the US, White, nuclear family centered around two married individuals of the opposite sex. When Ofelia heard such doctrines, however, her first thought was not of some future marital togetherness. She thought only of her daughter.

I might say, "As soon as I close my eyes, I'm going to the Celestial Kingdom," but, how do I know if Heavenly Father will consider me qualified? Maybe there are some things I've forgotten?

My biggest worry was, how am I going to get sealed, I mean, with my daughter?

Because I'm not sealed in the temple, I'm not married, and so my worry was always that: "Wow, so that means I have to get married if I want to get sealed to my daughter?"

Ofelia and her daughter Shannon were more than just temple-worthy. They lived their religion more fully than anyone whom I had ever met, they were more unified than any married couple that I had ever known, and they made the sixteen-hour bus ride to the Lima temple and performed more proxy ordinances there for deceased others than anyone else with similarly scant financial means in Barrio Periféricos. Yet, they could not perform the most vital of those ordinances for themselves. Simply because Ofelia was not sealed to a man, she could not be sealed to her own daughter, the person whom she loved the most. She was not permitted to make the "covenants" involved in eternal mother-daughter sealing that not only would allow for togetherness in the next life but also would build heaven during this one. As one Mormon theologian, Rosalynde Welch (2020), explained regarding the types of families that temple sealings were thought to form, "the resulting network is not only a cosmic familial structure but a salvific medium: the sealing bonds are sacramental conduits through which divine grace flows. As dramatized in the endowment rite, each individual's access to God routes through the social ties performed by the sealing. Heaven itself is structured—indeed, is brought into being—by sealed familial relationships" (499).

As a result of their improperly nonlinear, matriarchal relationality, Ofelia and Shannon's heaven would have to be postponed, at least in their current official church's linear version of marriage. Their current Prophet continued to heighten the temporal stakes of that postponement in his Sad Heaven speech. Speaking to all those who knew that they had to make marriage covenants in the temple in order to seal the Anglo-defined family, but who, for whatever reason, had not yet made those covenants, President Nelson (2019) stated:

[T]hey have chosen not to make covenants with God. They have not received the ordinances [one-time rites] that will exalt them with their families and bind them together forever. . . .

They need to understand that while there is a place for them hereafter— with wonderful men and women who also chose not to make covenants with God—that is *not* the place where families will be reunited and be given the privilege . . . of never-ending progression and happiness.

Those consummate blessings can come only by living in an exalted celestial realm with God . . . and our wonderful, worthy, and qualified family members. . . .

As you choose not to make covenants with God, you are settling for a most meager roof over your head throughout all eternity. . . .

If you truly love your family and if you desire to be exalted with them throughout eternity, pay the price now. (90)

Ofelia did truly love her family, but if the price involved marrying the next Mormon guy who came along, she was not willing to pay it. The crux of the matter was that for the Prophet and Ofelia, the word "family," and by extension "marriage," did not mean the same thing. Ofelia's strongest familial bond was to her daughter. Her strongest love lay therein. In the Prophet's category of family, however, such love was dangerous to the correct, holy order of things. It polluted the purity of eternal, patriarchal categories. Ofelia's love would not have been pathologized had Ofelia been a non-Mormon in Peru where mother-child love could never be too much. Her love was only a problem in a US patriarchal religion with a fundamental phobia of mother-child love. In any marriage-centric patriarchy, the husband needed a monopoly on love, and in a capitalistic corporate church obsessed with self-reliance, love was imagined as a scarce commodity. What little there was to go around had to go to the husband.

Reflecting on this, I thought of the ways Peruvian Mormon expressions of love contrasted with my own Anglo Mormon upbringing. I experienced a flashback, a memory of something my mother told us kids on multiple occasions, something so uncharacteristic of her that I doubted my recollection. I decided to corroborate it with others who might have had similar memories, so I asked one of the Anglo Mormon feminist Facebook groups of which I was a member: "Growing up Mormon in Utah, my mom (who is now single) would often make a point of telling us the order of her love. She loved God the most, her husband the second most, and us kids the third most. Was anyone else told this or something similar? Is this a Mormon thing? A White people thing? Do you tell your kids this?"

I had posted often across various Facebook groups during my study as a way of taking the pulse of the global Mormon supranation. However, I rarely got more than two likes and, if I was lucky, a single comment. Usually, I got nothing. This post, by the very next day, had 177 comments. In my world, it went viral. The mode comment was almost identical to this: "I'm a White, American, former Mormon and I was told that I was loved less than my parents' spouse constantly." Some thought of this hierarchization of love as a good thing: "I was taught this, but in a way that made me feel happy to have parents who loved each other. White, raised in Utah." A significant minority tended toward this assessment: "There was at least one talk I remember hearing in the 80s where a prophet told women to love their husbands more than their children. Even as a teen, I recognized that as self-serving bullshit." Yet, given Ofelia and Shannon's practice of good relations, I was most struck by the following reply to my query:

> I was raised by a single mother who was active in the church. I don't remember being told this (because it did not apply) but I do remember the quest for her to find a spouse and feeling like that love was tantamount to mother-child love. As a White, married mother myself I am ashamed to say this hierarchy of love resonates true to my processing, *but* your question makes me look at it, and I do not like that hierarchy of love. I will work to consciously unprocess this. I hope that I have not portrayed this hierarchy to my children. My love for them is never in last place.

A combination of forces related to whiteness and patriarchy may have created a love hierarchy in the United States within the category of marriage, one to which Ofelia was not about to conform. As a non-White, unmarried, non-man, her official church triply marginalized her (Francke 1990). Her thrice multiplied distance from full sainthood demonstrated the limits of Mormon marriage and the precise location of the borders around love that Zion was not supposed to have. Ofelia embodied the difficulty of reconfiguring Zion's marriage category for the inclusion of Peruvian Mormons because she was both the most saintly person I knew and the furthest from sainthood.

That was why she was my principal study participant. Anthropologists often looked for the nonperson in the society that they studied because that person's situation revealed what the rules were for full personhood, exposing the society's secrets of relatedness and the true permeability of its categories. For example, during anthropologist Sandra Bamford's (2007) work among the Kamea of Papua New Guinea, she noticed a young man, Netsap, who seemed disconnected from society. She discovered that he was cut off from the male line that would have granted him land. This was not because he was an illegitimate son who did not know his father's identity, it was because his father died before transmitting to him the specific cultivation knowledge of the landscape that he was to inherit. For the Kamea, then, it was the sharing of ecological teachings rather than the sharing of genetic substances that created father-son relations. Instead of transferring to Netsap at the moment of conception the stuff that would create a relationship between them, his father was supposed to transfer it later in life. He died before that was possible, and so Netsap never had a father.

Under One Roof

If Netsap's nonpersonhood revealed that the shared substance of relatedness for the Kamea was ecological knowledge rather than gametes, what did Ofelia's incomplete sainthood in Barrio Periféricos reveal about Mormon marriage? For one, it revealed just how inextricably linked Mormon notions of marriage were to US notions of marriage and that the difficult work in which Peruvian Mormons were engaged consisted of impossibly extricating the one from the other so that they could follow what they knew in their hearts to be right—an abundance model of love—without disobeying the church that they knew to be true. Their extraction work within the category of marriage generated a dynamic Andean Mormon model of forever familia that was both abundant and scarce. What Andeans knew to be right regarding familia did overlap in some areas with the church, for example, in the eventual importance of marriage. Yet, in the Andean cosmovision, marriage had no urgency because it was not a stage on a timeline of progress. "In Andean reflections, pacha . . . is considered qualitatively both a 'before' and an 'after.' Another characteristic of time in the Andean conception is that it is not thought of unidirectionally; rather, it is conceived of in a cyclical form: the future is really found behind and the present ahead, and vice versa" (Mallku Bwillcawaman 2015, 72).

In this Andean conceptualization, time was multidirectional. Contrary to Delia's motivational speech that opened this chapter, there was no such thing as "being on time." Therefore, marriage was not a train with a scheduled departure time for which Pasi and Ofelia were always already late. Nor was marriage a vehicle for leaving familia and cleaving unto a spouse as it was in biblical time. For many Andeans, marriage was an intensely communal event even though there was often no ceremony that Mormons would recognize as a wedding. In fact, what categorized a sexual relationship as a true marriage, rather than what Anglo anthropologists of the Andes called a "trial marriage" (Price 1965), was the place wherein it was carried out: inside the spatial locality of the ayllu. When sexual intercourse was experienced outside of the ayllu's precinct, it was simply a rehearsal, meaningful only to the copulating couple. The ayllu did not care about sexual relationships until they were carried out inside it and with its assistance, traditionally through a festival of ritual drunkenness. "It [wa]s thus through fiestas and the sharing of food, alcohol, and coca with each other and spirits that the community and its identity [wa]s created and affirmed," (Canessa 2012, 123) and through which conception was achieved.

This meant that conception, within many Andean communities, was already "assisted reproduction," which was partially why IVF among Christians in Ecuador was not an aberration as it often was among Christians in the United States (Roberts 2012). It was also why Jaqi copulation within the town was itself the wedding (Canessa 2012). No ceremony was required to further seal the couple together because they already existed in interdependence—pacha— with each other and with the ayllu that constructed them.

What was important for Andean relatedness was being in place, not being on time. This was precisely where Andean relations came into conflict with the separate-unit dwelling arrangements of the self-reliant Mormon nuclear family ideal that distilled all relations down to a single category: marriage. For a Jaqi (human) person, living in President Nelson's heaven would have been very sad indeed, not because failing to marry within the specific allotted window of JAS-time (ages eighteen to thirty) would have made it difficult to qualify for a heavenly mansion instead of a heavenly hut, but because both a hut and a mansion implied independence from the ayllu, from pacha, and from familia—the very things that made people human. As Indigenous humans and Peruvian Mormons, Pasi and Ofelia were not only caught on a harshly individuating timeline—concerned only with their capacity as potential reproductive units for future Zion families—but they were caught between independence and interdependence.

In Peru and Utah, Peruvian Mormon members of what "The Family" considered a mere contingency called the "extended family" often formed expansive, site-bound domestic units where they lived, ate, and—most importantly—loved together. Again, as Andean philosopher Conibo Mallku Bwillcawaman (2015) mandated, "pacha should be understood as home, within which everything and everyone belongs to one family under one roof" (81).

However, as I discuss in the next chapter, contesting the appropriateness of those living arrangements—and the anti-self-reliant *inter*dependence that they implied—points to the refurbishing of a final category: independence. I worshipped with Peruvian Mormons as they worked to both expand and contract that category so as to control who got to dwell under the one roof of Zion.

CHAPTER 7

Independence

I say unto you, be one; and if ye are
not one, ye are not mine.
—*Doctrine and Covenants of the
Church of Jesus Christ of Latter-
Day Saints* (J. Smith et al. 1835, 119)

Interdependent Independence

Mormons like Ofelia and Pasi, whether single or married, often continued living well into adulthood and sometimes for the rest of their lives with the people whom they grew up calling "hermanos," a broad kin term in Peru including siblings, half-siblings, stepsiblings, cousins, parents' godchildren, and anyone within one's generational group with whom one was raised "under one roof" (Mallku Bwillcawaman 2015, 81). During my study, Pasi resided in Cusco in a six-story structure (with rebar for a seventh) inherited from her parents, who were still alive in a distant Runasimi-speaking village. She had six hermanos. Some were Mormons, some had kids, some had spouses, but all were adults living on different floors of the same, perpetually growing, concrete-enforced, brick complex.

This was a highly common living arrangement during my study, not only in Peru, but among Peruvian Mormons in Utah. While stringent zoning restrictions did not allow Peruvian Mormons in Salsands to literally extend their roofs to accommodate growing familia, they still lived close enough to eat under the same roof on a regular basis. In other words, Peruvian Mormon familias somehow managed to live intersubjectivity—pacha—in a religion that simultaneously valued both independent subjectivity and, as the epigraph from the *Doctrine and Covenants* commands, oneness.

Mormonism was an unusual form of Christianity in that respect. According to anthropologist of Christianity Joel Robbins (2004), "in modern Western culture, individualism is a paramount value" (290) borrowed from Christianity. Distinct from individualist cultures, there existed what Robbins called "relationist" (292) cultures, a label that he applied to all "Melanesian cultures"

(292). According to Robbins, pre-Christian Melanesian relationist culture was diametrically opposed to the individualist Christian culture that Melanesians later adopted.

Like Melanesian culture, Peruvianness was relationist in many respects, but, unlike Christianity, so was Mormonism. Per Robbins, Christianity was so utterly individualistic that, "as Christians see it, families, churches, denominations and towns do not get saved, only individuals do" (293). Conversely, as Mormons see it, individuals may very well get saved, but only families get exalted, and exaltation is an even higher form of afterlife than salvation. Furthermore, Zion, Mormonism's ultimate "unit of salvation" (295), is a town that will one day be exalted as a collective.

When Peruvians were Mormons, these hierarchized modes of afterlife, interpolated within simultaneously relationist and individualist "cultures," created a dialectic more complex than simply that which existed between relationist dependence and individualist independence. I mention this complexity not to debate the existence of "cultures" as discrete, countable entities, but to demonstrate how Mormonism's uniquely relationist sort of individualism accentuated one of the few differences between Peruvian Mormon relationality and Anglo Mormon kinship of which Peruvian Mormons were highly aware and critical. For Dutch Mormons, the "backward American ideology" (Maffly-Kipp 2020a, 14) of the official church was its homophobia. For Peruvian Mormons, the backward American ideology of the official church was its individualizing kin system.

As an arm of the greater US colonial project with a long history of pathologizing Indigenous kinways in order to "cure" them (Baca 2018), it was not surprising that Anglo Mormonism (SL) pathologized Peruvian Mormonism's familial interdependence. After all, the thrust of "The Family" was to shift dependence away from conglomerated, extended families (AL) and onto individualist, nuclear ones. This shift was so important to the Peruvian leaders of Barrio Periféricos that they portrayed a suggestion in "The Family" to only resort to dependence on extended family support "when needed" (First President and Council 1995, para.7) as a commandment tantamount to Moses's big ten. In espousing such commandments, some Peruvian Mormons seemed highly invested in learning to become staunch individualists within nuclear families.

It became all the more surprising, therefore, to discover just how deeply pathological those same Peruvian Mormons considered other instantiations of Anglo Mormon individualism. Peruvian Mormons' criticisms of Anglo Mormonism paralleled those that the Mapuche harbored toward Chile's wingka (non-Indigenous), with whom they associated "lying, practicing trickery, being stingy, and focusing on individual gain rather than the collective good" (Bacigalupo 2016, 118). The complexity surrounding the question of whether a Saint in Zion was to be independent or dependent, individualist or relationist, exhibited in the ways that Peruvian Mormons alternately extolled and decried what some in Utah called "la gringada"—the society of the Anglos who baptized them.

In this chapter, I take a closer look at the nature of that intrareligious and intercultural conflict in order to elucidate another of Zion's categories: independence. How can a religious society defined (in the epigraphic scripture) by interdependence "be one" through division into individualized families, selves, and souls?

Homes versus Units

Jacoba Arriátegui and Arcadio Costa met Anglo Mormon missionaries in New Jersey in the 1970s and, through negotiations with one of them, started an upholstery business in the suburbs forty miles north of Salt Lake City, Utah. In the decades since, their kids, grandkids, and great grandkids—the Costa family—rarely moved more than five miles from the site of that original business. Dozens of other primos, tías, hermanos, concuñados, entenadas, and people holding myriad other kinterms without English equivalents whom La Familia helped immigrate—or whom its network helped immigrate without Jacoba's matriarchal consent—also all lived in the same five-mile radius.

Salsands lay at the epicenter of that radius. Salsands had a very low Latin American immigrant population compared to the conglomeration of arbitrarily bounded small cities that formed the uninterrupted swath of suburbia connecting the metropolises of Salt Lake City in the south to Ogden in the north. Salsands was a flat, lakeside city that, during the lifetime of its mayor, had gone from largely agricultural lands to rapidly built subdivisions advertising neighborhoods with "homes in the $450,000s," twice as expensive as new houses in nearby cities. Salsands was proud of its exclusivity.

I interviewed Mayor Woods (in English) in the Salsands City Hall during one of his final days in office in November 2017. He was an old friend to the Costa family—part of La Familia—and we first met at the one-year anniversary celebration of the graduation from branch to ward of the Spanish-speaking congregation to which the Costa family belonged—the Pioneer Trail Ward. It was the only Spanish-speaking congregation of any religion in Salsands and one of the latest of Utah's 150-plus Spanish-speaking, Mormon congregations to have achieved a high enough concentration of active, male priesthood leadership in a specific residential area to have advanced to ward status. The new English-speaking congregations that sprouted from newly built residential subdivisions in Salsands usually started out with enough membership to be considered wards from the outset. They rarely had to pass through the branch phase of congregational adolescence, which, in the case of Spanish-speaking branches in the United States, was a phase of "weaning" (I. M. García 2015,

156) members from their Latinx Mormonism and acculturating them to Anglo Mormonism, a process understood to represent "progress in the kingdom" (156) of Zion. People like Mayor Woods helped naturalize the superior ward status automatically inherent to English-speaking congregations by carefully zoning new neighborhoods to systematically saturate them with Mormons of a certain desired family type: nuclear, wealthy, and White.

Mayor Woods, a generational Anglo Mormon from Arizona, told me that when he moved to Salsands in the seventies, the population was 2,000 and 92 percent Mormon. Now it was 29,000 and 70 percent Mormon. He said that 95 percent of "our homes" had been built since 1990. Since my nuclear family and I had to move within the Pioneer Trail Ward boundaries so that we could officially join the ward for the Utah phase of my fieldwork, I found out firsthand the difficulty of finding a place to rent in Salsands. There were only two apartment complexes—or "multifamily units," as the mayor called them—so I knew that by "our homes" he must have meant free-standing, single-family houses with yards. Though I was only asking about how his spirituality affected his political decisions, he revealed instead the "spiritual and temporal" reasons why the "multifamily unit" did not compute as "home" in his mind: "Well, I think it all has a spiritual and a temporal basis to what I've done, okay? You know, developers coming in and stuff like that, right? I still look at the development of this city, that I want it in a way that is more amenable to, uh—people living good lives. I'll put it that way."

When he said, "good lives," I thought of the times that he had used the word "good" previously in the interview and how he seemed conscious that he was using it to carefully obscure what he really meant. This was why he said, "I'll put it that way." He did not want to put it the other way because to do so would have been politically incorrect. Previously in the interview, he gave a clue as to what that other way might have been. "So, if we talk about what kind of people are moving here, uh, I would tell you this: high quality. Really, really good. Good people are moving in here. And I'm not going to define, you know, what 'good people' are. Uh, but typically people are moving here because there's good neighborhoods, there's good families. I do think the quality is still here that was here in 1976 when we moved here."

It was clear to me at this point in the interview that by "good families" he meant, consciously or subconsciously, "White families." He knew that I had grown up like him in a US system wherein race mapped almost perfectly onto class and in a religion of prosperity theology wherein class further mapped almost perfectly onto perceived righteousness. From one White Mormon man to another, it went without saying that "good" meant "White." We did not need the statistical evidence from geographers like George Lipsitz (2011) in his book *How Racism Takes Place* to know that cities like Salsands were not built for people of color. However, I was not sure how conscious Mayor Woods was of how his zoning decisions solidified Salsands as a White space. Similar to the situation that anthropologist Seth Holmes (2013) described in his ethnography of how racial and labor hierarchies overlapped on a berry farm in Washington such that all administrators happened to be Japanese Americans, all foremen happened to be US Latinos, and all field hands happened to be Triqui-speaking Mexicans, perhaps Mayor Woods was simply inhabiting the strata on the hierarchy that symbolic violence built for him.

Per Holmes, symbolic violence happened when people internalized their assigned rung on a historically constructed hierarchy to the extent that they adopted roles associated with defending it from lower rungs. Hierarchies were designed to keep people who were in a lower rung from infiltrating the purity of a higher rung, and so the inhabitants of that higher rung—irrespective of their own oppression from those in still higher rungs—adopted the gatekeeping role assigned them. Perhaps whiteness was so naturally a part of his own upper middle-class rung that the mayor was not cognizant of its being the de facto deciding factor as to whether or not a family was "good" enough to enter his city. Therefore, unable or unwilling to focus on whiteness directly as the prerequisite for Salsands residence, he focused instead on two other factors tied directly to whiteness in the US psyche: ownership and low crime rates (Harris 1993).

WOODS: So, did I fight some type of development coming in? Yes, I did. Because I felt like it was best for the city. Um, and did I not want to have big apartment buildings come into the city? Yes, I did that too. Because I would prefer ownership. I want people coming in to want to own the properties. Does that make sense?

JASON: Sure.

WOODS: So, and to me, I think there is some spiritual nature to that, you know. There was probably a lot of people that would disagree with that. . . . And I don't have a great argument against them, except for that it goes back to ownership. I believe—it makes a lot of difference—if people—so I own a few rental houses, and I own two in Salsands, and I own my business place here.

There is a difference between people who buy a house and take care of it compared to people who rent a house and don't take care of it.

Uh, so, I would, I would leave it at that.

Uh—I, I do believe that, that is what makes Salsands, uh, to have the rural feel and the same feel that it had forty-one years ago.

JASON: Yeah. 'Cause when you think of large apartment complexes, that's kind of an inner-city, urban kind of a feel.

WOODS: Well, well, the argument would be that it would bring in crime, more crime into the city. We would need more police officers. They say, you know, for every apartment building you bring in, you need three new police officers.

The mayor got to "leave it at that," only because "racialized space enables the advocates of expressly racist policies to disavow any racial intent. They speak on behalf of whiteness and its accumulated privileges and immunities, but rather than having to speak as whites, they present themselves as racially unmarked homeowners, citizens, and taxpayers whose preferred policies just happen to sustain white privilege and power. One of the privileges of whiteness, as Richard Dyer reminds us, is never having to speak its name" (Lipsitz 2011, 35). As prison abolitionist Jerome Miller stated, "there are certain code words that allow you never to have to say *race*, but everybody knows that's what you mean—and *crime* is one of those" (Szykowny 1994, 11). Focusing on factors associated with people of color, rather than focusing on the people of color themselves, the mayor was able to shrug off as coincidental the fact that he had designed Salsands in a way that disproportionately excluded people like his good friends in La Familia. Though affecting largely non-Black people of color (NBPOC) in the case of Salsands, his colorblind focus was intensified by a Pan-American ethos of antiblackness "that has identified Blacks with disorder and danger in the city" (Haymes 1995, 4) despite the fact that those who deliberately caused that disorder through urban disinvestment were usually White. In this way, the mayor's development of the suburban private family disguised the public underdevelopment of urban space that created the conditions for suburbia in the first place. Within the subtext of the mayor's words, "housing project geography is revealed as yet another alibi for antiblackness" (Shange 2019a, 14), an alibi that he skillfully extended to anti-NBPOC policy during his tenure as mayor.

Tests of implicit association showed that people across the US racial matrix associated people of color with crime (Sawyer and Gampa 2018), whiteness was a de jure requirement for land ownership during much of US continental imperialism (Saito 2015), and post-depression federally subsidized home ownership was widely available only to Whites (Breen 2019). Since I knew those data points before our interview, the two characteristics—low crime and ownership—that the mayor used to define "good families" seemed to me so obviously racist that they nearly distracted me from a more insidious racial code word enshrining the principal defining factor of goodness around which our whole conversation revolved: "home."

His nostalgia for the "rural feel" of 1976 Utah was complex. Perhaps it expressed White nostalgia for the "Dixie land" times of chattel slavery when everyone lived in a "unit" befitting their social status relative to the master's "home." Had the mayor been Peruvian, he might have expressed criollo nostalgia for a time when he would have been recognized as "el buen patrón" (the good boss) of hacienda slavery (M. E. García 2021, 54). While these historic sentiments may have been miles from his mind, he certainly was nostalgic for an affect that they both shared. He was nostalgic for a time when everyone knew their place, both socially and habitationally. The mayor longed for a bygone era when certain people automatically knew to stay out of towns like Salsands, an era before mayors had to do the settler colonial work of deliberately zoning them out.

At the conscious level, his rural nostalgia did not index a desire to return to the social hierarchies of quasi-feudal farming, which in Salsands were associated with illegally employed and disorderly housed Mexican sugar beet laborers who fled the Bracero Program (Solórzano 2014). Instead, he was nostalgic for something closer to his heart: the nuclear family and its postwar architectural instantiation in the free-standing, single-family home. In the United States, such a home historically implied a White family, and in a long-held US paradigm that "makes it possible to declare pathological almost any family feature that distinguishes minority families from White families" (Sarkisian and Gerstel 2012, 15), the "multifamily unit," or apartment complex, called to the mayor's mind a hotbed of non-White pathology defined against the "single-family home." Multifamily units, therefore, did not compute as "home" in his mind.

Multifamily units were undesirable in the United States, not because of crime or careless renters, but because they were associated with people of color and their allegedly pathological dependence on coresident "extended family" (López 2015). In order to doctrinally pathologize "extended family" dependence, the church's First Presidency published "The Family" in 1995, and the United States created the Personal Responsibility and Work Opportunity Reconciliation Act of 1996. I believe that both the Anglo-run church and the Anglo-run state put forth those remedies primarily for reasons relating to race. Sociologists found that many US citizens, a demographic that included most of the church's top leaders during my study, "pathologize[d] the Latino/a cultural preference for 'clannishness' . . . that they assert[ed] characterizes high levels of attachment to extended families. According to this view, Latino/a 'clannish' families impede assimilation and upward mobility in US society" (Sarkisian and Gerstel 2012, 14–15). Naturally, if they saw Latinx family types as impediments to capitalist accumulation, then the church and the state would want to remove those family types. They would, therefore, be motivated to logistically prevent the entry of Latinx families into new suburbs like Salsands. They would also be motivated to erase clannish sentiments from Latinx families through reeducation schemes such as "The Family."

Ironically, proto sociologists accused Anglo Mormons of clannishness 100 years before they achieved the individualistic "goodness" for which Mayor Woods was so nostalgic. His own ancestors were barred from inclusion into the whiteness to which their skin tone might have entitled them because their solidarity (and later polygyny) marked them in the national and international media as having devolved to the stage of "clannishness" on a teleology of family-type evolution (Bunker and Bitton 1983). On that teleology, increasing individualism was meant to correlate perfectly with decreasing melanin. This meant that, in scientific racism's nascent imagination, early Anglo Mormons were dark-skinned (Reeve 2015).

As Utah territory became less clannish in order to be included in whiteness and be admitted as the forty-sixth state of a White-imagined nation, it dissociated the church from nonwhiteness by structurally excluding (while discursively including) dark-skinned Mormons, such as the Costas, Mormons who clannishly misused Utah's single-family homes in the late 2010s. Yet, far from impeding assimilation, it was precisely the stigmatized "clannishness" of the Costa family, and a few other Latinx Mormon familias who made up the Pioneer Trail Ward, that allowed them to pool their resources and purchase huge single-family homes in Salsands. Never mind that their White neighbors defined the Costa clan as an "extended family" rather than as a "good family," or that their ownership represented an improper mismatch of home-shape to family-shape, La Familia transcended stereotypes and lived collectively in the most upwardly mobile city around.

When my properly nuclear family moved into one of Salsands' two over-priced multifamily "units" rather than into a single-family "home," we represented the opposite sort of mismatch. Shortly after we moved in, Jacoba's fifty-year-old newlywed son, Santiago, moved out of the spacious—but still crowded—single-family home that Jacoba shared with her daughter's large family and into our apartment complex. Santiago's wedding to a newly immigrated Peruvian woman who had daughters from a previous relationship took place in the Pioneer Trail Ward chapel. Living right next to him, I would watch his minivan depart every morning up the road before mysteriously circling back and going the opposite direction toward his work at an autobody shop. Through our friendship with him and his family—his new stepdaughters were the same ages as our daughters—I resolved the mystery. Jacoba would prepare a lunch for him to take to work every day, so he had to go fetch it every morning. Despite finally living somewhat independently from his parents, sister, brother-in-law, nieces, and adult sons from previous partnerships, and despite having a Peruvian wife who spent a large portion of her day cooking, he remained dependent on his mother's food.

That dependence, combined with his lack of ownership, placed Santiago on the wrong side of Mayor Woods's definition of "good family." The mayor attended Santiago's festive wedding reception—after all, he loved Peruvians and their food—but the White space that he helped design came close to excluding Santiago's new nuclear family entirely. They secured the very last rental vacancy in all of Salsands. Santiago might have mused, along with Chicano Mormon Ignacio García (2017), that Anglo Mormons "will . . . appreciate our culinary skills and our quick feet, but not our history or our thoughts" (16) or, for that matter, our dwellings.

Shattering Collective Selves

Before Santiago and I became neighbors, he was already my brother in our ward family, not to mention my primo. "Primo" was a highly inclusive kinterm in Spanish. In English, I would say that Santiago was "my spouse's cousin." However, in a Peruvian kin system refracted through Spanish that, in some instances, did not distinguish between cognates and affines but assigned everyone in the same generational group to a single kinterm, Santiago was no more my spouse's primo than he was mine. In fact, though we spoke English among ourselves, we always called each other "primo" in Spanish because "cousin" did not make sense. The language that Spanish/English bilingual Peruvians chose to use to express kinterms evinced the incommensurability between what they perceived to be a harmfully individualistic Anglo family and a healthy, collectivist, Peruvian familia.

Before moving in next to our apartment, Santiago kept me up to date on his search for a place to rent. When I suggested that he broaden his search to include the city of North Salt Lake where he worked, he immediately cursed la gringada that would put such a preposterous notion into my head. Santiago said "la gringada" in the same accent that he reserved for the Mexican epithet "la chingada" (the screw-up), undoubtedly la gringada's etymological inspiration. He, unlike some anthropologists that he knew who uprooted their kids every six months to live in "the multisite" between Peru and Utah, was not about to leave "tú sabes, La Familia" to live twenty-five miles away. The "tú sabes" (you know) that often preceded "La Familia" when members of the Costa family talked to me in English about why they chose to remain in Salsands—often despite lucrative opportunities elsewhere—was one of their more subtle ways of reprimanding my spouse and me for not adhering geographically to what we should have known emotionally: membership in La Familia required a certain amount of interdependence, which required a large amount of coresidence.

Peruvian Mormons in Utah diagnosed the lack of interdependence among la gringada as one of its most serious diseases. Yet, as I will now explore, in an economy controlled by la gringada, living for La Familia tended to reinstall the same glass ceiling that many Peruvian immigrants had to uproot themselves from Peru in order to shatter in the first place.

On my first trip to Arequipa in June 2016, I told Mormons that I was interested in Peruvians with connections to Utah. They told me to visit a ward named Barrio Umacollo. They also told me a joke: Umacollo was Zion because there was a scripture that described Zion's communal citizens as having "no poor among them," and Umacollo was wealthy. Of course, everybody knew that Umacollo had not achieved its elimination of poverty as Zion had done—through a unity so intense that all wealth was distributed evenly—hence the humor. It turned out that in Barrio Umacollo, there were not only Peruvians with connections to Utah, but actual Anglo Utahans who cycled through supervisory positions at the local mine, Cerro Verde—Arequipa's greatest source of wealth.

During my study, many of Thacker, Arizona's residents were Mormon because Thacker was originally one of Brigham Young's colonial projects. It later became a mining town under the same company that owned a large share of Cerro Verde (Knowlton 2016). Ted Parker was from Thacker, and I met him in Barrio Umacollo. He served a mission in Peru as a young man and, in 2016, then a father of four tow-headed children, wanted his family to imbibe the Peruvian hospitality that he remembered from his mission, so he bid to transfer his engineering supervisory position to Cerro Verde. Their "Peruvian experience" was disappointing on multiple fronts. Foreign Cerro Verde employees were thought to be prime targets for kidnapping, so they could not even go for a morning jog without bodyguards. This, and the general opulence that surrounded them in their 5,000-square-foot chateau on an immaculately landscaped, half-acre garden, was not exactly exposing Ted's spouse to the type of Peruvians that he wanted her to meet. "I was really hoping that she would be able to come and kind of have some of the experiences that I had in Piura [in northern Peru] and was expecting to have here. Some people, even though they don't have a lot, they'd give you the shirt off their back, right? And I really love that about the culture."

Though there was a disappointing lack of poverty, the experience was still a bit too cultural for his uprooted kids who were the only non-Spanish-speakers in their high-tuition, arequipeño private schools. All of this explained why, on the day that I interviewed him (in English) only one year into his two-year contract with Cerro Verde, his family had already gone back to Thacker, and he was packing up to follow them. As we talked in his temporary dwelling—the most luxurious single-family home that I had ever entered in my life—I asked why the mine would put up with so much transience among its top supervisors, not to mention the cost of housing, transporting, and protecting them, when they could hire local arequipeños, especially since arequipeño universities supported the nation's top mining-engineering programs, and also since Peru had proven time and time again that it did not need foreign "know-how" (an English loan word in Peruvian Spanish) to extract its own wealth (Rubio 2021). After a lot of hemming and hawing, trying to not make his mining company sound too racist, he finally formulated an answer.

It is a bit of a struggle jobwise for some of the Peruvian people to see that a lot of the leadership is—implants [laughs] from the United States. . . . There's been a little bit of reluctance to fill all of leadership with Peruvians and I don't—I don't know some of the answers on that.

They've had some—they've gotten burned in the past with—with some individuals that, ah—it's a little bit more accepted in Peruvian culture that, "hey, I scratch your back you scratch mine."

In other words, within Cerro Verde company politics, the primacy of Peruvian interrelated reciprocity was pathologized as nepotism and corruption much as it was within the Anglo Mormon category of leaders (Knowlton 1996). Peruvians could not be allowed to ascend ranks in the mine because they would likely help friends and familia do the same. In Cerro Verde's eyes, Peruvians were pathological backscratchers because they cared too much about the collectivities of which they formed part and not enough about the success of the individualized corporation. That pathologizing created a glass ceiling in Peru that ironically motivated immigration toward the source of the pathologizing.

Extractive powers accusing those from whom they extracted of clannishness and nefarious backscratching was a tactic as old as extraction itself. Cerro Verde's Mormon-influenced, anti-Peruvian policies were so expected as to be academically uninteresting. What was interesting in Peruvian Mormonism was that, when Peruvians went to Utah and confronted la gringada face-to-face, the pathologizing was reversed. Peruvian Mormons like Washington Tapia found that Anglo Mormons exhibited an appalling lack of mutual backscratching. Washington also belonged to Barrio Umacollo, and I interviewed him in his comparatively modest, but solidly arequipeño neto home a few days after I interviewed Ted. Washington had teenage children who, as he was proud to mention, were fourth-generation Mormons since Washington's great-aunt was the very first person to be baptized in Arequipa. When Washington was himself a teenager, his father immigrated to Utah and eventually became a US citizen, able to sponsor his own children. Washington spent his formative years knowing that one day his immigrant visa petition would go through and that he too would move to Utah.

This did not happen as fast as he would have liked, so he moved to Utah on a tourist visa, which he overstayed for eight years, until, as he put it, he could no longer stand the illegality of his situation and the hypocrisy that he felt that it generated within himself. He returned to Peru. Two years after our interview, his father's original immigrant visa petition finally went through, amended to include Washington's wife and children, and they returned to Utah. In this interview, Washington drew on the experience of his years of illegality in Utah from 2000 to 2008.

JASON: What was it like to deal with church leaders in Utah?

WASHINGTON: In reality it was the same as it is in Peru, no difference. Leaders are leaders. You feel the Spirit in those who have authority even if they speak English. That is, assuming you yourself have the Spirit with you. You know that he is an authority, so it's the same.

Where there's a difference is that the Americans—not all of them, mind you, not the Leaders, usually—when Americans are outside of church, they are different. And that is something that really struck my family. The Americans in our church are very good at church, but in the workplace, they are despots. They don't care at all about you.

The Latinos here in Peru, when we are faithful members inside the church, we are about the same inside the workplace. But not Americans. The American says, "Church is church, but business is business."

And it doesn't seem right to me that there be a break [quiebre] there because supposedly the principles are to be practiced in all arenas.

"I scratch your back, you scratch mine," inasmuch as it indexed the privileging of reciprocity and indebtedness over profit, contrasted sharply with the axiom that Washington noted among Anglo Mormons: "Church is church, but business is business." That motto captured the sentiment that while collectivism was all well and good in a religious setting of spiritual siblingship—reminiscent of the pre-Earth, preexistence wherein all humans existed as hermanos to each other in one giant nuclear family headed by Heavenly Father and Heavenly Mother—reinforced through constant ecclesiastical use of the kin titles, brother and sister, things were different in the corporate world. In Washington's expressiveness, "Americans" in Utah would say the following: "You might be my brother at church on Sunday, connected to me through the primordial substance of the pre-Earth life, but on Monday you are my underling, connected to me only as long as you bring money into my company." In Washington's Utah, profit trumped brotherly love and any reciprocity that love might have implied.

Part of the staunch individualism that Washington recognized as despotism was what many Latinx Mormons in Utah characterized as White stinginess in my study. In Utah's lawn care business, Anglo Mormons were notorious for being spendthrifts at best and cheats at worst. Another arequipeño Mormon in Utah, Aaron, wanted to write a thesis on why that was. His theory was that it stemmed from a harmful individualism that he noticed, not only among his clients, but also among his coworkers, all of whom were Anglo Mormons. Our interview took place in the unfinished basement of his former mission companion's house in Provo, Utah, where he was staying in August 2017.

JASON: So why would it be the topic of a whole thesis?

AARON: Why a thesis? Because a lot of times a question pops up here in the United States which asks, "Do we need Latinos?"

And I didn't have the answer to that, but now I do. What the Latino does, he does because—for example . . . in Peru, when you become part of a company, you make friends and among those friends you have each other's backs. There is a comradery. If I break something or cause something to go wrong, it's, "hey, let's all try to fix it before the boss finds out."

It's all for one.

But here, it is not like that.

Here, everyone throws water on his own mill.

You go to the restroom for a second, and everyone is thinking you are "*lazy*" [English] and reporting you to the manager, right?

And lately at my work, they started sectorizing. They say, "We are going to do a huge residence, so one of you grab the *push mower*, one get the *weedwhacker*, another grab the *ride-on*"—Right?

So, I get the *weedwhacker*, I'm cutting along, and I finish cutting early. One would assume that I'm not supposed to just go sit in the truck and sleep for the rest of the time while the others finish. Of course not, right?

So, I grab the extra *push mower* and I assess, "Okay, what still needs to be done? Oh, he needs help over there, I'll go support him," and I go and help.

But what do they do? They jump on the *ride-on*: cut, cut, cut, finish that, and they think they've done their part for the day. So that disturbs me as well.

One time—and this is an example of a lack of something that I call, "initiative"—I accidentally left a *weedwhacker* somewhere because I forgot to put it back in the truck. Every single one of my coworkers walked by it. We went from Orem to Lindon. When we got to Lindon, we needed that *weedwhacker* and it wasn't there. I was like, "Where is it?"

And everyone told me that it was left behind in Orem. And I said, "But, why didn't any of you pick it up if you all saw that I had left it behind?"

One said, "Not my problem, I'm not the one who used it."

That is when I got angry, and I argued with the supervisor and even with my former mission companion who owns the business. It's just that I don't understand why there is no comradery.

I mean, why is there no initiative to help?

But now, like I was saying, it is going to be a thesis because I also want to break that myth that a lot of Peruvians tell about what it's like over here: "Oh, if you are in the United States, the money comes to you easily." Yes, you make your money. But you have to break yourself here.

Aaron's mill metaphor was apt. A water-run mill is a public utility—community capital—that depends on the collective force of billions of individual molecules flowing as one. If every individual person diverts the stream in order to "throw water on their own mill," each gets a trickle. However, if the full force of the river is allowed to run a community mill, it will grind more than enough corn to make a profit for each capitalist individual who joins forces to maintain the mill.

Aaron's mill metaphor demonstrated that his critique of Utah's individualism did not stem from an ancient Andean ideal wherein humans, water, and corn were all one indistinguishable commune called the ayllu, distinguishable from other ayllus only through the practice of ayni (reciprocity). Rather, Aaron shared the same capitalistic ontology with his Anglo Mormon coworkers that humans were individuals; he simply saw Utah-style individualism as a short-sighted, counterproductive instantiation of that ontology that ensured lower profits for everyone involved.

For Aaron, that was why the United States needed "Latinos." In Aaron's experience, Latinos were socialized to understand that collective reciprocity and individual profit were not mutually exclusive. That also may have been why Aaron, and most other Peruvian Mormons in my study with some US experience were excited to identify as Latinos instead of Indigenous people, mestizos, or any of the other categories available in Latin America that seemed to them stale and problematic. In the United States, "Latino" was more an ethnicity adhering to one's heritage homeland than a race adhering to one's skin tone (Barth [1969] 1998). In fact, on many official US government forms, "Hispanic" (similar to Latino except that it included Spain and excluded Brazil) was the only "ethnicity" box available during my study. If checked, it often still required the additional selection of a "race."

Therefore, in US documentation and imagination, Latinos came in many races. Latino, therefore, was a less racialized identity than mestizo. For this reason, perhaps adopting the fresh, US label of Latino—or the gender-neutral version, Latinx—allowed for "the possibility of subordinating one's phenotype and emphasizing instead one's intelligence" (De la Cadena 2000, 9). Many self-identified Latinx Mormons in my study felt that such a possibility was important in marshaling a "de-Indianized" (6) united front against the diametric opposite of the collectivist, enterprising Latinx community: the individualistic, complacent "American."

This is not to say that Aaron had much of a choice in how he would ethnically identify. Earlier in the interview, he told me that his "American" coworkers automatically identified him as a Latino, a word that they used pejoratively by mentioning that Aaron was "one of the good Latinos, not like the Mexicans." Aaron's "American" coworkers—some of them Spanish-speaking returned missionaries—stigmatized his new Latinx ethnicity, counterintuitively motivating him to fall back on the united front of that very ethnicity for solidarity and comradery. Their stigmatization of Latinx identity oozed between the lines in the interview excerpt above. Notice that one of the few English words that Aaron heard often enough to incorporate into his vocabulary during his first months in Utah—along with "weedwhacker" and "push mower"—was "lazy."

Yet, from Aaron's perspective, they were the lazy ones. If Aaron's "American" comrades would have simply practiced a bit of "Latino" reciprocity, the value of every individual's labor would have increased. Instead, their whiteness fractured reciprocity. Aaron spoke of this fracturing as a breaking of self and Washington spoke of it as a rupture in the continuity of practice between church and profession. The poet Vivek Shraya (2016) defined whiteness itself by this fracturing: "whiteness [:] the meteor that fractured our planet" (68). Therefore, the Utah religion wherein, as the Endowment ritualized, "all truth may be circumscribed into one great whole" (Packham 2009, cell 4B)—symbolized by the mark of the compass on Mormon sacred, white undergarments—sometimes portended instead, for Washington and Aaron, a great break into independent shards.

Food-Dependent Sainthoods

Anthropologists often consider tension between dependence and independence—or intersubjectivity and subjectivity—to be a common condition in the category that they call "kinship." Imagining the Peruvian Mormon person to have embodied a blend of Mormon kinship and Andean Catholic kinship would have been complex enough had Mormonism sat squarely on the side of individualism while Andean Catholicism sat squarely on the side of collectivism. Those academic pairings, however, did not map onto each other in my experience. Not only that, but they created a false binary relationship between religion and kinship that muddied the waters further. There was no name for the space between religion and kinship wherein I encountered Mormon kinship, let alone Peruvian Mormon kinship. Yet, those categorical binaries created mental pathways that tricked my mind into seeing religion and kinship not only as identifiable entities but as completely separate ones.

Anthropologist John Jackson's (2013) ethnography of the African Hebrew Israelites of Jerusalem (AHIJ) offered me a way around that trick. It demonstrated how such pathways could be rewired, even among those coming from "the West," through an AHIJ reality expressed by one of its princes: "We DESPISE religion! . . . Isn't the detachment and compartmentalization of spirituality—as something unrelated to every aspect of our daily life—about as Eurocentric a concept as they come?" (171). The AHIJ's immigration from Chicago to Israel was not a pilgrimage to a land that they believed to be holy, it was about being in a place that was ancestrally home because of who they knew themselves to be, not racially, but through a conflation of both biogenetic Israelite lineage and a conscious decision to follow Yah. That focus on who they were—rather than on what they believed and to whom they felt they were related—explained why the AHIJ paralleled the LDS in so many respects: their exodus beyond national borders, their polygyny, their health code, their anthropological theorization of their own "culture" as divine, and—most importantly—their designation of who they were: Saints.

Like Jackson, I settled on "personhood," or "sainthood," as a way of investigating phenomena that were once taxonomized separately as either religion or kinship. For me, personhood hinged on "social relations predicated upon cultural conceptions that specif[ied] the processes by which an individual [came] into being and develop[ed] into a complete (i.e., mature) social person" (Kelly 1993, 521—22). In that sense, the complete development of a Saint, partially a "religious person," involved not only "social relations" but spiritual relations. Living those spiritual relations in a religion wherein "spirit is matter" (J. Smith [1844] 2013b, 266) among fellow Saints—neither humans nor gods—generated intense ambiguities. Per anthropologist Eduardo Viveiros de Castro (1998), such ambiguities belonged not to European ontologies like Mormonism but only to "Amerindian perspectivism." This was why anthropologists influenced by his theory of separate ontological worlds took for granted that the constant effort to clarify those ambiguities—through the gaze, for example—defined personhood, but only among people like the Jaqi, not among people like the Mormons.

According to those anthropologists, Jaqi people constructed personhood while Western people were born with its essence. However, on that continuum of the constructivist subject versus the essentialist subject, Mormons—though "Western"—appeared to be somewhere in the middle. They considered themselves to be both essential humans and constructed Saints. Nevertheless, where relatedness to other individuals was concerned, Anglo Mormons drifted significantly "West" on the continuum.

The Andean notion that relatedness needed to be cultivated in place and over time rather than established only at the biological moment of conception or the legal moment of marriage was the ontological ground upon which Peruvian Mormon criticism of la gringada's category of independence was founded. When I stayed in Pasi's building in Cusco in June 2016, she gave voice to that ground. She said, "You guys break the family bonds when you leave home at such an early age. That is why you consider your family only to be your wife and kids. For us it is our grandparents, cousins, and even more and more. We all live together." What struck her during her yearlong sojourn in Utah was that even though people had huge homes with more than enough space to house their family members, they would relegate their old people to senior living centers and forget about them. She considered that to be a great failing and cried tears of anger when she saw it. I asked her, "Don't you think that the Mormon church fosters that behavior through its promotion of only the nuclear family type?"

She resisted saying anything bad about the church but did admit that its lowering of the missionary age worldwide was a very US-centric thing to do. Her former mission companion in Utah told her that the reason that the official church lowered the mission age for males from nineteen to eighteen in 2012 was so that they would not stray from the church by doing a year of college before going on their missions. After the change, they could serve missions right out of high school. Pasi explained to me her disagreement with the church's new missionary age policy: "It reflects only a US reality. It has nothing to do with us in Latin America where we don't have the expectation that at eighteen you are going to leave home. We don't have that ripping apart. Americans have that expectation regardless, so moving off to college or moving off to a mission is going to be the same thing as far as homesickness."

I told her that ever since the mission-age change, a lot of eighteen-year-old Latinx youth whom I knew in Utah and California were getting sent home from their missions because of medical diagnoses of anxiety. She thought the anxiety was due to the fact that they were not raised with the expectation of absolute independence, of emotionally gearing up for that eventual "ripping apart."

I think Pasi's explanation of the missionary age policy change reflected her understanding of independence. Where relatedness is cultivated through food and coresidence over time, the longer one is with someone, the more one is related to them. For this reason, separating oneself—or, as many Peruvians in my study viscerally described, wrenching or ripping oneself away—from eighteen-year-old children whom la gringada arbitrarily considered adults, often became more complex than leaving very young children. Many upwardly mobile Peruvians in my study left young children behind for years in the care of grandparents, nuns, comadres, or godmothers for any number of reasons, many of which the Anglos in my study would not consider commensurate to the toll on the nuclear family. For example, my primo Santiago, who could later not fathom living more than a few blocks from his mother Jacoba, was left in the care of a Catholic school in Peru while Jacoba established a life for him in New Jersey. He did not see her from the ages of three to six. In contrast, I could not bear to leave my eight-, ten-, and twelve-year-old kids behind during my fulltime fieldwork year for this project.

It is tempting to theorize that the Andean notion of depositing relatedness over time compared with the Anglo notion of establishing relatedness at conception would translate into similar feelings of ripping away among the two groups, only with the timeframes reversed. If ripping away was more painful for Jacoba when Santiago was an adult than when he was a child, for me and my daughters it will likely be the opposite. For us it is early childhood; for them it is early adulthood. However, when this us/them distinction was stretched across the core/periphery power dynamic that Mormonism brought, it translated into the double pathologizing of Peruvian Mormon love: Peruvians loved their kids both too much and not enough. Just because Peruvians in my study left toddlers behind even as they criticized gringos for callously shipping their kids off to college at age eighteen, did not mean that they found separating from toddlers easier than separating from adults. Anglos in my study criticized the aforementioned separations through migration as unnecessary, especially given that the Peruvians in question were not living in dire poverty. However, what is or is not "necessary" is itself a situated construct of personhood, not a universal human archetype.

Within a framework of interdependence, Andeans did not "leave their toddlers behind" at all. Instead, they deposited them inside the specific nodes of transnationally interrelated networks of care that happened to be the most necessary for the continuity of that cycle of relatedness upon which their toddlers' very personhood depended (Roberts 2012). Similar realities unfortunately got overlooked in the deservingness discourse of purportedly objectifiable "need" that determined US immigration law designations of refugee and asylee during my study (Menjívar and Abrego 2012).

During the literature review aspect of my study, I learned that the place where people fell on a spectrum between individualism and collectivism often determined their definition of "need." For example, in Senya Beraku, Ghana, a cellphone was a need that motivated many to risk their lives crossing the Mediterranean Sea to work in Italy. Said one migrant,

> "instead of saving money, we're going for new phones." Sporting an older, larger phone with no camera or radio, a "cassava stick," is to call into question not only one's financial capacity but also one's very existence. [A Ghanian immigrant to Italy named] Samuel was coming home one day on the bus, having borrowed an old phone from a friend because his new phone had been stolen, when his friend remarked, "So, Samuel, have you come to the end of your life?" (Lucht 2012, 90–91)

So integral a part of personhood was a new cellphone—and the maintenance of relatedness to home that cellphones facilitated—that to have an old one was to sever personhood, to end life. Likewise, in Egypt, there "are things one must buy, even if they may seem a dispensable luxury to an outsider. Dining tables, glasses, and coffee sets . . . must be part of the apartment of a newlywed couple. . . . Consumption is not a choice. It is a necessity" (Schielke 2015, 115). In the same vein, the reasons that lower-class but professional, college-educated Peruvian Mormons in my study separated from young children were never trivial. In fact, the very thing that created the child's personhood and that made the mother related to the child was often at stake: food. Many of my Latin American study participants felt that recycling food between a locality and its people joined them all into one relatedness, one pacha. This feeling determined the value that they assigned to "good" food. Through methodological faith, I observed love being transmitted through food, food quality, and food preparation. Of course, this was also a common Latin American stereotype captured in popular literature, such as that of Gabriel García Márquez ([1988] 2007): "At the mere hint of a doubt, he would push aside his plate and say: 'This meal has been prepared without love.' . . . Once he tasted some chamomile tea and sent it back, saying only: 'This stuff tastes of window.' Both she and the servants were surprised because they had never heard of anyone who had drunk boiled window, but when they tried the tea in an effort to understand, they understood: it did taste of window" (289).

Apparently, food could capture both love and the desire of the preparer to escape domesticity through the window. As with most humor, the words of García Márquez only work because they arrive at a societal truth. In this case, the truth was a common tension in Latin American personhood that was laid bare when coresidence and the right kind of food became mutually exclusive keys to relatedness. Cristina Alcalde (2018) found that the importance of food within personhood was not merely a condition of subsistence-level existence in Peru. She distributed an open-ended survey to upper-class Peruvian migrants. They were supposed to fill in the following blank with a single word: "What I miss most about Peru is _____" (145). Instead, most participants wrote unsolicited comments in the margins of the survey about the unfair impossibility of having to choose between the two words that they would have needed to fill in the blank to make the survey at all accurate: food/family.

In her book *Sacrificing Families*, sociologist Leisy Abrego (2014) documented the globalized construction of the conundrum of having to choose between food and family among impoverished Salvadoran mothers who immigrated to the United States to find work in order to send back money to their children to buy food. In some cases, the need was "biological" in that the children would physically starve without the remittances, but when the children themselves recognized the need as constructed, they questioned it. Like the Ghanaian with an old cellphone, just plain old food was insufficient. Full personhood required proper food. A Salvadoran mother thus complained of her child's reaction to her absence, "he still says that it would have been better for me to be there and to eat rice and beans, but to have someone there" (128). This mother needed for her child to have expensive beef with his rice and beans more than she needed him to have her present. This was because in El Salvador as in Peru, "they are not just consuming food for survival: theirs is a cuisine that emphasizes taste and creativity. Moreover, culinary traditions matter beyond 'security.' They carry important cultural, religious, and social significance, and nourish not just the individual body but also ancestral spirits" (M. E. García 2021, 149). The stuff of Salvadoran interrelatedness—good food, and the care that it symbolized—was more important for the mutual connection of their personhoods than proximity in place. Through remittances and the quality food that they bought, mother and child maintained the "substance" of their intersubjectivity across distance.

Substantial Dividuals

This ontology has been dubbed "substantialism," which anthropologist Cecilia Busby (2006) defined as "the tendency to imbue qualities that Western ethnoscience would consider abstract or nonmaterial with a certain material essence and a concern with the effects of flow or exchange of such qualities between people and things" (85). Within this perspective, "the person is *substantially* connected to others and is not therefore a stable, bounded individual but rather a 'dividual,' constantly giving out and receiving parts of the self from others" (86). Mormonism's belief in spirit matter appeared to make it a substantialist religion. For my Mormon study participants, all humans were made of a material spirit inside spiritualized flesh. This duality was called a soul. In some ways, a soul was clearly a subject. However, discerning which of its heritable traits descended from which bio-spiritual objects to make up the Mormon self was never clear to me. For anthropologist of Mormon kinship Fenella Cannell (2013), the ambiguity of the Mormon soul's independence from materiality was what gave Mormon sainthood its mystery and, for some, its irresistible draw.

Since a principal purpose of the Enlightenment was to separate the spiritual from the material, the ambiguity of subject versus object captured in the Mormon idea of "soul" was represented as a natural, clear dichotomy for the rest of modern Christianity. Such clarity was nonexistent in communities, such as those in Melanesia (Whitehouse 2006), with an exclusive group potential divvied up differently among "dividual" roles that, to Christian eyes, confused agents with things (brides that could be bought) and objects with people (stones that were ancestors). Anthropologist Webb Keane (2007) explored this semiotic question of object and subject among the Sumba Island dwellers of Indonesia whom Calvinists were missionizing. He concluded that the true convert was not so much the one who believed in a Calvinist god, but the one who was able to distinguish between subject and object in a way that satisfied the missionaries.

Ironically, Calvinists would have probably accused my Anglo Mormon study participants of being unable to make that distinction. The Mormons in my study were not clear about whether they were objects or subjects of salvation. Jesus saved Mormons, yet at the same time, Mormons were "saviors" (J. Smith [1844] 2013b, 204) to their family members, including their dead, autonomous, individualized ancestors. Since Mormons were responsible for the salvation of their families—making them not only gods in embryo, but saviors in maturity—Mormon futures were collective. Tensions within sainthood, therefore, stemmed from pitting that collectivism against an equally vital Protestant injunction to "work out your own salvation" (Philippians 2:12) and be self-reliant.

Therefore, the Mormon person—a Saint—was made up of constructed parts and essential parts; dividual parts and individual parts; material parts and spiritual parts; but all those parts combined to form one whole soul. Peruvians in Arequipa, on the other hand, were made up of many parts as well, but souls were just some of those parts, not the whole person. A living Mormon body was a soul. A living arequipeño body contained many souls. One of those could flee the body and get trapped elsewhere, leaving the body alive but sick. Another could stick around after the body had decomposed. Some went to Christian heavens while others went to deified mountain peaks, but many merged back into collective ancestral inner worlds that produced the material of new human bodies.

Though she was Mormon and had lived in middle-class Salsands, Utah, for decades, Jacoba still retained parts of a cyclical ancestral idiom that complicated the individuated family. When she talked to me of her ancestors, she tore the Western arboreal analogy apart at the middle. She once said to me, "I always tell human beings, 'Look. Plant: Your kids are your branches, and your grandkids are your roots. And they remain there, planted.'" As a Mormon, she had seen countless family tree depictions wherein grandchildren fell below children. Those trees sprouted individual ancestors as branches and individual descendants as roots. Yet, Jacoba placed descendants (kids and grandkids) as both the branches and the roots: the future and the past. Hers was a familia rhizomatic web, not a family tree. Children could give parts of themselves to parents, making parents descendants as much as antecedents. Furthermore, since her cyclical cosmovision had only somewhat to do with genetics and vertical blood descent, nonblood kin who gave and took of the substance of relatedness and coresidence could become dividuals within Jacoba's genealogy.

Individuals incorporated parts to delimit wholes while dividuals gave up parts to expand wholes. Dealing with parts of dividual people was a matter-of-fact aspect of living in Arequipa in the late 2010s, even for Mormons whose doctrine of pre-Earth individuality did not seem capacious enough to allow for such agentive parts of self. For example, Ofelia had many experiences with dividual souls: "In our enclosed courtyard we saw a man who was over by the fig trees. He was tall with his white shirt and straw hat. When we saw him, I said, 'Shannon, look.' And we both saw the man hide among the trees. . . . 'Who is there?' Nobody answered, and nobody ever came out."

The next afternoon, Ofelia's grandmother, who lived next door, came to tell her that her uncle, who also lived next door, had died that morning.

JASON: You mean that the spirit in the orchard was your uncle, but that your uncle was still alive at that moment?

OFELIA: In that moment he was still alive, but we saw his spirit walking. That is why there are some Catholic beliefs [laughs] that say that the spirit makes its last rounds to say goodbye to people.

Ofelia dismissed as pejoratively "Catholic" the belief that part of a live person could wander unbeknownst to the person's other parts. Though Ofelia may have found the belief connected to it laughable, the fact of clothed spirits walking was such a standard part of her social milieu that it went unquestioned. Among many rural and urban societies of the greater region of Arequipa in the late 2010s, a soul supporting the weight of an object, such as a straw hat, was a mundane occurrence. Among such societies, "the surface of the skin does not mark the person's bodily boundaries. That which is inside and outside are connected, and a human being is primordially defined by his or her mutable social environment" (Theidon 2013, 59).

In a non-Mormon instantiation of this dividualism, the Parent Teacher Association (PTA) at my oldest daughter's school in Arequipa celebrated a huatia (earth meal) requiring the improvisation of a brick earth-oven in which to cook our chicken and potatoes. The PTA president, an Aymara-speaking grandmother who always dressed in her town's traditional clothing, sent her unassuming husband to go look for bricks in the back of the schoolyard. He returned saying that he had found some bricks, but that a human baby was crying beneath them. To him, the crying implied that the baby might have died in a long-ago collapse or that it was still alive somewhere, but that one of its souls somehow got stuck to the bricks. Either way, he did not want to disturb it. His wife scolded him, "It's just a baby's pining soul. Go get the bricks!" Before eventually complying, he mumbled that perhaps the bricks themselves had taken on soul and that he would not be held responsible if our chicken got baked back into animation. Though only a passing comment, likely a joke, the danger that bricks or stones might become subjects, thus making humans their objects, was real in his altiplano village.

In such an environment where subject and object designations were vital but transitory, the ayllu—or in this case, the PTA—guaranteed trust and evinced personhood through ayni. As Viveiros de Castro (1998) wrote, "He who responds to a 'you' spoken by a non-human, accepts the condition of being its 'second person.' And when assuming in turn his position of 'I' does so already as a non-human" (483). Therefore, in order to be a human, it is important to be a "you" to a human, and the only way to truly tell if someone is a human is through ayni. Instead of the individualist sentiment, "I think therefore I am," ayni expresses the collectivist sentiment, "you are, therefore we are." Ayni meant that my working relationship to the human PTA president was what made my personhood emerge in the first place in that site of food-sharing. In contrast, British kinship—the system that gave Mormonism a large portion of its kin concepts—posited that the individual person in a relationship existed "somehow prior to the relationship" (Strathern 1992, 53). Indeed, in Mormonism, individuals existed prior even to their relationship to God (Smith 1851).

"Mamá, I'm Home"

Understandably, contradictory opinions among my study participants further complicated the category of "independence" as it stretched across dividual and individual sainthoods. These opinions were not confined to the divide between Peruvians and la gringada. The extreme to which Mormonism took "independence" within its theology of a paradoxically interdependent Zion refracted into Peruvian Mormon arguments both for and against individualism. Pasi thought that la gringada's obsession with independence and ripping away bordered on the pathological. Ofelia, however, was of the opposite opinion—at least discursively.

Ofelia, who had never been to Utah, did not know Jacoba, who had never been to Arequipa. Yet, as our dialogue below makes clear, Ofelia would have considered fifty-year-old Santiago's reliance on Jacoba's cooking in Salsands a sad commentary on the retrograde dependence of Peruvianness. However, she might have pointed to the couples mission that Jacoba and Arcadio served together as evidence that living in Utah could begin to cure Peruvian dependency. Though Jacoba and Arcadio achieved neither an empty nest nor the financial independence to retire, leave everything behind, and preach the gospel together for two years in the Peruvian rain forest, they sold their upholstery business and went anyway. Jacoba was one of the most vocal critics of la gringada's pathological independence in my study, yet she served a couples mission, which was something that usually required such independence.

In other words, like Aaron, Jacoba saw individuality as beneficial, but only when paired with a collectivity that made it mutually beneficial. So, if individuality and collectivity were not mutually exclusive, why did Saints in Barrio Periféricos not serve couples missions? Wondering how that most saintly of retirement goals related to arequipeño sainthoods and their versions of independence, I asked Ofelia why I had not observed elderly couples in Barrio Periféricos exhibit the slightest ambition to serve couples missions.

OFELIA: There have been many brothers and sisters that very well could have gone on missions with their spouses, but the vision of these brothers and sisters is *not* that once your kids turn eighteen it's, "Chau, have a nice life."

JASON: You mean, they still have responsibility for their adult children?

OFELIA: That is the effect of these "hen parents" as they are known, who want to flutter around their sixty, seventy, eighty-year-old "little children." It's a very harmful thing because they don't let their children develop. Even if the son is married, they're always going to be there: "Oh, goodness! His wife doesn't know how to prepare his meals, I must go make my little boy his lunch."

So that is what happens when you don't release your children.

My mom—I mean, "Mamá Hen"—never let her children become independent. To this day, none of my hermanos know how to do something even as simple as getting their DNI [Peruvian national identification card]: "Let's go together, I'll get it for you." She even signs for it instead of them!

So, I tell her, "Mamá, stop doing things for them." . . .

Even my daughter sometimes asks me, "What flavor ice-cream would you like me to eat?"

And I ask her, "How old are you again?" [laughing]

"Twenty-one."

"There's your answer. Don't go asking me permission. You have to be independent," I tell her.

It bugs me when she asks those questions because it reminds me that we have that type of overprotective culture. I don't understand it because I personally have always been unattached to my mother. My younger brother and I have the same father, and we were left alone with our ancient grandmother to fend for ourselves. But my sisters were raised together with my mom. Nothing more than, "I'm hungry," and my mom was there to cut up their food into small bites. I, on the other hand, had to learn to turn on the stove, boil water in a pot, and everything. The rest of them have become spoiled.

I have an uncle who still lives with his parents and he's always, "Mamá, Mamá, Mamá," living under the skirts of his mother even now.

He makes long trips to Cusco, but when he's at home [in Arequipa], my grandmother waits on him hand and foot. She even made these special little tablecloths to keep food warm because she still doesn't want microwave technology.

She bundles up the food and keeps it nice and warm in its little winter coat just like in the old days, and so when my uncle comes—"Mamá, I'm home"—all he has to do is sit down, and my little grandmother, with all her pains and everything, gets the plate out of the warmer, puts it in front of him just so, and then he eats.

After, "thanks," is all he says, upon which my grandmother goes back in, washes the plate, puts everything away, and cleans the table. I mean, my uncle is almost sixty years old. You'd think he'd be able to wash a plate, right?

I just sit there and observe and think to myself, "how horrible."

But that is the kind of rearing that we continue dragging along with us. That is how closeminded we are despite living in this twenty-first-century age of globalization. We still live closed off. A lack of modernization, right?

And when I hear my mother say, "Ay, no, my poor little boy!"

I say, "What kind of a person are you raising? A useless person, that's what."

"But it's that he's in the university."

"And what does that have to do with anything?"

My daughter is in the university as well, and she comes home, "Mamá, I'm hungry."

"Oh, look in the *fridge* [English] and see what you can make for yourself."

"But can't you make me something?"

"No, Hijita [dear daughter], it's all there, just heat something up. There's milk, heat it up."

"But Mamá, can't you heat it up?"

"No, Hijita, you can heat it up!"

Sometimes she gets mad: "Mamá, why is it that you warm up food for the missionaries, but you won't do it for me?"

"Because the missionaries go out to work."

"But don't I work, Mamá?"

"It's very different. You are one day going to get married and become self-reliant, so I am teaching you. You should thank me." [laughs].

I am grateful to my mother. I used to criticize her and say, "But why did you abandon me at such a young age with so many responsibilities?"

But now I thank her for not worrying so much about me. I mean, she gave me meals—well she didn't "serve" me the meals, she'd leave them for me and say, "Prepare them however you want, they are your meals."

But thanks to that, I became very independent. I never depended on people even though I was alone with Shannon.

And having Shannon also helped me mature even more. Just because she's my only daughter doesn't mean that I spoiled her. She has always been responsible for her own things, and maybe that is why she was able to go on a mission without thinking twice. She never suffered the separation from, "who is going to clean for me, who is going to cook for me, who is going to wake me up early?"

None of that. She already knew how to run her schedule. She was even economically independent because she began working at age sixteen. She learned how to save her money and everything. So, these things have helped her, and I know that she is going to do a better job than I did when it comes time to form her family. She is going to know how to teach her children the principles of independence.

Ofelia seemed to lose sight of the original question, which had to do with why elderly couples in Arequipa did not serve missions. Yet, she intuitively cycled back to the topic by linking her daughter's gospel-preaching missionary skills to the mastery of the principles, not of the gospel, but of independence. Usually when Mormons used the word "principles" in my study, they followed it with "of the gospel," as part of a pat phrase that was also the title of a Sunday School manual. Instead, Ofelia said, "of independence." It would appear that in Ofelia's ontology, the principles of the gospel were the principles of independence. Mormons certainly valued independence—the nuclear family being the appropriate unit of individuation—and Ofelia was a very faithful Mormon, so it should not have seemed contradictory that she too would have valued independence. It should also not have seemed contradictory that Ofelia would have understood Shannon's eventual marriage to mean Shannon's eventual self-reliance and formation of a new family independent of Ofelia: "her family."

However, in other ways, Ofelia's anti-dependence discourse seemed too exaggerated to be a genuine reflection of her category of independence. It was almost as if she were trying to discursively swing the pendulum into the furthest reaches of theoretical individualism so that, in praxis, it would oscillate back to a level of moderate collectivism that could fit in Arequipa while still honoring her official church's principals of independence. I believe such was Ofelia's aim in our interview because in her selection of anecdotes, she portrayed herself as valuing independence from her family to such an excessive extent that she related familial independence in every single one of her examples to the very actions that constructed her kinship to familia in the first place: choosing, storing, warming, eating, and even anthropomorphically bundling up "in its little winter coat" a key substance of pacha relatedness—food.

Ofelia praised individualism to the extreme that she advocated becoming independent from the very foodways integral to arequipeño kinship, the same sort of kinship that structured her relationships to her mother, grandmother, hermanos, and daughter. I know she valued those interdependent relationships, so I sensed a lack of sincerity in her praise of independence from them. The confirmation of my theory that her praise of independence was not completely genuine came embedded within the contrasting context of our interview itself: her supremely interdependent living situation. Ofelia's dwelling was not exactly what Mayor Woods would have considered indicative of "people living good lives." Ofelia's "unit" would not have merited his designation of "home." Ofelia lived under the same roof with her nine adult hermanos, their families, and parts of their families' families. The mayor of Salsands, like many US sociologists, would have pathologized Ofelia's domestic situation as stereotypically "non-White" meaning "disorganized, as indicated by high rates of out-of-wedlock births, sexual promiscuity, marital instability, and matriarchal families characterized by 'strong and domineering' . . . women who prefer to head families on their own" (Sarkisian and Gerstel 2012, 14). As a matriarch who led her entire household, Ofelia proudly owned some aspects of that stereotype.

Therefore, while Ofelia's discursive preference for independence in a highly interdependent home was contradictory, her Mormon matriarchy was a paradox (Palmer 2022). Ofelia valued independence so much that she took it beyond the bounds of proper sainthood. She was independent from the one thing upon which all Mormons—Anglos and Peruvians—were supposed to depend: patriarchy. Her rhetorical individualism made her extremely Mormon, but her lived extension of that to include independence from husbands and from the nuclearization of family that husbands brought into being made her almost anti-Mormon. Furthermore, while Ofelia might have required her university-attending daughter to prepare her own food, they still lived under the same roof. In fact, they both lived under Ofelia's mother's roof, the very mother who purportedly gave Ofelia her appreciation for independence.

Good Relations

Ofelia's female-dominated, interdependent living situation in the background of her fierce critique of dependence was a microcosm of the tension between subjectivity and intersubjectivity that generated energy for Zion's category of independence. In this, Ofelia was not unique. Her daughter, her mother, and the majority of Peruvian Mormon women who participated in this study somehow meshed their matriarchal homes with an independence-focused religion that was dependent on patriarchal power. This tension between dependence and independence was felt by all Mormons in my study, not just Peruvian Mormons. This meant that the ways in which Peruvian Mormons lived in familias could not be easily parsed onto one side or the other of a battle between Anglos and Peruvians over what truly got to count as forever family.

Still, as Ofelia's living arrangements exemplified, the Peruvian Mormon work to expand independence so as to include pacha, coresident siblingship, and other conglomerative, non-arboreal forms of familia upset Zion's carefully constructed façade. That façade depicted a natural balance between dependence and independence. The existence within Mormonism of rhizomatic familias like Ofelia's and La Familia chipped at that façade, exposing how centuries of European global dominance had hegemonically set the purportedly natural balance to whatever la gringada (whiteness) considered proper. As it was extremely easy for the central church—controlled by well-intentioned Anglo Mormons like Mayor Woods—to tip that balance to the detriment of Peruvian Mormons, it was unlikely that Peruvian Mormon forever familias would be considered forever families as long as Anglos remained in control of Zion.

In the evolution of Zion as I observed it from 2014 to 2021, Peruvian Latter-day Saint familias were excluded from forever family status in their own religion. But, as the AHIJ Saint voiced, was not religion already an antiquated, Eurocentric category better off despised? Could not Peruvian sainthoods exist within their own lifeways and cosmologies unbeholden to the Utah church? Had not Peruvian Mormons demonstrated that they held the power to reach out and take the statuses that they desired while completely ignoring what their central church leaders thought of them? In these questions, tensions between mutually backscratching Peruvian mining engineers and despotic Utah bosses scale to broader zones of applicability than simply to local intercultural and intrareligious conflicts across Peru and Utah.

The tension between dividuality and individuality encapsulated in Zion's category of independence evokes the greater problem of good relations in today's world, especially as it connects to the hegemony of whiteness in categorizing what is "good." Since whiteness undergirded every category analyzed in this book, I conclude by facing it head on.

Whiteness

Leaving things undone and
uncomfortable is preferable to forcing
closure at the cost of the *testimoniante*.
—Pascha Bueno-Hansen, *Feminist and
Human Rights Struggles in Peru* (2015, 157)

Longing and Hate

Pioneer indigeneity is uncomfortable. Forever familia is undone. This conclusion will not resolve things. In fact, it will further entangle the one ingredient that all of this book's Mormon categories—leaders, government, legacy, holiness, future, marriage, and independence—have in common: whiteness.

During my study, Mormon Zion privileged whiteness. Therefore, the relationship that non-White Mormons in my study had to whiteness was—like Zion itself—paradoxical. Peruvian Mormons were engaged in a series of recategorizations that involved subtracting, adding, and reconfiguring whiteness as they attempted to expand their US religion to allow for some Peruvianness. Meanwhile, la gringada was remodeling its own categories, incorporating whiteness in ways that both inadvertently and deliberately facilitated and thwarted Peruvian Zion-building.

In this book's glossary, I define whiteness as pertaining to the elite group of people who benefit from the perpetuation of class-based hierarchies of oppression that they disguise as racial and, therefore, natural or God-given. Other researchers have defined whiteness differently. For an African American context, Africana scholar Theresa Perry (1998) defined whiteness as "that complex admixture of longing and hate that white people have for African Americans, their cultural formations, and their cultural products" (15). That definition is a perfectly contradictory fit for the sort of whiteness foundational to Zion, a city founded by Peruvian Mormons, African American Mormons, and unmarked Mormons alike on a "complex admixture of longing and hate," religion and kinship, holy and sacred, story and history, reciprocity and alienation, essentialism and constructivism, future and past, indigeneity and coloniality, dependence and independence, scarcity and abundance, singleness and matrimony, and, ultimately family and familia.

I have explored in this book many research questions in terms of how Peruvian Mormons navigated the difficulties that the complex admixtures reflected in that long list of binary constructs caused in their daily lives. My macrolevel question has basically been, how do Mormons excluded from the category "Mormon" change the category so that it includes them? In this conclusion, I provide personal examples of whiteness that dig into the roots of that question and funnel its dialectical tension into a smaller question. I hope that the smaller question serves as a satisfactorily uncomfortable concluding microcosm of the role whiteness played during my study relative to pioneer indigeneity and forever familia. The question is, in order to achieve the categorical inclusion of Peruvianness into Mormonism, did the norms of Peruvian Mormonism consider it preferable for Peruvian Mormons to marry Anglo Mormons?

White Genealogies

Given official Mormonism's predilection for whiteness and its cofounding of US whiteness, you might have expected that when the marriage-hungry Peruvian Mormon immigrants to Utah in my study sought the right person, they were also seeking a White person. The truth is that, regardless of whom they sought, right automatically had a high numerical probability of coinciding with White. For many Mormons, "right" meant marrying not only a fellow Mormon, but a Mormon who was born in the covenant, meaning someone who was born into a forever family. Though demographics were rapidly become more racially diverse among non-Mormon millennials in the United States in the late 2010s, born-in-the-covenant, single Mormons of marriageable age in Utah were still disproportionally White (Knoll and Reiss 2020).

To help you visualize the question of whether White was right for my Peruvian Mormon study participants, allow me to lead you through an exercise of imagination. Imagine that you are a first-generation arequipeña Mormon woman marrying off your dark-pigmented, second-generation Mormon son to a sixth-generation Mormon daughter-in-law who, if her high generational stage is any indication, is almost certain to be an Anglo Mormon.

Imagine the offspring of that union. You will suddenly have seventh-generation Mormon grandkids. You will have caught up to the Anglo Utah-Mormon future. Since your daughter-in-law's Anglo Mormon great-grandparents did their own family history, you stand amazed at the sheer size of the maternal side of your grandkids' fully brachiated and foliated family tree complete with names, dates, and photographs for every individual in each succeeding, numbered generation. You salivate before the immensity of all the ancestral lines that could be mined for names, which could then be shipped to the temple—a veritable ancestor-processing plant—to be given proxy rites and sealed to your forever familia.

Recalling the frenzy of family history that descended upon your fellow arequipeño Mormons when the rumor spread that temple construction had been delayed because of your ward family's failure to collect enough ancestor data to keep a temple running, marrying your son off to a generational Mormon becomes a genealogical windfall. I have known Peruvian Mormons to feel guiltier about not having "four generations back" filled out on their Familysearch.org family tree—a feat that was not yet on the official list of questions for temple-recommend interviews in the late 2010s—than they did about lacking feats that *were* on that list. Seeing a half-Anglo, half-seventh-generation Mormon grandchild's family tree is enough to make you, a Peruvian Mormon grandmother—ashamed as you may be over your own comparatively puny branch of that tree—beam with pride.

Furthermore, your grandkids will now be on the cusp of actually reaching the "day of the Lamanite." Their skin will be a shade lighter, meaning that they will have simultaneously fulfilled Mormon prophecies of curse cancelation and Latin American projects of national whitening. Plus, most pragmatically, your half-White grandchildren—assuming that your daughter-in-law was acquired after your son's immigration to Utah—will be birthright US citizens. They will be full members of the most developed and self-governing "first world" nation on the planet; the nation with, in the words of Alba from chapter 5, "much future going forward"; and the nation that *The Book of Mormon* prophesied would be "lifted up by the power of God above all other nations" (J. Smith 1830, 30). In short, your grandchildren will be in the present progressive state of blossoming as the rose, instead of being perpetually counted among those Lamanites like yourself, trapped in the static future tense, who always and only "shall blossom" (J. Smith et al. 1835, 192).

You can stop imagining now because, as a testament to the myriad categorical mismatches underlying Peruvian Mormon Zion and despite the tantalizing pulls of Mormon whiteness in the above thought experiment, there was no Peruvian Mormon in my study whose sentiments remotely approximated those of that hypothetical grandmother. What explains this? Why did the penchant for whiteness among Mormons in my study not translate into a sentiment among Peruvian Mormons that to marry the right Mormon one must marry a White Mormon? According to anthropologist Aihwa Ong (2003), Cambodian Mormon women in California did think that the right Mormon had to be a White Mormon. Ong was not the only one with that assumption. Katari, a Bolivian Mormon, lived with that assumption every day and blamed it for his ongoing singleness.

In 2016, Katari told me what it was like to be an unmarried Latino Mormon living in Utah. His principal complaint was that "Utah girls will only marry a

Moroni with a Lamborghini. "He explained that the Moroni half of that bipartite requirement indexed more about the ancient American prophet Moroni than just his impeccable righteousness. Moroni after all—as the last Nephite and the one who witnessed the dark-pigmented Lamanites eliminate his entire nation—was light-pigmented, or at least he was so depicted in many *Book of Mormon* illustrations infused with "arresting images of robust masculinity . . . [and] chiseled bodies" (Campbell 2020, 251). Furthermore, assuming that he took after his father, Mormon, he was "large in stature" (J. Smith 1830, 520). Katari, in contrast, and by his own estimation, was brown and short. In Katari's eyes, Mormon women, be they Andeans or Anglo Utahans, were looking to marry Mormon men who were righteous, rich, tall, and—therefore—White.

However, in my experience with specifically Peruvian Mormons and, even more specifically, with La Familia, the whiteness that they sought in a marriage partner had to be so tempered with Peruvianness that it ended up being easier to find a proper mate in Peru than in Utah. Jacoba made many a matchmaking trip back to Peru for that very purpose on behalf of her children and grandchildren. To appreciate the irony behind how it was possible that both Mormonism and Peruvianness could love whiteness even as their admixture concocted a Peruvian Mormonism that rejected Anglo Mormon marriage partners, you must undergo a short lesson on how whiteness manifested among Peruvians.

Cholo con Plata

During my study, the well-known idiomatic expression "cholo con plata" (formerly Indigenous person with money) worked as an oxymoronic joke in Peru that exposed the hiding places of whiteness. Cholos in Peru were characterized as people who grew up in autochthonous mountain villages but then "invaded" the cities. In the city, cholos tried to live a modern Peruvianness that was imagined as raceless but that was deliberately patterned after a US-style nation-building initiative that favored whiteness (Gandolfo 2009). Cholo con plata referred to the futility of the effort to join that simultaneously raceless and White national body. It was as if a White employer advertising a position were saying, "I need someone with plata," but then along came a cholo with money who was obviously not what the employer meant because cholos were, by societal definition, sin plata (penniless). Therefore, "cholo con plata" humorously revealed that the employer might have saved herself the effort of using a code wherein money equaled whiteness by simply admitting, "I will hire a White person like me."

However, had that conjectural employer herself been in the United States, she might have been considered a Latina and even a person of color. In Peru, on the other hand, as long as she was not Afroperuvian, she would have had no racial designation even as she inhabited the rung reserved for whiteness on the social hierarchy. This is because, for many Peruvians, that rung had more to do with perceived decency than verifiable skin tone. Thus, one could inhabit whiteness without being light-pigmented. The French Antilles had a similar racial arrangement. As Frantz Fanon ([1952] 1994) noted, "the Antillean . . . feels . . . that one is a Negro to the degree to which one is wicked, sloppy, malicious, instinctual. Everything that is the opposite of these Negro modes of behavior is white. . . . If I order my life like that of a moral man, I simply am not a Negro" (192). Similarly, in the modes of Peruvianness that coined "cholo con plata," if one lived above a certain economic and moral level—and one was not an Afroperuvian—one was understood to be "white" (Fanon [1952] 1994, 43).

Therefore, it is quite possible that the hypothetical employer herself was originally a chola who had been able to pass as a raceless—White—limeña. If someone from her ancestral village were to see her in her office in Lima, they might remark on her hobnobbing with upper-class executives just as a José María Arguedas ([1941] 2011) fictional character did in similar circumstances: "these cholos only just arrived [from the village to the city] and, even so, they move around the Sub-Director as if they were VIP's; . . . Isn't it true that their own parents are still alive wandering around their villages in their raggedy traditional garb?" (129, translation mine). Similarly, Kimberly Theidon (2013) commented about one of her study participants, a government-funded death squad member during the Shining Path War, that "although his skin color was no different than that of the *campesinos* [peasants] with whom I worked, his uniform and education made him a *mestizo* on the fluid continuum of 'racial' categories in Peru. Joining the military was one strategy of social whitening for young men. . . . He was handsome: . . . a full set of teeth. I realized how much I noticed teeth; they said so much about where one was positioned on the fluid continuum" (280).

Likewise, among my Peruvian study participants, skin tone did not determine whiteness (Burns 2011). In Peru, only Afroperuvians were "people of color." My Peruvian study participants, 90 percent of whom fit the US imaginary of "little brown people," reserved that diminutive moniker, "morenitos" or, even more derogatorily, "morochitos," for Black people. At the same time— and this is where whiteness in Peru becomes paradoxical—the extremely small percentage of Peruvians who actually fit the US imaginary of White people, many of whom were criollos, were referred to with an epithet: "pitucos."

My Peruvian study participants did not consider pitucos to be moral people. They thought them to be stingy, greedy, and individualistic opportunists. Unlike the Antillean definition wherein whiteness equaled morality, pitucos did not embody whiteness despite their "White" phenotype. Put differently, whiteness could sometimes connote immorality in Peru, not just morality. For another example, during the Path War, average members of communities became Shining Path militants, but some of their anti-Path neighbors considered all Shining Path militants to be foreign gringos or some other sort of pale-skinned monstrosity (Theidon 2013). Furthermore, the principal antihuman vampire of the Andes, the pishtaco or kharisiri—who sucked the substance of collectivist relatedness in the form of body fat and sold it to individualist capitalists to lubricate their machines—often took the form of a White male. He was "whitened by his sexual aggressivity and masculinized by virtue of his whiteness" (Weismantel 2001, 169). Therefore, "white," the skin color, while clearly associated with high economic status in Peru, was ambivalently associated with the moral status of "White," the race. This meant that whiteness, as a clear moral requirement for all the Anglo Mormon categories in this book, took on a different meaning when those categories met Peruvianness.

At first glance, light skin pigmentation was the most salient of the characteristics associated with societal superiority in Peru during my time there. For example, to be screen-worthy in Peru—meaning to have one's face on billboards, advertisements, films, and talk shows—usually one had to either have extremely pale skin (which could then be painted brown for anti-Indigenous buffoonery) or be a professional soccer player (Falcón 2016). In fact, since most Peruvians exhibited little to no phenotypic European admixture, it helped one's modeling career to not be Peruvian at all. I saw dozens of window posters promoting products through Peru's historic rise to the 2018 World Cup with text stating "The Coast, The Mountains, The Jungle: We are all ONE Peru" only to have it foregrounded with a diverse array of Nordic models who were drinking Inka Kola while dressed in Peruvian national team merchandise.

In Peru, though physical beauty was almost completely synonymous with pale skin color, the beauty of whiteness was often considered skin deep. Another reason for that was that pale skin color was associated with the United States. Peruvian Mormons bundled wealth, beauty, height, and many other attributes with whiteness's positive valence. However, the United States, despite its being the cradle of their religion and the architect of the White nation-building that they sought to emulate, was not fully part of that positive bundle. As I demonstrated throughout this book, there were things about "gringolandia" (the United States) that Peruvian Mormons were not willing to accept no matter how closely associated those things were to their beloved, new US religion.

So, why did Peruvian Mormon acceptance of that religion reach its limit at the precise latitude whereupon all the religion's advantages could have intersected: marrying a White, US citizen Mormon? A partial answer is that Peruvian Mormons in my study were already so exhausted from squaring with their spiritual lives what they considered to be Anglo kin pathologies that they had no energy left to square them with their familias. They certainly had no energy left to fully embrace them. Rather than fully embracing the faith of la gringada, many of my Peruvian Mormon study participants simply paused their acceptance of the divinity of the gringo kin notions that came attached to it and postponed that acceptance into the intangible, distant future. They often did this by claiming that their official church's unacceptable kin notions and temple-sealing strictures would "all be worked out in the Millennium," the 1,000 years of peace brought in by Christ's Second Coming.

However, when they were confronted with the prospect of a marriageable child being torn away into a cold, distant, sui generis, Anglo Mormon, nuclear, forever family right here and now on this Earth, things got real tangible real fast. When Peruvian Mormon familias lived in the largely Anglo Mormon society of Utah, such a ripping away was an ever-present possibility and it required a highly conflicted redrawing of the boundaries of anthropological endogamy. Mormons were already supposed to marry outside the kin group (exogamy) but inside the religion (endogamy). Inasmuch as Mormonism was a kin group, the blurry boundary of exogamy/endogamy between the colonializing categories of kinship and religion provided complexity enough. However, once in Utah, in order to preserve any semblance of familia, many Peruvian Mormons added another layer of complexity to their endogamy that trumped any desire for marrying a US citizen, a Moroni with a Lamborghini, or someone born in the covenant. That level of complexity was a criterion that nullified many of the mate-finding reasons for which unmarried Mormons immigrated to Utah in the first place: ideally, Peruvian Mormons in Utah needed to marry Peruvian Mormons.

Proving Peruvianness

In the Mormon context, Anglo/Latinx interethnic marriage implied the crossing of two estranged Israelite lineages in Mormon discourse: Ephraim, represented in White people from the United States, and Manasseh, represented in anyone with phenotypically discernable ancestry Indigenous to Abya Yala or the Pacific Islands. Joseph Smith prophesied that those two sons of the biblical Joseph of Egypt would come together in the Earth's final days, uniting their separate but somehow equal roles that, in poetic scripture and song, sounded strikingly similar to the unequal gender roles that one might find in a 1950s US marriage. Ephraim was the supervisor, and Manasseh was the builder. Ephraim was the vanguard, and Manasseh was the rearguard. And, in the most "matronizing" of those metaphors, Ephraim was the nursing mother and Manasseh was the baby. As I briefly described in chapter 5 regarding the Utah genocide of the 1850s, this coming together rarely ended well for Manasseh.

During my study, Manasseh's descendants were living among Ephraim like never before, but intratribal Mormon kin battles were no longer fought to the death, and the Ephraim versus Manasseh sides of the ancestral sibling rivalry were more porous. Yet, the rivalry remained. Manasseh, even when represented by Americanized Peruvian youth who grew up in predominantly White, Mormon, Utah public schools, did not often capitulate to Ephraim's kinways to the extent of physically marrying into them.

At least, not if Jacoba had anything to say about it. Jacoba demonstrated how "the family . . . [became] a key site of resistance" (Theidon 2013, 216) to Mormonism even as it became Mormonism's main attraction. Jacoba ran a semiofficial wedding reception decoration business in Salsands, Utah. It just so happened that three of her grandsons and one of her sons got married during the six-month, Utah phase of my fieldwork, so I had occasion to participate in many a Costa-style, Peruvian Mormon wedding reception designed by Jacoba. Jacoba had all the materials and know-how necessary to turn a Mormon chapel's cultural hall into a dance hall aglow with enough white Christmas lights and draped with enough tulle to make one forget about the basketball hoops above and the free-throw lines below. She even covered the invariably stained, scratched, and dented metallic folding chairs—the setting up, sitting in, and taking down of which have become part of a global Mormon habitus (Inouye 2015)—with custom-fit, pearly white sheaths.

Jacoba was my spouse Elvira's tía, so when my future spouse and mother-in-law were planning our wedding reception back in 2001, they naturally asked Jacoba for decoration help. Instead of help, Jacoba gave my fiancée urgently needed advice—"Do not, under any circumstances, marry a gringo." My fiancée—saints be praised—refused to follow that advice. Jacoba, therefore, refused to decorate our reception and also made sure that none of the Costa side of my fiancée's familia attended our wedding. Due in part to that symbolic protest, I was not included as a member of the Costa faction of La Familia until my preliminary research for this project began sixteen years later.

Of course, Jacoba had not expected our marriage to last that long. As a pioneer of the Latinx Mormon church in northern Utah and as an entrepreneur of the very idea of Latinx-centered Mormon activities, Jacoba had seen plenty of failed interethnic Mormon marriages and she attributed most of those failures to the pathological whiteness of one of the partners. One problem that Jacoba had seen multiple times was that the Anglo groom, despite knowing that marrying a Latina meant marrying into her familia rather than starting his own family, was never prepared for what that actually entailed. This was something that Peruvian Mormons whom I had only just met often felt the need to tell me even when they knew that my spouse was Peruvian. In other words, they perceived that I still, after almost two decades of marriage to a Peruvian, had not fully learned what the category of marriage was for a Peruvian.

On my very first Sunday at Barrio Periféricos in Arequipa, Flavio Abedul, fresh off his mission, asked for my advice about whether or not he should follow his mission president's counsel and get married right away at age twenty. I started explaining that it was his own personal choice, and that the best advice was to ignore other people's counsel. Older men standing around us during this conversation jumped in to get me up to speed on some information that they assumed that I would need to mitigate the damage my advice was apparently causing. They correctly assumed that I, though a fellow Mormon, probably had a rather different categorization of marriage than Flavio did by virtue of my whiteness. They explained, "When Anglos get married, they think of themselves as starting their own little family of two, but when Peruvians get married, they think of it as the merging of two large familias."

The compatibility of the two familias was just as important as the compatibility of the two individuals because the two separate familias would have to become one at parties—through Peruvian food and Peruvian dancing—that would mark the major life events of the couple and their children from then on: baby showers, birthdays, baptisms, mission call email-openings, mission farewells, mission homecomings, and wedding receptions. Therefore, since the couple's individual decision was only one of many factors to take into consideration, my advice to ignore counsel extraneous to individual choice was inappropriate in Peruvian Mormon gospel culture.

Peruvian food and dancing (but not alcohol) were key factors in marriage alliances for Peruvian Mormons because they were part of proximity. Potential new members of La Familia had to live close enough to Salsands to party often. One could not become a member of La Familia until one had been to enough of its almost weekly parties to prove one's Peruvianness through adequate dance skills and proper food preferences. This represented the other reason for our forever family's initial estrangement from the Costa clan's forever familia. Not only did we leave northern Utah, something that was almost unheard of in La Familia, but we left the United States entirely for eight years. I played right into Jacoba's stereotype of the gringo who could not hack it in a Peruvian familia and so either got divorced or took his Peruvian wife as far away from her familia as possible (we moved to Turkey).

However, other than their boycott of our wedding, our marriage began happily enough. We started out a few miles from the Costas. We lived in a house shared with Wendy—another of Elvira's many tías—Elvira's brother, his Salvadoran wife, and their baby daughter. I learned a lot about my whiteness during the year that we were there, and so did Wendy. She, incidentally, was still reeling over her own violent divorce from a gringo Mormon. Things were never great between them, but when more and more of her adult children immigrated to the United States and came to live with them in Utah, the gringo realized that the warning, "when you marry her, you marry her family," was not metaphorical. However, thanks to the gringo's personification of whiteness at its most individualist, I did not look half bad in comparison. In Wendy's eyes, I was not nearly as "White" as he was. What was my advantage?

I could speak Spanish and had lived in Latin America for two years as a missionary. I was so "down" with Peruvianness that I had even acquired a taste for chuño, a freeze-dried, fermented potato that was "a living, sentient being" (M. E. García 2021, 151) in some Peruvian ontologies and a staple of many highland cuisines. While living in Arequipa, I observed Ofelia periodically serving chuño to the gringo missionaries who ate daily in her large familial complex. She did so partially as a lighthearted torture and partially as a litmus test of their nascent Peruvianness.

Since food was one of the principal substances of Peruvian relatedness, it was no surprise that in my first year of living with a Peruvian tía, it was over food that we had the inevitable falling out that would spiral into a breach of coresidence between her and her niece. Though every adult in the home worked, including the aging Wendy (twelve-hour shifts at the Skyline Select food factory), she was the only one who cooked, and we would occasionally eat together as a household. I felt like Wendy had a sixth sense when it came to scrutinizing what I ate. I could not extract a single chicken vertebra from my plate of arroz con pollo without her noticing and commenting on the thinly veiled insult of her cooking that such an extraction implied.

Low-grade battles over food culminated in the closest that I have ever come to a fistfight with a Peruvian brother-in-law. Since we all used the same kitchen, there was always a conflict over who did the dishes. I had the brilliantly individualistic idea that everyone could use their own distinctive set of dishware and wash their own. I assumed that the virtues of my All-American plan would speak for themselves, so I taught it through example one night by serving up Tía Wendy's famous tallarín verde on my own personal aluminum camping plate—complete with matching spork—rather than using the family dishware. Big mistake. My brother-in-law took it as a personal afront to his tía and a subversion of her ultimate authority over the kitchen. He also took it as a rupture of the collectivity that was supposed to be inherent in communal eating. Most of all, he took it as a sign that I still concealed—below my Spanish-speaking, Peruvian food-eating surface—a pathological amount of whiteness.

When we came back to the United States for the purpose of my preliminary investigations for this project sixteen years later, time had healed most wounds, and the Costa clan of the greater group that called itself La Familia invited us to their annual campout. I had heard a lot about Jacoba, the matriarch of the Costas, but had not actually met her before this. During the campout, which included a dance-off, the faithfully Mormon Costa clan finally approved of our marriage and with it, my insertion into La Familia. My inclusion did not happen because I proved myself to be sufficiently Mormon, but because I proved myself to be sufficiently Peruvian. Despite the high value that whiteness, variously defined, had in both Mormonism and Peruvianness, my whiteness was not an asset in the eyes of those Peruvian Mormons. It was a handicap that I had to overcome in order to join La Family. Legally marrying a biological member of La Familia was not enough to grant me entry even though our marriage sealing was performed inside the Salt Lake City temple, the Peruvian symbol par excellence of Mormon forever familia worthiness. Instead, to be granted entry, I had to show that I understood what familia truly meant, and that required that I become as "Peruvian" as possible.

Immanent Obligation

Under my settler gaze, it would seem that La Familia (kinship) was ultimately more important than the church (religion) in creating Peruvian Mormon Zion. However, under La Familia's gaze, there existed no binary construct that pitted kinship against religion in the first place. Since the division between kinship and religion was colonial, removing it meant that the church *was* La Familia, just as it meant that the true translation of Abya Yala's many Indigenous words mistranslated as "sacred" *was* in fact "relatedness." The logical conclusion of those ontological equivalences further meant that Peruvian Mormon Zion *was* pioneer indigeneity, and that pioneer indigeneity *was* forever familia.

I capitalized La Familia in Spanish throughout this book to distinguish constructed membership in my in-laws' familial network from an essentialist membership that one might experience when one simply happens to be born into a societal arrangement called "my family." Jacoba's English-preferring grandkids demonstrated a linguistic awareness that there was something different between the way that they spoke of family and the way that their Anglo peers spoke of family. Even when speaking English to monolingual English speakers, those in La Familia's youngest generations would almost always use the Spanish kin terms of tía and primo when referring to members of what they called, always in Spanish, La Familia, by which they meant their large conglomeration of interrelated kin groups, including the Costas. When they said "my family" in English, they indexed the nuclear sense of family, the sense that they had in common with Anglo peers. But when they said La Familia, they indexed a special association. It was an association that evoked a higher and deeper level of relatedness to which they had to earn access. It represented a kinship that granted them a "holy" and "sacred" belonging above and beyond that which either of those two colonial terms could contain and stronger than that which their Anglo Mormon peers experienced.

Members of La Familia could not fathom why people would want to wrench themselves away from such belonging as gringos notoriously did when they moved away from their families at age eighteen. They could not conceive of how it would even be possible to raise children away from La Familia as Elvira and I had done. Most of the questions that Jacoba and her eldest daughter,

Lori, had for me when I finally became a member of the Costa faction of La Familia revolved around how I could justify raising my daughters so far away from La Familia. Jacoba was particularly intent on convincing me to get a job at a local university in Utah because perhaps there would still be time for my daughters to be raised up properly, meaning within the space of La Familia. This might have seemed hypocritical coming from the woman who had left three of her kids, including Lori, in Peru for three years while she attempted to start a new life in the United States, but Jacoba's actions were perfectly in line with her kinship ideals. She left her children precisely so that they could reside longer with La Familia in Peru until a remote offshoot of La Familia could be formed for them in the United States. Her actions in leaving her young children near the place from whence their greatest relationality emanated only proved the point that "familia" did not include simply her, her antecedents, and her descendants in the way that "family" did for the Anglo Mormons in my study.

Familia, in Peruvian Mormonism, was a much larger, deeper, and broader network than "family" was in the Anglo Mormonism in which I was raised. For Jacoba, familia was her connection to the multitemporal places of Zion, be they in Peru or Utah. As such, familia was a connection to her pioneer indigeneity that was intimately interwoven with her claims of being first in the land of Zion and her claims of being "prior" even though those claims were difficult to historically prove in ways that US modernity would find satisfactory. Jacoba's conception of familia and its conflation of time and place—pacha—involved what Elizabeth Povinelli (2011) called "immanent obligation."

> By "immanent obligation" I am referring to a form of relationality that one finds oneself drawn to and finds oneself nurturing or caring for. This being 'drawn to' is often initially a very fragile connection, a sense of an immanent connectivity. Choices are then made to enrich and intensify these connections. But even these choices need to be understood as retrospective and the subject choosing as herself continually deferred by the choice. I might be able to describe why I am drawn to a particular space, and I may try to nurture this obligation or to break away from it, but still I have very little that can be described as "choice" or determination in the original orientation. (28)

Immanence evokes magnetic innateness flowing out to include unchosen human and nonhuman others (people and places) within a connection. Obligation imposes itself from the outside to exclude threats to that connection. In this sense and inasmuch as immanent obligation is familia, familia is a microcosm of Mormonism itself and of the exclusive inclusivity of Zion's categories. Seen from the level of quotidian interactions among La Familia teeming with immanent obligations toward each other, toward their sacred church, and toward their holy places, the meanings of their categorical difficulties change. The supposed tribulations involved in reconfiguring the official church's categories to make way for Peruvian Mormonism within them lose their uniqueness to Zion and become part of "original people's ancestral memories of being 'human'" (Hernández 2021, 3). Thus understood, the constant effort to reconfigure categories such that they simultaneously include kin and exclude threats is simply part of good relations.

La Familia, like Mormonism itself, functioned on some levels almost as a tribe of people in a place of intimate interaction, rather than as a nation in a space of "stranger sociality" (Povinelli 2011, 28) wherein complete strangers could be group members. Like a tribe, La Familia was so extremely exclusive that it provided extra satisfaction and protection to those who were able to pass through its borders. Requirements for passage included a sort of immanent connection to the modern nation-state of Peru and to the modern/antimodern religion of Mormonism. Entry into La Familia was neither completely based on biological essentialism nor completely based on constructing relationships and proving Peruvianness through eating and dancing. As such, La Familia did not conform to either side of the kinship binaries that pitted indigeneity against coloniality, constructivism against essentialism, history against myth, and stranger sociality against proximal relationality. La Familia, as Elvira would say, was a mezcolanza (complex admixture) of all those things.

Cholo sin Plata

Yet, the mixture had to be balanced lest La Familia and other Peruvian Mormon constructions deem it unacceptable. Whiteness was an important ingredient of all mixtures involving La Familia and Peruvian Mormonism, but what was the right ratio of whiteness to other, non-White assemblages, such as indigeneity?

I already established that my whiteness was an obstacle in my path to full fellowship in La Familia, but that did not mean that a potential in-law without any whiteness at all would be received with open arms. Crossing into La Familia required the right amount of whiteness. At first, I had too much, but my primo Basilio Corimayta had too little. Basilio grew up in the small village of Madrigal in southern Peru's Colca Canyon near the city of Arequipa. As a young adult, he moved to Lima to live with his uncle, converted to Mormonism, served a two-year mission in Ayacucho, Peru, and immigrated overland to the US/Mexico border. He was called as the first councilor in a Mormon bishopric in Nogales, Mexico, while he worked in a maquila (factory) for six months to save up money to cross into Nogales, Arizona. He eventually made it to Utah to the home of one of his former mission companions. He then joined the only Spanish-speaking Mormon congregation north of Salt Lake City, Utah, at the time (the 1980s). The leader of that congregation was none other than Arcadio Costa. At a Young Single Adults Family Night in the Costa family home, Basilio saw before him many young Peruvian Mormon women from whom to choose as potential targets for courtship.

In his version of the story, he chose the most beautiful of them all. That this happened to also mean the lightest-complexioned of them all was a phenotypic fact not lost on the artist who painted a portrait of the couple after their Salt Lake City temple wedding and who, it seemed, had a flare for accentuating both ancestral and complexion contrasts and for sensationalizing those into a racialized, stylistic affect. The painting depicted the parents of the very light-complexioned bride and the very dark-complexioned groom hovering above them in the background as properly arboreal antecedents. The bride's father was a mustachioed Spaniard with a linen suit and a dark necktie. The bride's mother had curly, strawberry blond hair, bright white skin, and long pearl earrings. The groom's parents' facial features were darker and blurrier than those of the bride's parents. They blended into the black background. His clean-shaven father was dressed like a hacienda peasant with drab, course clothing and a rounded bowler cap. His mother, sunk further into the background than anyone, was a young black-haired girl wearing a tunic and hat identical to those of her much older husband.

I rediscovered Basilio's wedding portrait as part of the home décor analysis aspect of my study. It was not hanging on the walls with depictions of the Salt Lake Temple, motivational quotes about families being forever, a giant US dollar bill with the inscription "financial self-reliance is within reach," and the commemorative plaques, medallions, and photographs of his children's missionary and Boy Scouts of America achievements. Instead, it was in the closet behind the vacuum cleaner. I would not have found it at all had I not deliberately asked him to include it in the digitally recorded tour of his walls, and I would not have asked about it had I not remembered it hanging prominently on the walls of his previous house in Ogden. I asked him why he shoved it in the closet. He told me that he had always hated it and that, since his wife put him in charge of decorating their new apartment in Salsands, he finally had the chance to hide it away. I asked him why he hated it. He said, "Because honestly, it makes me look like a cholo. Not that there is anything wrong with being a cholo. You know the song, 'Yes, I'm a Cholo, Stop Feeling Sorry for Me?' Well, I love that song, and I'm proud to be a cholo, but I didn't come to this country to wallow in my cholo-ness, so to speak. You know?"

The beautiful member of La Familia whom Basilio married was Vilma, Jacoba's niece. When Basilio first saw her at the Family Night, she had only recently emigrated from Lima to reunite with the Utah band of La Familia. As a result of her distinctive skin tone's mismatch with her lower-class status,

Vilma had grown up being called "la gringa" in Lima-Callao even before she knew about the existence of gringolandia. Basilio and Vilma's coupling, inasmuch as it epitomized the melding of the Two Perus dichotomy between the "white" coast and the "brown" highlands, presented a constant challenge to La Familia's inclusiveness. Basilio and I were both retornados—meaning that we were supposed to be "more attractive to faithful, Mormon women" (Patterson 2020, 66)—and we were both married in the Salt Lake City temple to members of La Familia. However, Basilio's ostentatious indigeneity presented a much larger obstacle to his inclusion into La Familia than my ostentatious whiteness presented to mine. This was because, despite Mormonism's hierarchy-flattening mechanisms—namely, the mission's comunitas and the interclass, Latin American solidarity of Spanish-speaking wards—there was an underlying "process of exclusion at the heart of Peruvian racial-gender-class hierarchies in the realm of migration" (Alcalde 2018, 33).

Though largely through jest, La Familia did not let Basilio forget for one moment that he grew up in an adobe hut, that he was completely undocumented in the United States until 2018, that he was a cholo perpetually sin plata, and that, as such, he was not worthy of Vilma. Resisting full capitulation to whiteness was vital to Peruvianness, but "assimilation to some form of whiteness" (I. M. García 2020, 731) was equally vital to "non-black Saints of color" (731) in the United States. Unfortunately, Basilio, in the La Familia's imagination, was unassimilable. This is all to say that La Familia—and Zion and Peru before it—was shot through with as much race-based exclusivity as it was with universal fellowship.

However, La Familia—again, like Zion—could also exude good relations. For example, La Familia included two large generational groups called Los Primos and Los Tios. Elvira and I were members of Los Tios along with most members of La Familia in our generation or older. Our daughters were members of Los Primos along with most members of La Familia who were one or more generations younger than us. Many fully fledged members of those groups did not share DNA with any members of La Familia, others did not share DNA with any Peruvian at all, but they all had constructed their relatedness to La Familia, sharing the substances of Peruvian food and Inca Kola through Peruvian Mormon partying (Palmer 2023). Many of Los Primos, including the four products of Basilio Corimayta and Vilma Arriátegui's complex admixture, had the privilege of calling Jacoba "abuela" (grandmother) even though, in the case of the four Corimayta siblings, she was technically their great aunt. Being able to call Jacoba "abuela" rather than simply "tía" as my daughters did, was always a great comfort to the US-born Corimaytas since both sets of their biological grandparents (caricaturized in the aforementioned painting) stayed in Peru and died without ever meeting them in person. Comfort, therefore, was one positive biproduct of La Familia's efforts to recategorize Anglo Mormonism's kin categories in order to fit Peruvianness into Zion.

"Tortillas and Rice"

Professional wedding photographers captured the generational groupings of Los Primos and Los Tios on multiple occasions during my study. One particular occasion occurred on the Ogden, Utah, temple grounds in the summer of 2017 after Jacoba's grandson Jericó's temple marriage. The events and discussions leading up to the ritual sealing of his fiancée into La Familia were emblematic of the contested amount of whiteness required to belong in Peruvian Mormon Zion.

I had the privilege of observing Sylvia, Jericó's fiancée, navigate her own probationary stage of construction as familia. First, you must understand that Lori, Jacoba's eldest daughter, was slated to become the de facto matriarch of the Costa cadre of La Familia upon Jacoba's death and that Jericó was Lori's only son. Jericó was also Jacoba's only "full-blooded" grandson who spoke Spanish and was a retornado. Though Jacoba had a few other grandsons who had been married, Jericó was the first to get married in the temple. Furthermore, Jacoba had no qualms about telling everybody that Jericó was her favorite grandson. She would even say this in the presence of the Cori-mayta siblings whom she allowed to call her "abuela" even as she made clear that she was not "really" their abuela. There was also a transparent sentiment from everyone in La Familia that Jericó was the most righteous among us. Even though all four of the Corimayta siblings had also served and honorably returned from missions—a sure sign of righteousness—Jericó remained the sole Moroni of La Familia's second to youngest generation. Like his grandfather Arcadio, Jericó was destined to become a future leader in the church and in La Familia. This meant that the woman whom he chose to marry could very easily become destined to be Lori's successor, the future matriarch of the La Familia's Costa clan.

A lot was riding, therefore, on Jericó's chosen mate. It went without saying that for Jacoba to approve of her, she had to be Mormon. What apparently required reiteration was the second requirement. His chosen mate had to carry the innate essence of Peruvianness. She could not simply be constructed as "sufficiently Peruvian" like I had been. Part of her Peruvianness had to include the right amount of whiteness: not too much, but certainly not too little. So, though Jericó at least had the good sense not to get involved romantically with an Anglo, Jacoba did not take kindly to his choice of a Mexican American.

Sylvia, though Latina enough on her exterior to be perceived as someone who understood the true "familia" meaning of family, seemed to Jacoba to be way too White on her interior. Jacoba was not the only one with that view.

I talked to Carol (Mido's Catholic spouse from chapter 5) about her perception of Sylvia's very "Peruvian Mormon" bachelorette party. In our conversation, Carol was effusive in her pity for Lori at having to deal with such a "gringuificada" (Americanized) daughter-in-law. Apparently, Sylvia did not like to dance, she did not like to eat in large groups, she did not like to speak Spanish, and she did not like to party. In fact, Sylvia left early from her own bachelorette party. Not only was she not Peruvian, but she did not appreciate any of the things that, for La Familia, made a Peruvian a Peruvian. In other words, her perceived whiteness served to cancel out her sainthood in Jacoba's matchmaking rulebook rather than bolster it.

From that angle, it seemed that Sylvia's US attitudes and comportment would add too much whiteness to the already complex admixture that was La Familia. However, in Jacoba's categorization, Sylvia's Mexican ancestry gave her too much indio as well. When I asked Jericó how he ended up procuring Jacoba's blessing to marry Sylvia, I was not surprised that she used a culinary metaphor in her ensuing advice on kin-formation. Jacoba warned Jericó, "You know, Hijito, tortillas and rice don't mix." As I will explain below, her forbidden fusion recipe was her way of saying that Mexicanness (tortillas) and Peruvianness (rice) should not mix. It was her way of saying that Mexicanness and Peruvianness would concoct the wrong kind of indigeneity.

Upon arrival to the United States, Peruvian migrants were often lumped in with Mexican migrants as "Latinos," a nationally stigmatized identity group coded as "illegal" in greater US media and political discourses (Hallett 2012). Newly immigrated Peruvians in my study often resented this lumping and all associated with it, including Mexican people and, tellingly, Mexican food. I was able to predict with great accuracy that, regardless of class, race, age, religion, or gender, if Peruvian immigrants had less than two years in the United States, they would claim to despise Mexican food. After a few years, the Peruvians in my study usually ended up loving both Mexican food and Mexican people, especially as they realized the political advantages that came with the solidarity of Latinx identity in the United States. I believe that their initial distain stemmed from the symbolic linking of Mexicanness with abjectivity in greater US discourses (Gonzales and Chavez 2012), from the fear that Mexicans might infuse that abjectivity into their familia, from the ontological fact that food *was* familia, and from the reality that only Peruvian food was La Familia. "In this sense, food [became] a powerful site for the construction of particular brands of Peruvianness in Peru and abroad" (Alcalde 2018, 143).

In Salsands, these "brands" indexed a phenomenon whereby La Familia, after decades of interacting with other Latinx people at church and in the workplace, persisted in using food to police Latinx identity's effects on Peruvianness. Furthermore, La Familia did so in ways that privileged whiteness and deprecated indigeneity. Part of their policing involved the "Peruvian gastropolitical complex" (M. E. García 2021, xiii). As a self-assigned agent of that complex, Jacoba—before reminding Jericó that it was ultimately his decision to marry a Mexican and that, of course, she would respect it—warned him of the volatility of mixing corn tortillas with rice.

The corn tortilla was the uncontested millenarian staple of the Mexican diet, as it was of the ancient Mexica diet, and Sylvia was a Mexican American. The somewhat hidden staple of what counted during my study as Peruvian haute cuisine on a global culinary stage was arguably rice. Such was at least the case in Jacoba's performance of Peruvian gastropolitics, which, on her trip to Hawaii, involved packing her own rice cooker despite expensive luggage limitations. Similar to Mandarin Chinese, in the language of La Familia, "meal" was synonymous with "rice." Yet there was a recent historic process whereby the coastal staple of rice rather than the highland staple of chuño achieved hegemony within Jacoba's configuration of Peruvian cuisine.

Since the award's inauguration in 2012, Peru has won the World Travel Awards' (2021) annual designation as "South America's Leading Culinary Destination" eight out of ten times. Through Peru's rise to world gastronomic stardom and its Marca Perú (Peruvian Brand) advertising campaign, "Peruvian ingredients and dishes from the Andes and Amazon [were] transformed via Lima at the hands of white-mestizo chefs to present a whitened (largely male) urban version of national identity to the world" (Alcalde 2018, 149). The culinary evolution of cuy (guinea pig) was symbolic of this larger, national whitening of foodways that were once considered Indigenous. For example, Lima's "Mistura" gastronomy festival was an open market venue including workshops wherein "chefs" (coded as White) trained "producers" (coded as Indigenous) on proper culinary comportment. At Mistura, María Elena García (2021) observed how both cuyes and cuy vendors were reaffirmed as authentically Indigenous even as their indigeneity was sanitized, urbanized, romanticized, and otherwise tamed for White tastes. Discussing a Runasimi-speaking vendor who had the audacity to ambulate around the festival selling whole, skewered cuyes, one trainer remarked, "We don't eat [the cuy] whole, certainly not with its head still on. People don't want to look at the face, especially tourists or Peruvians from a certain class. Her actions are taking us backwards" (97).

Unlike corn tortillas, chuño, and cuy, white rice is not indigenous to Abya Yala, and it does not cook well at high altitudes. This, combined with its ubiquitous use on the Peruvian coast (racialized as White) and its global familiarity, gave white rice the power to silently de-Indianize (SL) many of Peru's dishes for unmarked "cosmopolitan" (i.e., White) tastes. If White chefs had left chuño in the dishes, then the dishes would have remained uncivilized. Likewise, if Jacoba had admitted that choclo (corn) dominated in both

Mexican and Peruvian foodways, then La Familia would have opened itself up to a potentially destabilizing influx of Mexican indigeneity.

Thus, in ways deemed safely exotic, rice whitened both La Familia and Peruvianness. White rice made both of their newly branded indigenizations—the former in the figure of the de-*ite*-ed Lamanite, the latter in the figure of the beheaded cuy—palatable to whiteness. Therefore, the comment that corn and rice did not mix, coming from a Peruvian Mormon neo-Indianist Lamanite like Jacoba, was meant to strike Jericó at the ontological level of his being. Jericó—in La Familia's version of Peruvianness—*was* rice. His relatedness to others—the relatedness that made his personhood emerge in the first place—depended on shared rice. The "complex admixture" of corn and rice—brown, Indigenous Mexicanness and white, upwardly mobile Peruvianness—seemed so potentially volatile to Jacoba that she could not remain silent. Jericó had her permission to marry Sylvia, but he had to be told in the culinary terms of constructed kinship that doing so would put his relatedness in La Familia at risk. The migratory context intensified this risk because, as Erica Vogel's (2020) Peruvian study participants in Korea also demonstrated regularly, food was an even more important marker of Peruvianness in the global Peruvian diaspora than it was in Peru. Furthermore, since La Familia was the driving force behind much of Spanish-speaking Mormonism in Salsands, Utah, Jericó's citizenship in Zion would ironically be at risk as well despite the fact that he, a born-in-the-covenant retornado, was planning on starting a forever familia with a born-in-the-covenant, Latina Mormon by being sealed to her in Zion's holy temple.

Reminders

In this conclusion, I analyzed the reasons why Peruvian Mormons avoided both excessive whiteness and excessive indigeneity in the construction of their category of sainthood, which was a category generated through the dialectical tension between relatedness and cosmology. In Jacoba's understanding, finding people who were sufficiently Mormon in their conception of "family" without being too White or too Indigenous in their conception of "familia" was only really possible if those people were innately Peruvian Mormons. However, words like "White," "Indigenous," and "innate" evoke biological essentialism, the sort of essentialism that Jacoba's husband, Arcadio, refuted when he shot down my focus group question around the campfire in chapter 3: "What is it like to be a Peruvian Mormon in Utah?"

When he replied that there was no such thing as a Peruvian Mormon or any other "kind of Mormon" he wanted to uncomplicate the admixture that I was creating with all my talk of Peruvian Mormonism and its categorical battle with Anglo Mormonism. For Arcadio, Saints were Saints, plain and simple. He wanted to remind me that all Saints were part of the same universally inclusive siblingship. He wanted to remind me that we were all hermanos spiritually born of the same heavenly parents before this world even existed.

Yet, I wanted to remind him that, according to the official church's depiction of that preexistence, even though the material world did not yet exist in that spacetime, the material categories of race, gender, and kinship somehow did. I wanted to remind him that though the church to which we both belonged understood those categories as existing without beginning or end and as applying to all beings equally, they sure seemed remarkably similar to the culturally specific categories of Anglo settler colonists living on planet Earth in a particular time and place. I wanted to remind him that the categories that central church leaders considered universally inclusive only ended up including certain people. After all, only certain people fell effortlessly into the unmarked category of Mormon. Only a certain culture got categorized as gospel culture. Only a certain, ill-appropriated indigeneity got categorized as the governing prior. Only certain sacrifices got categorized as building legacy. Only certain sacred places got categorized as holy. Only certain temporalities got categorized as punctual. Only certain relationships got categorized as exalted. Only certain dwellings got categorized as home. Only certain families got categorized as forever.

I also wanted to remind Tío Arcadio and Tía Jacoba of all the work that they did not realize they were doing in trying to mesh their Peruvian categories with Mormon ones so as to categorize themselves and La Familia as they saw fit. I wanted to remind them of the immense energy that they had to expend in order to become actors who categorized rather than objects who got categorized. Finally, I wanted to remind them that though La Familia will likely never count as a Mormon pioneer family or as a forever family on Anglo Mormonism's terms, Jacoba and Arcadio had their own categories of pioneering—pioneer indigeneity—and of family—forever familia—that exceeded both this book and the Church of Jesus Christ of Latter-day Saints and overwhelmed our terms entirely.

Glossaries

Mormon Lingo

This glossary is for Mormon lingo (ML) that members of the Church of Jesus Christ of Latter-day Saints (alternately, church members, Mormons, Saints, or LDS) who participated in this study used in either English or Spanish regardless of nationality. The definitions of the management structures and leadership hierarchies in this glossary have been simplified.

Active: Mormons who remain involved with their congregation's activities.

Apostle: A member of the Quorum of the Twelve Apostles (alternately, the Twelve) headquartered in Salt Lake City, Utah. The Twelve has authority over all **General Authority Seventies**.

Area: A group of many **stakes**. Peru is part of the South America Northwest Area.

Area President: Supported by two councilors in the Area presidency and by men known as Area Authority Seventies, an area president has authority over all stake presidents in an area. Area Authority Seventies in South America tend to keep their secular employment. Area-level callings are considered temporary, but often lead to higher callings.

Army of God: The Mormon missionary force.

Auxiliary Organizations: Later additions to the church that function as appendages to the core priesthood hierarchy. Females are often called to leadership positions in auxiliary organizations.

Bishop: A calling with authority over all **ward** members. Bishops tend to keep their secular employment. Bishop is a temporary calling.

Born in the Covenant: Born of temple-sealed parents. Children so born are automatically eternally bound to their parents without the need of an additional temple rite.

Branch: A small, not fully organized congregation of Mormons often led by fulltime missionaries who hail from places where Mormon congregations are larger and more established.

Brother: The title, followed by a surname, used to refer to adult male Saints who do not hold a calling-specific title such as **elder, bishop,** or president.

Calling: A specific organizational post and responsibility that God Himself assigns to each actively participating, adult member of the church regardless of ecclesiastical training. Callings are usually temporary. Generally, they are not to be requested, rejected, or remunerated. Other forms of the verb "to call" denote the same divinity that is behind "callings."

Called to Serve: Assigned by God Himself to preach His gospel in a specific place to a specific group of people, among whom an elect few will be awaiting His message.

Chapel: A religious and recreational meeting house open to all visitors.

Companion: The temporary partner assigned to each fulltime missionary. Fulltime missionaries live and proselytize in pairs called companionships.

Couples Mission: The type of fulltime mission that a married couple, usually elderly and retired, can serve together.

Cultural Hall: A large, stage-equipped indoor multipurpose room inside most **chapels** that can function as a gymnasium, dance hall, conference room, or wedding reception salon.

Deacons: Members of the eleven- to thirteen-year-old male age cohort. Deacons hold the priesthood keys that include the authority to ceremonially distribute the sacrament bread and water to their ward's members during **Sacrament Meeting.**

Dedication: A ceremony whereby a completed **temple** becomes a literal house of God that can abide His physical presence. Once a temple is dedicated, only temple-worthy Mormons may enter.

Doctrines: Aspects of church rulemaking and administration that the church's top leaders consider unchanging and preexisting human decision making.

Elder: The only term in this glossary that is the same in both Spanish and English. Elder is the title given to members of the **First Presidency,** the Twelve, and male missionaries. It is also the title given to members of each ward's age-cohort called Elders Quorum who have undergone the rite of passage open to all males eighteen years old and up that confers upon them a higher level of priesthood with permission to conduct more rituals than that of the younger age cohorts, **deacons, teachers,** and **priests.**

Endowment: Considered one of Mormonism's most sacred ceremonies, it ritualizes the eternal nature of the male-over-female gender hierarchy as well as many other holy binaries. It is only conducted inside temples.

Eternal Progression: A phrase that depicts humans as proto gods who will never stop increasing in knowledge, power, and possessions as they expand their individual realms throughout the universe.

Family Night: Also called Family Home Evening, it is one night designated per week, often Monday, when Mormons devote time to sharing spiritual, recreational, and culinary activities with their families.

First Presidency: The president of the church (the **Prophet**) and his two high counselors make up the First Presidency. Members of the First Presidency are also considered **apostles.**

For Time and All Eternity: A phrase taken from the temple-marriage sealing ceremony implying that the temple-sealed conjugal relationship will continue beyond Earth's temporality.

Gathering of Israel: The prophecy that all members of the church around the world will unite into one physical or metaphorical place on Earth before the Second Coming of Christ.

General Authority Seventy: A calling to a quorum that has authority over all Area-level leadership in the world. The callings at the level of General Authority Seventy and higher up the leadership hierarchy are considered permanent and fulltime. While they are not technically remunerated, they include hefty living stipends and board memberships within the church's many for-profit enterprises. Most **area presidents** are also General Authority Seventies.

General Conference: A weekend series of globally broadcasted and livestreamed talks given from Salt Lake City, Utah, by the church's top leaders every April and October.

Gift of Discernment: An attribute attached to certain leadership positions that gives the occupier of those positions special insight into unseen thoughts and complex quandaries.

Gospel Culture: The tacit understandings, norms, sentiments, and commonsense notions of how to go about daily family life thought to automatically accompany membership in the church.

Holy: Pertaining to that which is orderly, imposed, rote, controlled, whole, and divine.

Inactive: Members who no longer participate in their assigned **ward's** activities.

Keys of the Priesthood: Jesus Christ's symbolic authority given to males to manage His church on Earth in ways that are also binding in heaven. Different keys are given to the different offices of the priesthood.

Lamanites: A nation of people who play a key, often antagonistic, role in many of the events and battles depicted in *The Book of Mormon*. They descend from Laman, the son of Lehi who descends from the biblical Israelite Joseph of Egypt's son Manasseh.

Laying On of Hands: An aspect of many Mormon rituals whereby males holding the priesthood place their hands upon a subject's head to confer power, positions, talents, or health.

Legacy: A term that connotes the importance of connecting ancestors to descendants and of keeping future families faithful to official church teachings.

Less Active: A phrase used to describe church members whom fellow **ward** members perceive as not participating in ward activities often enough.

Mission Call: A letter or email from the **Prophet** himself assigning a Saint to serve a fulltime mission to a specified place.

Mission District: A group of **branches** that has yet to be deemed a **stake of Zion**. Branches are to **wards** as mission districts are to stakes of Zion as children are to adults.

Mission President: Flanked by many administrative assistants and secretaries, some occupying paid positions in the church corporation rather than ecclesiastical callings, a mission president has authority over and responsibility for all fulltime missionaries in his assigned region. Mission presidents retire from or suspend their secular employment for three years in order to physically migrate to their mission areas and dedicate themselves fulltime to their missionaries.

Moroni: The son of Mormon. Moroni was the last prophet to make an addition to his father's compendium of ancient "American" writings compiled on gold plates. In 1830, 1,409 years after Moroni's addition, the Prophet Joseph Smith translated and published a portion of those ancient writings as *The Book of Mormon*. Smith found the plates because Moroni himself, in resurrected form, showed him where they were hidden in upstate New York, USA.

Peru, Arequipa Mission: An official mission region of the church's global missionary program. It overlapped with Peru's departments of Arequipa, Moquegua, and Tacna during my study.

Pioneers: Saints who were willing to make significant sacrifices to build **Zion**.

Policies: Aspects of church rulemaking and administration that the church's top leaders consider adaptable and open to human decision making.

Preexistence: A spacetime before the existence of the material world when Earth's future humans existed in gendered bodies made of spirit matter as siblings to each other.

Priests: Often members of the sixteen- to seventeen-year-old male age cohort. Priests hold a higher level of priesthood with permission to conduct more rituals than that of the younger age cohorts. For example, priests have the power and authority to baptize.

The Prophet: The leader of the Quorum of the Twelve Apostles and the president and sole owner of the church as a legal, US corporation. The Prophet and his two councilors make up the **First Presidency**. Many members of the church consider the fifteen men who constitute the First Presidency and the Twelve to be God's sole mouthpieces on Earth today.

Quorum of the Twelve Apostles. *See* **Apostle**.

Releasing: When a Saint is ritually relieved of a **calling**.

Relief Society: An **auxiliary organization** that females founded but that the church's male-only priesthood hierarchy coopted. The Relief Society is a **ward's** organization for adult females.

Returned Missionary: A Saint who has completed a fulltime mission. As gendered designations are more concise in Spanish, this book sometimes uses the Spanish-speaking Mormon term, retornado, to designate male returned missionaries and retornada to designate female returned missionaries.

Sacrament Meeting: Similar to Catholic mass, but far less scripted. Mormon Sacrament Meeting happens almost every Sunday in each Mormon **chapel's** sacrament hall and includes announcements of recreational activities, recognitions of individuals who have shifted from one leadership position to another, prayers, hymns, the silent distribution of bread and water in representation of Jesus's sacrifice for sin (the eucharist), speeches by members of the **ward family**, and, monthly, an open mic sharing of spiritual experiences and professions of belief.

Sacred: Pertaining to that which is secret, creative, insurgent, volatile, material, and spiritual.

Sealing: A rite whereby two or more Mormons immortalize their familial relationship to one another so that it remains binding after death. Couples can be sealed in matrimony. Such couples are deemed "temple-married" or "temple-sealed." A couple can also be sealed to its children.

Seminary: A course of high school study designed to be concurrent with the four years of US-style high school. Each year's curriculum focuses on one of Mormonism's four canonical books.

Single Adults: SA, an organization for unmarried adults ages thirty-one and up. In Spanish, the acronym is AS (Adultos Solteros).

Sister: The female equivalent to **elder** as a missionary title. Saints also call all adult female Saints "Sister" followed by her surname or husband's surname.

Stake of Zion: Alternately, "stake." It is a group of seven or eight **wards** in a particular geographic area. A US school is to a US school district as a **ward** is to a stake.

Stake President: Flanked by his two councilors and twelve high councilors, a stake president has authority over all **bishops** in a stake. They tend to keep their secular employment. Stake president is a temporary calling.

Sunday School: Usually taking place after **Sacrament Meeting**, it is an aspect of each **ward's** Sunday worship services—which were reduced worldwide from three hours to two hours during this study—wherein ward members of both genders learn from a manual produced in Salt Lake City and usually express their full agreement with that manual's teachings.

Teachers: Members of the fourteen- to fifteen-year-old male age cohort. Teachers hold a higher level of priesthood with permission to conduct more rituals than **deacons**.

Temple: A building that, once dedicated, only temple-worthy church members may enter. Temples are the only places wherein the sealing rites and marriages key to familial togetherness in the afterlife are performed. Worldwide, the church's construction department builds approximately one temple for every 180 congregations.

Temple-Recommend: A card that members must present upon temple entry to validate their temple-worthiness as ascertained through two worthiness interviews, one with their **bishop**, and the other with their **stake president** or his representative.

Temple-Sealed. *See* **sealing**.

Temple Work: Performing sealings and other temple rites on behalf of dead ancestors who are considered individuals with static identities, genders, names, and dates.

Too Sacred: A designation implying that certain people must not witness the phenomenon so described.

Trek: An official youth program that simulates the mid-nineteenth-century Mormon exodus from Illinois to what would later be known as Utah.

The Twelve: *See* **Apostle.**

Ward: A larger, fully-fledged Mormon congregation to which all Mormons in a specific, bounded geographical area belong every day of the week, not simply during Sunday worship services.

Ward Family: How members of wards often refer to their fellowship with each other. Since some ward members recreate, worship, and serve together often, they consider themselves to be an organization similar to a family.

The Word of Wisdom: The Mormon health code, often interpreted as prohibiting the following in any amount: alcohol, tobacco, tea, coffee, and recreational drugs.

The World: Relating to the imperfect, non-Mormon, or evil aspects of mortal existence.

Worthy, Worthiness: A ward member's status within Mormon society as deemed by that ward's **bishop.**

Young Single Adults: YSA, an organization for unmarried adults ages eighteen to thirty. In Spanish, the acronym is JAS (Jóvenes Adultos Solteros).

Zion: Metaphysically, it is a group of people who are pure in heart. Geographically, it is wherever a significant body of Saints organizes into congregations. Prophetically, it will one day be Jackson County, Missouri, USA. Mythologically, it is Utah. Architecturally, it is any city with a Mormon temple at its center.

Peruvian Lingo

This glossary is for Peruvian lingo (PL) that Peruvians who participated in this study used regardless of religion. I have translated some of the terms below into English.

Abya Yala: A placename for what Indigenous rights activists of the Andes consider a single landmass: the Americas North, South, and Central.

Anglo: The label that many Peruvians in my study used for North American White people.

Arequipeño Neto: A quasi-indigenous identity expressing a person's provenance as being completely and innately from Arequipa, a Spanish-founded city.

Ayllu: A group of humans connected both to each other and to the land that creates their connection.

Cholo: A racial epithet referring to Indigenous people who live too indigenously in the epithet user's opinion. Many Peruvians have coopted cholo as a token of Indigenous pride.

Criollos: Peruvians who understand themselves to be descendants of the first Spaniards born in Peru. Criollos inhabit the apex of Peru's class hierarchy.

Decent: The way gente decente (decent people) act. This is often a racial code word that denotes whiteness as opposed to **indigeneity**.

La Gringada: The culture, especially its negative aspects, of the people whom Peruvians in this study called "**Anglos**" when they were trying to be polite and "**gringos**" when they were not.

Gringo: The less polite version of "**Anglo**" that Peruvians use to refer to North American White people.

Hacienda: A form of plantation that enforces hierarchies of difference through multiple forms of indoctrination and forced labor.

Hermanos/Hermanas: A broad kin term in Peru including siblings, half-siblings, stepsiblings, cousins, parents' godchildren, and anyone within one's generational group with whom one was raised in the same household.

Indio: A sixteenth-century term from Spain's official caste system denoting a person indigenous to the Americas.

Invasions: New, squatter communities without public utilities on the outskirts of Peruvian cities.

Mestizo: A sixteenth-century term from Spain's official caste system denoting the offspring of a Spaniard and an Indigenous person.

Negros: A sixteenth-century term from Spain's official caste system denoting people indigenous to Africa and their descendants.

Pachacuti: One of a series of world-changing historical events that do not necessarily proceed in chronological order.

Peruvianness: More than simply being from the nation-state of Peru, Peruvianness connotes a fragile oneness achieved between influences both foreign to Peru and originating in Peru.

Pituco: An epithet used to insult social elites, usually understood as immoral, stingy, and White.

Prima: Most nonsibling, female family members in one's own generational group.

Primo: Most nonsibling, male family members in one's own generational group.

Puneños: People from the Peruvian city of Puno. The "-eño" suffix in Spanish—as in **arequipeño**, cusqueño, and limeño—signifies being from the attributed place, in this case: Arequipa, Cusco, and Lima respectively. Placed identities are not capitalized in Spanish.

Tía: Most nonmother, female family members older than one's own generational group.

Tío: Most nonfather, male family members older than one's own generational group.

Yunza: A type of Andean Catholic patron saint festival involving ritual drunkenness wherein a tree laden with gifts is slowly chopped down throughout the night.

Peruvian Mormon Lingo

This glossary is for Peruvian Mormon lingo (PML) that Peruvians who were also Mormons tended to use in this study.

Familia: All who eat, drink, party, and live together under one roof often enough to construct relatedness with each other.

Leaders: A term (used in Spanish and designated in this book with a capital L) often referring to church leaders who are male, Anglo, and descendants of early Great Plains–crossing **Mormon Pioneers** even though none of those attributes are official requirements for leadership positions in the church.

Anglo Lingo

This glossary is for Anglo lingo (AL) that Anglos who participated in this study used regardless of religion.

Empty Nesters: Married couples whose children have gone off to form their own distal nuclear family homes.

Extended Family: A kin group defined against the nuclear family, the extended family includes relatives related by DNA or legal documents who should ideally live outside the nuclear family home.

Mormon Pioneers: The US Great Plains–crossing heroes of Manifest Destiny as mythologized in many US grade school history texts.

Anglo Mormon Lingo

This glossary is for Anglo Mormon lingo (AML) that Anglos who were also Mormons tended to use in this study.

Family: A heterosexual, monogamous, legally married couple, its individualized dead ancestors, and its legally adopted or biological coresident minor offspring.

Forever Family: An advertising slogan with no real translation in Spanish, a "forever family" is an ideal Mormon nuclear family that, because of its worthiness of the temple-sealing ceremony, will be able to strengthen family ties during life and continue family ties after death.

Singles Wards: Rather than being organized solely around cartographic demarcations as are most **wards**, singles wards are also organized around civil status and age demarcations. Singles wards are congregations comprised almost entirely of unmarried adults. *See also* **Single Adults** and **Young Single Adults**.

Scholarly Lingo

This glossary is for scholarly lingo (SL) that scholars used in the literature that I reviewed for this study. It is also for terms that I used or coined during this study.

Anglo Mormonism: The ways in which Mormonism is practiced among Anglos.

Coloniality: Pertaining to the activity of profiting from while eliminating the relationships between people and the ecosystems of which they form a sustainable part.

Constructivism: A cultural tendency to consider reality as being brought into existence through human and nonhuman interactions and volition.

De-Indianization: Attributed to anthropologist Marisol De la Cadena, it refers to the process that Indigenous people undergo when they acculturate to settler society or to a new form of Indigenous society that settler society accepts as sufficiently hygienic, orderly, and decent.

Essentialism: A cultural tendency to consider reality as an unchanging, universal framework externally imposed upon all humans equally.

Forever Familia: A term deliberately in Spanglish so as to denote its incommensurability with the church's official advertising slogan, "forever family." "Forever familia" recalls two intersecting difficulties. One is the difficulty that Peruvians encounter when trying to make their familias legible as Mormon families. The other is the difficulty they encounter when trying to force a "forever" sort of future onto Peruvian temporal categories that contain no stark divisions between past, present, and future.

Government: Connoting rule, sovereignty, and organization.

Indigeneity: Pertaining to people who have formed a sustainable part of a particular, sited ecosystem since time immemorial.

Matrilocality: A social form wherein a husband moves into a household led by his mother-in-law or another female leader in his wife's family.

Methodological Faith: Attributed to anthropologists Rane Willerslev and Christian Suhr, it is the faith that scholars studying communities of faith must adopt in order to use the tools of study appropriate to the community. It involves experiencing the same otherworldly otherness that study participants experience in order to take their truth claims seriously.

Nephite Immunity: The tendency of elites to think of their elite status as having been earned through their unique capability of knowing when it is morally permissible to bend or break rules, not recognizing that such a capability comes only from the fact that they, as elites, made the rules.

Pacha: Attributed to philosopher Conibo Mallku Bwillcawaman, it connotes a cyclical interrelatedness between humans, their relatives, and the Earth itself.

Peruvian Mormonism: The ways in which Mormonism is practiced among Peruvians.

Pioneer Indigeneity: An important aspect of Mormonism for all Saints regardless of nationality. Pioneer indigeneity is present when Saints benefit from both indigeneity and its antithesis.

Siblingship: When modified as "coresident siblingship," it refers to a family form common in Peru wherein siblings live together as adults. When modified as "universal siblingship," it refers to the Mormon belief in a pre-Earth life when all soon-to-be humans lived together as siblings.

Tele-territoriality: The cultural ability to condense or undermine geography so that two or more lands can share one cultural category.

Trans-temporality: The cultural preference to adapt the category of time itself in order to incorporate new information into societal knowledge.

Whiteness: Pertaining to the elite group of people who benefit from the perpetuation of class-based hierarchies of oppression that they disguise as biological and, therefore, natural or God-given.

Notes

Introduction. Categories

1. All interview transcripts in this book were originally in Spanish unless otherwise noted. All translations are mine.

2. All study participant names are pseudonyms other than Elvira, my spouse. For all study participants, especially those whose positions or relationships might make them recognizable despite their pseudonyms, I have fictionalized aspects of lives, merged situations, and otherwise obscured identities to protect anonymity. Part of these layers of anonymity include pseudonymous placenames (Salsands), congregation names (Pioneer Trail and Barrio Periféricos), company names, and other identifiers. The effect is that nobody, not even my study participants themselves, will be able to accurately match a character in this book to a person in real life.

3. Incidentally, as I was finishing up my fifteenth draft of this introduction on October 1, 2022, Tracy Browning became the first Black woman to speak at General Conference (González 2022).

4. Naming wards is a common LDS practice.

Chapter 3. Legacy

1. Alcohol in any quantity was forbidden in the official church's health code.

2. Between their completion and their dedication, temples have open houses, which are the only windows of time wherein non-Mormons and unworthy Mormons may enter.

Bibliography

Abrego, Leisy. 2014. *Sacrificing Families: Navigating Laws, Labor, and Love across Borders*. Stanford, CA: Stanford University Press.

Adams, James Truslow. 1932. *The Epic of America*. Boston: Little, Brown, and Company.

Agamben, Giorgio. 1998. *Homo Sacer: Sovereign Power and Bare Life*. Stanford, CA: Stanford University Press.

Aikau, Hokulani K. 2012. *A Chosen People, A Promised Land: Mormonism and Race in Hawai'i*. Minneapolis: University of Minnesota Press.

Alcalde, M. Cristina. 2018. *Peruvian Lives across Borders: Power, Exclusion, and Home*. Urbana: University of Illinois Press.

Alexie, Sherman. 1996. "How to Write the Great American Indian Novel." In *The Summer of Black Widows*, 95. New York: Hanging Loose Press.

Allen, Catherine. 2014. "Ushnus and Interiority." In *Inca Sacred Space: Landscape, Site, and Symbol in the Andes*, edited by Frank Meddens, Katie Willis, Colin McEwan, and Nicholas Branch, 71–77. Oxford: Archetype Books.

Allen, Julie K. 2020. "Mormonism, Gender, and Art in Nineteenth-Century Scandinavia." In *The Routledge Handbook of Mormonism and Gender*, edited by Amy Hoyt and Taylor G. Petrey, 114–28. New York: Routledge.

Allen, Julie K., and Kim B. Östman. 2020. "Mormons in the Nordic Region." In *The Palgrave Handbook of Global Mormonism*, edited by R. Gordon Shepherd, A. Gary Shepherd, and Ryan T. Cragun, 533–58. New York: Palgrave Macmillan.

Altamirano, Teófilo. 1999. "Los Peruanos en el Exterior y Su Revinculación con el Perú." In *Comunidades Peruanas en el Exterior: Situación y Perspectivas*, edited by Academia Diplomática del Perú, 26–45. https://www4.congreso.gob.pe/historico/cip/materiales/imigra/Peruanos_exterior_revinculacion.pdf.

Anderson, Kim. 2010. "Affirmations of an Indigenous Feminist." In *Indigenous Women and Feminism: Politics, Activism, Culture*, edited by Cheryl Suzack, Shari M. Huhndorf, Jeanne Perrault, and Jean Barman, 81–91. Chicago: University of Chicago Press.

Anzaldúa, Gloria. (1987) 2012. *Borderlands/La Frontera: The New Mestiza*. San Francisco: Aunt Lute Books.

Appadurai, Arjun. 1991. "Global Ethnoscapes: Notes and Queries for a Transnational Anthropology." In *Recapturing Anthropology: Working in the Present*, edited by Richard G. Fox, 191–210. Santa Fe: School of America Research Press.

Ara, Luis, dir. 2017. *Perú: Tesoro Escondido*. Documentary. Netflix.

Arguedas, José María. (1941) 2011. *Yawar Fiesta*. Lima: Editorial Horizonte.

Arguedas, José María. (1964) 1973. *Todas las Sangres*. 2 vols. Lima: Ediciones Peisa.

Arguedas, José María. (1966) 1975. *Dioses y Hombres de Huarochirí*. México City: Siglo Veintiuno Editores S.A.

Babb, Florence E. 2018. *Women's Place in the Andes: Engaging Decolonial Feminist Anthropology*. Oakland: University of California Press.

Baca, Angelo, dir. 2008. *In Laman's Terms: Looking at Lamanite Identity*. Documentary. Native Voices Documentary Program, University of Washington.

Baca, Angelo. 2018. "Porter Rockwell and Samuel the Lamanite Fistfight in Heaven: A Mormon Navajo Filmmaker's Perspective." In *Decolonizing Mormonism: Approaching a Postcolonial Zion*, edited by Gina Colvin and Joanna Brooks, 67–76. Salt Lake City: University of Utah Press.

Bacigalupo, Mariella. 2016. *Thunder Shaman: Making History with Mapuche Spirits in Chile and Patagonia*. Austin: University of Texas Press.

Bamford, Sandra. 2007. *Biology Unmoored: Melanesian Reflections on Life and Biotechnology*. Berkeley: University of California Press.

Barth, Fredrik. (1969) 1998. "Introduction." In *Ethnic Groups and Boundaries: The Social Organization of Culture Difference*, edited by Fredrik Barth, 9–38. Long Grove, IL: Waveland Press.

Bartholomew, Ronald E. 2020. "The Gathering of Scattered Israel: The Missionary Enterprise of the Church of Jesus Christ of Latter-Day Saints." In *The Palgrave Handbook of Global Mormonism*, edited by R. Gordon Shepherd, A. Gary Shepherd, and Ryan T. Cragun, 57–90. New York: Palgrave Macmillan.

Basquiat, Jennifer Huss. 2004. "Embodied Mormonism: Performance, Vodou, and the LDS Faith in Haiti." *Dialogue: A Journal of Mormon Thought* 37 (4): 1–34.

Benally, Moroni. 2017. "Decolonizing the Blossoming: Indigenous People's Faith in a Colonizing Church." *Dialogue: A Journal of Mormon Thought* 50 (4): 71–78.

Bennion, Janet. 2004. *Desert Patriarchy: Mormon and Mennonite Communities in the Chihuahua Valley*. Tucson: University of Arizona Press.

Bennion, Michael Kay. 2012. "Captivity, Adoption, Marriage, and Identity: Native American Children in Mormon Homes, 1847–1900." Master's thesis, University of Nevada, Las Vegas.

Berg, Ulla D. 2015. *Mobile Selves: Race, Migration, and Belonging in Peru and the U.S.* New York: NYU Press.

Berkes, Howard. 2013. "A Woman's Prayer Makes Mormon History." *The Two-Way*, April 8. National Public Radio. https://www.npr.org/sections/thetwo-way/2013/04/08/176604202/a-womans-prayer-makes-mormon-history.

Bernard, H. Russell. 2011. *Research Methods in Anthropology: Qualitative and Quantitative Approaches*. Lanham, MD: AltaMira Press.

Bessire, Lucas. 2014. *Behold the Black Caiman: A Chronicle of Ayoreo Life.* Chicago: University of Chicago Press.

Bhabha, Homi K. 1984. "Of Mimicry and Man: The Ambivalence of Colonial Discourse." *October* 28: 125–33.

Bialecki, Jon, Naomi Haynes, and Joel Robbins. 2008. "The Anthropology of Christianity." *Religion Compass* 2 (6): 1139–58.

Bighorse, Eva. 2021. "Columbus Day and the 'Rest of the Story.'" *Dialogue: A Journal of Mormon Thought* 54 (2): 114–16.

Bitsoi, Alstair. 2017. "Greenthread: Bears Ears to Brooklyn." In *Edge of Morning: Native Voices Speak for the Bears Ears*, edited by Jacqueline Keeler, 44–49. Salt Lake City: Torrey House Press.

Black, Kristeen Lee. 2016. *A Sociology of Mormon Kinship: The Place of Family within the Church of Jesus Christ of Latter-Day Saints.* Lewiston, NY: Edwin Mellen Press.

Bluehouse, Philmer, and James W. Zion. 1993. "Hozhooji Naat'aanii: The Navajo Justice and Harmony Ceremony." *Mediation Quarterly* 10 (4): 327–37.

Boateng, Boatema. 2019. "Black Indigeneities and Regimes of Sovereignty." Paper presented at Troubling the Grounds: Global Configurations of Blackness, Nativism, and Indigeneity, University of California, Irvine, May 24.

Boesten, Jelke. 2010. *Intersecting Inequalities: Women and Social Policy in Peru, 1990–2000.* University Park: Penn State University Press.

Bonilla-Silva, Eduardo, and Tukufu Zuberi. 2008. "Towards a Definition of White Logic and White Methods." In *White Logic, White Methods: Racism and Methodology*, edited by Eduardo Bonilla-Silva and Tufuku Zuberi, 3–27. Lanham, MD: Rowman & Littlefield.

Bordo, Susan. 2004. *Unbearable Weight: Feminism, Western Culture, and the Body.* Berkeley: University of California Press.

Bourdieu, Pierre. 1990. *The Logic of Practice.* Translated by Richard Nice. Stanford, CA: Stanford University Press.

Bourdieu, Pierre. 1994. "Social Capital: Preliminary Notes." In *P. Bourdieu: Sociological Texts*, edited by Nikos Panagiotopoulos, 91–95. Athens: Delfini.

Bowman, Matthew. 2020. "Mormon Gender in the Progressive Era." In *The Routledge Handbook of Mormonism and Gender*, edited by Amy Hoyt and Taylor G. Petrey, 129–42. New York: Routledge.

Boxer, Elise. 2009. "'To Become White and Delightsome': American Indians and Mormon Identity." PhD diss., Arizona State University.

Boxer, Elise. 2015. "'The Lamanites Shall Blossom as the Rose': The Indian Student Placement Program, Mormon Whiteness, and Indigenous Identity." *Journal of Mormon History* 41 (4): 132–76.

Boxer, Elise. 2019. "The Book of Mormon as Mormon Settler Colonialism." In *Essays on American Indian and Mormon History*, edited by P. Jane Hafen and Brenden W. Rensink, 3–22. Salt Lake City: University of Utah Press.

Breen, Deborah. 2019. "Mapping Inequality: Redlining in New Deal America; Renewing Inequality: Family Displacements through Urban Renewal." *Journal of American History* 106 (2): 548–50.

Brekhus, Wayne. 1998. "A Sociology of the Unmarked: Redirecting Our Focus." *Sociological Theory* 16 (1): 34–51.

Brooks, Joanna. 2018. "Mormonism as Colonialism, Mormonism as Anti-Colonialism, Mormonism as Minor Transnationalism: Historical and Contemporary Perspectives." In *Decolonizing Mormonism: Approaching a Postcolonial Zion*, edited by Gina Colvin and Joanna Brooks, 163–85. Salt Lake City: University of Utah Press.

Bueno-Hansen, Pascha. 2015. *Feminist and Human Rights Struggles in Peru: Decolonizing Transitional Justice*. Urbana: University of Illinois Press.

Bunker, Gary L., and Davis Bitton. 1983. *The Mormon Graphic Image, 1834–1914: Cartoons, Caricatures, and Illustrations*. Salt Lake City: University of Utah Press.

Burns, Kathryn. 2011. "Unfixing Race." In *Histories of Race and Racism: The Andes and Mesoamerica from Colonial Times to the Present*, edited by Laura Gotkowitz, 58–70. Durham, NC: Duke University Press.

Busby, Cecilia. 2006. "Renewable Icons: Concepts of Religious Power in a Fishing Village in South India." In *The Anthropology of Christianity*, edited by Fenella Cannell, 77–98. Durham, NC: Duke University Press.

Bushman, Richard Lyman. 2007. *Joseph Smith: Rough Stone Rolling*. New York: Vintage.

Call, Daniel Glenn. 2021. "Rubik's Palimpsest: Searching for My Indigeneity." *Dialogue: A Journal of Mormon Thought* 54 (2): 65–80.

Campbell, Mary. 2020. "Mormonism, Gender, and Art." In *The Routledge Handbook of Mormonism and Gender*, edited by Amy Hoyt and Taylor G. Petrey, 239–57. New York: Routledge.

Canessa, Andrew. 2012. *Intimate Indigeneities: Race, Sex, and History in the Small Spaces of Andean Life*. Durham, NC: Duke University Press.

Cannell, Fenella. 2006. "Introduction: The Anthropology of Christianity." In *The Anthropology of Christianity*, edited by Fenella Cannell, 1–50. Durham, NC: Duke University Press.

Cannell, Fenella. 2013. "The Blood of Abraham: Mormon Redemptive Physicality and American Idioms of Kinship." *Journal of the Royal Anthropological Institute* 19 (May): 77–94.

Cannon, Brian Q. 2018. "'To Buy Up the Lamanite Children as Fast as They Could': Indentured Servitude and Its Legacy in Mormon Society." *Journal of Mormon History* 44 (2): 1–35.

Carsten, Janet. 2000. "Introduction: Cultures of Relatedness." In *Cultures of Relatedness: New Approaches to the Study of Kinship*, edited by Janet Carsten, 1–20. New York: Cambridge University Press.

Caspary Moreno, Hans Ralf. 2021. *Las Ruinas de Tiwanaku y el Libro de Mormón*. La Paz, Bolivia: Ediciones Daimon.

Castañeda, Heide. 2019. *Borders of Belonging: Struggle and Solidarity in Mixed-Status Immigrant Families*. Stanford, CA: Stanford University Press.

Chamberlain, Beverly, and Jonathan Chamberlain. 2009. *Happy Is the Man: A Social Biography of Thomas Chamberlain, 1854–1918*. Provo, UT: Brigham Young Printing Services.

Chamberlain, Jake, dir. 2019. *For the Love of God*. MFA thesis, Stanford University. Documentary. Vimeo. https://vimeo.com/350848067/5544e5f84e.

Chavez, Leo. 2013. *The Latino Threat: Constructing Immigrants, Citizens, and the Nation*. Stanford, CA: Stanford University Press.

Chen, Chiung Hwang. 2008. "In Taiwan but Not of Taiwan: Challenges of the LDS Church in the Wake of the Indigenous Movement." *Dialogue: A Journal of Mormon Thought* 41 (2): 3–31.

Chen, Chiung Hwang, and Ethan Yorgason. 2020. "Intersectionality." In *The Routledge Handbook of Mormonism and Gender*, edited by Amy Hoyt and Taylor G. Petrey, 38–49. New York: Routledge.

Christensen, Dale. 1995. *History of the Church in Peru*. N.p.: CreateSpace Independent Publishing Platform.

Church News. 1997. "All Cultures Are Children of One God." August 2. https://www.thechurchnews.com/archive/1997-08-02/all-cultures-are-children-of-one-god-12076.

Church of Jesus Christ of Latter-Day Saints. 1999. "Remain in Homelands, Members Counseled." *LDS Church News*, December. http://www.ldschurchnews archive.com/articles/36891/Remain-in-homelands-members-counseled.html.

Church of Jesus Christ of Latter-Day Saints. 2011. *For the Strength of Youth*. Salt Lake City: Church of Jesus Christ of Latter-Day Saints.

Church of Jesus Christ of Latter-Day Saints. 2017. *Starting and Growing My Own Business: For Self-Reliance*. Salt Lake City: Church of Jesus Christ of Latter-Day Saints.

Church of Jesus Christ of Latter-Day Saints. 2018. *Saints: The Story of the Church of Jesus Christ in the Latter Days*. Vol. 1: *Saints: The Standard of Truth, 1815–1846*. Salt Lake City: Church of Jesus Christ of Latter-Day Saints.

Church of Jesus Christ of Latter-Day Saints. N.d. [2018]. "Lamanite Identity." *Church History Topics* (blog). https://www.lds.org/study/history/topics/lamanite-identity?lang=eng.

Clayton, William. 1985. "Come, Come, Ye Saints." In *Hymns of The Church of Jesus Christ of Latter-Day Saints*, 30. Salt Lake City: Church of Jesus Christ of Latter-Day Saints.

Colavito, Jason. 2020. *The Mound Builder Myth: Fake History and the Hunt for a "Lost White Race."* Norman: University of Oklahoma Press.

Colloredo-Mansfeld, Rudi. 2009. *Fighting Like a Community: Andean Civil Society in an Era of Indian Uprisings*. Chicago: University of Chicago Press.

Colvin, Gina. 2017. "There's No Such Thing as a Gospel Culture." *Dialogue: A Journal of Mormon Thought* 50 (4): 57–70.

Comaroff, John L., and Jean Comaroff. 2009. *Ethnicity, Inc*. Chicago: University of Chicago Press.

Cook-Lynn, Elizabeth. 2001. *Anti-Indianism in Modern America: A Voice from Tatekeya's Earth*. Chicago: University of Illinois Press.

Coontz, Stephanie. 2016. *The Way We Never Were: American Families and the Nostalgia Trap*. New York: Basic Books.

Cooper, Rex Eugene, and Moroni Spencer Hernández de Olarte. 2020. "The Church of Jesus Christ of Latter-Day Saints in Mexico." In *The Palgrave Handbook of Global Mormonism*, edited by R. Gordon Shepherd, A. Gary Shepherd, and Ryan T. Cragun, 369–96. New York: Palgrave Macmillan.

Coulthard, Glen Sean. 2014. *Red Skin, White Masks: Rejecting the Colonial Politics of Recognition.* Minneapolis: University of Minnesota Press.

Council on Biblical Manhood and Womanhood. 1988. "The Danvers Statement on Biblical Manhood and Womanhood." November. https://www.grbc.net/wp-content/uploads/2015/09/The-Danvers-Statement-on-Biblical-Manhood-and-Womanhood.pdf.

Coutin, Susan Bibler. 2003. *Legalizing Moves: Salvadoran Immigrants' Struggle for U.S. Residency.* Ann Arbor: University of Michigan Press.

Crawford, Rebekah Perkins. 2020. "Gender and Mental Health in Mormon Contexts." In *The Routledge Handbook of Mormonism and Gender,* edited by Amy Hoyt and Taylor G. Petrey, 378–91. New York: Routledge.

Crenshaw, Kimberlé. 1991. "Mapping the Margins: Intersectionality, Identity Politics, and Violence against Women of Color." *Stanford Law Review* 43 (6): 1241–99.

Crowfoot, Monika Brown. 2021. "The Lamanite Dilemma: Mormonism and Indigeneity." *Dialogue: A Journal of Mormon Thought* 54 (2): 57–64.

Decoo, Wilfried. 2013. "In Search of Mormon Identity: Mormon Culture, Gospel Culture, and an American Worldwide Church." *International Journal of Mormon Studies* 6: 1–53.

Decoo, Wilfried. 2015. "Mormons in Europe." In *The Oxford Handbook of Mormonism,* edited by Terryl Givens and Philip Barlow, 543–58. New York: Oxford University Press.

De la Cadena, Marisol. 1995. "'Woman Are More Indian': Ethnicity and Gender in a Community Near Cuzco." In *Ethnicity, Markets, and Migration in the Andes: At the Crossroads of History and Anthropology,* edited by Brooke Larson and Olivia Harris, 329–43. Durham, NC: Duke University Press.

De la Cadena, Marisol. 2000. *Indigenous Mestizos: The Politics of Race and Culture in Cuzco, Peru, 1919–1991.* Durham, NC: Duke University Press.

De la Cadena, Marisol. 2005. "Are Mestizos Hybrids? The Conceptual Politics of Andean Identities." *Journal of Latin American Studies* 37 (2): 259–84.

De la Cadena, Marisol. 2008. "Alternative Indigeneities: Conceptual Proposals." *Latin American and Caribbean Ethnic Studies* 3 (3): 341–49.

Delaney, Carol. 2004. *Investigating Culture: An Experimental Introduction to Anthropology.* Malden, MA: Blackwell Publishers.

De la Puente, Robert, dir. 2012. *Choleando.* Documentary. Taller Antropología Visual.

Delgado, Richard, and Jean Stefancic. 2017. *Critical Race Theory.* New York: NYU Press.

Deloria, Ella Cara. 1988. *Waterlily.* Lincoln, NE: Bison Books.

Deloria, Philip J. 1999. *Playing Indian.* New Haven: Yale University Press.

Deloria, Vine Jr. 1969. *Custer Died for Your Sins: An Indian Manifesto.* Norman: University of Oklahoma Press.

De Mello e Souza, Laura, and Christine Robinson. 1997. "Demonology, the Devil, and the Image of America." *Portuguese Studies* 13: 159–79.

Deranger, Eriel. 2018. "Tar Sands Operations and Waterborne Exposure and

Subsistence Food Supply in Canada." Paper Presented at the International Society for Environmental Epidemiology Annual Meeting, Ottawa, August 26–30.

Desai, Kiran. 2006. *The Inheritance of Loss*. New York: Grove Press.

De Soto, Hernando. 1986. *El Otro Sendero: La Revolución Informal*. Lima: Editorial el Barranco.

Douglas, Mary. 1966. *Purity and Danger: An Analysis of the Concepts of Pollution and Taboo*. London: Routledge & Kegan Paul.

Dow, James W., and Alan R. Sandstrom, eds. 2001. *Holy Saints and Fiery Preachers: The Anthropology of Protestantism in Mexico and Central America*. Westport, CT: Praeger.

Dubisch, Jill. 2005. "Healing 'the Wounds That Are Not Visible': A Vietnam Veterans' Motorcycle Pilgrimage." In *Pilgrimage and Healing*, edited by Jill Dubisch and Michael Winkelman, 135–54. Tucson: University of Arizona Press.

Duffy, John-Charles. 2008. "The Use of 'Lamanite' in Official LDS Discourse." *Journal of Mormon History* 34 (1): 118–67.

Dunbar-Ortiz, Roxanne. 2021. *Not "A Nation of Immigrants": Settler Colonialism, White Supremacy, and a History of Erasure and Exclusion*. Boston: Beacon Press.

Durán, Diego. 1967. *Historia de las Indias de Nueva España e Islas de la Tierra Firme*. México City: Porrua.

Durand, Jorge. 2010. "The Peruvian Diaspora: Portrait of a Migratory Process." *Latin American Perspectives* 37 (5): 12–28.

Eastman, Charles Alexander. 2003. *The Soul of the Indian*. New York: Dover Publications.

Easton-Flake, Amy. 2020. "Mormon Women and Scripture in the Nineteenth Century." In *The Routledge Handbook of Mormonism and Gender*, edited by Amy Hoyt and Taylor G. Petrey, 100–113. New York: Routledge.

Embry, Jessie L. 1997. *In His Own Language: Mormon Spanish-Speaking Congregations in the United States*. Provo, UT: Signature Books.

Escárcega, Patricia. 2020. "Newsletter: Here's Why We Stopped Italicizing 'Foreign' Foods." *Los Angeles Times*, January 4, Food sec. https://www.latimes.com/food/story/2020-01-04/foreign-foods-tasting-notes-newsletter-patricia-escarcega.

Estes, Nick. 2020. "Fighting Trump's Border Wall w/ Nellie Jo David." *The Red Nation Podcast*. https://directory.libsyn.com/episode/index/show/therednation/id/12705440.

Eyring, Henry. 2011. "Poderoso Mensaje a los Misioneros." *YouTube*. https://www.youtube.com/watch?v=3c8fQM9vsiU.

Falcón, Sylvanna M. 2016. *Power Interrupted: Antiracist and Feminist Activism inside the United Nations*. Seattle: University of Washington Press.

Fanon, Frantz. (1952) 1994. *Black Skin, White Masks*. New York: Grove Press.

Farmer, Jared. 2008. *On Zion's Mount: Mormons, Indians, and the American Landscape*. Cambridge, MA: Harvard University Press.

Fenton, Elizabeth, and Jared Hickman, eds. 2019. *Americanist Approaches to "The Book of Mormon."* New York: Oxford University Press.

Ferguson, James, and Akhil Gupta. 2002. "Spatializing States: Toward an Ethnography of Neoliberal Governmentality." *American Ethnologist* 29 (4): 981–1002.

First Presidency and Council of the Twelve Apostles of the Church of Jesus Christ of Latter-day. 1995. "The Family: A Proclamation to the World." https://www .lds.org/topics/family-proclamation?lang=eng.

Fletcher Stack, Peggy. 2007. "Single Word Change in Book of Mormon Speaks Volumes." *Salt Lake Tribune*, November 8. http://archive.sltrib.com/article.php? id=7403990&itype=NGPSID.

Foucault, Michel. (1977) 1995. *Discipline and Punish: The Birth of the Prison*. Translated by Alan Sheridan. New York: Vintage Books.

Francke, Marfil. 1990. "Genero, Clase, Etnia: La Trenza de la Dominación." In *Tiempos de Ira y Amor*, edited by Carlos Iván Degregori and Marfil Francke, 79–106. Lima: DESCO.

Gallango, Richard. 2019. *Diario de Caminos*. N.p. [Peru]: Madreselva.

Gandolfo, Daniella. 2009. *The City at Its Limits: Taboo, Transgression, and Urban Renewal in Lima*. Chicago: University of Chicago Press.

García, Ignacio M. 2015. *Chicano While Mormon: Activism, War, and Keeping the Faith*. Madison, NJ: Fairleigh Dickinson University Press.

García, Ignacio M. 2017. "Thoughts on Latino Mormons, Their Afterlife, and the Need for a New Historical Paradigm for Saints of Color." *Dialogue: A Journal of Mormon Thought* 50 (4): 1–29.

García, Ignacio M. 2020. "Lamanitas, the Spanish-Speaking Hermanos: Latinos Loving Their Mormonism Even as They Remain the Other." In *The Palgrave Handbook of Global Mormonism*, edited by R. Gordon Shepherd, A. Gary Shepherd, and Ryan T. Cragun, 727–50. New York: Palgrave Macmillan.

García, María Elena. 2021. *Gastropolitics and the Specter of Race: Stories of Capital, Culture, and Coloniality in Peru*. Oakland: University of California Press.

García Márquez, Gabriel. (1988) 2007. *Love in the Time of Cholera*. Translated by Edith Grossman. New York: Vintage Books.

Garcilaso de la Vega, Inca. (1609) 2009. *Comentarios Reales de los Incas*. Arequipa, Perú: Biblioteca Juvenil.

Gardner, Ruth M. 1985. "Families Can Be Together Forever." In *Hymns of the Church of Jesus Christ of Latter-Day Saints*, 300. Salt Lake City: Church of Jesus Christ of Latter-Day Saints.

Gardner, Susan. 2009. "Introduction." In *Waterlily* by Ella Cara Deloria, v–xxxvi. Lincoln: University of Nebraska Press.

Gilio-Whitaker, Dina. 2019. *As Long as Grass Grows: The Indigenous Fight for Environmental Justice, from Colonization to Standing Rock*. Boston: Beacon Press.

Glick Schiller, Nina, Linda Basch, and Cristina Blanc-Szanton. 1992. "Transnationalism: A New Analytic Framework for Understanding Migration." *Annals of the New York Academy of Sciences* 645 (1): 1–24.

Golding, David. 2020. "Gender and Missionary Work." In *The Routledge Handbook of Mormonism and Gender*, edited by Amy Hoyt and Taylor G. Petrey, 169–86. New York: Routledge.

Gómez Páez, Fernando Rogelio. 2004. *The Church of Jesus Christ of Latter-Day Saints and the Lamanite Conventions: From Darkness to Light*. México City: El Museo de Historia del Mormonismo en México, A.C.

Gonzales, Roberto G., and Leo R. Chavez. 2012. "Awakening to a Nightmare: Abjectivity and Illegality in the Lives of Undocumented 1.5-Generation Latino Immigrants in the United States." *Current Anthropology* 53 (3): 255–68.

González, Sydnee. 2022. "First Black Woman Speaks during Latter-Day Saint General Conference." *KSL.Com*, October 1, News/General Conference. https://www.ksl.com/article/50487085/first-black-woman-speaks-during-latter -day-saint-general-conference.

Gooren, Henri. 1999. *Rich among the Poor: Church, Firm, and Household among Small-Scale Entrepreneurs in Guatemala City*. Amsterdam: Thela.

Gooren, Henri. 2003. "The Religious Market in Nicaragua: The Paradoxes of Catholicism and Protestantism." *Exchange* 32 (4): 340–60.

Gooren, Henri. 2008. "The Mormons of The World: The Meaning of LDS Membership in Central America." In *Revisiting Thomas F. O'Dea's "The Mormons": Contemporary Perspectives*, edited by Cardell K. Jacobson, John P. Hoffmann, and Tim B. Heaton, 363–89. Salt Lake City: University of Utah Press.

Gordon, Sarah Barringer. 2002. *The Mormon Question: Polygamy and Constitutional Conflict in Nineteenth-Century America*. Chapel Hill: University of North Carolina Press.

Green, Rayna. 1988. "The Tribe Called Wannabee: Playing Indian in America and Europe." *Folklore* 99 (1): 30–55.

Hafen, LeRoy R., and Ann W. Hafen. (1960) 1992. *Handcarts to Zion: The Story of a Unique Western Migration, 1856–1860*. Lincoln: University of Nebraska Press.

Hales, Robert D. 1996. "The Eternal Family." *Ensign*, November. https://www .churchofjesuschrist.org/study/ensign/1996/11/the-eternal-family?lang=eng.

Hallett, Miranda Cady. 2012. "'Better Than White Trash': Work Ethic, Latinidad, and Whiteness in Rural Arkansas." *Latino Studies* 10 (1/2): 81–106.

Harris, Cheryl I. 1993. "Whiteness as Property." *Harvard Law Review* 106 (8): 1707.

Harris, Lacee A. 2021. "The Lamanite Dilemma: Mormonism and Indigeneity." *Dialogue: A Journal of Mormon Thought* 54 (2): 87–100.

Harris, Olivia. 2006. "The Eternal Return of Conversion: Christianity as Contested Domain in Highland Bolivia." In *The Anthropology of Christianity*, edited by Fenella Cannell, 51–76. Durham, NC: Duke University Press.

Hartman, Saidiya. 1997. *Scenes of Subjection: Terror, Slavery, and Self-Making in Nineteenth-Century America*. New York: Oxford University Press.

Haymes, Stephen Nathan. 1995. *Race, Culture, and the City: A Pedagogy for Black, Urban Struggle*. Albany: State University of New York Press.

Hein, Annette. 2014. "Journey to Martin's Cove: The Mormon Handcart Tragedy of 1856." *WyoHistory.Org: A Project of the Wyoming State Historical Society* (blog). November 8. https://www.wyohistory.org/encyclopedia/journey -martins-cove-mormon-handcart-tragedy-1856.

Hendrix-Komoto, Amanda, and Joseph R. Stuart. 2020. "Race and Gender in Mormonism: 1830–1978." In *The Routledge Handbook of Mormonism and Gender*, edited by Amy Hoyt and Taylor G. Petrey, 26–37. New York: Routledge.

Hernández, Daniel. 2021. "A Divine Rebellion: Indigenous Sacraments among Global 'Lamanites.'" *Religions* 12 (280): 1–14.

Hernández de Olarte, Moroni Spencer. 2018. "Si Pudimos con una Revolución, Podemos con una Iglesia: Zapatismo, Mormonismo y la Tercera Convención." PhD diss., Universidad Nacional Autónoma de México.

Hill, Jane H. 1998. "Language, Race, and White Public Space." *American Anthropologist* 100 (3): 680–89.

Hinckley, Gordon B. 1986. "Dedicatory Prayer: Lima Peru Temple, January 10, 1986." *Church of Jesus Christ of Latter-Day Saints: Temples* (blog). https://www.lds.org/temples/details/lima-peru-temple/prayer/1986-01-10.

Hinderaker, Amorette. 2015. "Severing Primary Ties: Exit from Totalistic Organizations." *Western Journal of Communication* 79 (1): 92–115.

Holmes, Seth. 2013. *Fresh Fruit, Broken Bodies: Migrant Farmworkers in the United States*. Berkeley: University of California Press.

Horne, Gerald. 2020. *The Dawning of the Apocalypse: The Roots of Slavery, White Supremacy, Settler Colonialism, and Capitalism in the Long Sixteenth Century*. New York: Monthly Review Press.

Hoyt, Amy. 2020. "Femininities." In *The Routledge Handbook of Mormonism and Gender*, edited by Amy Hoyt and Taylor G. Petrey, 50–59. New York: Routledge.

Hurwitz, Laura Sarah. 2017. "Settler Colonialism and White Settler Responsibility in the Karuk, Konomihu, Shasta, and New River Shasta Homelands: A White Unsettling Manifesto." Master's thesis, Humboldt State University.

Iber, Jorge. 2000. *Hispanics in the Mormon Zion, 1912–1999*. College Station: Texas A&M University Press.

Inouye, Melissa Wei-Tsing. 2015. "Building Zion: Folding Chairs." In *A Book of Mormons: Latter-Day Saints on a Modern-Day Zion*, edited by Emily W. Jensen and Tracy McKay-Lamb, 5–11. Ashland, OR: White Cloud Press.

Isasi-Diaz, Ada Maria. 1996. *Mujerista Theology: A Theology for the Twenty-First Century*. Maryknoll, NY: Orbis Books.

Jackson, John L. 2013. *Thin Description: Ethnography and the African Hebrew Israelites of Jerusalem*. Cambridge, MA: Harvard University Press.

Jennings, Chris. 2016. *Paradise Now: The Story of American Utopianism*. New York: Random House.

Johnson, Elizabeth A. 1996. *She Who Is: The Mystery of God in Feminist Theological Discourse*. New York: Crossroad Publishing.

Johnson, William. 1831. Cherokee Nation v. Georgia 30 U.S. (5 Pet.) 1 at 27 (Johnson, W., concurring), 5 Richard Peters. U.S. Supreme Court.

Keane, Webb. 2007. *Christian Moderns: Freedom and Fetish in the Mission Encounter*. Berkeley: University of California Press.

Kelly, Raymond C. 1993. *Constructing Inequality: The Fabrication of a Hierarchy of Virtue among the Etoro*. Ann Arbor: University of Michigan Press.

Kerns, Virginia. 2021. *Sally in Three Worlds: An Indian Captive in the House of Brigham Young*. Salt Lake City: University of Utah Press.

Kimball, Spencer W. 1960. "The Day of the Lamanites." In *One Hundred Thirtieth Conference of the Church of Jesus Christ of Latter-Day Saints*, 32–37. Salt Lake

City: Church of Jesus Christ of Latter-day Saints. https://archive.org/details/conferencereport1960sa/page/n33/mode/2up.

Kimball, Spencer W. 1975. "'Why Call Me Lord, Lord, and Do Not the Things Which I Say?'" *Ensign*, May. https://www.lds.org/ensign/1975/05/why-call-me-lord-lord-and-do-not-the-things-which-i-say?lang=eng.

King, Farina. 2019. "Indigenizing Mormonisms." *Mormon Studies Review* 6 (January): 1–16.

Kline, Caroline. 2020. "Global Mormon Perspectives and Experiences of Familial Structures." In *The Routledge Handbook of Mormonism and Gender*, edited by Amy Hoyt and Taylor G. Petrey, 321–35. New York: Routledge.

Knoll, Benjamin R., and Jana Riess. 2020. "Changing Religious and Social Attitudes of Mormon Millennials in Contemporary American Society." In *The Palgrave Handbook of Global Mormonism*, edited by R. Gordon Shepherd, A. Gary Shepherd, and Ryan T. Cragun, 293–320. New York: Palgrave Macmillan.

Knowlton, David. 1996. "Mormonism in Latin America: Towards the Twenty-First Century." *Dialogue: A Journal of Mormon Thought* 29 (1): 159–76.

Knowlton, David. 2008. "Go Ye to All the World: The LDS Church and the Organization of International Society." In *Revisiting Thomas F. O'Dea's "The Mormons": Contemporary Perspectives*, edited by Cardell K. Jacobson, John P. Hoffmann, and Tim B. Heaton, 390–412. Salt Lake City: University of Utah Press.

Knowlton, David. 2016. "What Happened When Mormons Came to Mine and Build Peru?" *Clouds, Storms, and Power* (blog). http://stormsandpower.blogspot.com/2016/04/what-happened-when-mormons-came-to-mine.html.

Kohn, Eduardo. 2013. *How Forests Think: Toward an Anthropology beyond the Human*. Berkeley: University of California Press.

Krakauer, Jon. 2004. *Under the Banner of Heaven: A Story of Violent Faith*. New York: Anchor.

Krögel, Alison. 2010. "Quechua Sheepherders on the Mountain Plains of Wyoming: The (In)Hospitality of U.S. Guest Worker Programs." *Journal of Latin American and Caribbean Anthropology* 15 (2): 261–88.

Lajimodiere, Denise K. 2019. *Stringing Rosaries: The History, the Unforgivable, and the Healing of Northern Plains American Indian Boarding School Survivors*. Fargo: North Dakota State University Press.

Larson, Brooke. 2005. "Redeemed Indians, Barbarized Cholos." In *Political Cultures in the Andes, 1750–1950*, edited by Nils Jacobsen and Cristóbal Aljovín de Losada, 230–52. Durham, NC: Duke University Press.

Lipka, Michael. 2016. "U.S. Religious Groups and Their Political Leanings." *Pew Research Center* (blog). February 23. http://www.pewresearch.org/fact-tank/2016/02/23/u-s-religious-groups-and-their-political-leanings/.

Lipschütz, Alejandro. 1967. *El Problema Racial en la Conquista de America y el Mestizaje*. Santiago, Chile: Editorial Andres Bello.

Lipsitz, George. 2011. *How Racism Takes Place*. Philadelphia: Temple University Press.

Lomawaima, K. Tsianina. 1994. *They Called It Prairie Light: The Story of Chilocco Indian School*. Lincoln: University of Nebraska Press.

Longley, Kyle. 2009. *In the Eagle's Shadow: The United States and Latin America.* Wheeling, IL: Wiley-Blackwell.

López, Ian Haney. 2015. *Dog Whistle Politics: How Coded Racial Appeals Have Reinvented Racism and Wrecked the Middle Class.* New York: Oxford University Press.

Low, Setha. 2009. "Maintaining Whiteness: The Fear of Others and Niceness." *Transforming Anthropology* 17 (2): 79–92.

Lucht, Hans. 2012. *Darkness before Daybreak: African Migrants Living on the Margins in Southern Italy Today.* Berkeley: University of California Press.

MacCormack, Sabine. 1991. *Religion in the Andes.* Princeton, NJ: Princeton University Press.

Maffly-Kipp, Laurie F. 2020a. "Gender and Culture in a Global Church." In *The Routledge Handbook of Mormonism and Gender,* edited by Amy Hoyt and Taylor G. Petrey, 11–25. New York: Routledge.

Maffly-Kipp, Laurie F. 2020b. "Pulling Toward Zion: Mormonism in Its Global Dimensions." In *The Palgrave Handbook of Global Mormonism,* edited by R. Gordon Shepherd, A. Gary Shepherd, and Ryan T. Cragun, 143–62. New York: Palgrave Macmillan.

Mahmood, Saba. 2005. *Politics of Piety: The Islamic Revival and the Feminist Subject.* Princeton, NJ: Princeton University Press.

Mallku Bwillcawaman, Conibo. 2015. *Filosofía Tawantinsuyana: Una Perspectiva Epistémica.* Lima: Juan Gutemberg Editores Impresores.

Manrique, Nelson. 2003. "Memoria y Violencia: La Nación y el Silencio." In *Batallas por la Memoria: Antagonismos de la Promesa Peruana,* edited by Marta Hamann, Santiago López, Gonzalo Portocarrero, and Víctor Vich, 421–33. Lima: Red para el Desarrollo de las Ciencias Sociales en el Perú.

Marley, Jennifer. 2018. "Ending Heteropatriarchy in Pueblo Communities." *Indigenous Goddess Gang* (blog). March 1. https://www.indigenousgoddessgang.com/land-water-dignity-1/2018/2/28/jennifer-marley.

Martins, Marcus H. 2020. "An Oak Tree Bearing International Fruit: The Church of Jesus Christ of Latter-Day Saints in Brazil." In *The Palgrave Handbook of Global Mormonism,* edited by R. Gordon Shepherd, A. Gary Shepherd, and Ryan T. Cragun, 421–30. New York: Palgrave Macmillan.

Mauss, Armand L. 2003. *All Abraham's Children: Changing Mormon Conceptions of Race and Lineage.* Urbana: University of Illinois Press.

Maxwell, Neal A. 1985. "In Memoriam: Spencer W. Kimball, 1895–1985. Spencer, the Beloved: Leader-Servant." *Ensign,* December. https://www.churchofjesuschrist.org/study/ensign/1985/12/spencer-the-beloved-leader-servant?lang=eng.

Mayer, Enrique. 2009. *Ugly Stories of the Peruvian Agrarian Reform.* Durham, NC: Duke University Press.

McBride, Jane. 2018. "Finally a Forever Family." *Liahona* 47 (7) (June): 68–70.

McDannell, Colleen. 2020a. "Global Mormonism: A Historical Overview." In *The Palgrave Handbook of Global Mormonism,* edited by R. Gordon Shepherd, A. Gary Shepherd, and Ryan T. Cragun, 3–34. New York: Palgrave Macmillan.

McDannell, Colleen. 2020b. "Mormon Gender in the Mid-Twentieth Century."

In *The Routledge Handbook of Mormonism and Gender*, edited by Amy Hoyt and Taylor G. Petrey, 143–56. New York: Routledge.

McGuire, Randall H. 1992. "Archeology and the First Americans." *American Anthropologist* 94 (4): 816–36. https://doi.org/10.1525/aa.1992.94.4.02a00030.

McKay-Lamb, Tracy, and Emily W. Jensen. 2015. "Afterword." In *A Book of Mormons: Latter-Day Saints on a Modern-Day Zion*, edited by Emily W. Jensen and Tracy McKay-Lamb, 191–92. Ashland, OR: White Cloud Press.

Means, Bill. 2022. "The Black Hills Is Our Jerusalem." *Landback Magazine* 1 (1): 34–39.

Menjívar, Cecilia, and Leisy J. Abrego. 2012. "Legal Violence: Immigration Law and the Lives of Central American Immigrants." *American Journal of Sociology* 117 (5): 1380–1421.

Mignolo, Walter D. 2003. *The Darker Side of the Renaissance: Literacy, Territoriality, and Colonization*. Ann Arbor: University of Michigan Press.

Mignolo, Walter D. 2009. "Epistemic Disobedience, Independent Thought, and De-Colonial Freedom." *Theory, Culture & Society* 26 (7–8): 159–81.

Moffat, Riley M., and Fred E. Woods. 2020. "The Church of Jesus Christ of Latter-Day Saints in the Islands of the Pacific." In *The Palgrave Handbook of Global Mormonism*, edited by R. Gordon Shepherd, A. Gary Shepherd, and Ryan T. Cragun, 431–54. New York: Palgrave Macmillan.

Morales, Alejandro. 2010. *Hombres de Ladrillo*. Houston: Arte Publico Press.

Mormons in Transition. (1990) 2011. "The Mormon Temple Endowment Ceremony." Institute for Religious Research. http://mit.irr.org/mormon-temple-endowment-ceremony.

Moslener, Sara. 2020. "Sexual Purity and Its Discontents in Mormonism." In *The Routledge Handbook of Mormonism and Gender*, edited by Amy Hoyt and Taylor G. Petrey, 271–83. New York: Routledge.

Mueller, Max Perry. 2017. *Race and the Making of the Mormon People*. Chapel Hill: University of North Carolina Press.

Murphy, Thomas W. 1997. "Fifty Years of United Order in Mexico." *Sunstone* 20 (3): 69.

Murphy, Thomas W. 2003. "Simply Implausible: DNA and a Mesoamerican Setting for 'The Book of Mormon.'" *Dialogue: A Journal of Mormon Thought* 4 (36): 109–31.

Murphy, Thomas W. 2018. "Decolonization on the Salish Sea: A Tribal Journey Back to Mormon Studies." In *Decolonizing Mormonism: Approaching a Postcolonial Zion*, edited by Gina Colvin and Joanna Brooks, 47–66. Salt Lake City: University of Utah Press.

Murphy, Thomas W. 2020. "Views from Turtle Island: Settler Colonialism and Indigenous Mormon Entanglements." In *The Palgrave Handbook of Global Mormonism*, edited by R. Gordon Shepherd, A. Gary Shepherd, and Ryan T. Cragun, 751–80. New York: Palgrave Macmillan.

Museo Cultural de Arequipa. N.d. "Etapa Hispánica: El Primer Proceso, El Asentamiento (1540–1687)." Arequipa, Perú.

Nelson, Russell M. 2019. "'Come Follow Me.'" *Ensign*, May. https://www.church ofjesuschrist.org/study/general-conference/2019/04/46nelson?lang=eng.

Newcomb, Sarah. 2019. "Speculation of Lamanite Identity." *The Lamanite Truth Project: The Truth about the Lamanite Myth and Why It Matters* (blog). March 11. https://lamanitetruth.com/blog-2/.

Newcomb, Sarah. 2021. "Considering the Next Generation of Indigenous Children." *Dialogue: A Journal of Mormon Thought* 54 (2): 111–12.

Ngai, Mae M. 2004. *Impossible Subjects: Illegal Aliens and the Making of Modern America*. Princeton, NJ: Princeton University Press.

Nieves y Bustamante, Maria. (1892) 2010. *Jorge, el Hijo del Pueblo*. Arequipa, Perú: Biblioteca Juvenil.

Niumeitolu, Fuifuilupe. 2019. "The Mana of the Tongan Everyday: Tongan Grief and Mourning, Patriarchal Violence, and Remembering Va." PhD diss., University of California, Berkeley.

Oaks, Dallin H. 2012. "The Gospel Culture." *Ensign*, March. https://www.church ofjesuschrist.org/study/ensign/2012/03/the-gospel-culture?lang=eng.

O'Brien, Hazel. 2020. "Institutional Gender Negotiations within Irish Mormon Congregations." In *The Routledge Handbook of Mormonism and Gender*, edited by Amy Hoyt and Taylor G. Petrey, 405–18. New York: Routledge.

Okazaki, Chieko. 1995. "A Living Network." *Ensign*, November. https://www .churchofjesuschrist.org/study/ensign/1995/11/a-living-network?lang=eng.

Oman, Heather Bennett. 2015. "Of Chicken Salad Sandwiches." In *A Book of Mormons: Latter-Day Saints on a Modern-Day Zion*, edited by Emily W. Jensen and Tracy McKay-Lamb, 76–82. Ashland, OR: White Cloud Press.

Ong, Aihwa. 2003. *Buddha Is Hiding: Refugees, Citizenship, the New America*. Berkeley: University of California Press.

Packer, Boyd K. 1991. "How Does the Spirit Speak to Us?" Paper Presented at a Seminar for New Mission Presidents, Salt Lake City, June 19. https://www.churchof jesuschrist.org/study/new-era/2010/02how-does-the-spirit-speak-to-us?lang=eng.

Packham, Richard. 2009. "Similarities between the Freemasonry of the 1830s and the Mormon Endowment (Pre-1940)" (blog). http://packham.n4m.org/mason -endow.htm.

Padilla, Elaine. 2013. "Expanding Space: A Possibility of a Cavernous Mode of Dwelling." In *Contemporary Issues of Migration and Theology*, edited by Elaine Padilla and Peter Phan, 53–72. New York: Palgrave Macmillan.

Paerregaard, Karsten. 2008. *Peruvians Dispersed: A Global Ethnography of Migration*. New York: Lexington Books.

Palmer, Jason. 2020. "Peruvian Mormon Matchmaking: The Limits of Mormon Endogamy at Zion's Border." In *The Routledge Handbook of Mormonism and Gender*, edited by Amy Hoyt and Taylor G. Petrey, 419–31. New York: Routledge.

Palmer, Jason. 2021. "Be Careful, Ye Catholic: The Entanglement of Mormonism and Money in Peru." *Religions* 12 (4): 246–68.

Palmer, Jason. 2022. "La Familia versus The Family: Matriarchal Patriarchies in Peruvian Mormonism." *Journal of the Mormon Social Science Association* 1 (1): 123–51. https://doi.org/10.54587/JMSSA.0105.

Palmer, Jason. 2023. "Tiny Papers: Peruvian Mormon Substances of Relatedness." *Dialogue: A Journal of Mormon Thought* 54 no. 4 (Winter 2023): 82–123.

Palmer, Jason, and David Knowlton. 2020. "Mormons in Peru: Building Temples with Sacred Cornerstones and Holy Drywall." In *The Palgrave Handbook of Global Mormonism*, edited by R. Gordon Shepherd, A. Gary Shepherd, and Ryan T. Cragun, 397–419. New York: Palgrave Macmillan.

Parry, Darren. 2019. *The Bear River Massacre: A Shoshone History*. N.p.: By Common Consent Press.

Patterson, Sara M. 2020. "Masculinities." In *The Routledge Handbook of Mormonism and Gender*, edited by Amy Hoyt and Taylor G. Petrey, 60–72. New York: Routledge.

Pereyra, Omar. 2015. *Contemporary Middle Class in Latin America: A Study of San Felipe*. Lanham, MD: Lexington Books.

Perry, Theresa. 1998. "'I'on Know Why They Be Trippin'": Reflections on the Ebonics Debate." In *The Real Ebonics Debate: Power, Language, and the Education of African-American Children*, edited by Theresa Perry and Lisa Delpit, 3–16. Boston: Beacon Press.

Peruvian Truth and Reconciliation Commission. 2003. *Informe Final de La Comisión de Verdad y Reconciliación*. Lima: Comisión de la Verdad y Reconciliación.

Peterson, Mark E. 1981. *Children of Promise: The Lamanites: Yesterday and Today*. Salt Lake City: Bookcraft.

Pierre, Jemima. 2012. *The Predicament of Blackness: Postcolonial Ghana and the Politics of Race*. Chicago: University of Chicago Press.

Povinelli, Elizabeth A. 2002. *The Cunning of Recognition: Indigenous Alterities and the Making of Australian Multiculturalism*. Durham, NC: Duke University Press.

Povinelli, Elizabeth A. 2011. "The Governance of the Prior." *Interventions: International Journal of Postcolonial Studies* 13 (1): 13–30.

Prashad, Vijay. 2008. *The Darker Nations: A People's History of the Third World*. New York: New Press.

Pratt, Parley P. 1888. *The Autobiography of Parley Parker Pratt*. Chicago: Law, King & Law.

Price, Richard. 1965. "Trial Marriage in the Andes." *Ethnology* 4 (3): 310–22.

Pulido, Elisa Eastwood. 2020. *The Spiritual Evolution of Margarito Bautista: Mexican Mormon Evangelizer, Polygamist Dissident, and Utopian Founder, 1878–1961*. New York: Oxford University Press.

Quijano, Aníbal. 2019. "Colonialidad del Poder, Eurocentrismo y America Latina." *Espacio Abierto* 28 (1): 255–301.

Quinn, D. Michael. 1994. *The Mormon Hierarchy: Origins of Power*. Salt Lake City: Signature Books.

Radke, Andrea, and Rebecca Cropper-Rampton. 2005. "'On the Outside Looking In': A Gendered Look at Sister Missionary Experiences." In *New Scholarship on Latter-Day Saint Women in the Twentieth Century: Selections from the Women's History Initiative Seminars, 2003–2004*, edited by Carol Cornwall Madsen and Cherry B. Silver, 141–51. Provo, UT: Joseph Fielding Smith Institute for LDS History.

Recacoechea, Juan de. 2007. *American Visa*. New York: Akashic Books.

Red Nation. 2021. *The Red Deal: Indigenous Action to Save Our Earth*. Brooklyn, NY: Common Notions.

Reeve, W. Paul. 2015. *Religion of a Different Color: Race and the Mormon Struggle for Whiteness*. New York: Oxford University Press.

Reeve, W. Paul. 2018. "Rethinking Pioneer Day." Paper Presented at Sunstone Symposium, Salt Lake City, July 25–28.

Reinaga, Fausto. 2010. *La Revolución India*. La Paz, Bolivia: Movimiento Indianista Katarista.

Renan, Ernest. (1882) 2018. "What Is a Nation?" In *What Is a Nation? and Other Political Writings*, edited by M.F.N. Giglioli, 247–63. New York: Columbia University Press.

Reséndez, Andrés. 2016. *The Other Slavery: The Uncovered Story of Indian Enslavement in America*. New York: Mariner Books.

Riess, Jana, and Benjamin R. Knoll. 2020. "Social Science Perspectives on Gender and Mormon Orthodoxy." In *The Routledge Handbook of Mormonism and Gender*, edited by Amy Hoyt and Taylor G. Petrey, 364–77. New York: Routledge.

Rifkin, Mark. 2017. *Beyond Settler Time: Temporal Sovereignty and Indigenous Self-Determination*. Durham, NC: Duke University Press.

Rivera Cusicanqui, Silvia. 2007. "Everything Is Up for Discussion: A 40th Anniversary Conversation with Silvia Rivera Cusicanqui by Linda Farthing." *NACLA Report on the Americas* 40 (4): 4–9.

Rivera Cusicanqui, Silvia. 2010. "The Notion of 'Rights' and the Paradoxes of Postcolonial Modernity: Indigenous Peoples and Women in Bolivia." *Qui Parle* 18 (2): 29–54.

Rivera Wright, Lesley. 2021. "The Broken Shelves: Ex-Mormon Reddit Narratives of Deconversion." Master's thesis, University of North Carolina.

Robbins, Joel. 2004. *Becoming Sinners: Christianity and Moral Torment in a Papua New Guinea Society*. Berkeley: University of California Press.

Roberts, Elizabeth F. S. 2012. *God's Laboratory: Assisted Reproduction in the Andes*. Berkeley: University of California Press.

Roberts, Elizabeth F. S. 2013. "Assisted Existence: An Ethnography of Being in Ecuador." *Journal of the Royal Anthropological Institute* 19 (3): 562–80.

Robinson, Cedric J. 1983. *Black Marxism: The Making of the Black Radical Tradition*. Chapel Hill: University of North Carolina Press.

Rodríguez, Efraín. 2018. "De Costa a Costa: Nuestro Viaje al Templo." *Liahona* 42 (3) (March): 44–46.

Romanello, Brittany. 2020. "Multiculturalism as Resistance: Latina Migrants Navigate US Mormon Spaces." *Dialogue: A Journal of Mormon Thought* 53 (1): 5–31.

Romanello, Brittany. 2021. "Not a Country or a Stereotype: Latina LDS Experiences of Ethnic Homogenization and Racial Tokenism in the American West." *Religions* 12 (5): 1–15.

Romero, Raúl. 2004. *Identidades Múltiples: Memoria, Modernidad, y Cultura Popular en el Valle del Mantaro*. Lima: Fondo Editorial del Congreso del Peru.

Rosa, Jonathan. 2019. *Looking like a Language, Sounding like a Race: Raciolinguistic Ideologies and the Learning of Latinidad*. New York: Oxford University Press.

Rosaldo, Renato. 1989. "Imperialist Nostalgia." *Representations*, no. 26: 107–22.

Rubio, Juan Manuel. 2021. "Mining Ecologies: Capitalism and the Environment in Peru's Central Highlands, 1884–1930." PhD diss., University of California, Irvine.

Sabogal, Elena. 2005. "Viviendo en la Sombra: The Immigration of Peruvian Professionals to South Florida." *Latino Studies* 3 (1): 113–31.

Said, Edward. 1993. *Culture and Imperialism*. New York: Knopf.

Saito, Natsu Taylor. 2015. "Race and Decolonization: Whiteness as Property in the American Settler Colonial Project." *Harvard Journal on Racial & Ethnic Justice* 31: 31–67.

Santos-Granero, Fernando. 2009. "Introduction: Amerindian Constructional Views of the World." In *The Occult Life of Things: Native Amazonian Theories of Materiality and Personhood*, edited by Fernando Santos-Granero, 1–23. Tucson: University of Arizona Press.

Sarkisian, Natalia, and Naomi Gerstel. 2012. *Nuclear Family Values, Extended Family Lives: The Power of Race, Class, and Gender*. New York: Routledge.

Sawyer, Jeremy, and Anup Gampa. 2018. "Implicit and Explicit Racial Attitudes Changed during Black Lives Matter." *Personality & Social Psychology Bulletin* 44 (7): 1039–59.

Schielke, Samuli. 2015. *Egypt in the Future Tense: Hope, Frustration, and Ambivalence before and after 2011*. Bloomington: Indiana University Press.

Scorza, Manuel. (1970) 2002. *Redoble por Rancas*. Lima: Piesa.

Shange, Savannah. 2019a. "Black Girl Ordinary: Flesh, Carcerality, and the Refusal of Ethnography." *Transforming Anthropology* 27 (1): 3–21.

Shange, Savannah. 2019b. *Progressive Dystopia: Abolition, Antiblackness, and Schooling in San Francisco*. Durham, NC: Duke University Press.

Shepherd, Gary, and Gordon Shepherd. 1998. *Mormon Passage: A Missionary Chronicle*. Urbana: University of Illinois Press.

Shepherd, R. Gordon, A. Gary Shepherd, and Ryan T. Cragun, eds. 2021. *The Palgrave Handbook of Global Mormonism*. New York: Palgrave Macmillan.

Shraya, Vivek. 2016. *Even This Page Is White*. Vancouver, BC: Arsenal Pulp Press.

Shunn, William. 2015. *The Accidental Terrorist: Confessions of a Reluctant Missionary*. New York: Sinister Regard.

Silva, Noenoe K. 2017. *The Power of the Steel-Tipped Pen: Reconstructing Native Hawaiian Intellectual History*. Durham, NC: Duke University Press.

Singer, James. 2021. "Time to Let Go of Columbus." *Dialogue: A Journal of Mormon Thought* 54 (2): 117–18.

Smith, Christopher C. 2015. "Playing Lamanite: Ecstatic Performance of American Indian Roles in Early Mormon Ohio." *Journal of Mormon History* 41 (3): 131–66.

Smith, Joseph. 1830. *The Book of Mormon: An Account Written by the Hand of Mormon, Upon Plates Taken from the Plates of Nephi*. Palmyra, NY: E. B. Grandin. http://josephsmithpapers.org/paperSummary/book-of-mormon-1830?p=70&highlight=good%20nor%20bad#!/paperSummary/book-of-mormon-1830&p=70.

Smith, Joseph. (1830) 2013a. *The Book of Mormon: Another Testament of Jesus Christ.* Salt Lake City, UT: Church of Jesus Christ of Latter-Day Saints.

Smith, Joseph. 1842. "Church History." *Times and Seasons*, March 1. http://joseph smithpapers.org/paperSummary/times-and-seasons-1-march-1842#!/paper Summary/times-and-seasons-1-march-1842&p=8.

Smith, Joseph. 1844. *Doctrine and Covenants of the Church of Jesus Christ of Latter-Day Saints.* Nauvoo, IL: John Taylor. http://josephsmithpapers.org/paperSummary/doctrine-and-covenants-1844?p=428&highlight=hearts%20 of%20the%20fathers%20to%20the%20children#!/paperSummary/doctrine -and-covenants-1844&p=5.

Smith, Joseph. (1844) 2013b. *The Doctrine and Covenants of the Church of Jesus Christ of the Latter-Day Saints.* Salt Lake City: Church of Jesus Christ of Latter-Day Saints.

Smith, Joseph. 1851. *The Pearl of Great Price.* Liverpool: F. D. Richards. https:// dcms.lds.org/delivery/DeliveryManagerServlet?dps_pid=IE4501499.

Smith, Joseph, Oliver Cowdery, Sidney Rigdon, and Frederick G. Williams. 1835. *Doctrine and Covenants of the Church of Jesus Christ of Latter-Day Saints.* Kirtland, OH: F. G. Williams & Co. http://josephsmithpapers.org/paperSummary/ doctrine-and-covenants-1835.

Solórzano, Armando. 2014. *We Remember, We Celebrate, We Believe / Recuerdo, Celebración, y Esperanza: Latinos in Utah.* Salt Lake City: University of Utah Press.

Spalding, Karen. 1970. "Social Climbers: Changing Patterns of Mobility among the Indians of Colonial Peru." *Hispanic American Historical Review* 50 (November): 645–64.

Speed, Shannon. 2019. *Incarcerated Stories: Indigenous Women Migrants and Violence in the Settler-Capitalist State.* Chapel Hill: University of North Carolina Press.

Spotted Elk, Miacel. 2019. "The Making of a Lamanite: Popular Native American Cultural Efforts from the LDS Church." *Daily Utah Chronicle* (blog). February 23. http://dailyutahchronicle.com/2019/02/23/the-making-of-a-lamanite -popular-native-american-cultural-efforts-from-the-lds-church/.

Stanton, Megan. 2020. "Structures of Home and Family: North America." In *The Routledge Handbook of Mormonism and Gender*, edited by Amy Hoyt and Taylor G. Petrey, 336–49. New York: Routledge.

Stapley, Jonathan A. 2020. "Women and Priesthood." In *The Routledge Handbook of Mormonism and Gender*, edited by Amy Hoyt and Taylor G. Petrey, 569–79. New York: Routledge.

Stewart, David G. 2020. "The Dynamics of LDS Growth in the Twenty-First Century." In *The Palgrave Handbook of Global Mormonism*, edited by R. Gordon Shepherd, A. Gary Shepherd, and Ryan T. Cragun, 163–204. New York: Palgrave Macmillan.

Strathern, Marilyn. 1992. *After Nature: English Kinship in the Late Twentieth Century.* New York: Cambridge University Press.

Straubhaar, Rolf. 2018. "Unpacking White-Heritage Mormon Privilege: A Latter-Day Saint Pursuit of Critical Consciousness." In *Decolonizing Mormonism:*

Approaching a Postcolonial Zion, edited by Gina Colvin and Joanna Brooks, 103–13. Salt Lake City: University of Utah Press.

Szykowny, Rick. 1994. "No Justice, No Peace: An Interview with Jerome Miller." *Humanist* 54 (1): 9–19.

Tallbear, Kim. 2013. *Native American DNA: Tribal Belonging and the False Promise of Genetic Science*. Minneapolis: University of Minnesota Press.

Tallbear, Kim. 2021a. "Science v. the Sacred, a Dead-End Settler Ontology—and Then What?" Paper Presented at the History of Science Society Annual Meeting, Online, November 18–21.

Tallbear, Kim. 2021b. "We Are Not Your Dead Ancestors: Playing Indian and White Possession." *Unsettle* (blog). https://kimtallbear.substack.com/p/we-are-not-your-dead-ancestors#details.

Taussig, Michael. 1984. "Culture of Terror—Space of Death: Roger Casement's Putumayo Report and the Explanation of Torture." *Comparative Studies in Society and History* 26: 467–88.

Taussig, Michael. 1992. *Mimesis and Alterity: A Particular History of the Senses*. New York: Routledge.

Taylor, Lori Elaine. 2000. "Telling Stories about Mormons and Indians." PhD diss., State University of New York at Buffalo.

Thayne, Stanley J. 2019. "'We're Going to Take Our Land Back Over': Indigenous Positionality, the Ethnography of Reading, and *The Book of Mormon*." In *Americanist Approaches to "The Book of Mormon,"* edited by Elizabeth Fenton and Jared Hickman, 321–40. New York: Oxford University Press.

Theidon, Kimberly. 2013. *Intimate Enemies: Violence and Reconciliation in Peru*. Philadelphia: University of Pennsylvania Press.

Thomas, Philip. 2002. "The River, the Road, and the Rural-Urban Divide: A Post-colonial Moral Geography from Southeast Madagascar." *American Ethnologist* 29 (2): 366–91.

Thompson, E. P. 1967. "Time, Work-Discipline, and Industrial Capitalism." *Past & Present* 38 (December): 56–97.

Todorov, Tzvetan. 1984. *The Conquest of America: The Question of the Other*. Translated by Richard Howard. Norman: University of Oklahoma Press.

Toscano, Margaret. 2020. "Men and the Priesthood." In *The Routledge Handbook of Mormonism and Gender*, edited by Amy Hoyt and Taylor G. Petrey, 580–97. New York: Routledge.

Tristán, Flora. (1838) 2010. *Peregrinaciones de una Paria*. Arequipa, Peru: Biblioteca Juvenil.

Tuck, Eve, and K. Wayne Yang. 2012. "Decolonization Is Not a Metaphor." *Decolonization: Indigeneity, Education & Society* 1 (1): 1–40.

Tullis, F. Lamond. 1980. "The Church Moves Outside the United States: Some Observations from Latin America." *Dialogue: A Journal of Mormon Thought* 13 (1): 63–73.

Tullis, F. Lamond. 2018. *Martyrs in Mexico: A Mormon Story of Revolution and Redemption*. Provo, UT: Deseret Book Company.

Tupac Amaru Bastidas, Fernando. 2011. *Este Cautiverio y Agonía sin Fin*. Lima: A.F.A. Editores Importadores.

Ture, Kwame. 1990. *Zionism: Imperialism, White Supremacy, or Both?* Keith Hakim Workshops, University of Minnesota Law School. YouTube video posted by Pasma Sobukwe Branch on November 7, 2013. https://www.youtube.com/watch?v=yQrDBZfDjZA&feature=emb_logo.

Turley, Richard E., and Clinton D. Christensen. 2019. *An Apostolic Journey: Stephen L. Richards and the Expansion of Missionary Work in South America.* Provo, UT: RSC/BYU.

Turner, Victor. (1967) 1979. "Betwixt and Between: The Liminal Period in Rites de Passage." In *Reader in Comparative Religion: An Anthropological Approach,* edited by William Armand Lessa and Evon Zartman Vogt, 234–43. New York: Harper & Row.

Turner, Victor. 1969. *The Ritual Process: Structure and Anti-Structure.* London: Aldine.

Turner, Victor, and Edith Turner. (1978) 2011. *Image and Pilgrimage in Christian Culture.* New York: Columbia University Press.

Uchtdorf, Dieter F. 2015. "Dedicatory Prayer: Trujillo Peru Temple, June 21, 2015." *Church of Jesus Christ of Latter-Day Saints: Temples* (blog). https://www.lds.org/temples/details/trujillo-peru-temple/prayer/2015-06-21.

Ulrich, Laurel Thatcher. 2020. "Mormon Gender in the Age of Polygamy." In *The Routledge Handbook of Mormonism and Gender,* edited by Amy Hoyt and Taylor G. Petrey, 86–99. New York: Routledge.

US Census Bureau. 2010. "Census Congressional District Summary File (113th Congress): Hispanic or Latino by Type." *American Fact Finder.* http://factfinder.census.gov/faces/tableservices/jsf/pages/productview.xhtml?pid=DEC_10_113_QTP10&prodType=table.

Valandra, Edward. 2019. "Mni Wiconi: Water Is [More Than] Life." In *Standing with Standing Rock: Voices from the #NoDAPL Movement,* edited by Nick Estes and Jaskiran Dhillon, 71–89. Minneapolis: University of Minnesota Press.

Van Beek, Walter E. A. 2005. "Mormon Europeans or European Mormons? An 'Afro-European' View on Religious Colonization." *Dialogue: A Journal of Mormon Thought* 38 (4): 3–36.

Van Beek, Walter E. A., Ellen Decoo, and Wilfried Decoo. 2020. "Persisting in a Secular Environment: Mormonism in the Low Countries." In *The Palgrave Handbook of Global Mormonism,* edited by R. Gordon Shepherd, A. Gary Shepherd, and Ryan T. Cragun, 503–32. New York: Palgrave Macmillan.

Van Gennep, Arnold. (1908) 1961. *The Rites of Passage.* Chicago: University of Chicago Press.

Vargas Llosa, Mario. 1983. "Inquest in the Andes." *New York Times Magazine,* July 31, sec. 6.

Vega, Sujey. 2020. "Mujerista Theology." In *The Routledge Handbook of Mormonism and Gender,* edited by Amy Hoyt and Taylor G. Petrey, 598–607. New York: Routledge.

Viveiros de Castro, E. 1998. "Cosmological Deixis and Amerindian Perspectivism." *Journal of the Royal Anthropological Institute* 4 (3): 469–88.

Vogel, Erica. 2014. "Predestined Migrations: Undocumented Peruvians in South Korean Churches." *City and Society* 26 (3): 331–51.

Vogel, Erica. 2020. *Migrant Conversions: Transforming Connections between Peru and South Korea*. Oakland: University of California Press.

Walia, Harsha. 2021. *Border and Rule: Global Migration, Capitalism, and the Rise of Racist Nationalism*. Chicago: Haymarket Books.

Walker, Tai. 2017. "Whānau—Māori and Family—Contemporary Understandings of Whānau." In *Te Ara- the Encyclopedia of New Zealand*. http://www.TeAra.govt .nz/en/whanau-maori-and-family/page-1.

Waziyatawin. 2012. "Malice Enough in Their Hearts and Courage Enough in Ours: Reflections on US Indigenous and Palestinian Experiences under Occupation." *Settler Colonial Studies* 2 (1): 172–89.

Weatherford, Jack. 1987. *Indian Givers: How the Indians of the Americas Transformed the World*. New York: Crown Publishers.

Weismantel, Mary. 1995. "Making Kin: Kinship Theory and Zumbagua Adoptions." *American Ethnologist* 22 (4): 685–704.

Weismantel, Mary. 2001. *Cholas and Pishtacos: Stories of Race and Sex in the Andes*. Chicago: University of Chicago Press.

Welch, Rosalynde. 2020. "Theology of the Family." In *The Routledge Handbook of Mormonism and Gender*, edited by Amy Hoyt and Taylor G. Petrey, 495–508. New York: Routledge.

Whitehouse, Harvey. 2006. "Appropriated and Monolithic Christianity in Melanesia." In *The Anthropology of Christianity*, edited by Fenella Cannell, 295–307. Durham, NC: Duke University Press.

Willerslev, Rane, and Christian Suhr. 2015. "Is There a Place for Faith in Anthropology? Religion, Reason, and the Ethnographer's Divine Revelation." Paper Presented at the 114th American Anthropological Association Annual Meeting, Denver, November 18–22.

Winkelman, Michael, and Jill Dubisch. 2005. "Introduction: The Anthropology of Pilgrimage." In *Pilgrimage and Healing*, edited by Jill Dubisch and Michael Winkelman, ix–xxxvi. Tucson: University of Arizona Press.

Wolfe, Patrick. 2006. "Setter Colonialism and the Elimination of the Native." *Journal of Genocide Research* 8 (4): 387–409.

Woodson, Ashley N. 2019. "Racial Code Words, Re-Memberings, and Black Kids' Civic Imaginations: A Critical Race Ethnography of a Post–Civil Rights Leader." *Anthropology & Education Quarterly* 50 (1): 26–47.

World Travel Awards. 2021. "South America's Leading Culinary Destination." *Winners* (blog). https://www.worldtravelawards.com/award-south-americas -leading-culinary-destination-2021.

Yanagisako, Sylvia, and Carol Delaney. (1994) 2013. "Naturalizing Power." In *Naturalizing Power: Essays in Feminist Cultural Analysis*, edited by Sylvia Yanagisako and Carol Delaney, 1–22. New York: Routledge.

Yazzie, Melanie K. 2015. "Solidarity with Palestine from Diné Bikéyah." *American Quarterly* 67 (4): 1007–15.

Zahzah, Omar. 2022. "The Negation of the Negation of Meaning: Resisting Symbolic Settler Terror through Joint Struggle." *Landback Magazine* 1 (1): 42–47.

Zea, Irene. (1975) 2012. "U.S. Hegemony on the American Continent." In *Looking North: Writings from Spanish America on the US, 1800 to the Present*, edited by John J. Hassett and Braulio Muñoz, 90–108. Tucson: University of Arizona Press.

Zhang, Li. 2010. *In Search of Paradise: Middle-Class Living in a Chinese Metropolis.* Ithaca, NY: Cornell University Press.

Index

Basch, Linda, 34
Basquiat, Jennifer Huss, 155
Bautista, Margarito, 155, 157
believing-blood theory, 11, 57
benevolent colonialism, 13–14
Berg, Ulla, 100–101, 170
Berta, Luz, 185–92, 197, 198
Best, Efraín, 71
Bighorse, Eva, 195
Black Martinicans, 169, 171
Blanc-Szanton, Cristina, 34
Book of Mormon, The, 6–12, 59, 81, 83,
    88, 120, 218, 264; believing-blood
    theory and, 11, 57; connection of
    Native people to Israelites in, 140,
    142; Lamanite legacy and, 99; on the
    Lamanites as chosen people, 171–72,
    180, 263; martial metaphors in, 71;
    pageantry created from conceptions
    of indigeneity in, 114–15; Pascuala
    Cusicanchi on, 115–18, 121–22, 143;
    perceived skin tone and, 14; Peruvian
    cultural categories and, 21; on places
    in America, 155–56; prophecies about
    Latin American Mormons in, 56; on
    righteousness and prospering, 196;
    set in Peru, 146–50; tele-territoriality
    and, 144–45, 146; time metaphor in,
    226–27
*Book of Mormons: Latter-day Saints on a
    Modern-Day Zion, A,* 57
Bourdieu, Pierre, 116
Bowman, Matthew, 58
Brekhus, Wayne, 57
Bueno-Hansen, Pascha, 261
Busby, Cecilia, 252
Bwillcawaman, Conibo Malku, 31–32,
    232

Calvinism, 252–53
Canessa, Andrew, 100, 213–14
Cannell, Fenella, 252
Carnvales, 201–2
Catholicism, 122, 136, 140; converts to
    Peruvian Mormonism from, 102–5,
    154–55; original sin in, 227; saints
    shrines in, 162
Celestial Kingdom, 208, 228

cholo con plata, 264–67
cholo sin plata, 273–76
Christensen, Clinton, 153
Christensen, Craig, 191
Christensen, Dale, 19, 150
Christianity: concept of the soul and
    salvation in Enlightenment, 252–53;
    Mormonism as unusual form of,
    233–34; in pre-Hispanic America, 143
Church Education System (CES),
    200–201
Church Handbook of Instruction, The,
    64–66
clannishness, 239–40
Colloredo-Mansfeld, Rudi, 151
coloniality. *See* settler coloniality
Columbus, Christopher, 139
Córdoba, Pedro, 76
Corimayta, Basilio, 147
Costa, Arcadio, 98, 108–9, 112, 148–49,
    235, 274
Coutin, Susan Bibler, 193
Cowdry, Oliver, 11
culturing of leaders, 57–60
Cusicanchi, Pascuala, 114, 143, 249;
    on *The Book of Mormon* set in Peru,
    146–47; on Indigenous blood, 115–18;
    living arrangement of, 233; on sacred
    stones, 123–26; singleness of, 208–15,
    220, 221–22; tele-territoriality and,
    143–44; on transmission and dilution
    of legacy, 120–22
Cusicanqui, Silvia Rivera, 167

Daly, Collin, 112; on *The Church Hand-
    book of Instruction,* 64–66; on growth
    of Peruvian Mormonism, 69–70;
    on Indigenous government, 71, 72;
    temple construction in Arequipa and,
    60–64
Danvers Statement, 55
de Castro, Viveiros, 254–55
decolonization, 137–38
De la Cadena, Marisol, 101–2
Delaney, Carol, 111
Deloria, Ella Cara, 120, 139, 214
Deseret Book, 218
dividualism, 253–55

holiness: of *The Book of Mormon* set in Peru, 146–50; holy order of the Sun God, 140–42; holy-versus-sacred dialectic and, 162–63; Lamanite epistemology and, 153–58; Lamanite threat to colonial, 168–72; metaphysical, 155; of public land, 137–40; racism and disavowals of Lamanite, 158–61; versus sacredness, 134–36; in story versus history, 151–53; tele-territoriality and, 143–46; trans-temporality and, 142–43; Utah-centeredness and, 132–34, 137; whiteness and, 148, 153, 157–58, 164–68, 171; wild tongues and, 163–68

Holmes, Seth, 236

holy-versus-sacred dialectic, 162–63

How Racism Takes Place, 236

Humala, Ollanta, 142

immanent obligation, 271–73

immigration: illegality and meritocracy and, 195–96; Latinx identity and, 246–47; laws related to, 169–70, 191, 193–94; tourist visas and, 194–95, 209–10, 215–16

Incas, 140, 141

independence: couples missions and, 255–58; food and, 251–52; homes versus units and, 235–41; individualism and, 258–59; interdependent, 233–35, 259–60; kinship and, 247–49; opposing views on, 255–59; relatedness and, 248–52; shattering collective selves and, 241–47; substantialism and, 252–55

Indian Removal Act, 11

indigeneity, 4–6, 31, 261; folkloric dance and, 100–102; holiness and, 136; legacy and, 96–98; pioneer, 21–23; pioneering leadership and, 56–57; stigmatization of, 12–13

Indigenous government, 70–72; Shining Path movement and, 13–14, 21, 48, 70, 71–72

individualism, 258–59, 269

interdependent independence, 233–35, 259–60

Jackson, John, 247–48

James, apostle, 9, 23

Jefferson, Thomas, 8–9

Jehovah's Witnesses, 16

Jesus Christ, 3, 10, 80; in *The Book of Mormon,* 9; Nephites and, 152; resurrection of, 163; skin tone of, 165–66

John, apostle, 9, 23

Johnson, William, 140

Kimball, Spencer, 16–17, 152, 177

kinship, 247–49, 255, 258, 271–73

Knowlton, David, 67

Kuczynski, Pedro Pablo, 141

La Familia, 1, 95, 96, 134, 194–95, 235, 238, 270–71; cholo sin plata and, 273–76; immanent obligation and, 271–73; interdependence in, 241–42, 259–60; legacy and, 95, 96, 106–8; living in Utah, 24, 98–99, 132; marriage in, 274–75; migration and, 24, 31, 76; population and geography of, 35–36; sealed marriages and, 29; Spanglish used by, 34; transnationalism of, 34–35

Lamanites, 151, 167–68; *The Book of Mormon* on, 146–50, 171–72; disavowals of holiness of, 158–61; epistemology of, 153–58; as the future of Mormonism, 176–80, 198–200, 202, 263; holiness and sacredness and, 140–42; Jesus as, 166; legacy of, 98–106; tele-territoriality and, 143–46; as threat to colonial holiness, 168–72; whiteness and, 179–80. *See also* Cusicanchi, Pascuala

Landback Magazine, 139

Latinx identity, 246–47

LDS South Americanist School of Book of Mormon Geography, 148

leaders, Mormon: culturing, 57–60; gendering, 49–56; hierarchy of, 10, 16; indigeneity and pioneering, 56–57; reading, 64–68; tools of, 68; whitening of, 60–64

legacy: of Anglo Mormon Great Plains disasters, 95–96, 110–11, 130;

components of, 108–10; faithfulness to, 119–22; gendering of, 110–11; Indigenous blood and, 115–18; La Familia and, 106–8; Lamanite, 98–106; owning, 114–15; pageantry and, 114–15; pioneer, 94; of sacred stones at temple sites, 123–26; sacrifice and, 112–14, 119; tribulations and, 94–98; Utah-centeredness in placing, 111–12

Liahona, 16

Lipschütz, Alejandro, 6

Lipsitz, George, 236

Llosa, Mario Vargas, 71

local leadership in Peruvian Mormonism, 91–93

López, Leticia, 127–31

love and marriage, 227–30

MacCormack, Sabine, 143

Maffly-Kipp, Laurie, 66

Mahmood, Saba, 53

Manifest Destiny, 138

marriage: Andean conceptualization of, 231–32; Anglo/Latinx interethnic, 266–71; children of, 26–27; Endowment ceremony and, 221; forever families and, 33–35, 175–76, 180, 204; gendered leadership and, 54–55; ideal female age for, 210–13; Jaqi people and, 213–15; in La Familia, 274–75; love and, 227–30; making of a person through, 213–15; Ofelia Dominguez on singleness and, 222–32; polygamous, 195–96; punctuality and, 203–6, 231–32; requirements for Mormon, 208, 276–77; sealed, 23–28, 208, 227–28, 271; socially engineered retornadas and, 207–13; trial, 232; unsealability of, 25–28; wrongness of singleness versus, 205–206. *See also* family

Martínez, Virgilio, 142

Martin's Cove, Wyoming, 95–96, 109, 110–11, 152

Marxism, 93

masculinity, 264; missionaries and, 86–87; in settler coloniality, 58

Means, Bill, 139

meritocracy and illegality, 195–96

mestizos, 14–15, 101

Mexican Mormons, 74–75, 155, 157–58, 178

Miller, Jerome, 238

missionaries, Mormon, 10–11, 16–17, 20–21, 79–82, 186; elderly couples as, 255–58; female, 85–88, 211–12; hypermasculine, military metaphors of, 86–87; Latinx, 249; white male leadership of, 83–84

Monson, Thomas, 228

Monte, Ignacio, 96–98

Moroni, 153, 264

Native people, 138–39, 161; *The Book of Mormon* on connection between Israelites and, 140, 142

necropolitical legacy, 94–95

Nelson, Russell, 3, 16, 227–28, 229, 232

neoliberal capitalism, 199

Nephite immunity, 66–68, 168

Nephites, 151–52

Oaks, Dallin, 59

Ojeda, Ruth, 15–16

Okazaki, Chieko, 224–25

Oman, Heather, 57

Ong, Aihwa, 263

Our Heritage: A Brief History of The Church of Jesus Christ of Latter-day Saints, 108–9

Our Legacy, 120, 156

pageants, Mormon Miracle, 114–15

Parent Teacher Association (PTA), 254–55

Parker, Ted, 242

paternalism, Mormon, 16–20, 54–55

Path War. *See* Shining Path

patriarchy, 83–84, 225; love and, 227–30; misioneras and, 85–86; patriarchal blessing and, 224

Patterson, Sara, 110

Pearl of Great Price, 16

perceived skin tone, 14, 265–66

personhood: constructed parts and essential parts in, 253; food and, 251–52, 269, 277–79

Peruvian Mormonism, 1–2, 262, 279–80; in Arequipa, 20–21; *The Book of Mormon* set in Peru and, 146–50; cholo con plata and, 264–67; cholo sin plata and, 273–76; collective selves in, 241–47; culturing leaders in, 57–60; data collection on, 37; in de-Catholicizing Peru, 19; emergence of, 15–16; ethnic identity assigned to, 277; families in, 28–31, 208–9, 231–32; Family Night and, 218–20; festivals and, 185–90, 201–2; forever familia in, 33–35, 175–76; gendering leaders in, 49–56; glossaries of, 3–4; growth of, 17–18, 69–70, 84–85; holiness and sacredness in, 140–42; identification as Lamanites, 21–22; indigeneity and coloniality and, 4–6, 31, 56–57; interdependent independence in, 233–35; kinship in, 247–49, 271–73; marriage to whites, 266–71; missionary work by, 79–81; paternalism in, 16–20; pioneer indigeneity and, 21–23; pioneering of government and, 72–76; pioneer leaders in, 56–57; prophetic paternalism and, 16–20; reading leaders in, 64–68; relatedness in, 248–52; researcher positionality in studying, 37–39; research methodology on, 35–37; singleness in, 207–13; stagnant path in growth of, 69–70; in story versus history, 151–53; study participants on, 39–41; tourist visas and, 194–95, 209–10, 215–16; US-centrism of, 91–92; whitening of leaders in, 60–64, 171. *See also* Anglo Mormonism; government, Peruvian Mormon

Peruvianness, 1, 2–3, 12–16; Afroperuvians and, 264–65; anti-indigeneity and, 13; in Arequipa, 15–16; benevolent colonialism and, 13–14; class hierarchy and, 196–98; destruction and beauty in, 132–34; family in, 31–33; festivals and, 185–90; food and, 251–52, 269, 277–79; future of, 181–85; inferiority

complex and, 135; marriage conceptualization in, 231–32; mestizos and, 14–15; no future in Peru and, 181–85, 207–8; perceived skin tone and, 14; as pro-Indigenous, 4; proving, 267–71; relationist culture and, 233–34; Shining Path movement and, 13–14, 21, 48; slavery and, 13; unpunctuality and, 207–208; "whitening" and, 13

Peter, apostle, 9, 23

pigmentocracy, 6

polygyny, 195–96

Povinelli, Elizabeth, 57, 272

Pratt, Parley, 12

priesthood, Mormon, 9–10, 23

Protestantism, Latin American, 189, 199

public land, 137–40

Pulido, Elisa Eastwood, 99

punctuality, 198–200

racism, 6–12, 235–41; perceived skin tone and, 14, 265–66

reading of leaders, 64–68

reenactments, Pioneer, 46–48

relationist culture, 233–34

Relief Society, 53, 55, 205, 223, 225

Renan, Ernest, 137

Rites of Passage, The, 80–81

Robbins, Joel, 233–34

Roberts, Elizabeth, 214

Rosa, Jonathan, 202

rural nostalgia, 238–39

Sabogal, Elena, 193

sacredness versus holiness, 134–36, 161; holy-versus-sacred dialectic and, 162–63

sacrifice, 108–9, 112–14, 119, 120

Sacrificing Families, 251

Saints: The Story of The Church, 156, 163, 164

Salt Lake City, Utah, 12, 65, 155–56; in Anglo Mormonism origin story, 139–40

Schielke, Samuli, 175

sealed marriages, 23–24, 208, 227–29, 271; children born of, 26–27; forever familia and, 33–35

Self-Reliance Initiative, 206

Van Gennep, Arnold, 80
vernacular statecraft, 151
Vogel, Erica, 194, 199

Waterlily, 139
Welch, Rosalynde, 228
whiteness: acceptance into La Familia
  and, 273–74; cholo con plata and,
  264–67; holiness and, 148, 153,
  157–58, 164–68, 171; longing and
  hate in, 261–62; of Mormon leaders,
  60–64; racism and, 6–12, 235–41;
  Shining Path and, 75, 265–66; white
  genealogies and, 262–64
Whitmer, Mary, 156–57

Willerslev, Rane, 19
Williams, William Carlos, 7
women: marriage and ageism against,
  210–13, 217–18; as missionaries,
  85–88, 211–12

Yanagisako, Sylvia, 111
Young, Brigham, 3, 95–96, 177, 195; on
  the Lamanites, 179; on subduing the
  West and its Native inhabitants, 139

Zeballos, Delia, 77
Zion, 73, 175; Lamanite future and,
  176–80; whiteness of, 261–62
Zion's Camp, 46–48, 72, 91–93

JASON PALMER is an independent scholar.

The University of Illinois Press
is a founding member of the
Association of University Presses.

———————————————————

University of Illinois Press
1325 South Oak Street
Champaign, IL 61820-6903
www.press.uillinois.edu